Critical Cinema 4

I am deeply grateful to the National Endowment for the Humanities for its support of the Critical Cinema project, most recently in the form of an NEH Fellowship awarded at the end of 2003. Of course, it should be understood that any views, findings, conclusions, or recommendations expressed in this book do not necessarily reflect those of the National Endowment for the Humanities.

The publisher gratefully acknowledges the generous contribution to this book provided by the General Endowment Fund of the University of California Press Associates.

A Critical Cinema 4

**Interviews with
Independent Filmmakers**

Scott MacDonald

University of California Press
Berkeley / Los Angeles / London

University of California Press
Berkeley and Los Angeles, California

University of California Press, Ltd.
London, England

For a list of previously published material included in this volume, please see the acknowledgments of permissions section that begins on page 383.

The front cover image shows an eye with a poem written on it in Arabic. The poem, "I Feel Sorry for the Garden," by Forough Farokhzad, reads: "No one is thinking about the flowers / No one is thinking about the fish / No one wants to believe / that the garden is dying / that the garden's heart has swollen under the sun / that the garden / is slowly forgetting its green moments. . . ." Shirin Neshat, *Offered Eyes* (1993). Photo by Plauto. Courtesy Barbara Gladstone Gallery.

Library of Congress Cataloging-in-Publication Data

MacDonald, Scott, 1942–.
    A critical cinema : interviews with independent filmmakers / Scott MacDonald.
    Includes bibliographical references and index.
    ISBN 0-520-05800-3 (v. 1 : cloth)
    ISBN 0-520-05801-1 (v. 1 : paper)
    ISBN 0-520-07917-5 (v. 2 : cloth).
    ISBN 0-520-07918-3 (v. 2 : paper)
    ISBN 0-520-08705-4 (v. 3 : cloth).
    ISBN 0-520-20943-5 (v. 3 : paper)
    ISBN 0-520-24269-6 (v. 4 : cloth).
    ISBN 0-520-24271-8 (v. 4 : paper)
    1. Experimental films—United States—History and criticism.
2. Motion picture producers and directors—United States—
Interviews.   I. Title.
PN1995.9.E96M34   1988   87–6004
791.43'75'0973—dc21

Manufactured in the United States of America

13   12   11   10   09   08   07   06   05   04
10   9   8   7   6   5   4   3   2   1

For *Jonas Mekas, Gene Youngblood, Amos Vogel, Sheldon Renan, P. Adams Sitney, William Moritz, David Curtis, Malcolm LeGrice, Annette Michelson, Peter Gidal, Tom Gunning, Lucy Fischer, Jim Hoberman, David James, Paul Arthur, William C. Wees, Patricia R. Zimmermann, and all the other writers who have helped me find my way to the films and filmmakers I admire.*

Contents

Acknowledgments

A Critical Cinema 4 has been possible because of the many institutions and individuals who have provided support.

I am grateful to Bard College and to Hamilton College for allowing me to have both a teaching life and a research life.

As always, I am indebted to Canyon Cinema (especially to Dominic Angerame and Mark Toscano); to Anthology Film Archives (Robert A. Haller and Jonas Mekas); to the Pacific Film Archive (Kathy Geritz); and to the Museum of Modern Art's Department of Film and Media (Jytte Jensen), Video Department (Sally Berger), and Circulating Film Program (Kitty Cleary). Thanks, also, to the New York Film-makers' Cooperative (M. M. Serra), to Electronic Art Intermix, to the Video Data Bank, to the Robert Flaherty Film Seminar, to Blum and Poe Gallery (Santa Monica) and Barbara Gladstone Gallery (New York City), and to "Views from the Avant-Garde" at the New York Film Festival (and its curators, Mark McElhatten and Gavin Smith).

Many colleagues have provided various kinds of professional and personal support, among them David E. James (University of Southern California), R. Bruce Jenkins, Patricia O'Neill (Hamilton College), P. Adams Sitney (Princeton University), John Pruitt (Bard College), Patricia R. Zimmermann (Ithaca College), Don Fredericksen (Cornell University), Fred Camper, William C. Wees, Robert A. Haller (Anthology Film Archives), Ruth Bradley (Ohio University/*Wide Angle*), Chris Gehman (Images Festival, Toronto), Peter Hutton (Bard College), Steve Anker (California Institute of the Arts), Marie Nesthus (Donnell Public Library), Mary Fessenden (Cornell Cinema), Patricia Thomson *(The Independent)*, Lynne Sachs, John Hanhardt (Guggenheim Museum),

Mary Beth Haralovich (University of Arizona), Ann Martin *(Film Quarterly)*, and Richard Brennan at the print shop at Hamilton College.

Many friends have, often unknowingly, offered valuable support, including Larry Platt, Bryan Cressy, Robert Huot, Kim Landon, Terry Grimmer Krumbach, and David Gatten.

And my love and thanks to Patricia Reichgott O'Connor, to Ian MacDonald, to Ed Burg, Annie LaSalla Burg, Tia Burg, and Marli Patricia Burg; to Art Burg, to Winifred Driskill, Tim and Elaine Reichgott, Marc Reichgott; and to Sarah, Tim, Beth, Robert, and little Sarah Driskill, to Julie and Daniele Prieto, to Megan, Alyson, Amy, Emily, Anna, Eric, and John Reichgott—and especially to my aunt, LaMoss Messinger, whose longevity and high spirits are an inspiration.

Introduction

Critique and Creativity

Each time I have begun a new volume of *A Critical Cinema,* I have assumed it would be the last in the series, but in every instance, as the volume has begun to take its final shape, I have realized not only that I want to continue the series but that the field it serves *requires* another volume. As *A Critical Cinema 3* was taking shape, I saw it as a fitting conclusion for my project; the number (twenty-six) and international range of the interviews and discussions included in that volume provided not just a set of new perspectives on the history of alternative cinema but a metaphor for my basic assumption about this history: that it is an immense and expanding world that even film historians and lovers of cinema have only begun to explore. The fact that *A Critical Cinema 3* is longer and more fully international and multiethnic than *A Critical Cinema 2,* which was longer and more expansive than *A Critical Cinema,* was my way of suggesting that, whatever we think of the achievements of the late 1960s and early 1970s—and of course they were so many and varied that I am still catching up with them—they certainly were not a coup de grâce for the field. Indeed, more recent achievements allow us, in some cases *force* us, to rethink and reevaluate the earlier phases of this history.

Much the same experience has characterized the evolution of *A Critical Cinema 4.* As the interviews accumulated, I realized that alternative film (and video) is a hydra-headed monster. One might assume that after sixty-one interviews, the Critical Cinema project would at least have dealt with the classic figures in the field; but in fact here, finally, is a sustained interview with Stan Brakhage, a conversation with P. Adams Sitney about the film scene during the early 1960s when Gregory Markopoulos was such a crucial figure, and an interview with Peter Kubelka about *Unsere Afrikareise (Our Trip to Africa)* (1966). And, of course, during the past half century, and during the twenty-five years I have been working on the Critical Cinema project, many careers have matured and many others have emerged, sometimes extending the work of earlier decades, sometimes rebelling against the earlier work, and often both.

While the process of doing *A Critical Cinema 4* has been similar to the process that led to the three earlier Critical Cinema books, recent decades—even events during the past few years—have forced me to reevaluate my assumptions about alternative cinema, again and again, and to rethink even the moniker of this project. My original choice of "A Critical Cinema" was, of course, tactical. The crucial word was "critical"; it was chosen because the filmmakers I interviewed for *A Critical Cinema* seemed to have but one thing in common: an interest in offering implicit and explicit *critiques of* conventional cinema (which, of course, encodes larger societal patterns in simple and complex ways). My choice of "critical" was tactical in another sense, as well. During the 1980s and 1990s, as earlier volumes took shape, my assumption was that the best hope for an expanded audience and expanding uses of the field was within academe, where critique is de rigueur. My hope was that my interviews would provide a bridge between academics—not only in film studies but in a wide range of other academic fields (American studies, environmental studies, art history, for example)—and this remarkable film history.

The other words in the project title were also chosen carefully. "Cinema"—rather than "motion pictures," "film," "the movies"—seemed the best way of suggesting that *these* films were serious, worthy of respect. I decided on "*A* Critical Cinema," rather than "*The* Critical Cinema," or just "Critical Cinema," because I already knew that the field I had ventured into was larger and more varied than could be accounted for by any particular categorization or definition, and too extensive for any one scholar to chronicle adequately—that the best I could do was to chronicle *a* portion of it. That my use of "*A*" was also a form of rebellion, against Anthology Film Archives' "*The* Essential Cinema," is clear in the introduction to my interview with P. Adams Sitney.

As of 2004, only the "*A*" remains operative in the sense I originally meant; both "critical" and "cinema" have been rendered increasingly problematic. In recent years the distinction between film and video has narrowed, and to the extent that "cinema" suggests only film, it suggests an often pointless distinction. Often, interviewees in this and earlier Critical Cinema volumes are equally filmmakers and videomakers; and there is no function in acting as if their work in film is more accomplished, or critical, than their video work. Further, several interviewees have worked between film and video—shooting in film but presenting in video or DVD, or using film as raw material for video works. I am still comfortable with "A Critical *Cinema,*" but *only* in Gene Youngblood's useful sense of "cinema": "Cinema is the art of organizing a stream of audiovisual events in time. It's an event-stream, like music. There are . . . at least four media through which we can practice cinema—film, video, computer, holography—just as there are many instruments through which we practice music" (Youngblood, "Metaphysical Structuralism: The Videotapes of Bill Viola," *Millennium Film Journal,* no. 20–21 [fall/winter 1988–89]: 83).

I am less comfortable with "critical." For a number of years, I have been troubled by the way in which so many of us (and by "us" I mean those who are aware of alternative media) have relied on an essentially political justification for the noncommercial cinema we admire. In avant-garde film, at least American avant-garde film, a critique of capitalism—as exemplified and epitomized by Hollywood filmmaking—has been our mission. Now, I certainly do not want to suggest that this critique is no longer justified or useful. Indeed, few dimensions of modern American life are more embarrassing than the Hollywood blockbuster. One can only cringe at the implicit and explicit brutality, the xenophobia, and the astonishing, and astonishingly shameless, vacuousness of the American films that seem to dominate so much of the international marketplace. How can *anyone*—anyone interested in anything other than money—respect *these* films or want to emulate the lives they depict? Since Hollywood seems unable to effectively critique itself, those who teach film history must do what they can to model a thoughtful approach to the Hollywood product and the culture it represents.

The problem, of course, is that critique is, by definition, negative; it can help us understand what we are *against* and why we are against it, but it cannot by itself model a next step. But such modeling has always been another, albeit implicit, function of alternative media in general and of avant-garde film in particular. For much of the history of cinema, filmmakers working alone, or in small groups, with limited resources have found ways of creating inventive cinema within capitalist economies. Many of us have periodically made wry jokes about how the money spent on the most inexpensive Hollywood feature, even on a single shot in some Hollywood features, could finance the production of dozens of avant-garde films—and have forgotten to celebrate the fact that, despite this seemingly grim economic reality, the past half century has produced a body of work that is at least as aesthetically accomplished as the best of Hollywood cinema. I have come to feel that, whatever its (considerable) value for cultural critique, avant-garde cinema requires a new commitment on the part of scholars and exhibitors/distributors to exploring what these films *do* accomplish, and to developing a new appreciation for what this immense, complex history has to offer as a positive alternative to the film industry in Hollywood and its imitators around the world.

That more attention to the creativity (as well as the critique) offered by alternative cinema is necessary is particularly obvious right now, for the field is confronting a crisis that I could not have imagined during the years when I was first interviewing filmmakers.

16mm—and Film History—in Crisis

In the fall of 1982, I was invited to the conference "Cinema Histories/Cinema Practices II" hosted by the University of Wisconsin–Milwaukee, one of a number of attempts in those years by the new generation of film studies scholars and teachers to come to grips with two remarkable cultural projects that had seemed to burst upon the American academic scene during the 1960s and 1970s: a considerable body of new, alternative film practice (with a variety of monikers: the New American Cinema, Visionary Film, Structural Film, Expanded Cinema, the New Talkies, Feminist Cinema) and a challenging set of theoretical approaches arriving from Europe with a range of cinematic applications.

My paper offered one simple argument: that by discovering and exploring so many new ways of *writing about* film, we might soon find ourselves in the same cul-de-sac as other, more traditional academic disciplines. There would be so much writing about cinema that scholars/teachers with normal academic responsibilities and personal lives would need to choose between keeping up with scholarly commentary about film and keeping up with film history itself. To be more precise, I was already growing concerned that we would find ourselves needing to choose between producing a literature of theoretical conjectures and theoretically informed analysis of films/Film and using the screening space as a creative environment where various forms of film and film experience could critique and respond to commercial cinema and the audience that has developed for it.

Two decades later, I look back on my presentation with some embarrassment (it was more defiant than coherent), but I am surprised, and disappointed, to realize that my concerns about the impact of film scholarship on exhibition were so well-founded that with the turn of the new millennium we have arrived at a crossroads. If film studies continues on the path it has established during the past twenty years, we may soon see the disappearance of the very range of film practice that in 1982 seemed so exciting and invigorating to the film scholars who gathered in Milwaukee.

Simultaneous with the flowering of more sophisticated writing about film in the 1980s and 1990s was a decreased interest on the part of many teachers in maintaining the regular public exhibition of a substantial spectrum of cinema in and around colleges and universities. I say "maintain" because for a period at the end of the 1960s and into the 1970s, nearly every urban area and most colleges and universities had regular access not only to Hollywood first-run releases but to recent "foreign film," and to revivals of classics from here and abroad, even to new forms of documentary and a variety of forms of experimental and avant-garde work—what I call "critical cinema." Indeed, it became a prestige issue in some institutions to build theaters in which the very best screening conditions prevailed—conditions particularly necessary for those critical films that explored the edges of perception; and some filmmakers had the presumption not only to demand that their films be shown well but to interrupt screenings when a projection problem was evident and demand that the problem be fixed before beginning the screening again. That is, for a time, at least in some of those academic environments where film was finding a place, film was taken seriously both as a series of "texts" worth writing about *and* as a diverse set of in-theater experiences with the potential for perceptual, psychological, intellectual, and spiritual engagement and transformation.

The past twenty years have seen a radical change in the commitment of academe, and even among film studies academics, toward exhibition. This change is clear in the status of 16mm exhibition within educational institutions. For several generations 16mm was the gauge of home-movie-making and other more and less serious forms of amateur filmmaking; it was the gauge used by educational institutions for the presentation of nearly all forms of nonfiction film; and it was, and remains, the gauge of choice for most critical film artists who have used it and continue to use it for a broad range of explorations of perception, psychology, intellect, and spirit. Most critical filmmakers made (and still make) films in 16mm, with first-rate, 16mm theatrical presentation specifically in mind.

Yet it is increasingly common to learn that institutions of higher learning no longer have the option of 16mm exhibition, or at least are unaccustomed to using it. Nearly all colleges and universities still have decent 16mm projectors, though in many cases audiovisual departments feel under pressure or exert pressure to switch campuses entirely to VHS/DVD to avoid the expense of replacing older projectors and the ongoing costs of film rentals. The result is that manufacturers of 16mm projectors continue to disappear, and if the current trend continues, there will be no new 16mm projectors, and precious few who can service those still being used.

Were the arrival of new moving-image technologies a guarantee that even the core film history produced in 16mm could and would be passed on to the next generation, we could celebrate each nuance of technological development. But in this case at least, the de facto decision within academe to allow 16mm to be "replaced" by VHS/DVD is, in effect, the acceptance of a substantial narrowing of film history. Few who are even vaguely familiar with the world of critical cinema would be likely to argue that losing it would be a minor film-historical setback. Indeed, the accomplishments of filmmakers working in the field, and the incomparable pedagogical value of the films they have produced, make the critical cinema one of the supreme achievements in all of film history. Its disappearance would be comparable to the loss of modern poetry from literary history, or the disappearance of fresco painting from art history. To ignore the current film-historical crisis on the assumption that the better 16mm films will be preserved by the newer technologies is naive, both about the financial resources available for preservation and about the current academic commitment to this aspect of our cinematic heritage.

If, in fact, the abandonment of 16mm does result in the erasure of much of critical cinema from living film history, this would be the first major film-historical loss to occur since film studies became an academic discipline. Earlier losses of substantial dimensions of our cinematic heritage were caused by the instability of nitrate stock, by the refusal of many who had control of films to see that cinema might be more than a consumer good, by the devastation of war, and so forth, but the abandonment of 16mm and the loss of the film experiences it makes possible would be a function, it seems to me, of laziness and irresponsibility within American academe—an unusual but pervasive form of professional myopia that may be an unfortunate by-product of the widespread assumption that academic expertise is best demonstrated in scholarly publication.

Obviously I have no sweeping objection to this assumption. I have spent a good bit of my professional life writing about film, and I hope, like all scholars, that my writing is useful enough to help invigorate the field. But I do have concerns about what the current focus on written scholarship means for the ongoing potential for in-theater cinematic discourse, and I am increasingly troubled by what I see as not only a practical issue but an important ethical issue for those of us who mean to serve the field of film studies.

It is one thing to regard writing about cinema as a crucial demonstration of intellectual expertise in the field of film studies; it is quite another to assume that writing is the *only* important such demonstration and that writers are responsible only to the written discourse of which they are a part (of course, even if writing *were* the only possible demonstration of scholarship and expertise, the loss of that film history available only in 16mm would qualify the completeness and usefulness of this writing). As is true within any academic discourse about an art form, writers are, virtually by definition, dependent on those who produce the works they write about. Without filmmakers, there are no film scholars. Further, since filmmaking has been one of the more expensive artistic endeavors, this intellectual dependency has also meant that the filmmakers make the risky financial investments that provide academic writers with the potential for economically improving *their* situations. To put it more crudely, academic discourse exploits the labor and financial risk taking of filmmakers, and at least in the United States, this exploitation often seems accomplished with no apparent sense of responsibility to the filmmakers.

Of course, since a good many films that are the subject of written academic discourse are mainstream Hollywood productions, or the productions of major studios in other sectors of the world, the exploitation I am describing is hardly a cause for concern. In fact, as suggested earlier in this introduction, many of us see ourselves engaged in forms of intellectual protection against the cultural power of the film industry. Any exploitation *we* do is minor compared with the industrial exploitation of the mass audience and the toll on contemporary culture of its frequent sexism, racism, and xenophobia. We feel free, even righteous, about exploiting in a small way the industrial exploiters of millions; we are Robin Hoods deconstructing the rich in the name of the masses.

An often ignored paradox here is that in order to protect modern culture *from* the industry, we focus our attention *on* the industry and support what we are determined to expose, both in the literal sense (colleges and universities rent feature films and buy VHS copies or DVDs of major releases so they can be studied) and in the sense that ongoing academic attention in effect confirms the claim by the industry that it is the producer of virtually all films of any cultural import.

During the early years of film studies, this tendency to focus on mainstream cinema was, if not inevitable, at least understandable. There was an institutional necessity to demonstrate that film studies was intellectually respectable, and, of course, the traditional means of demonstrating this respectability was to produce written discourse. Mainstream film was not only comparatively accessible but eminently worthy of critique. The problem is that once film studies had become established, this tendency to focus on the commercial cinema, and to avoid less popular forms of film, had become habit. Some scholars continue to pretend that avant-garde film is simply a lesser art than sophisticated feature narrative cinema. Others, more interested in cultural critique than in film history, find more to work with in the commercial cinema than in the critical cinema, where patterns of sexism, racism, and xenophobia are not so obvious or influential. The bottom line is that, after thirty years of film studies, many younger film scholars and most undergraduate film students are only marginally aware that there is a substantial history of critical film.

The stockpile of 16mm critical cinema, which remains available through the major 16mm distributors—such as Canyon Cinema in San Francisco, the Filmmakers' Cooperative and the Museum of Modern Art's Circulating Film and Video Library in New York, and the Canadian Filmmakers Distribution Centre in Toronto (see the filmography for a more complete listing of distributors)—includes hundreds of films that provide illuminating interruptions in the smooth continuities and psychic repressions of industrial cinema, that model healthy defiance in a world addicted to easy compromise, that help us retrain and reinvigorate our perceptual capacities, and that reveal a sense of the sacred within a medium addicted to the profane. Critical cinema still offers the best possibility of energizing the theater space so that showing and seeing film becomes a theoretical *experience,* revealing the limits and possibilities of cinema. Here is the most underutilized major pedagogical resource available to film studies professionals, as well as to those in other disciplines who could and, I am sure, would use these films if only their colleagues in film studies would take the time to show them what is available.

At this crucial moment, I believe those of us who teach film history should use the academic purchase we have written so hard for to demand a new level of academic respect and resources for those cinematic contributions that have little chance of surviving to the next generation without our intervention. I am arguing for a last-minute rescue of 16mm that might take several particular forms.

First, while we can and should welcome new technologies that allow for more effective presentation and exploration of moving-image media, we need not, *must* not, allow an effective, proven technology, necessary for the correct presentation of crucial dimensions of alternative cinema, to disappear. Specifically, we need to protect and expand existing rental budgets for the classroom use of 16mm, so that both critical filmmakers and their distributors can remain economically viable. Certainly I understand the difficulties of expanding rental budgets during a period when many educational institutions are suffering financially as a result of a weak economy. Yet, given the necessity of protecting our film heritage, I continue to believe that most institutions can find a way to support reasonable rental budgets.

Second, many larger universities have what at one time were rental collections of 16mm prints. Often these collections are now seen as white elephants, taking up space and resources, in a world gone over to VHS/DVD and the Internet. And while it is true that many, even most, of the films in these collections are outdated educational documentaries, the collections often contain prints of films that (ironically *because* of the failure of film studies to commit to critical cinema) are sometimes in better shape than current rental prints of these same films. Surely, there is a film studies professional in every major institution who could retrieve these valuable prints before these 16mm collections are destroyed and make them available to those distribution organizations that specialize in avant-garde film.

Of course, a true rescue of critical cinema—and thus of Cinema itself—also requires a new commitment to academic exhibition. Again, in large measure because professional advancement does not require it, often does not even recognize it, programming beyond the classroom has often been left to students who—unknowingly following in the footsteps of many film studies professionals!—focus almost entirely on recent commercial releases. Those of us who teach film and video have the same obligation as professionals in other areas of the arts to provide expanded opportunities to campus and local communities. Obviously, maintaining a serious exhibition schedule for an imaginative range of critical cinema, along with video art and new digital work, requires not only research and creativity but also institutional resources, both money and time. Programmers need to be reasonably abreast of developments in media production; they need to create alliances across academic disciplines to develop audiences and financial resources for rentals and visiting artist fees; and they need to work with campus and local communications to alert the potential public about their programs. But surely, any serious department of film studies or communications ought to have a first-rate exhibition component that models the activity of creative exhibition.

Such labors in support of the full spectrum of cinema history should be rewarded not just financially but in recognition that the field of film studies cannot simply restrict itself to written discourse that is confined, for reasons of convenience, to the most easily accessible film history. We need to demonstrate to our students and colleagues in other fields that, while the popular cinema remains culturally influential and needs to be critiqued (and while it produces some remarkable films), an academically respectable, living film history must include the most inventive, accomplished work of all kinds.

A Critical Cinema 4

Chronicling the evolution of critical cinema, and of critical filmmakers' attitudes about their work, is certainly an act of hope: I *must* believe that academe will come to its senses before it is too late for 16mm and that in the coming years those of us who have access to the necessary resources will redouble our efforts to ensure that our students and colleagues have access to first-rate public presentations of the broadest range of cinema. Once this happens, we will be more likely to recognize and honor the history that has brought critical cinema to us—and not just the history of the filmmaking and the films themselves but the history of their exhibition, distribution, and preservation. This institutional history has informed the Critical Cinema project from the beginning.

The internal organization of *A Critical Cinema 4,* like earlier volumes in the series, is meant to evoke two attitudes toward the presentation of alternative film, one espoused by Amos Vogel (director of Cinema 16, author of *Film As a Subversive Art* [New York: Random House, 1974]—interviewed in *A Critical Cinema 3*), the other by Jonas Mekas (filmmaker, poet, critic, and guiding spirit of the New American Cinema—interviewed in *A Critical Cinema 2*). At Cinema 16, Vogel was interested in demonstrating the considerable variety of ways in which alternative film could function vis-à-vis audiences. The most characteristic dimension of his programming was a dialectical juxtaposition of types of film. Vogel was committed to what he considered the best avant-garde films, *and* the most remarkable documentaries, *and* the best experimental animation, *and* the most innovative and thought-provoking feature narratives, classic and modern. He admired and honored filmmakers at Cinema 16, but his more fundamental commitment was to the discourse of cinematic idea as a means of invigorating good citizenship within a modern capitalist republic, and in relation to nations across the globe. Mekas, partly in response to Vogel's programming and distribution strategies, committed himself to the individual avant-garde film artist and to the evolution and popularization of the most distinguished filmmaking careers. For Mekas these careers were not means to the end of a social discourse about cinema but remarkable cultural contributions in their own right that provided audiences with opportunities analogous to those provided by the great painters, poets, and composers. The New American Cinema was less about the use of film to provide a political critique of conventional society than about forming a new society around a particular set of filmmaking accomplishments.

In retrospect, it seems obvious that both Vogel's and Mekas's approaches to programming have proved their value and, indeed, need never have been seen as mutually exclusive. In fact, I have long believed that the inability of Vogel and Mekas to work together during the early 1960s to find a synergic balance of their approaches set the stage for an ongoing series of battles between groups of filmmakers and filmgoers that, in the end, contributed to the crisis I have just described. As a result, I have organized each of the Critical Cinema books so as to suggest that the Vogel and Mekas approaches might still be combined, and that the remarkable cinema history to which both men have devoted their lives might still take its rightful place in those institutions devoted to sustaining, expanding, and deepening an awareness of the arts and culture.

The individual interviews in *A Critical Cinema 4* are modeled on Mekas's passionate commitment to the individual film artist. That is, they are as extensive and as thorough in chronicling the evolution of individual careers as seems feasible and useful. In my interviewing and editing, I labor to provide each filmmaker with an extended (both in length and over time) opportunity to have a detailed say about particular films and about the general trajectory of her or his career.

While my work on the individual interviews is Mekas-like in its assumptions, the accumulation and organization of these interviews within each Critical Cinema volume are indebted to Vogel's work at Cinema 16. I arrange individual interviews in an order that is meant to provide a complex discourse about critical film history and current practice, and about Cinema itself—at least for that (probably rare) reader who approaches the book as a complete, integral work. For example, the opening filmmaker juxtaposition in *A Critical Cinema 4*—between Stan Brakhage and Jill Godmilow—is meant to dramatize the considerable differences in motivation and commitment, in filmmaking process and product, that characterize the wide world of critical cinema. The same is true of the subsequent juxtapositions of Godmilow with Kubelka, Kubelka with McBride, and so on. Of course, it is also true that as divergent as the juxtaposed careers included in *A Critical Cinema 4* may seem to be, there are often surprising continuities between them. For example, Brakhage is the epitome of the non-Hollywood, even anti-Hollywood, filmmaker, whereas Chuck Workman has spent much of his life in Hollywood, often producing filmic homages to the industry. On the other hand, Brakhage was always an inveterate moviegoer (during some periods of his life, he went to see a commercial film every day), and Workman counts Brakhage one of the major influences on his work. My hope is that as readers explore *A Critical Cinema 4,* they will discover the complex set of collisions and continuities that inform the volume, and that this process will produce serious thought about Cinema and the way it functions, and might function, in the world.

A Critical Cinema 4 builds on its predecessors not only by bringing new viewpoints to bear on the many issues raised and the many cinematic territories explored in earlier volumes but also by elaborating the network of explicit and implicit interconnections between and among the sixty-one previous interviews and twelve new ones. As the history of critical cinema has evolved during the past half century, filmmakers and those who have exhibited their work and responded to it have become something like a community with a shared personal and professional history, shared concerns, and a set of cinematic traditions. This implicit, and often explicit, community will be more evident in *A Critical Cinema 4* than in earlier volumes, in large measure because the number of interviews has finally reached the critical mass necessary for the many interrelationships to declare themselves. My hope is that this new volume will result in a fuller sense of the Critical Cinema series as a single, interlocked metaconversation.

As in each of the earlier volumes, certain themes or motifs characterize the discussions in *A Critical Cinema 4*. Generally speaking, the makers interviewed here choose among two approaches. Several take the earlier history of cinema in all its forms—or at least what has survived of that history—as raw material and recycle it into new, imaginative forms. Of course, "recycled cinema" or "found-footage film" is hardly new: Joseph Cornell, Bruce Conner (see *A Critical Cinema*), and Raphael Montañez Ortiz (see *A Critical Cinema 3*) had made it a valuable option for filmmakers by 1960. But during the final decades of the twentieth century, recycling became a dominant strategy, and *A Critical Cinema 4* includes a set of major contributors to it, remarkable for their diversity, including Chuck Workman, Peter Forgács, Abigail Child, and Lawrence Brose.

Other filmmakers have wrestled with the perennial question of how to merge aesthetics and politics in productive ways: how to create new forms of cinema that can allow filmmakers to express—and viewers to understand and enjoy—ideas, experiences, attitudes, commitments, concerns, needs, and frustrations that do not find expression within the commercial media. Obvious examples include Jill Godmilow, Peter Kubelka, Peter Forgács, Abigail Child, Chantal Akerman, Shirin Neshat, and Ellen Spiro—though all the filmmakers I have interviewed have engaged this question at some level.

Each Critical Cinema volume has also had a distinct "topography," both in terms of its relationship to previous Critical Cinema volumes and in terms of how the interviews are organized. The fact that until *A Critical Cinema 4* each of the volumes was larger than the previous one was my way of suggesting the continuing expansion and importance of the field the project surveys. While *A Critical Cinema 4* interrupts this pattern, this is only because at one point the book had grown so large as to be impractical—and bifurcated into two volumes.

A Critical Cinema 5, which so far includes interviews with Peggy Ahwesh, James Benning, Alan Berliner, Nathaniel Dorsky, Ernie Gehr, Kano Shiho, George Kuchar, Sharon Lockhart, J. Leighton Pierce, and Phil Solomon, will quickly follow *A Critical Cinema 4:* another way of suggesting how relentlessly this field continues to develop and expand.

A Critical Cinema 4 is rhythmically organized, moving back and forth between sets of extended interviews and pairs of shorter interviews focusing on particular films and videos. The organizational regularity and symmetry of the volume can be read as my way of trying to maintain a grip on a field that seems to be moving in many directions simultaneously, a field that continues to erupt with creativity despite periodic claims that it is on the verge of demise.

Obviously, the very nature of the Critical Cinema project—its pretense of surveying a field—has required that in each volume I explore a variety of kinds of career. *A Critical Cinema 4* includes interviews that discuss the careers of makers who have been productive for decades (the interview with Brakhage begins with his earliest films, made half a century ago, and concludes with films made in the late 1990s); interviews that honor recent contributions by makers who remain better known for earlier work (the interview with Chantal Akerman about her recent Place trilogy, for example); interviews that provide a new look at particular classic films (a conversation with Jim McBride about *David Holzman's Diary,* 1967); and interviews that focus on younger filmmakers or on filmmakers whose reputations have developed more recently (Shirin Neshat and Ellen Spiro). The emphasis certainly remains historical; though I continue to be interested in emerging makers, my primary concern is with those many productive careers that have not begun to receive the attention they deserve.

Each Critical Cinema volume includes interviews with filmmakers whose inclusion broadens the scope of "critical cinema" and hopefully along with it, the audience for these books, and for the wide world of cinema itself. Some might argue that my inclusion of Chuck Workman, Jill Godmilow, Ellen Spiro, and Peter Forgács in *A Critical Cinema 4* confuses the project's rationale. Workman is a Hollywood filmmaker in many senses; he does not produce big-budget features, though he has worked in and around the industry for decades, making, first, trailers for commercial films and, more recently, other kinds of sponsored projects. He is also an independent documentarian and an independent feature director. He is included in *A Critical Cinema 4,* however, because the compilation montages he makes for various commercial entities, including the annual Academy Awards shows (in 2003, Workman contributed five short montages to the awards show, one for each of the acting awards and a fifth, reviewing a history of the Best Picture awards), are a significant contribution to the history of "recycled cinema." Like Slavko Vorkapich and Saul Bass, Workman has found a way of working independently, and sometimes "critically," even within "the belly of the beast."

Godmilow and Spiro, and even Forgács, might normally be considered documentarians—though the distinction between "documentary" and "avant-garde" has never been less clear, as is obvious in such recent books as Catherine Russell's *Experimental Ethnography* (Durham, N.C.: Duke University Press, 1999); Barry Keith Grant and Jeannette Sloniowski, eds., *Documenting the Documentary* (Detroit, Mich.: Wayne State University Press, 1998); and Patricia R. Zimmermann's *States of Emergency* (Minneapolis: University of Minnesota Press, 2000). Ever since *A Critical Cinema 2,* I have implicitly argued that "critical cinema" includes a good many makers who are also included, or at least should be included, in histories of documentary (Ross McElwee, Trinh T. Minh-ha, Godfrey Reggio, and Peter Watkins are interviewees in *A Critical Cinema 2;* and William Greaves, Arthur Peleshian, Hara Kazuo, Watkins, and Mani Kaul are interviewees in *A Critical Cinema 3*). Indeed, much of the history of documentary might be considered critical cinema, since documentary has always offered at least an implicit critique of the popular fictions produced by the industry. On the other hand, there is no particular shortage of documentary historians and commentators; and I have tended to include only inventive documentarians who have not routinely received attention elsewhere and who have functioned somewhere in the gap between the historical categories of "avant-garde" and "documentary," as is certainly the case with Forgács, Godmilow, and Spiro.

It is also true that I continue to focus on *film*makers, rather than on *media*makers, despite the fact that in many cases, perhaps in the majority of cases now, the distinction between filmmaking, videomaking, and digital work is at best ambiguous. To champion filmmaking as somehow more important than video or digital work can seem hopelessly old-fashioned and theoretically unsupportable—and yet, there are a good many filmmakers who remain committed to the celluloid muse; and their accomplishments in what often seems to be a disappearing medium can seem particularly poignant, and worthy of documentation and discussion, in part *because* of its very precariousness. On the other hand, most of my interviewees have worked in both film and video, either in combination or as two distinct but equally viable cinematic options. Peter Forgács transforms home movies shot in various film gauges into "video operas"; Chuck Workman recycles bits of old Hollywood blockbusters into film montages for broadcast on television; Shirin Neshat exhibits her films as video installations or, more recently, as DVD projections. Abigail Child now works both in film and in video or digital formats, depending on the project and on the resources available at any given moment. And Ellen Spiro works entirely in video but thinks of what she produces as "films."

What strikes me as the accomplishment and ingenuity of the works I commit to must be reasonably durable: that is, generally I need to experience these works as remarkable, screening after screening, and ideally to continue to discover new and interesting dimensions of them, and/or I need to see that these works continue to have considerable value for my students. I would not say I never tire of the works that seem ingenious to me—most any work can lose its excitement if experienced too much, and some accomplished works are simply less dense than others—but I will say that in nearly all cases, if I come to admire a film or set of films to the extent that I feel I must interview the maker, my admiration for the accomplishment of this work tends to be comparatively long-lasting, and the work's value within a teaching context continues to be obvious to me.

From the beginning, I have always understood that, given my own predilections, to limit my project to filmmakers who make films relevant to the issues I personally care about, or even to filmmakers who make films that at any given moment I happen to love, would be counterproductive to my project as a whole. Like anyone who works in this field, I have come to understand that many of my most crucial, transformative film and video experiences do not begin as pleasure and, in some cases, may never inspire my personal affection.

My earliest experiences with the films of Stan Brakhage during the late 1960s did not result in my feeling that his films are remarkable. My utter boredom with nearly all the underground films I saw during those years is reflected in my inability to recall which particular Brakhage films I did see. On the other hand, I vividly recall my utter horror and outrage at Brakhage's *The Act of Seeing with One's Own Eyes* (1971) when I saw it in Binghamton, New York, soon after it was finished. For many of my interviewees, Brakhage's films were an immediate revelation and an ongoing inspiration, but my admiration for them was an acquired taste, one that grew slowly out of my fury at *The Act of Seeing with One's Own Eyes:* I simply could not stop thinking about the film and, in time, wanted my students to join me in grappling with this and other Brakhage films.

Of course, while my hope is that these collections of interviews provide a service to a remarkably underserved field, I am fully aware of the considerable limitations of the Critical Cinema project. I have interviewed a good many filmmakers—seventy-four, if we include *A Critical Cinema 4*—but there are certainly important makers not included in these volumes, among them, many who passed on before I could talk with them about their work. Looking back, I can only wonder why I did not act more quickly to interview Harry Smith, Sidney Peterson, Jack Smith, Shirley Clarke, Derek Jarman, Warren Sonbert, and so many others. Obviously, whatever ambition I have for the Critical Cinema project is terribly compromised by such gaps. Further, whereas my interviews are as thorough as I can make them, or at least as seems sensible at the time of the interview, the best any interview can do is evoke something like a clear sense of what a filmmaker has meant to accomplish and of the personal, social, aesthetic, and political contexts within which the filmmaker's contributions have developed. If the interview can provide a glimpse of the filmmaker as a person, so much the better.

Certainly, I recognize that while some of my choices of interviewees will seem appropriate to virtually everyone even vaguely familiar with the field of alternative media, other choices will seem surprising, even inappropriate. I am sure that to some readers, my selection of interviewees may seem not just eclectic but too inclusive or even, at times, "politically correct" in the worst sense: that is, a way of currying favor, especially within academe, by honoring makers primarily on the basis of their ethnicity, gender, or sexual orientation rather than for any real accomplishment in their work. I can only say that I am committed to talking with makers about works of quality and importance, and I never interview a maker whose work does not, at least in part, convince me of its accomplishment and significance. Obviously, few words are more charged than "quality" and "importance." How do we measure the "quality" of a film or of a filmmaking career? What makes a critical film or video "important," and important to whom? I certainly have no answer to questions that have confounded aestheticians for centuries. I do hope, however, that my introductions to the individual interviews and the interviews themselves provide adequate justification for my choices of interviewees.

It is true that I work to make the Critical Cinema books "politically correct," but not in the sense that I include interviewees who, as film artists, do not deserve whatever tiny bit of recognition these volumes provide. I *do* make sure that each collection includes a representation of women and men, of older, middle-aged, and younger makers, and, to the degree possible, of makers who come to make critical cinema from a variety of backgrounds. Indeed, my deepest reservation about *A Critical Cinema 4* is that it does not represent as wide a range of nationalities and ethnicities as I would have liked.

In the end, my hope is that the interviews in *A Critical Cinema 4,* and those in future Critical Cinema volumes, will be able to overcome, at least in some measure, whatever limitations are evident in my method and in my selection process, and will help to enlarge the reader's sense of a portion of a remarkable cinematic history. The voices represented here will, I trust, enlarge the reader's sense of that extended and continually extending community of mediamakers devoted to providing audiences with exciting, challenging, thought-provoking, sometimes life-changing moving-image experiences that are simultaneously valuable and memorable in their own right *and* a tonic for those frustrated with the more popular forms of media and looking for productive alternatives to experience and support. And should the reader be a teacher, I would hope that an exploration of the many approaches to cinema evident in these interviews and a more developed sense of the remarkable accomplishments of my interviewees might suggest new pedagogical strategies, might help to invigorate classrooms in a wide range of academic fields so that, in time, the astonishing contribution of critical cinema might achieve its rightful place in the history of culture.

P. Adams Sitney

When I was finding my way into the world of avant-garde cinema during the middle to late 1970s—going to screenings at Anthology Film Archives when screenings were held in the Invisible Cinema at the Public Theater (designed by Peter Kubelka) and later, after Anthology had moved, on Wooster Street— the most visible presence, aside from the ubiquitous Jonas Mekas, was P. Adams Sitney. In those days, Sitney was for me a problematic figure. Of course, I knew his groundbreaking *Visionary Film* (Oxford University Press), first published in 1974—a revised, expanded edition appeared in 2002—and the three collections he edited during the decade: *Film Culture Reader* (New York: Praeger, 1970); *The Essential Cinema: Essays on the Films in the Collection of Anthology Film Archives* (New York: Anthology Film Archive/New York University Press, 1975); and *The Avant-Garde Film: A Reader of Theory and Criticism* (New York: New York University Press, 1978). But I was also in a state of rebellion against what Sitney seemed to represent.

In *The Essential Cinema* there is a photograph of the Anthology Film Archives selection committee (Ken Kelman, James Broughton, Sitney, Mekas, and Peter Kubelka), the group that had selected "the Essential Cinema"—the "nuclear collection of the monuments of cinematic art," to use Sitney's phrase— that would become the repertory of Anthology Film Archives. Stephen Shore's photograph of the committee, it seemed to me then, perfectly captured the dimension of Sitney that I was rebelling against. There is something rather forbidding about the photograph, something arrogant, even hostile; and, in the 1970s, when so many of us were coming to grips with issues of gender and sexuality, and confronting whatever dimensions of patriarchy had infected us,

The Anthology Film Archives Selection Committee. *From left:* Ken Kelman, James Broughton, P. Adams Sitney, Jonas Mekas, and Peter Kubelka. Photograph by Stephen Shore. Courtesy Anthology Film Archives.

this photograph seemed particularly reactionary. The elaborately bearded Sitney, standing in the center of the photograph, seemed the patriarch among patriarchs. Of course, the committee's presumption in selecting *the* "monuments of cinematic art" seemed utterly typical of patriarchs everywhere. When I finally made what I hoped was a substantial contribution to the field in 1988, I decided on the title, "*A* Critical Cinema," in conscious contradistinction to the "*The*" in *The Essential Cinema.*

Looking back at that moment, and that photograph, from a quarter of a century later, I recognize that while some of my reactions to the essential cinema project may have been sensible, my hostility to Sitney was largely a function of my envy. I had come into the field not simply because of my growing passion for alternative cinema but because the field in which I had earned my academic degrees—American literature—was already so crowded with scholars that even when I did have something like a new insight into a Hemingway short story (my Ph.D. thesis focused on Hemingway's use of narrative perspective in his short stories), I lived in fear that another scholar would have that same insight and would get it published before I did. This situation was very frustrating, even embarrassing, since it meant that when someone *did* have a new insight, I was *disappointed!* What kind of a teacher *was* I, if I was *un*happy when colleagues in the field shared my understanding?

By the late 1970s, I had come to feel that whatever small, scholarly contribution I might be able to make would be of considerably more use in the field of avant-garde film than in American literature. I thought I had taken to heart Nam June Paik's famous advice to "go where there's no competition," but, of course, once I began exploring this new field, I discovered that there *was* competition, and formidable competition at that. If, from the beginning, my Critical Cinema project was designed as a counterpoint to *Visionary Film* that would model a different way of doing scholarship—oral history—and bring a broader spectrum of film artists into the historical repertory of avant-garde film, I recognize now that my hostility to Sitney's fine work was ungenerous and counterproductive.

In the early 1970s, it was possible to imagine that the cultural, and especially the academic, visibility of avant-garde film would expand and, if not replace the widespread cultural focus on Hollywood, provide a powerful and pervasive response and corrective to it. Indeed, that very somber look on the faces of the Anthology selection committee was, I can see now, directed at the commercial cinema and its assumption of cinematic preeminence. Of course, as years have gone by, our early hope that critical cinema would become a major cultural force has come to seem, if not a silly fantasy, at best a tenuous possibility; and my youthful sense of the field, in which Sitney seemed an adversary, has evolved. For a variety of reasons, some of which are discussed in the general introduction to this volume, the remarkable and continuing growth of the field of avant-garde film (and video) through the 1970s, 1980s, and 1990s was not attended by a comparable development of cultural, or academic, attention. Indeed, there are times when this entire cultural project seems poised to disappear. And, of course, this very precariousness has helped me to appreciate those who have devoted themselves, in whatever ways, to the development and maintenance of the field—and especially Sitney, who is as supportive and generous a colleague as one could have.

My decision to interview Sitney for *A Critical Cinema 4*—he is the second nonfilmmaker interviewee included in the project (Amos Vogel was interviewed for *A Critical Cinema 3*)—was a function of my recognizing so recently what many must have known all along: that Sitney seemed to be a patriarch in the early 1970s in part because he had been a wunderkind in the 1950s and 1960s. By the early 1960s, when he was still in his midteens, Sitney had made himself a fixture in the alternative film scene, and, when he completed *Visionary Film* at the ripe old age of twenty-nine, it incorporated well over a decade of passionate engagement with nearly all facets of the avant-garde film scene, including his seeing and studying hundreds of films; writing extensively about many film-makers and the issues raised by their films; founding and editing *Filmwise,* and subsequently editing *Film Culture* (when it was this nation's most interesting film periodical); and traveling the world with programs of avant-garde film that were to have considerable impact on fledgling filmmakers in many cultures.

I realized that my project would profit from a discussion with Sitney about his early experiences in the field; and in fact he was able to offer a valuable per-spective on a largely underchronicled moment in the history of alternative media: the late 1950s and early 1960s. Sitney and I talked at his home near Princeton in May 2000 and refined the resulting interview by mail.

MacDonald: Most people are aware of your contributions to avant-garde film history during the late sixties and early seventies, especially in a series of books: *Visionary Film, Avant-Garde Film: A Reader,* and *The Essential Cinema.* But by the time you were making those contributions, you had already been on the scene for years. In fact, you had found your way to avant-garde cinema at an unusually young age. I'm curious how a high school student from New Haven got involved with avant-garde film.

Sitney: My father owned a "bodega"-sized, one-person grocery store two blocks from the Yale campus. As a streetwise kid, I began to use Yale Univer-sity. I started entering the buildings when I was ten years old, and soon I was attending classes. Professors thought I was the son of a graduate student, and graduate students thought I was the son of a professor.

At ten, I was mostly interested in collecting rocks and fossils, so I would hang out in the geology department. Later, I attended other kinds of events at the university. As a teenager, my idea was to go to Harvard, become a Greek professor, and be a poet. I didn't do any of those things.

More to the point, I began attending screenings at the Yale Film Society, when I was fifteen.

MacDonald: This is when?

Sitney: 1958, 1959. I was born in 1944. I remember seeing *Un Chien Andalou* [1929], which utterly enthralled me, for all of the adolescent reasons: the vio-lence, the sexuality, the mystery.

At that time I was working at an after-school job at the university, in a med-ical lab, injecting rats and pigeons with LSD—long before anyone was taking LSD. Those psychology lab experiments had a formative effect on my life. I was just a lab assistant, but I was involved in all the processes. We'd have to decapitate the rats and analyze their brains. As a result, in the sixties I never, ever took drugs, and I begged my friends not to take LSD, but they were mostly just astonished that I had had access to a little safe with a hundred thousand dol-lars' worth of LSD.

My working at the university allowed me to have a library card. I couldn't take books out of the library, but I read the *Art in Cinema* catalogue [Frank Stauffacher, ed., published by the San Francisco Museum of Art, 1947] and Manvell's *Experiment in the Film* [London: Grey Walls Press, 1949] with adolescent intensity, and that gave me a need to see the films that were described.

MacDonald: Besides *Un Chien Andalou,* what do you remember seeing at the Yale Film Society?

Sitney: Everything from *Casablanca* [1942] to *Rashomon* [1950], the standard repertory of the late fifties.

MacDonald: Other experimental films?

Sitney: They had one experimental film night, and the university owned prints of *At Land* [1944] and *A Study in Choreography for Camera* [1945].

During high school I earned money as a projectionist for the film society and discovered that the art history department had no interest in the films that Maya Deren had sent them. They let me take the films out as long as I brought them back every week, so I was able to look at them over and over.

In 1958 or 1959 I started my own film society at the local YMCA where we showed exclusively avant-garde films.

MacDonald: How many people came to those events?

Sitney: Between fifteen and thirty. One of the regular viewers was a very individualistic and eccentric playwright from the drama school named Ken Kelman. He had a remarkable ability to write very, very quickly and very well, and I encouraged him to write on some of these films for the little newsletter we had started, which was called *Filmwise.*

Around 1959 a graduate student at the Yale School of Art, named Thomas Mapp, a painter who had come from the University of Colorado, organized a big series of experimental films, which included a number of Brakhage films (he had been in close contact with Brakhage in Colorado) and Bruce Connor films, and much of the Cinema 16 rental collection. Just by being in New Haven at the right time, I had this extraordinary access to a preliminary cinematic education.

Later, Brakhage arrived in New York to show some films, and I got a friend to drive me to New York. I was very taken with Brakhage. He was about ten years older than I was, so I must have been about sixteen. He had just finished *The Dead* [1960], and I wanted to do a show of his work in New Haven, but he was leaving to go back west. We began to correspond, and he sent me all these writings that he had been unable to publish, and I decided to do a special issue of *Filmwise.* As I worked on the issue, it got bigger and bigger. People were sending me things that I hadn't expected. Kelman wrote something; Willard Maas sent a memoir; Parker Tyler contributed; and my high school friends, a miniature subculture of nerds, contributed things too. Of my friends none would become known, except George Landow, my oldest friend from babyhood, who was interested, above all, in *making* films of this kind. This issue of our little journal, which we called *Filmwise 1* (because it would be the first we had sold outside the film society), was unbelievably successful.

During this time I was writing my own criticism, but for a while I had fantasies of being a filmmaker. I made a couple of films, which cured me of *that* desire. It turned out to be a great gift for me to realize that what I could do best was be a writer and scholar of these films. When you're a teenager, or even older, it's very hard to make the move from the obviously sexier position of the artist, to the scholarly and critical role. But once that happened, my mission was pretty clear.

MacDonald: Could you talk about your experience of the New York scene during those early years.

Sitney: Probably the most important single figure in encouraging me to do the Brakhage issue of *Filmwise,* and in encouraging any number of other young people, was Gregory Markopoulos. He responded very early to my request for a New Haven show. He had finished a 35mm film called *Serenity,* that we couldn't show, and was working on *Twice a Man* [1963], and agreed to show *Twice a Man* with us as soon as it was finished—which wasn't to be for a couple of years.

Gregory was an enormously generous person. When I had originally begun to correspond with filmmakers, Markopoulos was the first to respond. He invited me to stop by Brentano's bookstore, where he worked, and I did, and spent most of a day talking to him when there weren't customers. He had very little money—I think he was earning forty dollars a week, and he lived in a very modest, though elegant, apartment—but when he realized that I was trying to put together a magazine on Brakhage and that I couldn't come up with twenty dollars to mimeograph a hundred copies, he said that if I kept it a secret, he would pay for the printing, so there could be a couple of hundred copies instead of the ten or fifteen that we normally made. The Gotham Book Mart bought all the copies, so it was immediately out of print. Then, almost immediately, copies were worth several dollars apiece.

MacDonald: Why did he want it to be a secret?

Sitney: He didn't want to be seen as the patron of the magazine or have people misinterpret his motives. It was just a generous gesture. He didn't want anything for it.

The Brakhage issue was such a success that we decided we would do a Maya Deren issue. Then came a Willard Maas and Marie Menken issue. By this time, through Markopoulos, I had met Jonas Mekas and was going to his presentations at the Charles Theater. Because I was collecting so much material for *Filmwise,* Jonas asked me to join the editorial board of *Film Culture. Filmwise* came to an end with the Maas-Menken issue, and *Film Culture* became more receptive to publishing the kind of material that had been appearing in *Filmwise.*

Gregory had a way of treating young people as though they had a full roster of accomplishments behind them. He would introduce me as a film critic. He had also gathered around him a number of other young people: Nick Dorsky and Jerry Hiler, Warren Sonbert, Tom Chomont, and ultimately Robert Beavers, Gerard Malanga, Andrew Meyer, David Brooks, and others whose names I've forgotten. There were many, many people that he was constantly encouraging, loaning his camera to, giving an extra roll of film to, putting their films on the same show as his. In general, he was a kind of a spiritual leader to all of these young people.

Now, by and large, these were gay young men, though this wasn't in any sense a requirement. David Brooks and I were not gay. There was no sexual component to Markopoulos's enthusiasm and support. And while the group around him was almost all men, it wasn't exclusive in that respect. At various times there were young women in that circle. There was a critic named Mary Batton, and Margot Brier, who worked at the Film-makers' Cinematheque and played Pandora in *The Iliac Passion* [1967].

Markopoulos was a crucial figure in terms of putting us in touch with each other and in introducing us into places that we could never have accessed on our own. He was extremely well dressed, very handsome, and very dignified. He had entrée almost everywhere, including all sorts of artsy parties on the Upper West Side and Park Avenue. He could create access.

The end of Markopoulos's career, and his later antagonism to the American avant-garde, his aloofness, shouldn't overshadow the historical record that he was this extremely generous figure. Even when he was dying, various Austrians and Germans whom he had helped were trying to be of some help to him—again, young people.

MacDonald: Why the change in attitude later on?

Sitney: I was not the witness to it. I'm the witness only to its effect. He met Beavers and established a relationship with him unlike any I had ever known him to have. He was intensely in love. At that time, he was one of the first film-maker teachers, traveling back and forth to the Art Institute of Chicago, which I think he didn't like doing. Beavers was going to Europe (Markopoulos had arranged some introductions for him), and Markopoulos decided to join him and then didn't want to come back. He believed that whatever had been going on in New York was over, had been corrupted. I would guess that there were all sorts of developments in the late sixties that he was very uneasy with.

MacDonald: Was his early influence a function of his films?

Sitney: One of the things he did that no one else had ever done, and it transformed the whole mode of seeing avant-garde films, was to show rushes. At the end of a regular show, an audience of twenty or thirty people might stay on (or may have arrived late, just for this) to see the dailies of *Twice a Man.* The dailies became a kind of ironical serial that was shown one episode at a time. It gradually became an event.

Jack Smith picked up on that, and I think Andy Warhol's *Kiss* [1963] was modeled on Markopoulos. In the minds of many of us, *Twice a Man* was *the*

Press conference on Underground Film at Overseas Press Club at the United Nations, December 1963. *From left:* Gregory Markopoulos, P. Adams Sitney, Andy Warhol, and Ron Rice. Photograph by Jonas Mekas. Courtesy Anthology Film Archives.

most exciting ongoing project, and part of the excitement was the ability to see it, section by section, as it developed. All during 1962 and 1963, one was seeing material shot for *Twice a Man,* and it was dazzlingly beautiful, which, of course, created an anticipation and interest in the finished film. *Twice a Man* was a transfiguring work in Markopoulos's own career. It was much longer than any of his previous 16mm films. It was finished in the fall of 1963.

One of the interesting things about the field in those days was the widespread myth that people were just about to move from making avant-garde films to making a new kind of commercial film. This notion has failed, decade after decade. There was a period in the early sixties when Shirley Clarke and Jonas, and any number of other people, thought the moment had come for a 35mm avant-garde cinema. Markopoulos was the first to realize that there was no possibility of this.

Markopoulos also went to everybody's screening and spoke enthusiastically to the filmmakers afterward. I think the whole scene would have been different without Markopoulos's presence. No one else—not even Jonas—was as influential in encouraging and bolstering young people to make films. Markopoulos also brought Leslie Trumbull to Jonas, and Leslie became the head of the Filmmakers' Coop. I'm sure I'm leaving out many people, because Markopoulos was *always* bringing in new people, new enthusiasts.

Also associated with Markopoulos was a group that published a magazine called *Scenario.* These were youngish filmmakers, who occasionally showed films in storefronts. Charles Levine was part of this group. Many of these people spent more time talking about the films they were going to make than actually making films, but a number actually did make films, including people we no longer hear from, like Joseph Marzano and Lloyd Williams. I spent a lot of time with these people, arguing with them about films.

Of course, as important as he was, Markopoulos was certainly not the only important presence. One evening, a young guy who had an extraordinary job at Sarah Lawrence College, then an all-women's school, came to New York to show his mythological film, *Icaris* [1960]. It was Brian DePalma. Also there was Dan Drasin at Harvard, who had made a film called *Sunday* [1961], documenting folk singers being violently ejected from Washington Square Park; Jonas proclaimed *Sunday* one of the four cornerstones of the "new cinema."

I wasn't introduced to Willard Maas and Marie Menken until I had been going to New York for a year or two. They had a "penthouse" in Brooklyn, actually a shack on top of a roof in Brooklyn Heights. It was filled with antiques, and there was *always* company there and *always* a dinner going on, and a great deal of drinking. Maas was both fascinating and scary to me, as were the aggressive attentions of Ondine (later Ondine became a friend). I had known many homosexuals, but I had never been in the company of someone as flamboyantly and publicly homosexual as Maas was. But there was always nourishment of some sort over in Brooklyn Heights at Maas and Menken's.

I think the very first time I met Maas was at the Charles Theater, at a screening of Marie's films. He was obviously inebriated and openly necking with Gerard Malanga, who was my age. I had never seen anything like that before. When I first went to his apartment, I was very uneasy, not knowing what was ironical and what was direct, and feeling very strange and threatened. But I quickly got over that.

Maas was also extremely helpful to me. He wrote amusing autobiographical texts for *Filmwise,* reflecting on Maya Deren or Brakhage. I believe it was with Maas and Malanga that I first encountered Andy Warhol, but I was already in college by then and familiar with most of the avant-garde environments in New York.

MacDonald: What do you remember from the screenings at the Charles?

Sitney: The Charles was very far east, maybe Avenue C around Twelfth Street, kitty-corner from Stanley's, a bar frequented by artists. Most of the time the Charles would show European repertory films and Hollywood auteurs, but at midnight on weekends, Jonas would present avant-garde film shows. You could either pay admission or bring a roll of film to show. Poets and filmmakers would gather for those screenings. One would see the poet Tully Kupferberg and Taylor Mead, and Ken Jacobs would show up. There would be either an open

Marie Menken and Willard Maas. Photograph by J. H. Hawkins. Courtesy Anthology Film Archives.

screening (that's how Jonas first discovered Ken Jacobs, who brought *Little Stabs at Happiness* to the Charles one midnight), or Jonas would have set up a program of films of, say, Ron Rice, or Marie Menken.

There was almost a kind of Moses and Aaron scene between Jonas and Adolfas. Jonas was very shy, spoke with a stammer, and worried about his English. Adolfas would stand around, very flamboyantly, in his tailor-made suit, with a cigarette holder, and was the mouthpiece. I spent time with Adolfas and eventually became quite close to Jonas, as well; but that was much slower: Jonas was much more reticent.

I proved myself to Jonas and Adolfas by being a willing laborer. I remember working all night on *Film Culture* on pasteups, cutting galleys. They would send me out at twelve o'clock at night because they had run out of rubber cement, and it would take me two hours to find rubber cement in Manhattan in the middle of the night. But it was the kind of thing I could do, and eventually it earned me my status at *Film Culture.*

Jonas was able to generate an audience because he was a film critic at the *Village Voice,* an extremely powerful position at that time. Week by week, crucial information on the avant-garde cinema was to be found in Jonas's column. One of the first major publications I wrote for was the *Voice,* when Jonas asked me to write his column while he went off to a festival for a couple of weeks. It was the first time I ever got paid for writing—ten dollars a column, I think, which in those days was pretty decent.

MacDonald: Were you aware of Cinema 16 at this time?

Sitney: I slowly began to realize that there was a kind of rivalry between the screenings at the Charles and Cinema 16.

During my high school years I would stay in New York until Sunday in order to attend the Cinema 16 screenings, which were set up long in advance and were designed as a smorgasbord of genres. You might see an exotic documentary— I remember one about people walking on fire—and an avant-garde film from America, and maybe something from the Polish Film School, and an extraordinary scientific film.

At this point, there seemed to be a division of filmmakers. Certain of the more established avant-garde filmmakers—Robert Breer, Ed Emshwiller, Stan Vanderbeek—would be more likely to be seen at Cinema 16 than at the Charles Cinema. But by the end of the Charles screenings, in 1962, it was clear that a major shift had occurred; all of those people were starting to show up at the Charles.

MacDonald: Tell me more about the division between the Charles screenings and Cinema 16.

Sitney: Well, it was a division I really didn't understand and had to intuit, because neither of the principals ever spoke directly about it. I would go over to Cinema 16, where I had rented a lot of films in the past, and had become friendly with Jack Goelman. I first understood that there was a problem when I realized Amos was annoyed because I hadn't told him that the Maya Deren issue of *Filmwise,* which Cinema 16 had supported, had also been supported by the Film-makers' Cooperative.

Then, one evening later on, I think I overheard Vanderbeek talking with Jonas and some other people, saying, "Now that we're doing this, we have to go tell Amos." I presume they were going to be distributing their films through the Film-makers' Cooperative, and if Amos insisted on exclusive distribution through Cinema 16—exclusive distribution was part of Cinema 16's way of working— they were going to leave him.

Again, since I wasn't a filmmaker, and since I was a kid, I was on the outside trying to feel my way around this. My sense was that Jonas thought that he was doing his own thing and didn't feel in competition with Cinema 16. Amos and Jack felt that they had carefully built up something that had a very delicate, minimal economy, and that this new development was disruptive and also bad for the field. There was also a real ideological difference: Amos and Jack seemed to think that if films like *Anticipation of the Night* [1958] were shown, audiences would stop being interested in avant-garde films, and, of course, that position fueled the moral polemic of Jonas and all the people who were wild about Brakhage.

Amos Vogel and American filmmakers in 1960 in Berlin's Sportspalast for an event organized by Cinema 16 and Literarisches Colloquium. *From left, front row:* Stan Brakhage, Carmen D'Avino, Stan Vanderbeek, and Ed Emshwiller; *from left, back row:* Bruce Conner, Shirley Clarke, Walter Hoellerer (of Literarisches Colloquium), and Vogel. Courtesy Amos Vogel.

MacDonald: Menken was involved in this, too, right? Brakhage told me that he rebelled because Amos wouldn't show Menken's films.

Sitney: I don't think it was because Amos wouldn't show Menken. You know, in support of Amos, plans for a Menken screening would usually begin with Willard storming in, often in a belligerent, inebriated mood, demanding that someone show something of Marie's. Of course, this film of Marie's wasn't even glued together yet, but Maas would demand that a screening be scheduled anyway.

Amos and Jack, who ran a business of sorts, programmed six or seven months in advance and of course would want to see a film before deciding to show it. And once they had seen it, they might say yes or no to any particular Menken film. Rejection, even hesitation, would send Willard into a terrible huff.

For Jonas, Willard's approach was fine. Jonas agreed to have a screening for Marie at the Charles, and I'd guess that a third of her films were made the night before that screening. She was up all night putting them together. Some had sound tracks, some didn't. Gerard Malanga was making titles; Willard was running around screaming and cursing out everybody involved. Cinema 16 simply couldn't operate that way, but Jonas could.

MacDonald: Were you a member of Cinema 16?

Sitney: Well for years I couldn't afford it. It cost something like fifteen dollars, a fabulous amount of money in those days. As I got to know Jack and Amos, they let me in free. In fact, one evening I absolutely saved a show for them. I forget what the film was, but they discovered it was on cores, and needed reels. This was the kind of thing I was good at. I went running out and remembering that Adolfas was editing *Hallelujah the Hills* [1965], ran to the editing room and grabbed all the 35mm reels I could get and rushed back down to the Needle Trades Auditorium so they could project the film. I always tried to make myself useful.

MacDonald: What do you remember about particular Cinema 16 screenings?

Sitney: They were so mixed. The Sunday morning screenings were at eleven o'clock, in what were then posh, new, uptown theaters, like the Beekman. Those screenings felt like going to church. The people would be dressed up in jackets and ties. They'd see the latest Japanese film or a collection of short films from the Polish Film School. The people looked interesting, but it was a little bit like going to the New York Philharmonic: there wasn't a lobby life.

If I saw someone I knew at a Cinema 16 screening, I might end up going out with them, but one didn't have the sense of being part of a community. Amos, and some of the people who were twenty years older, composers and writers and so on, knew each other; but these were the kind of people who had enough money to go to a restaurant. Of course, it turns out that many, many fascinating people were in those Cinema 16 audiences.

The more radical shows were on Wednesday night, down at the Needle Trades Auditorium. It was harder for me to get in from high school on Wednesday nights, but when I think about how often I played hooky and how often I managed to get to New York, I'm rather astonished now.

While Cinema 16 was Lincoln Center, the Charles was like a clubhouse. Down at the Charles, people who didn't even have enough money to go to Stanley's for a beer could hang out in the lobby after screenings.

This was the era of Horn and Hardarts, where you could buy one cup of tea and sit for hours, constantly resoaking the teabag in hot water. If you were really daring, you could use the free lemons and sugar to make yourself a lemonade. In those days it was possible to live in New York with no money. New York was a dying city. No one wanted to live there. George Landow's apartment cost nine dollars a month. The toilet was in the hall. There was a whole culture in New York of people living on next to nothing. When I worked at *Film Culture* full-time, we were opposite the Belmar Cafeteria, where you could get three vegetables for forty-five cents, a whole plate piled with vegetables. This was the main meal of the day.

MacDonald: You mentioned Markopoulos's generosity. Were there other people, filmmakers in particular, but other kinds of people too, who were well known in that moment that we no longer know?

Sitney: One important figure was associated with a film that never got made: a novelist named Harold Humes, known as Doc Humes. There was a wonderful obituary for Doc Humes by George Plimpton, in an issue of the *Paris Review* published five or ten years ago. Humes had written a novel called *Men Die,* and he was said to be shooting a film. He was a big, burly, outgoing man who, on most Sundays, had a big spread in his house. People could just come by, eat, and talk. It was a kind of salon. We'd go and stuff ourselves with cheese and shrimp—the meal of the week. I think in a number of instances bread and cheese were pilfered from the table. I remember one evening when Doc suggested that a bunch of us go to Chinatown. It was terrifying for me because I didn't have enough money, but he made it perfectly clear that *he* was going to pay for this. He was a charismatic figure.

There was an extremely beautiful young woman, who had starred in Jonas's *Guns of the Trees* [1961]—Frances Stillman. Occasionally she would give a party in her nice downtown apartment. She gave a party for me when I was taking films to Europe for the first time, in 1963. She had just come back from Mexico, and there was this big pile of brownies. Kelman and John Cavanaugh sat there stuffing themselves with brownies; and at a certain point, someone went to stop them. But Ginsberg said, "No, leave them alone." They became the center of the party, which consisted of the two of them laughing uproariously at all of the other guests—not being aware that their own laughter and their own naïveté about getting high for the first time was the subject of the whole party. Frances added elegance and glamour and fascination. She must have been twenty-five when I was nineteen, so she seemed an incredibly sophisticated, sexually mature woman.

On another horizon was a woman who lived in the Dakota named Pana Grady, who seemed to be a patron of Ginsberg, William Gaddis, and William Burroughs. Occasionally we would go up there for a dinner or a party or an event of some kind.

When Anais Nin was in town, Ian Hugo sometimes did something at his NYU apartment below Washington Square. There would be a mixture of poets and filmmakers.

There were different schools of filmmaking. I first came in contact with a kind of Beat culture when Ron Rice arrived from California. The focus of this group was Jerry Joffen, who had a loft in the Chelsea district—an incredibly crazy, messy loft where there were some rooms you were not supposed to go into. Once I mistakenly wandered into one of the rooms and saw a lot of women who seemed to be shooting up. In this particular loft you were likely to see a lot of jazz musicians and, often, Jack Smith and his flaming creatures, or Taylor

Mead. Rice lived there for months. Joffen himself was a filmmaker, but his "film," in those days, consisted of reels piled on tables and floor. He would say, "Here! Look at my film," which meant that for the next x number of hours, until you couldn't take it any longer, you'd look at one reel after another. Some of it was quite fabulous, but I'm afraid all of it was lost.

Joffen became a focus of attention and something of a mentor for David Brooks, a freshman at Columbia when I knew him (he was a year older than I), who started making films and became the first manager of the Film-makers' Cooperative. Initially, we were bound together as acolytes of Brakhage. Eventually he took a teaching position at Antioch, where he died in a car crash, very young, in 1969.

Another, completely different epicenter formed around Robert Breer, who had a spacious house in Sneden Landing, an artsy enclave on the other side of the Hudson about an hour from New York. Every year he'd hold a party for the Film-makers' Cooperative, and any filmmaker who wanted to could go. Breer was very close to Oldenburg, and John Cage and the pop art world, and Billy Klüver, who was an engineer at Bell Labs and much involved in connections between art and technology, and very big in the gallery world.

And there was Andy Warhol's Factory. I first saw Warhol, as a film personality, at screenings at St. Mark's Church. Word was out that he was making a film of someone sleeping. I went off to Europe, and when I came back, people were regularly gathering at the Factory, around Forty-seventh Street on the East Side. You just got on the elevator and went up, and there was *always* something going on. Warhol seemed to be able to work with crowds around, often quite indifferent to their presence. Street hustlers, debutantes, world-famous authors would all be there: Tennessee Williams would be next to Ron Rice, and Jack Smith's flaming creatures, next to society ladies. I never felt as comfortable there as in the other places.

So there were these intersecting worlds of cinema and the other arts, and we all wove various patterns among them.

Behind much of this activity, but unknown to me until 1963, was one fabulously wealthy person, Jerome Hill. Jerome paid for a number of things but didn't participate as an artist until the mid-1960s.

MacDonald: What did he pay for?

Sitney: He paid the rent at the Film-makers' Cooperative, which was initially the *Film Culture* office. When *Film Culture* had sort of gone under, Jerome paid the journal's basic costs. In 1964 he established a group called the Friends of New Cinema. Jonas had told him that for ten dollars a week, filmmakers could buy a roll of film and shoot. Jerome found it hard to believe that what was so little to him could be important to artists, so he made about fifteen anonymous grants. You couldn't apply for them; you didn't even know where they came from; checks for forty or fifty dollars a month would just start arriving. Kubelka lived for years in Vienna on those checks.

MacDonald: Who besides Kubelka?

Sitney: Landow, Brakhage, probably Markopoulos, Ron Rice, and probably Jerry Joffen. I recommended Landow and John Schofill at a certain point, and I know that they were put on the list, which varied from year to year, but was always based on need. I'm sure that Bob Breer was not on the list. Jonas kept it all pretty secret.

MacDonald: Why couldn't Jonas tell people that Hill provided the money?

Sitney: Jerome didn't want it known, which I think is characteristic of real money that has been real money for a long time. And Jonas didn't want anyone to know that he was more or less telling Jerome who should get money because Jonas couldn't guarantee what Jerome would decide.

MacDonald: When you first went to Europe in 1963, was there an avant-garde scene there?

Sitney: There was nothing! I didn't know Jerome Hill then, but he paid for that trip. I was traveling on an absolute minimum. I had arranged that each country would pay for my train from the previous country and for shipping the films, and for my hotel and food while I was there. I had been given five hundred dollars for the year, as my spending money, though at a certain point, very early on, Jonas needed some money, and I think a hundred of that went back to Jonas. We started at the Knokke-le-Zoute festival in Brussels, a big event organized by Jacques Ledoux. Then I went from city to city. There was a great deal of interest in avant-garde film at the time, largely spurred by the sensations and scandals in America around Kenneth Anger's *Scorpio Rising* [1963], Jack Smith's *Flaming Creatures* [1963], and the Warhol phenomenon. I was in an odd position, because I was not at all interested in the scandalous dimension of those films, but only in the high-art dimension.

I traveled from city to city, arranging publicity, introducing shows, often engaging in polemical arguments. To my great annoyance, Barbara Rubin decided to join me. Everywhere that Barbara went, she wanted to disrupt "the institutional." Some marginal institution would have invited us, but that marginal institution was always much *too* institutional for Barbara's taste, so there would be daily confrontations and eruptions. It was a constant struggle, and the way Barbara was leading her life made it completely unpredictable whether she would even be there the next day or the next week. Of course, people were completely fascinated with her; they'd never *seen* anything like her.

MacDonald: Where in the scene you've been describing did she come from?

Sitney: Barbara began to show up around 1963. I think she was the niece of the man that Jonas was renting the Gramercy Arts Theater from. The Film-makers' Cinematheque was located at the Gramercy Arts, a few blocks from the

Film-makers' Cooperative office at 414 Park Avenue South. Many films—*Scorpio Rising, Kiss, Chumlum* [1964]—premiered there.

You know, my concern in doing this interview is that I'm going to regret saying this or that or that I'm going to forget important things.

MacDonald: There's no way around that. By that logic, I should never do any interviews.

Sitney: No, no, no! When a *filmmaker* talks about what he did at a particular time, he could be lying, or he could be distorting things, but even if that's the case, you still get more of value for understanding his films than when *I'm* trying to recall the social environment of forty years ago!

MacDonald: I understand your reservations, but you were so crucial in witnessing and chronicling this whole phenomenon that it's become interesting to know something about where *you* come from.

Sitney: Maybe, but in those days, there were several areas of reticence on *my* part—particularly about sex and drugs—that seriously limit my memory. I was quite friendly with Gerard Malanga, who seemed to have none of my inhibitions. If *he* were describing the contours of the scene I've described, you would get a very different picture—because *he* wouldn't get up and leave at ten o'clock in the evening when something seemed dicey or scary to me. There are whole aspects of that environment that I simply didn't see or that I carefully avoided.

Have you ever interviewed Gerard?

MacDonald: No.

Sitney: That would be an interesting interview; he knew absolutely everyone.

MacDonald: We were in Europe with Barbara Rubin.

Sitney: Ah, yes! Looking back, I realize I underappreciated Barbara. I thought I had known people like her, that is, people of the type she *seemed* to me to be at that time: a celebrity-hunting, promiscuous woman who had grown up with considerably more money and privilege than I had, who was acting out for the attention, and who would be leading an utterly middle-class life five years hence. Also, I didn't appreciate her film [*Christmas on Earth,* 1963]. I thought it was sloppy.

She thought *I* was much too uptight and academic and uncool and conservative in every way. We were not ideal companions. I got to like her later.

Now, I realize that Jonas's thought in permitting this strange pairing on our tour was actually quite perspicacious: we presented an interesting, diverse spectacle to the people we encountered. I guess Jonas had seen us as two parallel phenomena of American child culture. As usual, Jonas's insight and wisdom proves itself in the end, although I certainly wasn't seeing it at the time.

MacDonald: You mentioned to me, after you read my book in manuscript [*The Garden in the Machine* (Berkeley and Los Angeles: University of California Press, 2001)], that I'd finally written a book that I'll be hated for.

Sitney: I told Jim Hoberman the same thing—that he'd be hated—when he took his job at the *Voice.* He didn't believe me, either.

MacDonald: Your remark suggests more about your career than mine—I doubt many people will even see my book. Obviously, you've had a good many negative experiences with filmmakers. When did that start for you? I assume not until the seventies.

Sitney: No, it started for me in 1963, in Paris. Standing outside the Cinemath-èque Française was a man handing out hate literature about me. I'm so sorry now that I listened to my French friends at the time, who said to ignore him. It was Maurice Lemaître, the lettrist filmmaker. He perceived me as an interloper and part of a giant conspiracy to deny his importance. And there was a certain amount of truth in his feeling. Many of the French were extremely hostile to the American avant-garde film, but those who *were* accepting of American work were dismissive of all *French* filmmakers who hadn't operated within the pre-scribed penumbra of *Cahiers du Cinema* and the French New Wave.

So that's where I first encountered that kind of intensity, although I didn't understand it at the time. I understand it now perfectly. When the stakes are extremely low, when there's absolutely *nothing* to be had—that's when the fight-ing gets most vicious.

I had been in Venice in 1964 when Rauschenberg won the Bienalle. Rauschen-berg, and Oldenburg, and Rosenquist, and Lichtenstein, Chamberlain, and Johns were all there, and were extremely friendly toward each other; there was a sense of camaraderie. But, of course, *all* of them were selling work, hand over fist. There wasn't a sense that if Johns gets a certain amount of attention, Chamber-lain—a sculptor who worked primarily with compressed automobiles—gets none. *Nobody* was getting *anything* from avant-garde film, but everyone *thought* that either Brakhage was getting everything he needed, or that Kenneth Anger was, and that I had some kind of control over who got what. With these very low stakes, people get extremely bitter.

I'd also learned from Robert Kelly, the practicing poet I knew best, the inten-sity of controversy within the various poetry communities—another instance where the stakes are almost nonexistent and the bitternesses and oppositions within and between schools quite considerable. I hadn't realized at first how intensely people would scrutinize any particular article or program of films to imagine why one person was included and another not, or why one person would have *two* films in a program rather than just one. This seems to be an intense mental activity for many filmmakers, especially when there is almost nothing to be gained or lost by being included *or* excluded.

To go back to your book for a moment, in the *Critical Cinema* books, you've done a series of interviews without producing a work that has anything like a com-prehensive shape. But the moment you do try to give a part of that history a com-prehensive shape—as you've done in *The Garden in the Machine*—you must leave people out, and it will be clear that you have made a decision to "leave them out," and *then* you open yourself to all the jealousies and angers. It's just part of what happens when you devote yourself to the criticism of such films. And by "criticism" I don't mean saying negative things. When you devote yourself to the elucidation of some of the films by some filmmakers, you earn the enmity of others.

Of course, we *really* brought enmity down on ourselves in 1970 with Anthology Film Archives.

MacDonald: Yes, "the Essential Cinema" and that picture of the selection committee was like throwing down a gauntlet.

Sitney: Well, it wasn't meant to be, but it *was* remarkably bad timing, historically.

MacDonald: I do understand your deciding that you believed in this body of work and challenging the film community to argue with you about it. I think that if a body of work is to become a field of study, at some point, somebody has to establish a canon. I remember when Andrew Sarris came out with *The American Cinema;* for years I'd go to the back of the book, where Sarris listed the most important and interesting films of the year—that is, the films that exemplified auteurship—in order of their importance. That listing was hugely important for me as a way of finding my way into the field. It wasn't that I necessarily ended up agreeing with Sarris, any more than I would agree with the Anthology selection committee that Frank Stauffacher is more "essential" than John Ford, but somebody has to say, "OK, *this* body of work must be accounted for if you are to understand the field."

Sitney: Well, there were different degrees of intensity and different kinds of commitment. At the time of the foundation of Anthology Film Archives, the person most concerned with the kind of evaluative discrimination Sarris did in his book was the one who ended up most unhappy with our list: Kubelka. For Kubelka, Anthology ended up being much too catholic and broad. He felt there was no distinction or point in showing *his* films, if Bresson, a filmmaker he abominated, was also going to be shown.

Brakhage also felt that the audience was being destroyed by our attention to junk. Ultimately, it's interesting that both Kubelka and Brakhage, two filmmakers who felt personally excluded by Amos Vogel, ended up taking what would be a version of the position that Vogel took, vis-à-vis the audience—not in terms of showing a mixture of genres but in their belief that quality distinctions were needed to keep the audience coming back.

At the time, we felt that we had done a very compromised and tentative thing, but this tentative thing appeared at a moment when, all through the culture, there was a naive revolution against canons of any sort. The opening of Anthology roughly coincided with the publication of *Visionary Film,* and I inherited a lot of the animosity that had been directed against Anthology.

Jonas ended up running Anthology, because I wasn't capable of it. I was the first director but was just no good at it. *Jonas* was the one who took the most catholic and open of possible positions.

The other day I was talking to a group of younger filmmakers about a current situation I simply cannot understand. There seems to be a tremendous revitalization of avant-garde filmmaking now, but there's absolutely no one publishing anything about it, *anything*. The filmmakers themselves do not seem compelled to have their own magazine or journal or even a Web page. None of the young people associated with this phenomenon seem to want to write about it, so all this work exists in what seems to be a vacuum. Actually, for the last ten years the nonartist personalities interested in the field have assumed *not* the role of critics but the role of "curators."

MacDonald: There does seem to be a lot of activity now, but I've never felt any waning of the number of quality works coming out during any particular period.

Sitney: Oh, *I* have! But I think things are better now than they were fifteen years ago.

MacDonald: There *is* a pulse, but I'm still finding my way to interesting work done in earlier decades. I think there *has been* a lot of interesting work, and there *still is* a lot of interesting work. But I agree with you about the paucity of writing about new work, and I don't get it either, especially since universities seem to be producing graduate students by the thousands, all of whom need thesis topics.

Sitney: That I understand entirely. The universities have completely imploded. They're the places to go if you believe that the media discourse of French philosophers is the only viable approach to film, and that the empirical relationship of the viewer to the work of art is utterly passé. A generation of followers of Foucault, Lacan, and Derrida has made the universities as hermetically sealed against the presence of this art as the universities in the fifties were. One can't expect this writing to come out of the university system.

I can only fantasize about young independent people who love these new films and want to write about them. Even the journals where you'd most expect this kind of writing, like *Millennium,* are much more likely to have an article on Yvonne Rainer or Brakhage than on this group of young filmmakers who are now about thirty years old.

But when these filmmakers *show* their works, people do come to see them. It's a situation I simply don't understand.

Stan Brakhage

When he died on March 8, 2003, in Victoria, British Columbia, Stan Brakhage was the preeminent figure in American avant-garde filmmaking. The quality of his best work and its influence, both within the history of alternative media and beyond, and the power of his voice and his example are unprecedented and unequaled in the field. Indeed, Brakhage's creative productivity has been so remarkable for so long—*The Canyon Cinema Film/Video Catalogue 2000,* the primary American rental resource for Brakhage's films in the United States, lists nearly three hundred titles—that few scholars have had the temerity to engage Brakhage's career, no matter how enthusiastic they are about the films. Of those who have worked at coming to grips with this immense oeuvre, P. Adams Sitney (see *Visionary Film* [New York: Oxford University Press, 2002]), Fred Camper (see his Web site: http://www.fredcamper.com/Brakhage), Bruce Elder (see *The Films of Stan Brakhage in the American Tradition of Ezra Pound, Gertrude Stein and Charles Olson*), and Marie Nesthus (see her Ph.D. thesis, "A Crucible of Document: The Sequence Films of Stan Brakhage, 1968–1984" [New York University, 1999]) have been the most successful.

My own experience with Brakhage's career, if not typical, is, I am sure, not unusual. Brakhage has been central to my thinking about alternative media and to my teaching since the early 1970s. As a result, I made a tentative move to interview Brakhage in the mid-1980s; at the time, he was not interested in being interviewed. I forswore further attempts to talk with him, partly because I did not see how I could come to an adequate enough understanding of this immense body of work to conduct anything like a useful interview; in fact, the very idea seemed to suggest something out of the Greek underworld—Sisyphus perhaps:

Stan Brakhage at work, hand painting a film, in Cambridge,
Massachusetts, in 1995. Photograph by Robert A. Haller.
Courtesy Robert A. Haller.

even if I did set out to come to grips with the entire collection of Brakhage films
available at any particular moment, by the time I had explored *those* films, fifty
more would have been deposited at Canyon. Further, since Brakhage had
written not only about his own filmmaking (in *Metaphors on Vision*—the complete version was published in *Film Culture,* no. 30 [fall 1963], edited by P.
Adams Sitney; a shorter version is included in Sitney, ed., *The Avant-Garde Film*
[New York: New York University Press, 1978], 120–28)—and in *A Moving
Picture Giving and Taking Book* [West Newbury, Mass.: Frontier Press,
1971]) but also about avant-garde filmmakers whose lives and work have been
important to him (in *Film at Wit's End: Eight Avant-Garde Filmmakers* [Kingston,

N.Y.: McPherson/Documentext, 1989], Brakhage discusses James Broughton, Bruce Conner, Maya Deren, Jerome Hill, Ken Jacobs, Christopher MacLaine, Marie Menken, and Sidney Peterson), and even about major contributors to the history of world cinema (in *Film Biographies* [Berkeley: Turtle Island, 1977]), and about these and a range of other topics (in Robert A. Haller, ed., *Brakhage Scrapbook: Collected Writings, 1964–1980* [New Paltz, N.Y.: McPherson/Documentext, 1982]), there seemed no need for any interview I might do. And then, in 1996, I learned, along with everyone else in the avant-garde film community, that Brakhage had bladder cancer.

The fact that Brakhage's life was threatened forced me to realize that, as a person for whom his work had been crucial and as a chronicler of avant-garde film history, I had a personal and scholarly obligation to come to grips with this remarkable career, in whatever limited way I could. I contacted Brakhage in the summer of 1996, and in November we began a series of phone conversations (and, in one instance, an in-person conversation with Don Fredericksen's film class at Cornell University) that resulted in the long interview that follows. As I reviewed the Brakhage films I had seen and taught, and explored dozens of films I had not seen before, in preparation for our conversations, I became clearer about some of the reasons why Brakhage has been so important.

During the 1970s, as I worked at becoming a capable college film professor, a certain set of early Brakhage films became crucial for me personally and in my teaching. While I have always recognized the importance of the two Brakhage films that are considered most pivotal by a good many of those who have written about and taught his work—the breakthrough *Anticipation of the Night* (1958) and Brakhage's first epic, *Dog Star Man* (1961–64)—my experience with Brakhage, at least until quite recently, has focused on other films: *The Wonder Ring* (1955), *Sirius Remembered* (1959), *Window Water Baby Moving* (1959), *Scenes from under Childhood,* especially *Section 1* (1967), *Three Films: Bluewhite, Blood's Tone, Vein* (1965), and *The Act of Seeing with One's Own Eyes* (1971).

As fully as any films I have ever seen, these helped me understand how the experience of alternative media can provide a powerful and memorable in-theater critique of conventional mass-media spectatorship. Following the lead of Marie Menken, Brakhage freed the 16mm camera from the tripod and embraced new orders of cinematic motion more akin to abstract expressionist painting and free-form poetry than to mainstream filmmaking. Film by film, he articulated what became a theory of sight and a new mission for cinema. Brakhage theorized that acculturation generally involves the gradual constriction of the freedom of sight we witness in young children so that, as we mature, we come to understand *what* is socially acceptable to look at and *how* we should look at what we see. Conversely, this process of acculturation also involves learning what dimensions of the visible we must *not* look at. Coming of age involves the constriction of sight and the development of visual taboos, many of which involve organic bodily processes—sex, birth, sickness, aging, death—the very stuff of life. Mass-market film and television are crucial institutions that help society to reinforce rigid, conformist, thoroughly materialistic ways of seeing and living.

Brakhage's response was to use the motion picture camera—the quintessential product of Western technological development—against the grain of its history and its usual functions, as a means of reaccessing at least an evocation of the world of childhood sight "before the 'beginning was the word'" (*Metaphors on Vision,* paragraph 1), that is, before the child's expulsion from the world "under childhood" into the world of language and social expectations. For Brakhage, the camera became a new pair of glasses that he could train on precisely those dimensions of real experience that his social training had argued were taboo, and he filmed them with a gestural freedom that itself evoked the freedom of the untrained baby's eye. The resulting films were painstakingly edited into complex montage structures that offered his personal interpretations of sex (*Loving* [1997]), birth (*Window Water Baby Moving, Thigh Line Lyre Triangular* [1961], *Bluewhite*); death and decay (*Sirius Remembered, The Act of Seeing with One's Own Eyes*); and the experience of losing childhood sight itself (*Scenes from under Childhood, Sections 1–4* [1967–70]).

In time, I came to depend on the Brakhage films to invigorate my classroom teaching not only in courses relating to avant-garde film, or even to film in general, but in nearly every course I taught. Confronting my first-year writing students with *Window Water Baby Moving,* and challenging them to come to grips with the visceral experience of the film and its implications for how we experience the world and how women are usually represented in commercial media, became one of the predictable high points of the semester. Asking my film students to retrain their perception and their consciousness of what they actually perceive and then confronting them with Brakhage's exploration of childhood sight in *Scenes from under Childhood* or of autopsies in the Pittsburgh morgue in *The Act of Seeing with One's Own Eyes* resulted in a level of student engagement always difficult to achieve. In my forty years of college teaching, I have discovered no filmmaker of greater pedagogical value.

As I continued to see new Brakhage films through the 1970s, 1980s, and 1990s, I came to realize that my experiences with Brakhage had impacted more than my teaching. When my son Ian was born in 1972, I was present, despite resistance on the part of the hospital—in large measure because Brakhage's birth films had demonstrated that, whatever restrictive rules were standard in American hospitals at that time, the personal experience of seeing a child come into the world was worth fighting for. And as I came to know the Brakhage films of later decades—*The Text of Light* (1974), for example, and *The Roman Numeral Series I—IX* (1979–80), *Unconscious London Strata* (1982), *A Child's Garden and the Serious Sea* (1991), and so many others—I realized that my day-to-day experience was continually enriched by my growing awareness of a good many perceptual subtleties that Brakhage's films had alerted me to, had trained me to notice and enjoy, and to consider.

By the 1990s, as a result of the increasing expense of shooting film and of changes in Brakhage's domestic life—his thirty-year marriage with Jane Collum Brakhage had come to an end—Brakhage turned his filmmaking attention to painting. Using a variety of approaches (painting directly on the filmstrip, painting on glass and recording it frame by frame), in dozens of films, he extended the history of the abstract expressionist painting that had fascinated him as a youth, though the discovery of his bladder cancer instigated a series of lovely photographed films, including *The Cat of the Worm's Green Realm* (1997), *Self Song/Death Song* (1997), and *Commingled Containers* (1997).

Commingled Containers in particular is a memorable confirmation of a crucial, if difficult to discuss, dimension of Brakhage's work: his commitment to using film as a means of representing his own spiritual quest and of capturing evocations of the spirit in the world around him. Brakhage regularly talked of his films as having been "given to him to make," as the products of spirit moving through him; and throughout his filmmaking career he articulated and elaborated on the metaphor of light as spirit. In the early *Mothlight* (1963)—still his most frequently rented film—Brakhage created a cinematic emblem of the essential romantic quest. Affixing the wings of dead moths, blades of grass, leaves, and tiny flowers to clear celluloid and printing this collage, Brakhage evoked Percy Shelley's "One Word Is Too Often Profaned"—

> I can give not what men call love,
> But wilt thou accept not
> The worship the heart lifts above
> And the heavens reject not,
> The desire of the moth for the star
> Of night for the morrow
> The duration to something afar
> From the sphere of our sorrow.

—envisioning himself as a moth struggling to reach the light/Light. This spiritual quest has been consistently evident during Brakhage's long career, in his fascination with the lovely worlds of light that exist just at the edges of our normal perceptual range and just beyond the camera's normal, "correct" focal points. Indeed, Brakhage's mature films are often meditations on the ineffable qualities of reflection and refraction.

Commingled Containers, made at a moment of considerable personal stress, is a quintessential film in this regard. In the face of possible imminent death, Brakhage immersed his camera lens in Boulder Creek and discovered there a spectacular lightscape, created fittingly by the friction of water against rock. In the opening image of *Potemkin* (1925), Eisenstein saw waves breaking against rocks as an emblem of the proletariat wearing away the power of the czars; for Brakhage, the meeting of water and stone is also an emblem of finitude, even of mortality, but *this* friction creates figures of light that function as metaphors of Light. It is, after all, the reality of material decay that makes transcendence possible. *Commingled Containers* can be seen as a talisman that expresses Brakhage's determination to continue his spiritual quest and to offer viewers something of Light, despite his fear of mortality, for as long as it was given to him to remain in the flow of life.

While Brakhage's prolific filmmaking career will continue to have an impact for years to come, his importance to the field of independent media extends well beyond his accomplishments as a maker. For nearly half a century Brakhage was one of the most passionate and articulate defenders of alternative cinema. Andrew Noren has described Brakhage's impact as a public speaker: "Brakhage would descend on New York from the mountains once a year or so, grandiloquent and Promethean, lightning bolts in one hand and film cans in the other, talking everyone under the table—what a talker! And in general burning the place to the ground. It's impossible to overestimate his influence on absolutely everyone: You could run, but you couldn't hide" (Noren in *A Critical Cinema 2,* 178).

As Brakhage often said, he made his artistic career with his eyes, but he made his living with his mouth. For well over a decade, beginning in the late 1970s, Brakhage commuted on a biweekly basis from his home in the mountains outside of Boulder to the Chicago Art Institute, where his lectures became legendary; and he continued to travel across North America and Europe to present his films, often despite the pressures of serious physical ailments and fatigue. Indeed, no avant-garde filmmaker I am aware of spent so much time in front of so many audiences, patiently answering questions and offering avenues into his films and generously extolling the accomplishments of other artists, writers, and filmmakers.

Because Brakhage lectured so widely and so often, it is no surprise that many of his stories, analyses, and conjectures have become nearly as stable as his films. When Brakhage spoke of his admiration for Gertrude Stein, he did not invent a new viewpoint each time but recycled his understanding of Stein in pretty much the same terms. We all do this to some extent, and to an increasing degree as we grow older; but because Brakhage made himself so available, was so committed to serving not just his own films but the field, it is no surprise that many of the stories he relates to me in this interview will be familiar to those who had the good fortune to hear Brakhage present his work. At the same time, since he always had so much of interest to say, my hope is that even veteran Brakhage aficionados may discover something new here. And, of course, for those who did not have the good fortune to hear Brakhage in person, his responses to my questions will be enlightening.

Brakhage's move in 2002 to Victoria, British Columbia, with his second wife, Marilyn Jull, and their two sons (Victoria is Jull's hometown) and his death the following year seemed to signal the end of an era in American independent cinema. A variety of factors, including considerable financial stress, led to this move, which serves as a reminder of how little support even the most accomplished American film artists can expect from their government and their cultural institutions. Brakhage, one of the greatest American filmmakers and one of our most remarkable artists, did not find it possible to continue living in his native land.

Throughout his battle with cancer, Brakhage remained high-spirited, available to friends and colleagues, and productive. Indeed, even as his life was slipping away, he was working on *The Chinese Series* (2003), scratching directly into the emulsion on 35mm filmstrips with his fingernails—holding on to life and creativity until the very end. Brakhage's death is an irreparable loss for our field but also an opportunity for a new beginning. There was no catching up with Brakhage when he was alive, but now perhaps we can begin to discover and understand the full breadth and depth of his remarkable cinematic legacy.

Because of the length of this interview, it seemed sensible to divide it into sections, based the dates of my several conversations with Brakhage (of course, each of these conversations evolved over time into the final form included here). My thanks to P. Adams Sitney and Fred Camper for their assistance in correcting this interview.

11/30/96

MacDonald: I've been fascinated with "Rip van Winkle" recently. I'm fifty-four, and a lot of my life now seems to involve revisiting things for the first time in a good many years and trying to adjust to the changes I see. One of the things that struck me about *Interim* [1952], when I looked at it recently, is that it's so much better than I remembered it. I remembered it as pretty rough, but this time it seemed good enough to make me doubt that it's your first film. *Is* it your first film, or just the first film you decided to distribute?

Brakhage: No, it is my first film. I also happened to see it recently and was embarrassed—as I was when it was made—about the chunks of dirt in the gate and other utterly unacceptable technical wrongs. But I was also moved by it; what it is in its innate being rings absolutely true for such a despairing, youthful love syndrome. It holds up. But, yes, it was very much my first film. Of course, a great deal of credit has to go to Stan Phillips, who was the cinematographer and who subsequently has gone on to devote a good deal of his life to animation and especially to animation in the service of ecological awareness. He was one of the major people involved in the *Captain Earth* series, and he is also in charge of the TV series *Madeline.* Several people contributed to making what, at that time, seemed an absolutely true, disparaging statement about the possibility of loving someone. Subsequently, thank God, we haven't found the possibilities of love as limited as they are in *Interim.* But in some rather cosmic sense, you could certainly say that love *is* very limited, a brief make-life fling on earth.

MacDonald: Knowing that you became the kind of filmmaker you are, it's easy now to read *Interim* as a visitation of the spirit. Your protagonist is on the main highway, where you/he is almost hit by a car. He comes down out of the mainstream space into the underground, a world underneath what modern life has created, and there he has the visitation.

Brakhage: Let me just say that my whole life's work has been a search among these themes that you have just expounded very well.

Perhaps the most vibrant, older-age exploration of the theme of love in *Interim* is *Untitled (For Marilyn)* [1992]—the parenthesis is there just so that while the film itself has no title, it reverberates with the dedication to Marilyn. I've come to a sense in which love is not only *not* despairing but is not even brief.

That other theme of the surface and the *under*surface, where things *really* happen, represented in *Interim* by the protagonist going down under the viaducts, is very much reflected in *Commingled Containers,* the first photographic film that I've made in a long time. I made it just before I went in for my bladder cancer surgery. *Commingled Containers* was shot in Boulder Creek here in town. The surface in this instance is the stream; the *under*surface is a series of beautiful, cellularly contained, semirepetitious but never repeating patterns of light, in great quietude. Now, this may seem too facile a comparison—going down under the viaducts in a dramatic sense with going beneath the surface of that creek to film the light and life of that body of water—but I believe that in both cases I was doing basically the same thing, and in fact the sense of desperation that drew me into Boulder Creek to shoot *Commingled Containers* was very similar to the desperation of the man in *Interim* being drawn to that plunge under the viaducts.

MacDonald: How did you come to make *Interim?*

Brakhage: Well, I had had a very rich life of movie viewing, unusually broad for those days. The movies were used as an inexpensive baby-sitting service by my mother after she separated from my father (you may know that these parents had adopted me; I was not their natural child). Anyway, when they separated, my mother would give me money to go to double features, which were quite ordinary in those days. I'd come out of one movie and have something to eat—a hot dog or whatever—and then go into the next, and sometimes a third. She would pick me up after the movies. Movies changed rapidly enough in those days that I rarely saw a movie more than once, unless I wanted to. We're talking about my life as an eight- or nine-year-old, or even a bit younger. I was constantly at the movies; and they were, in fact, my alternate parents.

MacDonald: Do you remember particular films?

Brakhage: Oh yes. *The Mummy* [1932, directed by Karl Freund] so moved me, created in me such identification with the monster, that I wrapped myself in sticky adhesive tape and went out on the street to frighten people. I hadn't realized how painful it would be to unwrap myself! And earlier than that, I remember being terrified of Disney's *Snow White and the Seven Dwarfs* [1937], which is, I believe, the first movie that I saw.

This was during the war years, and I remember the newsreels—there was a theater completely given over to newsreels—where I saw all the war news which, many years later, came to be the focus of *Twenty-third Psalm Branch* [1979]. At this newsreel theater, I also saw such things as a boa constrictor eating a lion, or whatever; a pig being stripped to the bone by piranhas in thirty seconds; and there were all these strange travel features. So that was also part of my moviegoing.

And then later in high school I had my experience with Jean Cocteau's *Orpheus* [1949] and knew that film could be an art—which was very surprising to me. By this time, I was very involved in the arts, in poetry primarily, but also in drama and music.

MacDonald: Who showed you the Cocteau film?

Brakhage: The Cocteau film came quite ordinarily to our local neighborhood theater during that brief period right after the war when European films suddenly poured into American theaters and people went to see them, because so many GIs had been in those countries and had seen those films while they were over there.

So first Cocteau's *Orpheus* and then a couple weeks later his *Beauty and the Beast* [1946] gave me experiences that were close enough to my involvement with poetry that I was certain that film could be an art. Then I began searching for it elsewhere, in Rosselini and DeSica, who were primary influences on *Interim,* and in Orson Welles, and so on.

Then later, during my brief stay at Dartmouth—the one uncompleted semester before my nervous breakdown—I saw certain silent classic films and other foreign films.

MacDonald: This is 1951?

Brakhage: Yes. I would have been class of 1955 had I come back to Dartmouth. Back in Denver, I remember sitting under those viaducts in *Interim* with my high school friends, in a car, all of us in various degrees of despair—myself from the loss of what I had thought a college education would be and hadn't been. As I remember, a friend in great despair, who had been in the marines (this was during the war in Korea), said, "It's too bad that artists can't work with film because it's too expensive." And I just saw red. I remember it vividly. I said, "We'll *make* a film." And, sure enough, we did find cameras—amateur cameras in people's attics—and started in.

MacDonald: Did *Interim* get shown in Denver?

Brakhage: It showed once and created a furor! The long kiss was supposed to have ruined the reputation of the beautiful young lady who appears in the film. Of course, part of my interest in making the film was to include her in it. In my shyness, I felt this was how I could begin to have a relationship with her. She was my first love, and our relationship was very much as is pictured in the film. We were in Saint John's Episcopalian choir together. Her parents called the preacher, who demanded to speak with me about how this film must be destroyed.

MacDonald: Where was the film shown?

Brakhage: In a church, actually. We were *that* innocent about it. We rented one of the rooms in the church, which you could do quite inexpensively, and invited everyone to come and see it—we had no sense of any wrongdoing. That the kiss lasted as long as it did was terribly shocking.

MacDonald: You know, it brought kissing back to me in a way. I had almost forgotten that that's what we did before there was birth control. Kissing was an extended experience and actually very sexy and a lot of fun.

Brakhage: Shortly after the furor over *Interim, The Outcast of the Islands* [1952; directed by Carol Reed] came to Denver, with a long kissing scene. I remember arguing with people, "Look, this is what they *do* in the movies." But it didn't matter.

Somehow this was my "you can't go home again." And I must say, in a sense, I haven't been back to Denver. The experience of *Interim* did for me what was done for/to Thomas Wolfe by the local people of Ashville when he exposed a dimension of their world that they couldn't face. It could have been New York; it could have been anywhere, but it was Denver. And it made me a persona non grata, absolutely.

When, shortly after that, I moved to San Francisco and came briefly back to Denver, all kinds of stories had circulated about me. One, believe it or not, was that I had married Jane Russell! That was fabricated on nothing more substantial than that she had married a man named Stanley. Another was that I had gone to a Tibetan monastery. Another was that I had raped a small child in Golden Gate Park and was in prison. Another, that I was a drug addict. I was pictured in the way people who are afraid of artists portray an artistic life.

MacDonald: *Interim* did show you that film was a medium you could work in.

Brakhage: Yes. For a long time, I thought of myself as a poet making films, like Jean Cocteau; but when it became clear that film was what I really *could* do, my life became devoted principally to film.

MacDonald: You became a relentless experimenter. Looking back, I'm surprised that I thought of *all* your early films as *Brakhage* films, without really conceptualizing what that meant. Now, what strikes me is the clear evolution toward that period in the late fifties and early sixties that produced, among other films, *Anticipation of the Night, Sirius Remembered, Window Water Baby Moving,* and what has come to be understood as your particular approach. Did you have a sense back then that you were moving toward something? Did you think about the overall process of your development?

Brakhage: Well, yes and no. Let's deal with "no" first. At that point, I'm just thrashing around, as most young people do—scrambling, trying to get some kind of toehold on a possible means of subsistence here on earth. And after all, I had failed: I was a scholarship student at Dartmouth and had failed at that miserably. When I met the poet Kenneth Rexroth in San Francisco, he said, "You better get a job, kid; and to get a job, you better go back to school, because the way this society is going, it's going to take a Ph.D. to run an elevator." Scary. So I did make an attempt to find another school that I could become part of, but never did succeed for more than one semester in the drama department at the University of Denver. Dartmouth asked would I want to pick up the scholarship again, but I couldn't really do so except under conditions that were not acceptable to Dartmouth.

MacDonald: I can imagine you having a problem with mainstream education.

Brakhage: Well, this goes back to your question about my development, which is really a question of formal development. What did I think about the process that led me to *Anticipation of the Night?* How can I be simple about that? I said I was just thrashing around, trying to find a purpose here on earth, but I had had a sense since I was nine years old that I was some kind of an artist. I had thought I was a poet, and I had continued to think so into my early twenties when I was living with Robert Duncan in the middle of the San Francisco Beat poetry movement. I met Michael McClure and Kenneth Patchen and Jack Spicer and Robin Blaser, Kenneth Rexroth and Louis Zukofsky and began having a sense of what a poet really was. All this powerfully confirmed my poetic aspirations.

But, more and more, I felt there was this *visual* possibility. As I began reading more and more about artists, it began to seem quite natural that, because my eyes were weak and because I had never been content to accept this weakness, and had continued to struggle against it (at seventeen I had even thrown my glasses away), the road of most possible creativity for me would be along the line of the eyes.

MacDonald: How bad were your eyes?

Brakhage: Pretty bad, actually. I had a bad astigmatism. I was walleyed: that is, my right eye was always adrift and didn't focus well. I had to really struggle to come to focus. I couldn't take focusing for granted. And much of what you and others have described as my experimentation is just a part of my scrambling to come to an understanding of how you achieve sight. Something that other people just have naturally, I had to *earn.* One time, an optician, on looking into my eyes, said, "Well, by your eyes, physically, you shouldn't even be able to *see* that chart on the wall, let alone read it. But, on the other hand, I have never seen a human eye with more rapid saccadic movements. What you must be doing is rapidly scanning and putting this picture together in your head." In knowing poets, I was discovering that many of them stuttered, couldn't speak easily at all. Robert Creeley hadn't come to speak in full sentences until he was seven or eight. The epitome was the poet Larry Eigner. You could barely understand what he had to say, and with his afflictions, he could barely type.

Now, I'm hardly speechless, as our conversation is demonstrating right now. All these years, I've earned my living essentially by talking. I will take credit for that, but it is also the reason I'm not a poet. It's so facile for me to talk that I don't honor talking, except in the sense that I have always tried to put it in the service of art. I have tried to do good with it. I haven't gone out and sold junk with it, as I might have.

Anyway, to get back to the question, I wasn't *trying* to invent new ways of being a filmmaker; that was just a by-product of my struggle to come to a sense of sight. And it seemed reasonable to me that film ought to be based on human seeing, and not just the physical eyes but the mind's eye: that is, what happens when the eye receives images from the outside and how they interrelate with remembered images on the inside of the mind. How do we arrive at our seeing and then imagine with our sight?—we put dove's wings onto a cat and "see" a griffin.

MacDonald: By the time of *Anticipation of the Night,* you're allowing yourself to represent the way you really *do* see, with all the supposed limitations, and to accept the reality of that as a means of making visual art.

Brakhage: Many years later, when I met the poet Charles Olson, he made quite clear the importance of accepting what's been God-given to you to work with, of accepting your limitations *as* the special gifts. My eyes were the weakest part of me really; either I was going to be destroyed by them or they were going to become the path through which my creativity could flower.

My sense, very early on, was to figure out what my talents were, what was God-given to me to do. Whatever you mean by God. I don't mean to sound religious, but there are certain things that *are* given, that are intrinsic within us; and that was very much Olson's message to me in that great encounter I had with him, and which is celebrated in the letter to Jane at the end of *Metaphors on Vision* about my being very clear about what my natural sight is and accepting it and going with that.

There *was* fear in doing this because I knew I was basing my life on an aberration, and that others were not going to understand. And to be sure, when it comes to the arts, people *are* very slow in understanding what you're doing. But over the years it has become clearer and clearer that the more I am true to my own particularities of being, and struggle for these, the more I become clear to everyone else. It's a wonderful irony.

MacDonald: When did you start to see underground films by Americans?

Brakhage: Shortly after making *Interim,* I went to San Francisco. I attempted to study at the California Art Institute, and then just ran off with a camera with another student—because they weren't teaching us anything. We brought it back, we didn't steal it; we just told them we were going out with the camera and would bring it back before they were ready to use it in class, and we did. We took it for a week and jammed one roll after another into it, and learned how to run it. That was during the same general period when I was meeting the poets.

Then I went back to Denver. With some of my friends, we formed a little film society and brought in Von Stroheim's *Greed* [1923], Kenneth Anger's *Fireworks* [1947], which was important, Maya Deren's *Meshes of the Afternoon* [1943], and several other classic movies.

MacDonald: Were you aware of Cinema 16, and Art and Cinema, and the film society movement in general?

Brakhage: Vaguely. But it seemed quite remote. When I went back to San Francisco the second time, I continued to make films, and discovered Art in Cinema, Frank Stauffacher's great series at the San Francisco Museum of Art. And he brought in Isadore Isou's *Venom and Eternity* [1951; aka *Treatise on Drivel and Eternity*], which caused a riot. It was a deeply meaningful film for me.

I also got to see Chris MacLane's *The End* [1953]. James Broughton. Sidney Peterson. At that point, I was living in the storage room where Broughton kept all his films, and I had access to Broughton's originals and outtakes and was studying those and the work he did with Peterson, also. I bounced back and forth between the West Coast and Denver for a number of years, and at one point I met Peterson in L.A., when I was working at the Coronet Theater for Raymond Rohauer, who was showing all kinds of banned and forbidden films from his vast collection. I swept up the theater and was a night guard in exchange for admission and access.

Gradually, God knows how, I made a series of films, shooting a roll at a time with whatever money I could beg or borrow. I didn't resort to stealing. I'd get odd jobs at times, doing some photography and this or that, and earn enough money to be able to make *The Way to Shadow Garden* [1954] or *Flesh of Morning* [1956, revised 1986].

MacDonald: Did you meet Kenneth Anger in L.A.?

Brakhage: I had met Kenneth Anger in San Francisco and saw him again in Los Angeles when he had his premiere of *Inauguration of the Pleasure Dome* [1954]. I was involved in the attempts that Kenneth made to have Harry Partch do the sound track for *Inauguration.* But Harry was just *so* offended by the movie. I tried very hard, under the influence of Robert Duncan, to resolve the difficulties between the two of them, but never could. [For further information about this incident, see Scott MacDonald, *Cinema 16: Documents toward a History of the Film Society* (Philadelphia: Temple University Press, 2003), 227–34.]

Anyway, at this time, I was toying with the idea of trying to see if I could work commercially. Some friends had arranged for me to meet Charles Laughton, and I was certainly moved enough by *The Night of the Hunter* [1955] to think that maybe I *should* work for him, if he'd have me. It looked like he would do *The Naked and the Dead.*

MacDonald: I can see why *The Naked and the Dead* would move you.

Brakhage: Yes. But by the time I got to meet Laughton, he was in complete despair. *Night of the Hunter* had failed at the box office; they had taken away *The Naked and the Dead* and given it to Rouben Mamoulian, destroying Laughton's dreams of having a great career as a director. And he just inveighed against L.A. and said, "Get out. Get out. They'll destroy whatever you want to do." He was just a mess, drunk on unhappiness.

But I did stay a while in L.A. and went to the studios and actually got an agreement that I could study under Hitchcock, and they would pay me (I forget what, something like five thousand dollars a week!) while I was studying. A certain number of people would be chosen to become directors of his television series. At the time, I was making *Flesh of Morning* and somehow I just couldn't get out of the track of making *Flesh of Morning* and onto a track that would provide them with a token sound film of a kind they would pay for. And I realized finally that if I stayed, I would be overwhelmed by that world. It was too powerful for me. I mean, if it could overwhelm Orson Welles, it would surely overwhelm me. He had such largesse, such sophistication; he was such a powerful man. What chance would *I* have?

Years later, when Werner Herzog was diddling with Hollywood to get money to finish *Fitzcarraldo* [1982], I said to him, "Look, you're talking about the MGM lion and the Twentieth Century Fox—beasts that have chewed up men like Von Stroheim and Orson Welles and spit them out. How do you think *you*'ll do?"

MacDonald: During this time you had started going to New York. I know you were at Cinema 16 in the fifties.

Brakhage: I went to New York maybe six months after finishing *Flesh of Morning* in L.A. and *Nightcats* [1956]. I had, in fact, been to New York before I made *Flesh of Morning.* I went to New York to try to get permission from John Cage for the use of his music in *In Between* [1955] and from Edgar Varèse to use *his* music in *The Way to the Shadow Garden.* Varèse refused but took me on as a student, to study music—he knew I did not mean to be a composer but to study the relationship between music and film. Cage did give me permission, and he sort of took me on, too, in the sense that he would take Jim Tenney and me out for beers and conversations that went on for hours. Merce Cunningham was often there.

MacDonald: So you already knew Tenney?

Brakhage: Yes. We went to the same high school in Denver. It's quite a mystery when you think about it. At this high school, South High in Denver, during

Stan Brakhage in *Flesh of Morning* (1956), his psychodrama about masturbation, no longer in distribution. Courtesy Anthology Film Archives.

this period, Jim and I were students. And Larry Jordan. Actually, Jim Tenney transferred there when I was at Dartmouth and graduated quickly; I knew him through my friends who were still there. Paul Sharits came to South High a year or so later. Also, Robert Benson, who is now a character actor in Canada. It was like a gathering place of . . . I don't know what. The same thing was happening in Wichita, Kansas, with Bob Branaman and Bruce Conner, Michael McClure, Lawrence Ferlinghetti, and Ronald Johnson, all growing up next to each other. You just wonder what causes that. Maybe it's just chance, but that seems a little preposterous, too.

Well, we can get lost in too many thickets of where I went and what I did and who I studied with. The main thing is that I was searching for a way to *see,* and I was recognizing that this search was a corollary to a realization of what film could be as an art.

I was also recognizing that while *Blood of a Poet* suggested the possibility of cinema art, in the sense that meant the most to me, as did Cocteau's *Orpheus,* I saw also that both those films were filled, as was Buñuel and Dali's *Un Chien Andalou* [1929], with Hollywoodisms. There was something very disturbing to

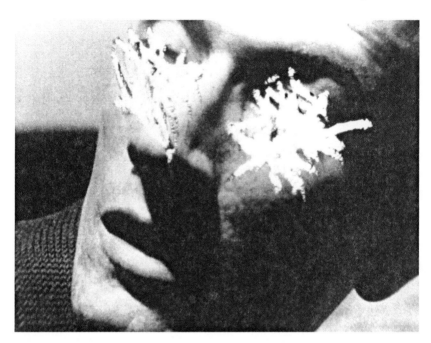

Scratching on film as metaphor for the filmmaker's and viewer's identification with a blind "seer" in Brakhage's psychodrama *Reflections on Black* (1955). Courtesy Anthology Film Archives.

me about this and about the overriding fact that narrative drama dominated everything. The dice were loaded clear back to the Greeks. Well, not just the Greeks, of course, because it's West *and* East, and it doesn't really matter whether you're dealing with a Kurosawa or a John Ford movie or with a Greek play. East and West, the world over, there's something intrinsically confining about narrative dramatics—and yet, of course, I also love them. I go to the movies all the time; and I care very deeply for drama. For years, I ran a theater in Central City, Colorado, staging Maeterlinck, Chekhov, and Stein.

Anyway, I had a sense that this loaded dice of drama could eventually destroy us all. I mean, if you think of all the forms of all the different arts, the one that changes the least is narrative drama. Because theater is also an edifice, and what is an *edifice* but something solid that doesn't change? Drama is always set up to come to the end—and the end can be happy or unhappy, or tragic, if you like, whatever—but there will be an end. Everything is designed like an equation, to come to the end.

Now, if you think about it, that is not true in the history of painting or music or poetry. These forms are ever more open and open-ended, especially as we come into full-blown romanticism. Somehow, the theater hasn't evolved in those directions, except perhaps through the not-very-often-staged work of Gertrude Stein, for example.

So I began to be more and more leery of narrative drama in my own work, and my evolution has been to try to find a way out of the dilemma of the dramatic in film. The whole concept of photoplay began to be embarrassing to me, and by the time of *Anticipation of the Night,* I had developed a form that had shaken at least some of the shackles off.

MacDonald: I understand that there was a break between you and Amos Vogel because he would not show *Anticipation of the Night* at Cinema 16. Is that true? What was your experience with Cinema 16?

Brakhage: Well, that's true about Amos and *Anticipation,* but it wasn't as simple as that. I mean, all along, Amos was the one hope. He had an audience of five thousand people to whom he would show works that my friends and I regarded as art. He showed it in a mix with scandal movies and documentaries of various shocking subjects and so on. In a way, Cinema 16 programs often didn't look all that different to me from the newsreels I had attended as a child during the Second World War.

MacDonald: Well, he showed a very wide variety of films, including newsreels and travelogues and cartoons . . .

Brakhage: Yes. His main concern and consideration was to show things that you could not see elsewhere. And that was what attracted his audience. They felt very special; they were seeing things that weren't allowed into the local neighborhood theaters and that you couldn't see on television: censored things, sexual subject matter, dog heads being kept alive on tables in a Russian laboratory—a mix into which was stirred some of the great American independent films.

Now, of course, the independent filmmakers felt there wasn't enough of *their* work and other work that they related to, and they often felt like they were being used in a freak show environment. In fact, the book that Amos finally wrote [*Film As a Subversive Art* (New York: Random House, 1974)] does show the freak show sensibility he had about film. On the one hand, he was bravely showing what was not available elsewhere; on the other hand, things got more and more strained with Amos across the years.

When the 1958 Brussels World Fair showings of American independent films occurred, I went to Amos to get money to buy a ticket so I could go. So I was still friendly with Amos and Marcia at that point, and am *still* friendly, and remember them *very* affectionately. That also permits me not to be too angry that Amos couldn't go as far as *Anticipation of the Night.* At that point, he just couldn't *see* it. His view was that it would destroy my reputation. I didn't see that I was having any kind of a reputation anyway, but in any case, Amos couldn't go that far. That was the end for him. But, in fairness to Amos, it was also the end for Parker Tyler and for many other people. They said, "Okay, that's

it, Brakhage has gone completely crazy and this is just degenerate work"—
not because of sexual subject matter; it was "degenerate" formally.

MacDonald: I can certainly see how Amos, audience-aware as he was, would
have trouble with the film. He didn't program to make his audience happy,
but he was certainly conscious of their boredom; and *Anticipation of the Night*
would have seemed, especially at that point, a long boring film, so slow as to
be impossible to show.

Brakhage: Oh, it created riots in Europe and wherever it was shown. People
came apart and threatened the projectionist and the screen. So, Amos couldn't
go that far, and that led to the break, but it wasn't just that. There were other
films that Amos refused to distribute or show, like Marie Menken's *Glimpse
of the Garden* [1957], and I said, "Until you distribute Marie Menken's new
work and *Anticipation of the Night,* I won't give you any of *my* new work." He
said, "Okay, then I don't take any of your work." So that was the break that
finally led to Jane and I advertising that we would distribute films, and our making an agreement with Bruce Conner and other people we knew, to distribute
from our home in the mountains.

At this point, I arrived in New York to begin showing some of my older work
that Amos *was* distributing and some work by other people, and at that precise
moment Jonas and Adolfas had decided to create the Film-makers' Cooperative. So, we more or less pooled our resources, and that's how the Film-makers' Cooperative began. Jonas and Adolfas were in a better position to do it: they
were in New York, they had backing of some kind or another, and eventually
they also came to have the support of Jerome Hill. Perhaps Jerome was already
involved. They were in a position to have a New York office and to distribute,
so I just became part of their efforts. Then gradually they—and I think to Amos's
bitterness—pushed him out and occupied his Cinema 16 offices.

MacDonald: There were—and are—some bad feeling about that.

Brakhage: I'm sorry that it created that bitterness for Amos and Marcia because
they did a great thing: they opened a gate without which there probably would
have been no American independent film movement. But that gate wasn't dedicated to the possible art of film as *we* understood it. Jonas at times wasn't either.
In those days, Jonas also could be very unsteady in that respect. Recently, a
lot of people find the word "art" problematic; but, by and large, Jonas has been
more artistically inclined than Amos. Art wasn't what Amos cared most deeply
about. So as our determination became more to see what an art of film might
be, Jonas became the obvious person to take over.

MacDonald: I think Jonas accepted certain kinds of work sooner. But I think
Amos also evolved into it and later was thoroughly enthusiastic about much
of that work; it's one of the bodies of work he feels most closely identified with.

Brakhage: Well, it's curious, you know. The qualities of a work that will make
it last often aren't visible to the makers either. They're just stuck with the work

that has come through them, usually in some degree of trance or some kind of desperate state. And even though they may feel obligated—as I certainly have often felt—to go out and speak for the work right away, to help give it a life on earth, the work is often very difficult for them, too. They are its first audience and find it as difficult as other audiences do. That's something I think a lot of people don't understand. You have to take the work on faith, both as an audience and as a maker.

Whatever faults there are in *Anticipation of the Night*—and there are many—it was produced through a process of *such* absolute sincerity. I mean, it was desperate making, and it was a gift to me and not one that I accepted easily, because it did start riots and lost me friends and brought every kind of abuse down on my head. But what am I to do? I have to trust my process. All I *can* trust is that this work continues to insist on being made, even when I'm passing through bladder cancer surgery, chemotherapy, and every other goddam thing—three operations in two months—and I'm still going to my office to make film splices! I know that I'm not mad. I may be a fool, but I'm not mad. There *is* an integrity to this process, and I will continue to struggle to try to raise the money to get the films printed—horrible as that struggle is going to be at this time—and to push the work out there where there are only about four places in the United States where it will probably ever be shown. It was the same with *Anticipation of the Night:* when I made *Anticipation,* there was *only* Cinema 16, and Amos wouldn't show it! In Europe it created a riot, and *that* was awful. I didn't enjoy any bit of it. It's always been just one kind of trouble after another, beginning with that long kiss in *Interim.*

I guess there's some deep fear of the new thing. Some artists, for their own reasons—and I've tried to express some of mine—feel they must work in a new way because the old way just won't do for their needs. From time to time, they end up creating something new and, sometimes, something that seems to last. Sometimes, much of the audience seems to know right away that it *is* going to last and because they can feel the power of this new thing, they try to destroy it and the person who made it. It seems to me that all my life I've been struggling with that syndrome, and of course I'm hardly alone.

MacDonald: When I show *Anticipation of the Night* now, this same overall history happens, but it happens in a microcosm. My students will revolt, and in discussion or in their formal journals, they'll try to think of new ways to tell me why this can't possibly be okay, why they are *not* going *this* far *this* time. But two weeks later a substantial number of them have come through that reaction and are feeling invigorated by the film. Over a generation there has been some movement, I think. The same thing does happen, but the pain is over quickly, and for at least some, the pleasure begins.

Brakhage: I'm delighted to hear that, not just for the usual reason—my own pride in having let that work come into being through me—but because the thought process embodied in *Anticipation of the Night* is far more important than the plot that ends with the hanging. This thought process is a way into new envisionment for people. I believe and hope that it can have its life on earth for the betterment of humans or at least for the reenergizing of humans—whether it's *betterment* or not, who can say?

We always need new vision. As Ezra Pound said, "The arts are the antennae of the race and cultures go blind without them." I feel that *Anticipation of the Night,* in its humble way (and along with so many other films by me and others), has had something to do with a new way of perceiving, which also means a new way of thinking about what you have seen. And I'm delighted if people can begin to get over the disturbance of the newness of it as rapidly as you say.

MacDonald: I've been thinking about the period from around 1957 through 1962 when you changed from being an inventive contributor to genres of independent cinema that other people had established to virtually a "genre" of your own, so that people could talk about a "Brakhage film," and we all knew what they were talking about. As you look back on it now, what were the pivotal moments that created the change that we see in *Loving, Anticipation of the Night, Window Water Baby Moving, Sirius Remembered...* ?

Brakhage: Well, I didn't know it when I made it, but *Nightcats* in 1956, though it's hardly avant-garde and not shocking to anyone, has a quality of aesthetics without which *Anticipation of the Night* is not imaginable.

MacDonald: The sensitivity to texture so clear in the work I'm talking about is there.

Brakhage: And a belief in the plastic cut, a belief that one form flowing into another is more visual than one scene being intercut with another, or being chopped into close-ups, long shots, and shot/countershot, and so forth. Narrative drama tends to be chopped up, chopped up, while *Nightcats* is much more intrinsically musical.

I didn't know and couldn't have said these things when I was making *Nightcats,* but the whole evolution of the relationship between film and music in my work came to bear on the making of *Nightcats,* which is curious because *Nightcats* was made very simply. In the Los Angeles neighborhood where I lived for a time, all these cats used to gather around the home of a couple friends who also had cats of their own. I just started taking floodlights out into the alleys at night and onto the porch.

MacDonald: It never occurred to me that the film was shot outdoors.

Brakhage: Yes, with Kodachrome and an ASA of 8 or something like that, very low, which gives the film its texture and vibrant color. But mainly it is the *musical* possibilities of film that are evident there, in contradistinction to *Flesh of Morning,* which is the film that I had just finished—the ultimate of what we used to call "psychodrama."

MacDonald: I often think of P. Adams Sitney's juxtaposition [in *Visionary Film*] of a shot from *Thigh Line Lyre Triangular* and an image of a de Kooning painting. How much was abstract expressionist painting in your mind at this point?

Brakhage: When I was a junior in high school, I was very, very involved in Jackson Pollock. I had not actually seen any abstract painting yet, but I was tremendously involved in reproductions of the paintings in books. By the time we're talking about, I had seen many of the paintings of Pollock and some of the earlier paintings of de Kooning and Kline and others. I haunted the galleries. I was very involved. But in those days (we're talking 1957–58, maybe until 1959), I began to be aware that a lot of what was called abstract expressionism was rooted in closed-eye vision, and I began consciously searching my own closed eyes for forms, shapes, areas that were related to de Kooning, as distinct from Pollock, and to Pollock as distinct from others, and so on. I was very centered on the *American* abstract expressionist movement; the Europeans, even Kandinsky, never held a great deal of fascination for me. I respected him, but my feelings about him or Klee were not at all comparable to what I was feeling about Pollock, de Kooning, and other Americans.

MacDonald: I feel that way, too, though I can't put my finger on why. It has something to do with a commitment to size.

Brakhage: I don't think that's the issue for me. It had more to do with the tendency toward the geometric, which certainly took over Kandinsky finally, and, of course, most famously, Mondrian. I was always interested in ineffable shapes that, if you were going to name them, would be biological rather than mathematical: shapes related to nerves, to cells, to the honeycomb of the bones, to the synapse system in the brain. That's how I found corollaries in Jackson Pollock and in some of de Kooning.

Of course, de Kooning had that whole other side of him that was interested in the figure, his so-called misogynist paintings. But he was important to me, just as Gorky was, and many in that movement. The early Philip Guston. Some of them came to very bad ends: violent suicide, extreme alcoholism.

The greatest of them for me became Joan Mitchell. To me, she was much more than a second-generation abstract expressionist; she was an epitome of something that grew out of the whole movement. She *included* both her teacher, Hans Hoffman, and everything that had been around her as she began her painting—all these others we've named.

But to come back to your question: for me, whether they were conscious of it or not, the abstract expressionists were always painting closed-eye vision, and I wanted to include that in film, since my impulse always was to include everything that you might *see* within the possibilities of filmmaking: closed-eye vision, daydreams, night dreams, and so on.

MacDonald: The conventional sense of your connection with those painters has to do with your gestural camerawork as an echo of their gestural painting.

Brakhage: There *is* something to the concept of the gesture. And it certainly relates to Jackson Pollock. Once I went out to Long Island with Parker Tyler and Charles Boultenhouse, who had been invited to Pollock's home along with some New York art critics, to see his new painting—what was, after his death, to be tabbed "the Cyclopean Painting" by *Life* magazine—because they never did see more than one eye in it, I guess. It was a return to the earlier totemistic work that Pollock had done.

I was too shy even to approach the man, and besides he didn't invite approach. He was dead drunk when everybody arrived, and he had a half bottle of whiskey beside him that he emptied. So the critics began browsing, and some of them began talking about "chance operations," and that threw him into a rage. And he said, "You see that doorknob over there?" It was about thirty-five feet away. He pointed to this doorknob, and drunk as he was, he did a swill around the bucket of paint beside him with the brush, flicked it across the room, and hit that doorknob. Then he said to this group of critics, "Don't give me any of your 'chance operations,' and *that* is the door out."

Parker and Charles and I got to stay a little longer and watch him drink a little more and look a little more at his painting. Within a year or so, he was dead.

So I had seen his ability to throw paint and the intensity of that kind of gesture. And certainly that was inspiring to me, as it was to everyone else—and I think it does have a lot to do with my handheld camera.

That, plus the newsreels: newsreels always looked more exciting to me when suddenly the camera would go off the tripod. There were a lot of other people, even in Hollywood movies, who were beginning to take the camera off the tripod and hand hold it. I'm thinking of Kubrick's first war movie, *Paths of Glory* [1957]. There's a lot of handheld camera in that. The handheld camera wasn't an invention of mine, but I certainly augmented it.

One thing I *did* do, and, until I started talking about it, I didn't know anyone else who did it, was to practice hand-holding the camera, with no film in it, for an hour or two a day so the camera could become one with my body. It wasn't to increase control, so much as to increase the possibilities of emoted feeling that might move through me into that camera when I was actually shooting. I wanted a degree of oneness with the camera. I didn't really think of that as gestural in the sense of hurling paint or anything like that. I think the connection with gestural painting is there, but overplayed. My reasons for hand-holding the camera were quite different from Jackson Pollock's reasons for throwing paint.

MacDonald: When you talk about trying to develop a way of empathizing with your subject by practicing these gestures, I immediately think of *Loving* [1956], which, when I saw it about a month ago, looked really wonderful. I had forgotten how lovely it is. There's a caress in the camera movement.

Brakhage: In *Loving* I was shooting outside again, seeing people who are in love and trying to comprehend them, trying to feel some empathy with their being. They were very close friends, Jim Tenney and Carolee Schneemann, who were about to break up, and yet, it seemed to me, they were terribly involved with each other as lovers.

MacDonald: I think Carolee never stopped being involved with James Tenney, or actually with any of the people she has been seriously involved with.

Brakhage: Well, she was in a bad way at the time. She had won a grant and was in Colorado trying to paint mountains. I went up into the mountains one day and asked Carolee and Jim if they would like to make this film. They agreed. I was desperate to connect with something of loving. I was very lonely and bereft in my life, and I felt they had something I didn't have that they were about to throw away. They used to joke—I don't know with how much truth—that making the film helped them to stay together for several more years. They liked the film very much.

MacDonald: How did you meet Carolee?

Brakhage: Jim and I went to New York about the same time, he to study with Varèse and Cage, and me to be allowed to sit in on these studies. We lived in a burned-out building on the Lower East Side together. Jim met Carolee in New York, and I got to know her about the time I made *Reflections on Black* [1955].

MacDonald: I have to confess that, as many times as I've seen *Anticipation of the Night,* I cannot get my eyes off the textures and the colors and the rhythms of the film; I can't *see* the story. I know from reading Sitney's analysis that there *is* a story, about suicide, but I cannot see it. I don't know if there's some kind of weird blinder in my brain, but every time, something carries me into these other dimensions of the film, and I just sit there thinking, "Wow, look at this! Look at that!" and then the film is over.

Brakhage: Maybe you're just wiser than most in your ways of viewing, because the truth is, the story is very insignificant and, in fact, is flawed because, in the end, I *didn't* commit suicide—though, of course, I *had* thought about it. I'm glad I didn't commit suicide, but all the same the film had come to a point where when my decision changed, it could not re-realize itself in a new mode. Otherwise, the film is music, visual music.

MacDonald: It's almost as though there was a battle between the new Brakhage and the old Brakhage. *Anticipation* completes the movement into a second way of doing things. And even though I can see that there is symbolic import to this or that detail, I'm immediately drawn back into the texture, the musical flow. Something in me fights seeing the film in that earlier way, as a psychodramatic story.

Brakhage: It's also true that music can be spoken of in terms of story. Some music lends itself more to that possibility; we call it "programmatic music." You tell a story, and the music is about that. In Debussy's *La Mer* (The Sea), there are the storms and the peaceful periods. That's a kind of story. And there's even a story dimension in Beethoven. There are themes and, if you can think of the themes as characters, they have interrelationships with each other and then come finally to a resolution. I don't see anything wrong with thinking of film in much the same way. The difference, of course, is that in music the sounds only rarely evoke with exactitude anything audible in the everyday, ordinary world, whereas with film, unless you are painting on film or really working hard to achieve something completely nonobjective, you *are* involved in pictures of things that are nameable.

Last Sunday, at one of our gatherings with friends, Phil Solomon made an interesting critique of narrative drama. He said, "When you see the first shot, very often you have a sense of infinite possibilities; by the time the film-maker has given you his/her second shot, your possibilities have been reduced to half. And so it goes. A fifth of the way through the movie, you're on a tread-mill that leads in an inevitable direction. And that is the limitation of narrative drama." I think that's quite true. He was comparing narrative drama with other modes of making, especially with the more poetic cinema where you can live in the continuous present and can always have an infinite number of possibilities.

MacDonald: That's certainly clear in *Anticipation of the Night,* as compared with your early psychodramas, which have to go somewhere. *Anticipation of the Night* can go where it wants.

Brakhage: I wish I had known that when I was editing! I was so hung up that *this* was the end. Partly, the idea of my suicide gave me the bravery to do all kinds of things with film that at the time were considered absolutely monstrous. Who could even imagine such editing? You almost had to be tilted on the edge of death in order to . . . but then actually I *didn't* have to die, except in the sense that you could say that we will *all* die in the end. So I guess there's nothing terribly wrong that there's a noose at the end of the film.

MacDonald: And since we do die in the end, the challenge is to see what we can see while we can still see it.

Brakhage: I guess I'm at peace with *Anticipation.* But I certainly prefer your way of looking at it.

MacDonald: Sirius Remembered, which was made right after *Anticipation,* is still one of my favorites of all your films. And it certainly goes in a very specific direction and has a very specific end, but somehow the development of layer after layer allows for a different kind of visual freedom to take place so that the film doesn't feel limited by its "story."

Brakhage: It also creates empathy for my grieving over the death of a pet; I'm not brooding over my *self.*

MacDonald: That's true. The film is also very positive. As Sirius decays, the film becomes increasingly dense. The form of the piece compensates for the loss of the dog, or at least for our confrontation of decay. And as the winter passes and we move toward spring, you create a sense of natural compensation.

Brakhage's signature, scratched directly onto the filmstrip, frame by frame, became an emblem of the filmmaker's commitment to handcrafted, personal cinema. Courtesy Anthology Film Archives.

Brakhage: You know, during that whole period of my life when Jane and I moved back east from Denver and ended up in Princeton, New Jersey—where *Sirius Remembered* was made and *Window Water Baby Moving* and *Cat's Cradle* [1959]—I was very haunted by and filled with the expectation of dying. At the same time, of course, the first baby was on the way, and Jane and I were trying to put together some kind of a life, but I was finding life very problematic, just in terms of surviving from day to day. I had jobs, pretty good jobs, too, and enough ability to rise very rapidly, in a commercial film company called On Film, located in Princeton. I had a responsible position and good salary.

But at the same time, I could never get my car started in the morning. I was always desperate to get Mr. Swing to come by and pull the car until it coughed into life somehow and could get me into Princeton, one more time, to go do these awful commercials. I remember one morning when the car started on its own and was doing fine, I had a flat tire, which felt so totally impossible to face that I drove all the way to work on the rim and parked it with the wheel smoking! I was hardly prepared to take on a family. I didn't even expect to keep living, really, and I became more shocked by life, every day. And the films showed it. Right after *Sirius Remembered* comes *The Dead* [1960].

MacDonald: I remember when my first wife was pregnant with my son, I could see that this oncoming kid was a kind of clock, and that I would now be living by *his* time instead of mine. I felt like he was going to throw me through life much more quickly than I wanted to go.

Brakhage: My feelings were different—complex and confused. Do I need to live anymore? Have I done enough? Perhaps that sounds odd, but a great center of my being is my compulsion to make films, to be an instrument for all these messages, many of which I do not understand at first, any more than anyone else in the audience does. I had such dissatisfaction with the human condition, and *my* human condition.

MacDonald: What was your filmmaking life like in those days? How much were you working? How did filmmaking fit into the rest of the life?

Brakhage: With few exceptions, I have almost always worked as much as I possibly could on my films. I was just making, making constantly, depending, of course, on how much time I was free from making a living, which was not a whole lot during the period we're talking about. But always if too much time goes by and I haven't been able to work on the film that I regard as given to me to make, it's as if I'm not having enough air and need to smash through the glass to be able to breathe.

MacDonald: What was your job at On Film?

Brakhage: Well, I did a number of jobs there. At first I was working on an animation stand doing what they told me. But it evolved very quickly. I was on a European shoot for the Atomic Peace Conference in Geneva, and I did all kinds of hotshot ads, like the *G.E. Theater* ad of the day, which was entirely designed by me.

I had a whole day, by the way, a wonderful and strange day, working with Boris Kaufman. He had won an Academy Award for his cinematography for *On the Waterfront* [1954], and On Film wanted his name for stature. They hired him to shoot a Scott toilet tissue box, and I was his assistant. I didn't even know about Dziga Vertov; I didn't know Boris *had* a brother, and no one else did in those days either. Well, I shouldn't say no one, but at the time very few Americans knew about Vertov. I did know the Vigo films Boris had shot [*A Propos de Nice,* 1933; *Zéro de Conduit,* 1933; *L'Atalante,* 1934], which not very many Americans knew anything about, so I could talk with him. He wasn't too anxious to talk about Vigo, but he did like to talk about qualities of light.

Then came my final job, when finally everything collapsed on me and I quit: I was director of a one-hundred-seventy-five-thousand-dollar documentary to make Pittsburgh look beautiful [*Pittsburgh,* 1957]. I had brought in Eugene Smith on that project. Smith was a still photographer who had spent a year photographing Pittsburgh and had made extraordinary images. I got to know him pretty well.

And Weegee. I got to spend a day on Coney Island with Weegee photographing through his kaleidoscopic box. And Len Lye—I brought him in, but he just sat and groused and picked up a consultant's fee—not that I blame him. Stan Vanderbeek was also brought in on that project.

MacDonald: Did the film get finished?

Brakhage: Not by me, but it did get finished. It's dreadful. Bob Haller [director of Special Programs at Anthology Film Archives in New York] can tell you all about it; he dug it up finally—it was sitting in somebody's attic—and he has it preserved at Anthology.

MacDonald: Is *Window Water Baby Moving* the most rented of your films?

Brakhage: No. Probably *Mothlight. Window Water Baby Moving* is still hard for some people to take.

MacDonald: That's a film I cannot teach without. I show it in nearly every course, partly because it's remarkable how little students know about the body and especially about the female body-in-process. During the sixties, it was hard to imagine that anything could be more conservative than the fifties but, on a certain level of colonizing the body, we may be worse off now than we were in the fifties.

Brakhage: I think so. There was a period when people began to be able to look at *Window Water Baby Moving* and feel it and see it as a film. But then that turned around to a large extent. I don't think this period is quite as bad as the fifties, but to some extent, people are removed from their bodies and, maybe it *is* getting worse now with the computer, which doesn't sweat, has no saliva, is not sticky, is so unproblematic. There's a science fictionish tendency to stop thinking about the body altogether.

MacDonald: I often show *Weegee's New York* [1954] in my classes. The second section focuses on Coney Island, where it appears that people actually have the revolutionary idea that when they are off from work, they should be able to take a vacation from how other people think they ought to look. They just stand there on the beach with their guts hanging out, being themselves—and to hell with everyone! Now, almost nobody can do that. Everybody has to have "million-dollar abs," and it's assumed that every part of the body has to be perfect by some standard, has to be under control. To show, as you do in *Window Water Baby Moving,* that the body is actually a process and that during the process of birth, things flow—many of my students are amazed, shocked; they swear off being parents! Anyway, forty years later it's still one of the most powerful films I can show.

Brakhage: They used to faint. We used to warn people. At almost every show of any size, someone would faint. They didn't crash down, but someone would end up lying on the floor. There was such fear.

MacDonald: How much legal resistance did you face?

Brakhage: Well, first off, I was certainly in danger of going to jail for having made *Window Water Baby Moving.* When I sent in the film to be processed, Kodak sent a page that said, more or less, "Sign this at the bottom, and we will destroy this film; otherwise, we will turn it over to the police." So then the doctor wrote a letter, and we got the footage back. But for years we lived under that threat.

Then, every time you showed the film in a public arena, there was a danger that someone would blow the whistle and you'd end up in jail. As you know, not too far down the line we were to have these big court cases with Jack Smith's *Flaming Creatures* [1963] and other films. Well, that could have happened with *Window Water Baby Moving* just as well. Nudity was forbidden, and only available in an underground way, in a gangster underground porn way. You could definitely go to jail for showing not only sexuality but nudity of any kind—though the idea of childbirth being somehow pornographic has always been offensive and disgusting to me.

MacDonald: It's remarkable.

Brakhage: I can't imagine how such an attitude could have existed, but it certainly did. Remember, I was alone during these years—there was no institutional support for independent filmmakers—trying to shepherd these films into the world. I'm also raising one child, then another, then three, then four, and finally five, and we always felt under threat, not only of me being thrown into jail but of my children being taken away from us, or whatever.

Window Water Baby Moving was often shown with George Stoney's *All My Babies* [1953], in an attempt to give it some aura of usability.

MacDonald: An interesting double bill.

Brakhage: It was a way to gentle it into people's cognizance. Whenever *I* presented the film, I talked to people about it, trying to make it easier for them, advising them to leave the room if they felt they couldn't take it. I don't recall any specific show, but New York City was always a worrisome place for the film. New York had a very uptight, highly developed censorship court, so whenever you showed in New York, you were running a risk, at least until 1963, 1964.

MacDonald: You know, I've often thought that that film might have had a substantial cultural impact. When my son Ian was born in 1972, I had to battle my way into the delivery room in our local hospital in Utica. It was still rare for a father to be present at a birth. I know that *Window Water Baby Moving* had a lot to do with my having the courage to confront the resistance, and I wonder how many people it might have taught, because suddenly delivery rooms became much more accessible to fathers.

Brakhage: It probably had some impact. Barney Rosset released that film in 8mm through Evergreen Press, and around five thousand copies sold. A lot of them were bought by clinics. It was very pleasing to me that maternity clinics, where they were training men and women to share this experience, were showing the film. It had a rich life in that sense.

One particular incident I remember happened at the post office in Boulder in the late sixties. A small-boned woman with a very large newborn baby stopped me on the steps and thanked me for *Window Water Baby Moving.* She said she wanted so much to have this baby without a cesarean, and it took her two days. "The last day and a half," she said, "I did not think of much, other than your film." Actually, I don't think it's feasible that *Window Water Baby Moving* would have made her decide to go two days struggling to give birth to this baby, but that the film inspired her and sustained her while she was doing what she was already determined to do means a great deal to me.

MacDonald: Ironically, when I did get permission to be in the delivery room when Ian was born, the hospital had all sorts of rules and regulations. I couldn't actually look directly at the baby coming out; I had to look at the whole thing in a mirror. On some level, it was like watching a movie!

Brakhage: My difficulty in just being at the delivery continued through all the births, and I imagine it still goes on today in some hospitals. They have their reasons: they're trying to avoid being sued or whatever, but the truth is that often it's not a human atmosphere; and here are people trying to share bringing a child into the world. Finally, I got to where I would say, "I know what you are saying, but I'm going in there. You're right, but I'm going in there, and you'll have to call the police if you want to stop me." Luckily, no one ever did.

MacDonald: One of the things that makes the film so powerful is that it's silent. Your shift into silent film has to do with a concentration on seeing, but was there a specific point in your life where you just said, "Okay, I'm not going to do sound anymore"?

Brakhage: Gradually it became more and more apparent to me that my abilities as a composer of sound were not keeping up with my abilities as a visionary; sound was tearing the films apart. I was desperately trying to keep up with my burgeoning envisionment, and as the films kept developing visually, I just had to forget sound. What sound can you put with *Loving? Anticipation of the Night* takes courage from that and just says, "Okay, we're just a silent film." Then *Wedlock House, An Intercourse* [1959], and *Window Water Baby Moving* go on from there: sound is hardly conceivable.

But then the question would rise again: *Shouldn't* I have sound? Fortunately, it didn't come up again until almost 1962, with *Blue Moses,* where the sound came *first,* and the picture is almost an illustration of the sound.

I never wanted to make a polemic against sound, you know. After all, I had done all this studying with Varèse and Cage, and I had great composer friends like Jim Tenney. But I was never capable of achieving adequate sound, except under unusual circumstances where the vision was either deficient or intentionally low yield, the way the visuals in *Blue Moses* are. I was perfectly aware of my own faults, as I had also become aware of my poetic limitations earlier, and had discontinued my pretensions to be a poet. Just because you *want* to write a poem doesn't mean you're going to be able to. It's like *wanting* to be in love. You may want to be, but you either are or you're not.

These days I would want to be almost anything *but* a filmmaker. Who wouldn't? I'm not even sure what a filmmaker *is* anymore. But I am what I am. It's always a question, do you accept what you are? Are you honest about that? And for me, anyway, the art gets a tremendous strength if one is honest about what one *cannot* do, and I simply couldn't do sound well.

3/23/97

MacDonald: At what point during that first pregnancy did you and Jane know you were making a film? Was it something you set out to do, the minute you found out Jane was pregnant?

Brakhage: It was more complicated than that. First of all, there was a strong desire on Jane's part that I be present during the childbirth, and I wasn't really wanting that burden. I thought I might faint. I rather think I would have had I not been making a film, and something in me knew that. Though that was not exactly how I came to make the film either.

In a way, it was suggested by the doctor: once he learned I was a filmmaker—he assumed a commercial filmmaker—he said, "Well, I always wanted a film of the childbirth process to show to women and their husbands." That's how I was able to come into the delivery room. The hospital, after agreeing at first, reneged on their offer, but the doctor was interested enough in having the film

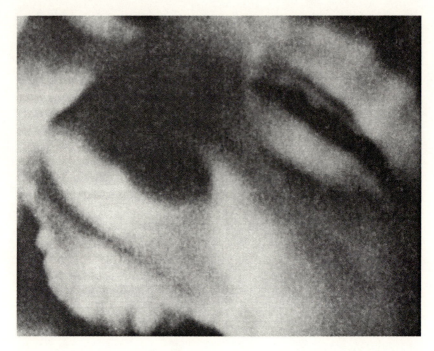

Jane Brakhage, in *Window Water Baby Moving* (1959). Courtesy Anthology Film Archives.

made that he agreed to come to our home. Then we had to hire a nurse and rent some very expensive emergency equipment. It got very complicated, but the possibility of my being in attendance when the child was born was dependent on my filming it.

So naturally enough, aside from whatever the doctor thought I was doing, what type of commercial film he thought I was making, I began wanting images previous to the birth.

MacDonald: When we look at *Window Water Baby Moving,* the domestic seems an idealized, comfortable, generally happy space for you. Is what we're seeing an idealization of what it was? Was there continual strife about the making of the film?

Brakhage: Well, as I said, I really didn't know if I could go through the birth without fainting. Every time they drew blood on me I used to pass out. I'd always tell them, "I am going to pass out," and they'd say, "Yes, yes, it's all right. It won't hurt." And they'd draw the blood, and I'd pass out! So basically, I'm not the kind to weather childbirth; but, in fact, two things were very important to Jane: one, that I *be* there and, two, that it be at home; and both of these were very hard to arrange at this time.

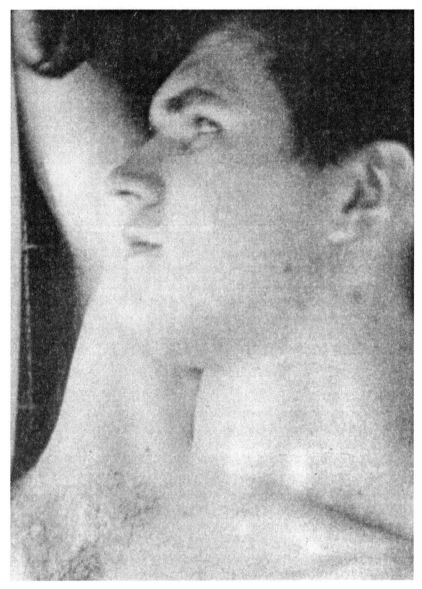

Stan Brakhage, filmed by Jane Brakhage, at the time of *Window Water Baby Moving* (1959). Courtesy Anthology Film Archives.

I wanted to take some images of Jane in the bathtub showing the pregnancy before the actual birth, and she got very, very shy—understandably. She had never been approached this way before in her life, and very few people have. And in her shyness she said, "Oh, I can't do this." So I said, "Okay, okay," and I tore the film out of the camera and spread it all over the floor and made a big dramatic scene and said, "All right, let's forget it!" And then a half an hour later she bravely relented. She had pulled her courage together and said, "Okay, we'll do this." That's pretty much the way my relationship with her was all along. Then she engaged in the work and even took the camera at the end and photographed *me*.

I would always show the edited sequences to her, not only of that film but of any film I made. I wanted some sense of the feminine to be in my work. I knew I wasn't a natural at it like D. H. Lawrence is said to have been. You know, many people think that *Women in Love* [1920] could have been written by a woman. He had that feminine side to him. I had *enough* to know I wanted more, so I was always open to Jane, and to women writers—certainly the most important to me is Gertrude Stein; I am always trying to get that balance into my work.

So in that sense Jane was deeply involved. She would come and look at things, and would say things, and often I would reedit things entirely, not that she ever said how to do anything or gave any instruction, but I got a feeling from her that something was missing here that needed to be added. It would be on a feeling level that I couldn't even put into language, nor did she, nor did she try. But we had that relationship, and sometimes she would also do photography: a lot of the photography in *Dog Star Man* and other films is by her. She's usually the one who was filming me.

There were other strains on our relationship during this time. Jane had had German measles at three months, and in those days, they thought this meant there was a much higher chance of giving birth to a monster. We were always concerned about that. When I first looked through the camera at the baby emerging, I thought, "This *is* a monster!" I had never seen a newborn baby before and thought this was a deformed monster, and I remember the thought passing through my head, "Then I will make a monster film!" and continuing to film in a kind of rage. Of course, it turned out much happier than that.

MacDonald: About the material before the birth that we see in the finished film: you went back after Jane relented and filmed again?

Brakhage: Yes. In fact, at that point she was quite open. It became an important bonding for us, too, in the sense that (except in a way in *Wedlock House,* where she was acting), she had never been involved to that degree in one of my films. In some way the idea overwhelmed her at first, and then she realized it was necessary for me, and from that point on, she was open to any photography that I would do.

Her holding the camera at the end of *Window Water Baby Moving* was at her insistence, not mine. I think it's pretty obvious I was too far out of my head to be able to do any directing—she said, "Give me the camera!"

MacDonald: After the birth, how long did it take to put the final film together?

Brakhage: I was working full-time (on a Scott toilet tissue ad, as a matter of fact), so I did whatever I could do in the evenings—I was usually pretty exhausted—and on weekends. I think it took a couple of months. Before I even started to edit, there was the delay caused by Kodak seizing the film. Once I did begin editing, it went rather quickly.

I was, as the title suggests, very loosened up and taught in new ways by Gertrude Stein's writing: I've been reading Gertrude Stein since I was about nineteen. She was coming into my aesthetics pretty strongly at that point.

MacDonald: Window Water Baby Moving not only gives birth to a new baby but pretty quickly to a whole new sense of who you are as a filmmaker. There's the obvious part—the whole theory of child vision—but also, soon after that film, you begin working on what becomes your first epic, *Dog Star Man. Dog Star Man* includes many of the kinds of work you had done up to that point, but it goes much further than just *including* it, it becomes a much larger, more expansive kind of vision. I'm curious about how that project took shape.

Brakhage: A number of things happened. First of all, *Sirius Remembered,* as its title suggests, is rather important here: Sirius is the "Dog Star." *Sirius Remembered* was made on the occasion of the death of our family dog. The ground was too frozen to bury Sirius, so we went out into the New Jersey woods with him and just laid him on the ground, so that he could have a natural setting and a going-back-into-the-earth, just like all the wild animals that die in the woods. Then, of course, for a time, I kept visiting his frozen corpse and finally was filming the corpse. So right after the childbirth film we have a consideration of death. Part of the tactic of that film reflected a wish to *revive* that dog (I feel tears coming to my eyes even now as I speak about that moment).

We had not had Sirius very long, but his death immediately followed my punishing him: I spanked him for having licked the new baby, and the next day he managed to get himself run over chasing a car. There was an enormous sense of guilt. I hadn't trusted him enough. I hadn't had *sense* enough to know that it might be all right for him to lick the baby. It might not have been; I might have been absolutely right to do what I did—I don't know. Sometimes a pet *can* be very dangerous to a new baby. In any event, there was not enough sensitivity, and then, coincidentally or because of that, he was dead. So those themes—of birth, of death—reverberated.

Certainly, *Sirius* is a very visceral, physical film that set off in my mind senses of the Dog Star, and therefore Orion, and a whole set of abstractions. But then it was my job to bring these abstractions back to earth, so I have a dog, a star, and a man. And I have a cat, an earth, and a woman. What happens to such an equation? Certain parallel themes started reverberating from what was probably just guilt over the death of this dog. How do you *envision* all that? *Dog Star Man* was almost like an equation, you see, a hieroglyphic, taking shape in the mind.

Also, I could no longer hold that job at On Film. It was driving me crazy. So we set off from the East to come back west, and since we had nothing left to fall back on, we moved in with Jane's parents.

Sirius was shot in Princeton, New Jersey. It was *edited* in Colorado, while I was starting to shoot *Dog Star Man.*

MacDonald: Is the superimposition in *Sirius* your first use of that technique?

Brakhage: Yes.

MacDonald: It's a beautiful and suggestive film in its use of layers. I interviewed Gunvor Nelson some years ago [see *A Critical Cinema 3*], and she talks about *Sirius* being a pivotal film in her experience.

Brakhage: It's nice to hear that. We know each other, but Gunvor and I have never discussed that film.

MacDonald: She told me that when she first saw *Sirius,* she couldn't *see* what she was seeing, and then years later, when she saw it again, it was totally clear to her. The idea of working through that many layers in a film—literally and intellectually—was a new idea.

Brakhage: Sirius was a much more important film than *Window Water Baby Moving,* in terms of my development as a filmmaker. *Window Water Baby Moving* was an anomaly in many ways, in terms of my later filmmaking. I don't mean that as anything *against* it, but it wasn't seminal like *Sirius Remembered* was.

Or, to give another example, you could say that *Nightcats* was seminal in the development of *Anticipation of the Night.* But *Loving,* which came right before *Anticipation of the Night,* I would *not* regard as a seminal work, but more the use of a mastery of certain things put in the service of some necessary revelation. A seminal work, to me, is something that cuts ahead: you don't know where it's going or what it is. *Sirius Remembered* was made in a trance, so I also didn't know really what it was.

We drove cross-country with a lot of footage that was later to be in *Scenes from under Childhood* [1969–70], *Sincerity* [1973, 1975, 1978], *Duplicity* [1978, 1980]. . . . I had piles of film, though often I couldn't afford to process it. And I began photographing our life more regularly. So while all these various reverberations off a thread of guilt are twanging in the brain, there's *also* a sense of rooting down, of photographing the *most* mundane things of everyday life, and a developing sense that there must be some relationship between the two.

Arthur Eddington's *The Nature of the Physical World* [Cambridge: Cambridge University Press, 1930] was an important book for me at this time. A number of science books began being important to me, and I subscribed to *Scientific American* for several years. Gertrude Stein was continuing to be more and more important, and also Pound and Joyce. The epic structures of the longer films began taking shape.

At any rate, here we were back in Colorado, living in my wife's parents' house in the mountains, and at some point I asked them, "What can I do to help out?" Jane's mother and father were teachers, and Jane had the baby, which was *her* life's work; and for a while I couldn't get a job of any kind. Her parents suggested I collect firewood. That became my job, and I did collect enough firewood so that they were still burning it five or six years later. Then I began sensing that the central character of a film could be a woodsman—the woodsman is certainly a central character in many fairy tales—and I began photographing myself.

Then I *did* get a job, which was to make two films based on Colorado legends—one about the Utes [*The Ballad of the Colorado,* 1961] and another about a couple of miners who fought over some gold [*The Colorado Legend,* 1961]—so suddenly I had the use of expensive camera equipment and film at below cost. Because I was doing these commercial films, I had a way to be working on *Dog Star Man.* And I was reading a lot of mythology: Graves's *The Greek Myths,* and so on.

MacDonald: I always think of Sisyphus when I see you climbing up that hill—

Brakhage: Yes, he was certainly a primary figure in my mind, but I wanted to embody legends from around the world. I was reading the Norse legends of Gilgamesh, and so on. My sense of it, in my bitterness, and there *was* coming to be a lot of bitterness in me by this time (despite the baby and my second baby coming and all that could have made life more joyful), was that the tree—the mythic structure, the metaphor for human culture—was dead, and all that it would be useful for was to chop up and burn for firewood. In a way, the story of *Dog Star Man* is a simplistic, embittered statement, something that someone might toss off at a bar, getting drunk. Remember, I was living in my wife's *parents'* house as a creature that they did *not* understand at all. I was *completely* suppressed in every part of my life except the filmmaking. And looking around me—we were coming out of the fifties, one of the most awful, intolerant times in the twentieth century—whatever felt brave or heroic *to me,* either culturally or aesthetically, seemed to be completely strange to the world around me.

MacDonald: I remember Carolee Schneemann talking about your battle to establish film as a visual art. It's easy to read this Sisyphus-like climb up the mountain as an attempt to drag film up onto the mountain and make it an art equal to other arts.

Brakhage: Well, that was certainly *always* in my mind, but the way I would have put it is that film *was* an art—from Méliès on, we had had obvious signs—and by now that ought to have been clear enough, though there *were* problems about how to make it *last.*

MacDonald: In the fifties there was still intellectual resistance to film, especially in the United States. I have a vivid memory from college—I believe it was in 1963—standing with a bunch of students and a professor, who said, "It would be interesting to have a film course," and all the students (and these were good students) laughed at the preposterousness of the idea that you could actually *study* something as frivolous as the movies.

Brakhage: I had heard stories, while Cinema 16 was still running, that some of the Tenth Street painters—heroes of mine like Kline and de Kooning and Pollock—used to go to Cinema 16 (or maybe they'd read about it or heard about it) and rail against the whole idea of film being an art. They made jokes about it and even used my name. I was *known* to them as that absurd kid who thought that movies were an *art.* So, yes, all those pressures were still very strong.

MacDonald: Dog Star Man has a very unusual structure that is evident even in the catalogue description of the film: *Prelude* is twenty-five minutes, *Part I* is thirty minutes, while *Part II, Part III,* and *Part IV* are quite brief (seven minutes, eleven minutes, and five minutes, respectively). I'm curious about how that structure developed.

Brakhage: Well, I had a belief in the compound. When you do lay out all the possible combinations of the superimpositions in those last three parts, of the A, B, and A, B, C, and A, B, C, and D rolls that are used in *Parts II, III,* and *IV,* you *do* get a proportion that is more classical. In other words, I start with the *Prelude,* which was put together just by a variety of chance operations—I was operating under some of Cage's ideas about chance—to try to create a dreamscape of the mind, to get a spill of the unconscious. I had a sense of the unconscious, not so much in the Freudian or psychoanalytic sense but as a chaotic world of chance operations.

Now, we all know that it's very Freudian to understand that things that you pass by quickly during the day, things you don't even notice, can create your dreams for that night, and as they do so, they can, and quite ordinarily do, reach back and touch your most ancient memories. But my sense was *also* that that *dream* you are having is affecting the whole *next* day.

So *Prelude* is the dream; then comes *Part I,* which is the actual attempt to climb this mountain. Of course, the mountain by this time has been so photographed and edited that, for one thing, its trees recapitulate, rather subtly, too subtly for most people, the history of human architecture and suggest Greek pillars at one point and Gothic stained glass windows at another. But all the way through, as this man climbs, there is an attempt to mimic the mud hut, the log cabin, the cathedral, eventually even the skyscraper. It is very important to me, by the way, that the Dog Star Man never climbs to the *top,* only somewhere up there, and this is after falling down, and the Armageddon of the forest fire (which *was* a real forest fire, by the way. I had to go and fight it, and when I finished fighting it with all my neighbors, *then* I photographed).

As you come to the later sections, things get more complicated. *Part I* has a lot of poetic complexity going on in it, and multiple meanings, but it's *dominated*

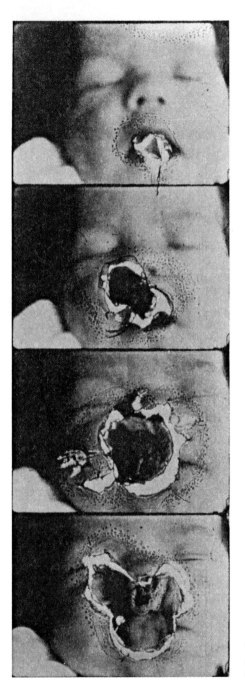

Collage of baby's cry in Brakhage's
Dog Star Man, Part II (1963).
Courtesy Anthology Film Archives.

by a narrative, so it goes along telling its tale, and everything is in the service of the tale of that climb up toward the plateau. *Part IV* suggests much more complex meanings. If one doesn't think *Part IV* is long enough, one could run it again and again and again.

Let me put it this way: as you add more layers, more rolls of superimposition, and if everything is stitched together in *meaning,* then *complexity* ought to be equal to *length.* Maybe you could say it's the difference between prose and poetry. Even an epic poem is always struggling to be brief, on the one hand, and to be Truth, which we know is full of complexity, on the other hand. What is great about a poem is that there are multiple layers of meaning so interlocked with each other that you could say *that* is the most exact and complete meaning that we can manage with language. In poetry a word will mean *exactly* something, something that could be thirty-five or fifty different things simultaneously, but then *that* will have exhausted that particular but complex meaning. And that one word is all tangled with all the other words that it is in alignment with, and all *their* alternative meanings.

This has always been my sense of working with superimposition, beginning with *Sirius Remembered.* In every superimposition you have an exact, finite number of possible meanings, far more than any single layer could produce. And so, each of the combinations of pictures in superimposition ought to be equal to a much longer, single, unlayered strand of image. The later sections of *Dog Star Man* may seem shorter, but once you begin to explore the many layers and the connections between them, what may seem to be short becomes far more substantial.

Fred Camper has always much preferred *The Art of Vision* [1965] to *Dog Star Man* because it *does* use a more classically proportioned presentation of the *Dog Star Man* material. All of the material *is* laid out at length; and when you show all the possible combinations of the four layers of superimposition possible with those four rolls, *Part IV* is about an hour and a quarter.

Another interesting question is, what *is The Art of Vision* vis-à-vis *Dog Star Man?* Is it a work that's become finally more outer than inner?

MacDonald: Could you talk about the sources of the other kinds of imagery in the film, especially the scientific imagery: the blood flowing and the images of the sun?

Brakhage: The next project that helped me make a living, while working on *Dog Star Man,* was a film for the physicist George Gamow, who was teaching at the University of Colorado. I had gotten to be, and still am, close friends with his son, Igor Gamow. Igor made it possible for me to know the father. Igor was a ballet dancer but had a trained scientific mind. He and I together photographed through a bat's wing to get the blood cells moving through the veins and arteries.

MacDonald: So you actually did that filming yourself? I've always assumed it was educational found footage.

Brakhage: No, that was my footage. I also went to the slaughterhouse and got some sheep hearts, which are the closest to the human, and Igor wore them like a glove and operated the valves—that's how I got *that* material.

The only thing that I *didn't* photograph in *Dog Star Man* are the high-altitude observatory images of solar flares. It was important to me that, among the other myths that were operative in this work, the life and death of a star as scientists picture it—*their* myth—be included. I have always viewed science as another set of myths, which are constantly changing. In order to use those images, I had to justify that they were being used correctly according to scientific views. It was quite a day when I went up to the high-altitude observatory and showed *Dog Star Man* with all these scientists gathered around, expecting another science film. I defended it on a symbolic and mythic level.

MacDonald: What was their reaction?

Brakhage: They were charmed and excited, and immediately gave me permission to use their footage. I got to know quite a number of scientists through George; that was always going on quite consciously in relationship to all the reading I was doing. I did not want the literary to dominate *Dog Star Man,* so in every way possible I am clashing symbols so that they reverberate. I wouldn't say it's an antisymbolic work because it *is* using symbols, but it's using them to "make it new," as Ezra Pound would put it.

There is also a lot of astronomy in the film. Someone (an amateur who had done a lot of stop-motion photography of clouds and stars) gave me a couple of Rube Goldberg–like boxes that allowed you to set your camera to make time-lapse material. That's my time-lapsed photography of the stars in the film. The moon was photographed through a child's telescope—just jammed up into the lens, and opening up and photographing, with a lot of luck.

And then, the main thing, to me, was to get the film down to earth, to daily living, so that's why you have all the images of the man and the woman and the baby at the hearth. That's what the wood is going to be chopped up *for:* to burn in that fireplace and warm that baby.

I was making *Dog Star Man* during the period before the hippies. And I'm walking around Boulder being very despised for my long hair. I remember I would cross the street to try not to go past a certain barber shop; they'd always break into laughter. One day I *was* walking past it, and this barber said, "Hey, wait a minute," and came up to me and *spat* on me. I couldn't rent a house, even when we got some money from these commercial jobs. Who would rent a house to a man with hair like that? Finally, I told some old lady who had a house for sale that I was making a religious film and playing Jesus Christ. That wasn't untrue, because Christ *was* another figure who was very prominent in my sense of who I was depicting in *Dog Star Man*. I wanted *Dog Star Man* to apply to as many male archetypes as possible.

MacDonald: Earlier, you were saying that, on one level, *Window Water Baby Moving* and *Loving* are outside the trajectory of your primary evolution as a filmmaker. It strikes me that *Bluewhite* [1965], *Blood's Tone* [1965], and *Vein* [1965] [distributed as *Three Films*] continue the earlier trajectory of *Window Water Baby Moving* and *Loving*. And this makes me think that, at least during that period, you alternated between two different kinds of exploration. One is clearly internal, an attempt to be true to the network of complexity within the psyche; and the other has to do with looking at particular dimensions of the world of human physical reality that conventional film ignores. Being *inside* for a long time working on *Dog Star Man,* there seems to have been this need to look at the outside of something that is fundamental and very important but is suppressed by society.

Brakhage: That seems like a reasonable hypothesis, but what bothers me is your leap toward a dichotomy, because there are other ways to view these more visceral, obvious films—one of which is that they are *sketches*. Before you take on some huge complexity, you do a sketch.

What you've hypothesized seems most relevant when I work more in the documentary mode—you could regard *Bluewhite* and *Blood's Tone* as documentaries. Certainly *Blood's Tone*. When I did the Pittsburgh films [*The Pittsburgh Trilogy: The Act of Seeing with One's Own Eyes* (1971), *Eyes* (1971), and *Deus Ex* (1971)], a lot of people said, "The camerawork is so focused, and, compared to *Dog Star Man* and other works of yours, it's so documentary." And I said, "Well, that's because I'm dealing with a social crisis, so I am suggesting more of an outerscape, whereas a lot of my work deals with an interior world and *isn't* so related to the social. I would suppose, in a way, this happens with a lot of artists. Every now and again, Picasso used to do very literal paintings, just to assure himself that he still *could* paint, or maybe he was moved to do so because he wanted a rendering of a child's face, one of his children's faces or something like that; and then he would go back to his struggles with complexity.

MacDonald: Well, I suppose the weakness of my hypotheses is that even when you go into the child's bedroom to film *Vein,* you are actually on an *internal* journey because you are trying to look at what the "Child" is. And the same thing with *Blood's Tone*. I mean, they're all archetypal, mythic images, at the same time that they're images of physical human realities that at a certain point in American history almost no one had seen in a movie.

Brakhage: There have been several different kinds of childbirth films in my making; one is wrapped up in *Dog Star Man* and is quite symbolic and complex, the way *Dog Star Man* is; and another that's hand painted—*Thigh Line Lyre Triangular;* and, of course, the original, more documentary *Window Water Baby Moving*. *Bluewhite* is an attempt to make a *brevity* of this, to do a quick sketch.

In *Blood's Tone,* there is the *voraciousness* of this child, attacking the mother's breast. There is the golden glow of her enjoyment and appreciation and the child's, but there is also something terrible about it, which is suddenly given as a vision.

In *Vein,* the boy child crawls up into my lap and begins masturbating. So I have a camera just sitting there on the table and I begin photographing, but that doesn't capture the intensity that he's emitting, so I mix it with the stars. I get out my boxes and photograph some stars, and so you go from the very most mundane thing, in some sense, to the cosmos.

These films are like little gifts. They're quickly made, and made in passing— and they will usually trigger further, more complex films.

MacDonald: In *Blood's Tone* I'm always struck by the voraciousness *of the camera.*

Brakhage: I was a bottle baby, and I know that the roots of your hungers, your lacks, your yearnings, are fuel for the making of any creative act. So it is perfectly reasonable to me to say, "Well, I am also participating in this vora-ciousness with the camera, with the *eyes.*" And the masturbation also. I'm feel-ing something of it. These are dangerous grounds because a lot of people, of course, would regard *Vein* as some kind of child porn. For *me,* this happened just like anything else might happen. Children also crawled up in my lap with a toy car or a picture they'd just painted or just to watch the fireplace, and so on, and were often photographed doing those things. It's a difficult question these days because I feel that the society has come again to where there is so little understanding of children's sexuality.

In fact, I have removed *Lovemaking* [1968] entirely from distribution.

MacDonald: I didn't know that.

Brakhage: The worst horror I can imagine is that some pornographer would try to use its stature to excuse *his* porn on the Internet, or wherever. It isn't just that I'd be afraid of the kind of trouble that the film might cause *me;* it's the horror that someone would use my attempt at a lovingly felt, deeply meant rev-elation of a human being for these horrible purposes and get it tangled up in the law. So I recently removed it, with great sadness. I could say, "Well, I removed it because people are not ready for these kinds of considerations," but how are they ever going to *get* ready for them? It's a dilemma for me.

MacDonald: There's a great courageous innocence in those films, in your being able to respond with artistic passion to obviously important moments in human development that this society has such a terror of facing and comprehending.

Brakhage: Well, we can hope for a world in which these visions can take their place. There was a great drive in the sixties to express sexuality, and also I lived in a very remote place. By the time *Vein* was made, I was living at nine thou-sand feet in the mountains, snowed-in six or seven months of the year. Often I would have the illusion that the society had evolved. I would get only the best of news out of New York or from the West Coast, and I would have the illusion that we were now free to express ourselves. I sat there in this innocence, and these films would come through me, and then I'd go out into society, and the films would begin reverberating with danger signals, and that's only *increased:* the suppression of real sexual information has only expanded during the past twenty years. I don't feel any hope of being able to release *Lovemaking* in my lifetime.

On the other hand, I certainly never expected the Berlin Wall to come down.

I want to add a few counterbalances, so we don't stay too stuck with the dichotomy we've been discussing. We were dividing works into what I call the sketches and the more complex works—you were saying the *inner* and the *outer.*

Consider the hand-painted work, which emerges first in *Dog Star Man.* My primary reason for doing hand painting has been to express hypnogogic vision. What is more real than *that?* What can be *more* of a reality or have more to do with the *external* than that we express the template of the nervous system *upon* the external reality we see?

And what do you do with *Eye Myth* [1967], which is nine seconds long and took about a year to make, which I think is intrinsically epic. In my view, epic isn't dependent on length. I argued this recently when I showed *Eye Myth* coupled with Jan Troell's *The Emigrants* [1968]. I was just trying to give my students a sense of epic, narrative filmmaking from the sixties and seventies, and I coupled Troell's film with mine and argued that if you give it a chance, the *weight* of this nine-second film will balance the length of the Troell film. Some students did feel that, but I have the proof of that pudding: later I took that nine-second film and made a twenty-six-minute film called *The Horseman, the Woman and the Moth* [1968] just by shifting those 180 or 190 frames around.

6/3/97

MacDonald: I'm interested in talking about *Scenes from under Childhood,* but I have a general question first. Are your films clear in your memory? You've made so many; how well can you remember them?

Brakhage: They're remarkably clear because I look at them constantly. For many years I went around the country, lecturing. I'd take trips that would combine four or five stops in a week, then I'd have three weeks off. All in all, I was averaging about one showing a week, and I showed mostly my own films, although I did also like to show other people's work—even preferred that, though understandably mostly I was asked to speak on my own work. So I became very familiar with the films. Now, of course, I still do some presenting, and I teach film at the University of Colorado. And I have my Sunday evening series. Recently, for example, I showed the whole *Scenes from under Childhood* series across four Sundays.

I'm always checking prints, too, to see what needs to be replaced.

MacDonald: I've taught *Section 1* of *Scenes* a lot, especially when I've talked about your theory of child vision, but it had been a while since I had seen *Sections 2, 3,* and *4.* One general question that comes up when I'm talking about those films with students is, how did this idea about child vision develop? And to what extent was it a function of seeing your own children born and watching what they were experiencing as they grew?

Brakhage: It was very largely that. I was very involved with the children and, at one point, was horrified to realize that I was guilty of what I came to call the "Shirley Temple syndrome": in other words, of finding them very cute and thinking of their lives as bucolic and happier than mine—in other words, not meeting them on the level of their own lives. And at that point I decided to start photographing them, because *that* enabled me to see more deeply into what they *were.* I had this sense in the back of my mind that a film might come out of it, but that was not the initial impulse. I wanted to *see* their world.

Now, I also understood that you can never really see inside another person's world; so at the same time that I'm looking at *them,* I'm remembering, as best I can, my own childhood. *Scenes from under Childhood* arises out of a superimposition of those two things. My children were providing tender material, which I gathered; and as it came into the camera though the lens and later, during the editing process, my memories of my own childhood were sparked by their activities and in one way and another found their way into the films.

MacDonald: The catalogue description of *Section 1* mentions fetal beginnings. I'm not clear how fully the four sections are meant to represent a chronology. Were you thinking that *Section 1* covers the transition from before birth to just after birth?

Brakhage: Well, not exactly. *Section 1* envisions fetal beginnings in the same way you might say something invokes something. And it seems a little odd, but you could say it is *me* remembering *them* remembering something of their fetal beginnings; or, better still, myself *imagining* them remembering fetal beginnings *and* also remembering some sense of such a thing in myself. My feeling is—though I have no way to prove it—that children close to their births are actually remembering something of their life in the womb and the birth itself, whereas adults can only imagine it—though some adults do claim they have a sense of these experiences.

MacDonald: Are you also conjecturing that, especially in the final months of prenatal development, babies see in the same way that we have closed-eye vision?

Brakhage: Yes. What we call "closed-eye vision" is for me the template in the mind upon which all further formative envisionment is to occur. So there is an outside limit to human seeing, which is implicit already in the womb.

My sense of that is fortified by scientific experiments that have shown that there is rapid eye movement in fetus eyes, very similar to the REM movement of dreaming in adults and in children, too, for that matter. The fetus can be said to dream, and it seems reasonable that very young children could be remembering something of their dreams in the womb. When children are very young, they remember things from a year or two earlier rather remarkably, and then there comes, gradually, a period where they don't remember much about the first several years. A four-year-old will remember a great deal of his or her one-, two-, or three-year-old life. Later, that is reduced to a very few scenes. I think it's because there is such a catastrophic shift in the psyche at that point.

MacDonald: As a result of learning words, language.

Brakhage: And the various other restrictions on the free flow of memory.

MacDonald: When I've taught *Scenes from under Childhood,* I've usually suggested that the opening passages of *Section 1,* where we're just seeing colors—very bright reds and then increasing varieties of color—have to do with the eyes adjusting to the overwhelming reality of light. After the womb, the sun would be incredible, shocking. The color red that dominates those early moments of the film has always struck me as the same color I see when I look at the sun with my eyes closed.

Brakhage: Yes. You've got exactly what I felt I was doing.

MacDonald: I have a lot of friends who are artists, and many of them have chosen not to have children because for them it was *either* children *or* their art. Others have one child who keeps them in a state of exhaustion. You and Jane had five kids. And you were and are a prolific artist. How did you *do* it?

Brakhage: I'm going to find that very difficult to answer because I feel very exhausted at the moment, now that I'm having my second family with Marilyn: Vaughan and Anton are six and seven, respectively. I feel exhausted most of the time, and mine is not the lion's share of caring for them. Marilyn is also exhausted.

When you're younger, you have more of a mad, hormonal strength, or even something more supernatural, like hordes of angels, helping to care for the children. Now that I'm older, it *is* very difficult, but I will say that I still go on with my work, despite my age, despite two boys fussing, playing, and enjoying but also scrapping with each other, despite my disabilities not only from age but also from the recent removal of my bladder and the chemotherapy I've just been through. I go on doing some making, however limited, and it turns out to be finally quite a lot, as always—more, in fact, than I can afford to process and print. So I suppose the answer for me is that I am just extraordinarily obsessed and didn't, and don't, have much, if any, choice in the matter. Most people seem to have more choice in the matter, even if they are artists; they can make fewer films and survive.

MacDonald: Was it possible in those days to have a regular schedule?

Brakhage: Not really, no. You never knew what was going to arise. I did have sort of a rule, once we got into that house in the mountains, that my work area was off-limits for the children. So I had a retreat. And I had a sensibility that let

From Stan Brakhage's *The Riddle of Lumen* (1972). Courtesy Anthology Film Archives.

me distinguish quite accurately, when children were shrieking in a game and when someone had actually gotten hurt or was in some kind of real trouble. And the minute someone *was* in trouble, I snapped out of whatever trance process I was in and went to their aid. But otherwise, I developed means to shut out the exterior world and be entirely concentrated on the filmmaking.

When I say these things, I'm talking mostly about the editing process. The photography, of course, was a direct engagement with that world of the children, and I think that's one of the reasons, perhaps the major reason, why so much of my work during that period was devoted to the children's world—not only *Scenes from under Childhood* but the *Sincerity* series [*Sincerity I* (1973), *Sincerity II* (1975), *Sincerity III* (1978), *Sincerity IV* (1980), *Sincerity V* (1980)] and a great many shorter films were integrally involved with family living, with the children growing up, with our immediate natural surroundings and the life within that house.

MacDonald: Was the camera always at the ready?

Brakhage: Yes. And the children's sense of it is that they grew up with father making movies of them being one of the most natural things.

MacDonald: How did you and the family survive financially?

Brakhage: Well, I was very fortunate. Economically, I could never do the things I did then, now. First of all, when I started, film was incredibly inexpensive: about eight dollars a roll and maybe two or three dollars for processing Kodachrome. Now it's hard to get a roll done for less than sixty or seventy dollars.

MacDonald: Still, it must have stressed you financially; you made *so* many films.

Brakhage: Yes. It did. It's just that there was always a way. First of all, there was a lot of money flowing through society, and it was post–World War II, when even the *trash* was excellent: you could live off of people's discards very easily, and I often did. I know something about comparing then and now, because I know a lot of younger artists and people in general, and I have grown children who have passed through life during the past several decades. Regardless of the economy, I know that I would probably have been obsessed and would have had to go on, but I would not have been able to make as many films. Who knows, that may have been better! But it would have been totally different because in those days I had so much access.

At times I engaged with commercial filmmaking and got film very inexpensively, even sometimes got short ends for nothing: the trash barrel of Western Cine, my lab in Denver, was something I could fall back on. And I had a Rockefeller grant for *Scenes from under Childhood* that went on for years.

That kind of funding was cut off because the government made it more and more difficult over the years for the foundations to give money to individuals. It became as expensive to give *me* a grant as it was to give millions of dollars to a hospital in Hawaii. The government took over funding of the arts, and, of course, that's almost always a complete disaster, as anyone who has studied governmental support of the arts could have told them—*unless* the government is going to spend an *enormous* amount of money, like Germany does. The city of Berlin alone spends more on the arts than the United States and Canada put together. Unless you are going to have *that* kind of outpouring, which essentially funds everybody to some extent, almost any bureaucratic selection of who shall be funded and who shall not is going to be a disaster. So when the government made it hard for the foundations to fund artists individually, the foundations rolled the money over into symphonies and other big institutions. There's been very little funding of individuals since then.

When the Rockefeller grant was no longer available, I had to bring *Section 4* to an ending that was reasonable. Originally, *Section 4* wasn't to have been the end of *Scenes from under Childhood*.

MacDonald: Did you finish *Section 1* before you did *Section 2* and so forth? It looks to me as if *2* and *3* were done almost in tandem.

Brakhage: Well, the same fund of material, which by this time had gotten to be five or six thousand feet of film, was being drawn on. In those days, unless something had a quality of envisionment that had been exhausted in some earlier work, I would save it rather than throw it away. So, yes, essentially, the sections are chronological; they're trying to show the progressive growing up of the children.

MacDonald: Recently, when I was looking at *Sections 2* and *3*—and this had not struck me before—the color range seemed to change. *Section 2* tends toward reds, and *Section 3* tends toward blues and greens. There also seemed to be other echoes between those two sections that aren't relevant in *Sections 1* or *4*.

Brakhage: What you said about *Section 1*—that it traces a recognition of the subtleties of colors coming out of this reddish field, which is like closed-eye vision of the sun (plus what I call the remembrance of womb life)—distinguishes that section. If you remember, the baby in that section is in an almost fetal position created by the distorting glass through which she is photographed. And so, all of *Section 1* is kind of a separating out of colors, a variety of colors, within this reddish field. Similarly, you could say that each successive section has certain biases of color, until you get to the fourth part, which has a wide spread of color, most obvious in the towel scene, where the various colored towels are going into blanks of color. There's an increasing accent on color recognition.

Also, in that fourth section I come to a suggestion of the larger world, with the city scenes at the end, the baseball, the model airplane.

MacDonald: Is some of the city material in *Section 4* actual home-movie material from your youth?

Brakhage: No, but that's a wonderful compliment! I did shoot it as an adult, but, of course, the main drive of this film is to give that sense of time travel, as if I were drawing from the inside of my brain the styles and qualities of life of my growing-up period. I'm delighted that you felt as if that imagery might have been photographed when I was young.

MacDonald: Even the cars participate; they don't look like late-sixties cars.

Brakhage: That would not have been a conscious thing, but unconsciously I'm sure I was trying to exclude anything that might look too flashily up-to-date. The model airplane certainly *was* something that began to be a fashion when I was very young. Also, the scene where the two boys hold the little model cars they are playing with against their penises is a suggestion of transition to adult empowerment, both physically and mechanically. So there are all those suggestions that permit *Section 4* to provide a closure appropriate to *Scenes from under Childhood*.

MacDonald: The film ends with photographs of buildings. Are *those* childhood photographs?

Brakhage: Those are from my childhood, yes. That's the house directly across the street from where I lived at 930 Washington Street in Denver, the house I was seeing from the porch of my apartment building. Another photograph shows a water tower that comes from Jane's childhood outside of Chicago. And there is a picture of an insane asylum that was a very haunting building when I was four or five years old, living in Bisbee, Arizona.

One of my most vivid memories is standing outside this asylum and seeing some poor man up in the tower screaming out to the people who were gathered watching him that he was going to come and kill them at midnight. For some reason my father took me for a walk down there, and it was a haunting and frightening scene for a child. So that picture, which I happened to have, of the insane asylum in the thirties helped take me back to touch those roots.

That's also the reason I included my own images at the beginning. If I include photographs of myself, mixed in with the imagery of the children growing up, then somehow it keeps things clearer *for me.* It isn't that anyone else looking at the film need even know that that is an image of *me* or that that's an insane asylum in Bisbee, Arizona. They *don't* need to know that. *I* needed it in there to have the right quality of feeling as I was making the film. Within the film it has no function other than as an institutional structure. The same is true of the picture of the house across the street from my own childhood home, which has no function but to point toward the idea of the city—because most of *Scenes from under Childhood* takes place in the mountains.

I must say, by the way, that there is so much magic in the creative process that I can only touch on it as we talk about these things. These works were made in a kind of trance state where I used various tactics just to keep from sliding completely into insanity, which is always a fear when you get into a really complicated, deep, lengthy work. Part of that process is the acceptance of what you might call "instruction from the outside." In *Scenes* those images from my past are meant merely to point in general directions, but their actual *existence,* how *I* happened to *have them,* is magic. That, for instance, among all the photos that were taken across my childhood, that picture of that *asylum* survived is magic.

I must say finally that accepting instruction from the outside also means that when the Rockefeller Foundation decided not to continue my grant, I had to accept that the work was in the hands of God and that it *should* end at that point.

I don't mean that acceptance was easy. There were the usual screams and whines and carryings-on, but when I am sane and when I am able to, I continue to work to accept what comes to me, what I cannot control. The struggle to pay for my work, to go on with this same struggle that I have had all these years— and sometimes much worse than when I made *Scenes from under Childhood*— could be very embittering, if I weren't operating under the sense that, well, something beyond me is shaping the kinds of film I make and how I make them, and I am merely the instrument for this process.

MacDonald: All of us who have grown up in a certain set of generations have these drawers or boxes or scrapbooks full of photographs that were taken in our childhood. You could exchange our drawers or boxes, and nothing would change, except the facial features. And it's almost as though—I don't assume this is conscious on your part—the photographs you use are referencing the way family life was conventionally envisioned photographically as an implied comparison with the much more elaborate exploration of childhood that your film is offering.

Brakhage: Oh, that's a nice thought.

MacDonald: Your films are the family movies maybe we wish we had.

Brakhage: Or do we? You may think you wish you had them, but the interesting thing is that my grown children are not very involved in looking at those films.

MacDonald: Were they ever?

Brakhage: Not really. They'd look at them when they came out, and that seemed okay. It was a normal part of their growing up, a daily activity. But they haven't shown much interest in their own photographed lives as children. Occasionally, they will ask to see the births, but otherwise they are not really interested—because, in a way, it isn't really *their* childhood. *They* are not remembering their childhood the way *I* was imagining them. The films confront them with *my* feelings about *my* own development, which they are only the occasion for.

And by the way, that was quite conscious. When I *first* started photographing, I got down on the floor and was rolling around with them with the camera, but I realized quickly that that was too much the Shirley Temple syndrome. So you'll notice that, pretty consistently throughout all of the footage in *Scenes from under Childhood,* the viewpoint is slightly above and looking down at the children, to keep that sense that this is *adult* envisionment, and that it is affected by and affects the quality of the *maker's* childhood coming through and coloring, shaping, twisting the forms—through apple jugs or whatever—into the production of an aesthetic.

MacDonald: You may find that as your kids get older, they'll get more interested. My son also doesn't go into the drawers where the images of his childhood are, but I think at a certain point he may become interested in reaccessing that material.

Brakhage: Perhaps you're right. We'll see. I continue to be interested in it, even in my own photographic representation in it, and I marvel as I look at the images and remember.

When I began to take *Scenes from under Childhood* on college lecture tours, I noticed that college-age people have *never* cared for this work. After talking to a number of people, I deduced that maybe it's because they're still too close to that period of their lives and *don't* want to remember. They're trying to climb up *out* of childhood. *Scenes from under Childhood*—unlike almost all envisionments of childhood, which are sugarcoated and nostalgic, and presented within a general aura that things were better then than they are now and that the soul was cleaner or purer in childhood—stands *absolutely* against that, and it gets some of its inspiration for doing that from Schumann, and, of course, from Freud, and from many other sources.

My own sense of it is that *to the children* childhood is very hard, grue-some, an often utterly impossible world, just as adulthood is for adults. Chil-dren are in a state of almost constant terror, mixed with hysterical happiness, which can also be terrifying in an instant. And childhood is grubby, and they sit sometimes as if in a haze (*Section 3* particularly is just this haze of repetitive slight shifts of tone and color) for long, dull periods, which people tend to con-nect with school but, in fact, are equally prevalent in home life. At home kids just sit around: "Mommy, there's nothing to *do*." The fact is that very often there *is* nothing to do; everything *is* boring.

MacDonald: I think that most people would assume that what *you* mean by the slower passages—I mean all the way through the film—has to do with the child's being more perceptive of the specific phenomena around him or her, not that it's boring or terrifying.

Brakhage: But that's exactly, from my viewpoint, what you *do* with bore-dom. You sink into it; you begin to be aware of the slight subtleties that are left in the gray field. The only thing that can be done with the dull civilization we are now having is to be fascinated by the *endless* riches of variance within the dullest, grayest field.

MacDonald: One of the techniques that is a motif through all four parts—this must have started earlier, but it strikes me as particularly connected with *Scenes from under Childhood*—is the use of both negative *and* positive, black and white *and* color. I assume that's partly a result of your having access to the Rockefeller grant.

Brakhage: Absolutely. Printing the light changes across all those superimpo-sitions was extraordinarily expensive at that time. In fact, there was a new machine that Western Cine advertised that could supposedly do up to five thousand light changes in an hour. I didn't have *that* many—I don't even know if you *could* have that many—but I did have two to three thousand in forty-five, fifty minutes, and it broke the machine, burned it out; they had to send it back. So this work was pushing the edge of technological possibility for light changes: light is changing constantly across one, two rolls, then three, then four rolls. Yes, that's why the work had to end when the Rockefeller Foundation ended their support.

MacDonald: There are a couple of places in *Scenes*—and again you can watch the film and understand a lot about it without knowing the specifics—where particular events stand out. I'm thinking about the beginning of *Section 4,* when Jane is crying and fingering a kind of pendant that she is wearing, and there's a photo in there that looks like it might be her father?

Brakhage: Yes, it is.

MacDonald: Was that a moment of specific loss or—

Brakhage: No. Her father, her mother, and her grandmother and her brother are a series of images that pass through that scene. It's helpful to me when you say that it looks like it might be her father, because you're doing what I don't know too many people can do, and that is recognize some family resemblance in the faces. When *I'm* invoking these images, I'm trying to feel *her,* to have complete empathy with Jane. During this period, she is very overloaded in the raising of the children, as am I for that matter, and that section invokes some of the feelings of frustration and quarrelsomeness during that period. She's breaking down and crying, and I am re-creating it or imagining it as best I can from what she was saying to me, and invoking her familiars, her family, to comfort her, to strengthen her, as part of this long tradition of generation. That pendant was something special that I had given her, but it also happens to be a wondrous light catcher/refractor.

MacDonald: Was your filmmaking—I assume it must have been—part of your relationship together? Obviously, for a lot people, one person being a filmmaker and the other one not would become a bone of contention.

Brakhage: Well, she agreed early on to engage with this. A lot of people think, "Oh, how could I be so cruel to photograph my wife when she's crying like that?" But that was also a way of comforting Jane, of saying, "It's going to be all right; we'll turn this into gold, and everything else, the really bad times, the sadnesses, we'll turn them into gold, too." It *was* collaborative in that sense.

Too much *has* been made of Jane as my *muse,* which is an idea *she* got going at some point. To call a human a muse or to try and take that attribute onto oneself is a blasphemous mistake, actually. In fact, the muse is quite nonhuman. There certainly *was* a collaborative element, but the art process, the aesthetics, were coming through me. I say this not to be piggish about it but because I was *born* to do what I do, obviously, or I wouldn't have done it all these years. A person would have to be *crazy,* after making a certain number of films, to persist in this hopeless career. So it was coming through me, but she was up for being a part of it, and she was open to it. She wasn't regarding it as a cruelty to her; it was a comfort; it was trying to make something out of a disaster, the way most people in a marriage do.

Marilyn, whom I am married to now, said—shortly after we began being really serious about each other—that she cannot stand to be photographed and could never live with anyone who wanted to be chronicling her life. That took me aback for. . . maybe ten seconds. And suddenly I felt an immense sense of relief. That meant I was *not* going to have to work in that autobiographical mode anymore, that it would not be appropriate for the life she and I are having together. So I don't photograph the children, her, or myself—almost not at all.

That *was* a process that Jane and I agreed to, and that Jane was very good for. I also tried to get the woman's view, what was specific to being a woman, into the films, during the editing process. Jane was advising me very often in that respect. In fact, Jane would grab the camera when I'd get angry and photograph *me* being angry, shaking my finger, just like she grabbed the camera right after giving birth to our first child in *Window Water Baby Moving.*

1/30/02

MacDonald: How did "the Pittsburgh trilogy" evolve?

Brakhage: Sally Dixon, when she was head of film programming at the Carnegie Museum, brought me in as a lecturer. She and her friend Mike Chakiris (a photographer for one of the local newspapers) picked me up at the airport and were asking me about films I wanted to make. I told them I had just tried to arrange to be in a police car in Boulder for several days, to photograph the ordinary, everyday activities of the police. I felt that the police were very maligned and that they weren't appreciated for what they primarily did. I wanted to try and *see* for myself if maybe they *were* as monstrous as many of my hippie friends told me they were. But I suspected maybe not, probably not. Certainly I, who was always subject to bullies, wouldn't want to live in a world in which there were no police to go to for protection.

So I was open, but at the same time, had a healthy paranoia about police—from use of police by mainstream society to put down protests and rebellions, from the beatings.

MacDonald: At this point, the only film imagined was a police film?

Brakhage: Yes. For some reason, I still remember also telling Sally and Mike that it was a big mistake for NASA not to send an artist to the moon, because all the pictures we were seeing were so dumb—like bad B-movie science fiction, Flash Gordon. I said you've got to remember that Columbus had Americus on his ship, after whom our country is named. Americus was the cartographer and also the one who made pictures so that people could have a sense of what had been discovered.

It turned out that Sally had connections, and she arranged for me to ride around in a police car. Mike agreed to go with me, which was invaluable, because he has a kind of spunky, easy manner and can interrelate with policemen. It's part of his job, actually: he's a photographer of city events.

We get into this police car, and they're driving us around, and after a couple of hours, nothing has happened, and I say, "Gee, things are really quiet in the ghetto here"—we were in the black ghetto of Pittsburgh. The two policemen looked at each other, pulled over to the curb, and said, "Well, we've been told just to drive you around until you get bored and then take you back, because nobody wants to open up the possibility of lawsuits. People are very leery because of the bad press we've been getting, but you guys seem okay"—I think they knew Mike from some previous experiences; he had a good reputation—"so we're going to tell everyone that we dropped you off, and then we'll start getting calls immediately." I said, "Well, should we duck down?" And they said, "No, everyone will know that you're *here,* but *on the record,* you won't be. If we do get into trouble, a riot or something, you'll have to look after yourselves.

So they called in to say we'd been dropped off, and immediately the calls came in. I began photographing, in the order in which you see it in the film, because the very first call took us to this dead man in the street. Everyone on the scene knew that we were okay and that they were to let us make imagery.

From that came Sally arranging that I could go into a hospital—on a later trip—and finally into the morgue. Sally had connections to Cyril Wecht, who is such an interesting character. He's still on TV all the time, one of the top autopsists in the country. He's the one who questioned all the Kennedy autopsy lies of the Warren Commission; he also put out a book, *Who Killed JonBenet Ramsey?* He's still very active. Anyway, the hospital was very open and excited, so long as I had signed releases from everyone who was photographed. The only similar complexity with the morgue was that I could not photograph the face of a corpse in a way that it would allow it to be recognized. And I understood that, perfectly well, and found it not too difficult a prescription.

MacDonald: When you were going into these institutions, it was still fairly unusual.

Brakhage: Forbidden.

MacDonald: Now it's hard to channel surf without seeing an operation or a police show.

Brakhage: Though I haven't seen one of those that can match *these* films. My secret was that I wasn't after what was making society so nervous, I was after an art. And all three situations provided me with the occasion to make art, and art that related to my own experiences: my own fear of police, and my dependency on them; my hospital experiences. I'd be dead many times over were it not for doctors and hospitals. Even at that time, I'd been in danger of death six or seven times.

Like the people who gave the process its beautiful name—"autopsis" literally means "the act of seeing with one's own eyes"—I *needed* to *see* these things, to see something of what it *was* to be just turned into furniture meat. After experiencing several days of photographing autopsies, I felt that suicide would be very difficult, if not impossible. There's something sadly ridiculous about the dead, and why would you turn this complexity of a wondrous human possibility into a hulk of decaying matter?

MacDonald: The structure of the three films varies. Both *Eyes* and *Deus Ex* seem to echo a day/night/day round-the-clock schedule. I've always figured that *The Act of Seeing with One's Own Eyes* was a much more difficult film for you than the other two—

Brakhage: Oh, much more difficult.

MacDonald: And that, as a result, its trajectory seems more involved with your coming to grips with the experience of being in the morgue.

Brakhage: But I think day/night/day *is* reflected in *The Act,* just more subtly. If you recall, there are bright, almost overexposed images where the white sheets and flashes of the still camera that someone's using create a lot of bright color; *and* there are also these dark areas, where the shutter closes up, and it's almost like falling into the pit of someone's chest, or whatever. There are lapses into the dark, almost like fainting, and I *was* close to fainting very often during the making of that film.

Part of the process of the film as an aesthetic structure is to allow the viewers to manage to accept what they're shown, so they can continue to watch.

MacDonald: One of the conjectures that often comes from students is that the experience of also hearing, and *smelling,* the autopsy space must have played a big role in your experience.

Brakhage: It was a terrible smell. I had to just accept that or quit, right at scratch. It was appalling. The whole rest of the building had been renovated, and air-conditioning had been put in, but this space, which is where the real work was done, was not repaired or fixed up, and didn't have air-conditioning. They sat in this stench, working day after day. In talks I had, later, with Wecht and the others, they admitted they felt that people despised the autopsists, and thought it appropriate that they live in their stench, that it was part of the job. It was almost as if they were being punished for doing the job they did.

The one thing I probably couldn't have survived is if a child had been brought in. I was told it was very rare that they had no children. They are required to autopsy all children and all public deaths of any kind.

MacDonald: I saw *The Act of Seeing* at an early screening, in Binghamton in 1972, and it was a transformative experience for me. You were not there. I was furious after the film and wanted to stand up and scream at the programmers for showing it—but within a few weeks, I was already thinking how it would be exciting and valuable to show the film to my students and to the public audience I was programming for. Am I right that *The Act of Seeing* has become one of the more popular of your films?

Brakhage: Yes. Also, of all the films I've made—and let me preface this by saying that I have always wished that I was not who I am, but the Hans Christian Andersen of film: I would easily give up everything to have been a great children's storyteller (of course, *Andersen* wanted to be Charles Dickens, so there we go: no one ever gets to be exactly what he wants to be)—this film was *the* film that our children always asked to see, and that they wanted to bring their friends in to see (I'd have to get permission of the parents, some of whom wouldn't give it). My children have always wanted to see this film, above everything else of my making, and see it over and over.

Children are always trying to figure out how bad things can get, and they love gruesome tales. And there *is* a fairy-tale quality to that film in a way. To all three of the Pittsburgh films.

MacDonald: When I was a kid and encyclopedia salesmen came by, the section of the encyclopedia I was most fascinated by was where the different systems

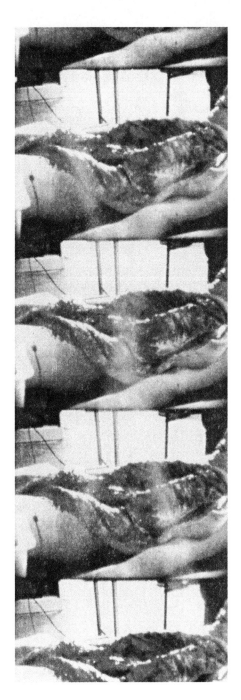

Cadaver during autopsy, from
Brakhage's *The Act of Seeing
with One's Own Eyes* (1971).
Courtesy Anthology Film Archives.

of the body were imaged on clear sheets of plastic; you could "enter" the body: skin, the muscles, nerves, organs, bones. So their reaction makes sense to me.

Brakhage: The children also accepted the form of the film in a way that some adults haven't been able to. It's a very dark vision and gets darker and darker as it moves along.

MacDonald: Though near the end you seem to have a kind of epiphany and become almost a child yourself in the excitement of exploring what seem to me to be landscapes. The camera becomes a plane swooping through these strange formations.

Brakhage: Oh, I'm glad for that. To me one thing that saves the film is this little tiny bit of reflected sky that's caught in a little puddle of liquid in the armpit of a corpse—a little blue ephemeral thing that can stand for all of Spirit, which otherwise would be missing.

Also, I think it's funny that at the end a little man in a little bow tie is seen reciting all this horror into a tape recorder. He turns it off, and the film is over. *The Act of Seeing* is full of jokes like that—it's black humor to be sure, but humor. The fly crawling on a toe. Or the zipping up of the body bag soon after a knife comes down and "unzips" a whole torso. Those moments are there to lighten the load of watching.

MacDonald: At what point did you think there would be a trilogy?

Brakhage: I knew by the time I was doing the third film that they would go together, and originally I thought there would be more. At first, I was thinking things like, "Oh, I should do *firemen* now." And there were attempts made to try to secure me a chance to film basketball, football, and other kinds of major social events. These would have been okay to do but wouldn't have had to do *at all* with what my deep unconscious had already recognized as three films that go together and that do not need anything else.

The trilogy begins with the police, who do what it is that the rest of us forgo doing: they go and deal with the misery and the blood and the suicides and the murders and the trash. We've hired these people to do that job, rather than reach out to our neighbors. They're the *eyes* of the society. I had a sense that there's the private eye and there's the public eye. These are the public eyes. "*Polis* means eyes," from Charles Olson, was also important to me.

Then you have the hospital, a stand-in for God—as you know, in Greek drama, when the playwright doesn't know what else to do, he brings in the deus ex machina: actors were swung out over the Greek stage and lowered onto the stage, where they spoke for the gods. In a way, our modern equivalent of that is the hospital. Watching the doctors, you almost get a sense of the Church. I feel that these hands moving to rescue this poor broken heart are kind of an epiphany of religious/spiritual feeling.

MacDonald: I like your metaphor in the Canyon Cinema catalogue of an Aztec ritual: the long shots of the operating-room work as a kind of elaborate ritual—

Brakhage: Except that instead of tearing the heart out; they're trying to revive it.

And then the third film is about the idea that nothing shall have died without our knowing why. The trilogy makes a circle at this point, because almost all murderers are caught by the autopsies. Usually, murderers make every attempt to disguise that a murder has even occurred. Many times, we wouldn't know there was murder at all without autopsy.

MacDonald: Did the various groups in the films see the results?

Brakhage: Oh, yes. The police loved *Eyes.* Cyril Wecht and his workers loved their film; they felt that their dignity had been restored, and that they had something they could be proud of to show to people. And even though their hospital was quite gloomy and old, the doctors saw the hospital as beautiful and loved all their machines. They were pleased with *Deus Ex.* That was important to me.

You know, at some point the Black Panthers in Chicago used *Eyes* to show what pigs the police are; on the other hand, the *police* used it to show how kind and gentle they are. I feel that this almost needs to be the credo for documentary: *both* sides should find in the film justification for their means and being. And I feel that's true of all three of the Pittsburgh films.

I felt this way about *The Governor* [1977] also. In fact, one of my dicta when I was working on that film was that if Governor Lamm [Richard D. Lamm, governor of Colorado, 1975–87] decided that the film was wrong as a portrait, then I would put it away and not release it.

MacDonald: Have you always thought of these films as documentaries? I see more and more documentary historians including you.

Brakhage: I always have, and for a while I hoped to be allowed to present my films at the Flaherty Seminar. In fact, Ricky Leacock, no less, fought for me, but we never got anywhere. Now I'm gradually winning the argument. I always had a documentary streak in me, and in fact, my biggest argument with P. Adams [Sitney] was about this issue. I said, "I am *foremost* a documentarian, among all the other things you might call me, because I photograph not only what's out there, but the act of seeing it. I'm documenting the very process whereby something is perceived." He always argued with that. He needed to keep the outside and the inside separate, I guess.

I love that you have the sense at the end of *The Act of Seeing* that it's landscape. There are wondrous landscapes inside this body, and it's a terrain that, yes, we need to *see.*

10/15/98

MacDonald: In your program note for *The Garden of Earthly Delights* [1981], you mention specifically that you used montane zone vegetation, so just out of curiosity, I asked a local biologist who does field guides of plants and trees to look at the film with me to see whether, if you were a biologist and you really knew plant life, you could identify what you're seeing when you're watching that film. He was thrown by the imagery because of course scale is very important in identification, and film projection totally transforms scale. When he got done, he said, "Well, it's very interesting, but I have absolutely no idea what plants I was looking at."

In the field of American studies, there's often a reaction on the part of westerners to easterners' assumption that *their* landscape, and plants, and seasonal variations, are the *real* American nature. I assume you're reacting to that tradition by specifying montane zone vegetation.

Brakhage: But in a friendlier way than you're thinking. Actually, the primary thing that got me thinking in the direction of photographing just what was in my backyard, at nine thousand feet in the Rockies, was Louis Agassiz's reply to some of his Harvard colleagues when they all came back from summer vacation. Some had gone abroad, traveling the wide Earth over, and they asked him where *he* had gone, and he said, "I worked my way slowly across half my backyard."—I'm paraphrasing, but pretty closely.

Also, at the time I made *The Garden,* I was very annoyed with Hieronymus Bosch's painting of the same name, which envisions nature as puffy and sweet, while the humans are suffering these torments. After all, nature suffers as well. As a plant winds itself around a rock, in its desperate reach for sunlight, it undergoes its own torments. We are not the only ones in the world.

4/12/99

MacDonald: How's your health, Stan?

Brakhage: Well, I'm okay. I keep taking these tests, and I keep passing. Thank God I don't have cancer. I'm a little upset at the moment that this colostomy has got a fungus or maybe a yeast infection or something and is giving me trouble; that always scares me. I'm never out from under the weight of it—let's put it that way. I'm frightened often, but you can't live that way, so you just keep going on.

MacDonald: At the moment when you made *The Text of Light* [1974], what was happening for you?

Brakhage: All during 1974 I was involved with light, even in *Dominion* [1974], which is a portrait of the American businessman Gordon Rosenblum, who owned the ashtray with which I photographed *The Text of Light.* I had known him since high school. Now, in *my* mind his "dominion," what he was lord of, was really some light moving across his desk. That's putting it far too simplistically, but you get what I mean.

MacDonald: When you began *The Text of Light,* did you know this was going to be a single large project?

Brakhage: No. I'd had a hard time shooting *Dominion.* Gordon was very uptight, and I was trying to get an image of him behind his desk in his office with the macro lens. I don't even know why I put that on, except that I was trying anything and everything. I was pretty desperate because it felt like a rare opportunity to get a portrait of a man of economic power. The same impulse had earlier sent me to do "the Pittsburgh trilogy" and would later result in *The Governor.*

So there I was, struggling. This macro lens kind of sags down onto his desk, and I remember it had a little bellows, and even the bellows kind of sagged down. And only because I had the habit of looking through a camera before I moved it (I often got gifts that way), I peeked into it and saw a whole forest of glassine trees. I looked up and said to Gordon, "My God, what I'm seeing is incredible. I don't know how this is happening!" I looked again, and this forest had changed slightly. And we finally figured out that it was light bouncing off the glass across his desk from underneath his glass ashtray. Then, as we watched, a little river seemed to appear and flow through it. I said, "Oh my God!"

I didn't do any thinking at all; I just gave up on the one project and started on the other. (I went back later and made *Dominion.*) Anyway, I'm in there with this camera, taking individual frames. Finally, over a period of time I accumulated several pieces of glass, all kinds of glass, and arranged them near this very fine crystal ashtray. I could move through the whole spectrum by shifting and adjusting pieces of glass. There were crystal glasses, and a cheap knickknack glass ball with some indentations on it, and the secretary would bring in this or that from her knickknack shelf, and we'd try it for a while. Some things were useful; most things weren't. I was always shooting into the ashtray, never into any of the other glass. These other kinds of glass were used to give me ways to affect the interior of this ashtray.

MacDonald: Did you shoot the whole film in his office?

Brakhage: All in his office. His office had windows all around the side so that you had the sun all day long as you moved from window to window. In the morning you got the early morning sun at one end of the building, and at sunset you would end up in the kitchen at the back with the sun setting. I moved the pieces of glass from window to window. A lot of the time I just used the ashtray, but I also had all these other objects to draw on.

MacDonald: How often did you shoot?

Brakhage: I would start shooting in the morning, usually. I had been in the habit of staying overnight at his office, which had a little guest room, on the way to my teaching in Chicago and on the way back, because often there were snowstorms. I didn't dare wait to the last minute to leave the house to go down to Denver to catch a plane because I could be stopped by a snowstorm.

So I would come into Denver, and Gordon and I would go out together to a movie or something, and I'd stay overnight in his office. I just began staying there rather regularly and would get up in the morning, start photographing, and then move from window to window and end up in the kitchen and have supper. It was a time of great ecstasy because the visions that were given to me through this process were just as you see.

The first shots I got back seemed way too smooth, and I never used them. What I began to do—we're talking daylight Kodachrome here—is to tap. The camera was screwed down with U joints, and I loosened those slightly, and by tapping slightly at the edge of the lens I could get it to move just a fraction to the left, then take a few frames, then a fraction more to the left and take a few more, and then tap it back the other way—so that the results had a handheld quality. A little way into the film I began thinking of it as a world, and just in order to hold my sensibilities together, I began thinking of myself as passing across a planet something like our own, but not entirely like ours, passing through its four seasons, and its mountainous and forested areas, and so on.

I wanted the film to be rough, not smooth and locked down. I owned a gadget with a timer that would have allowed me to just click off frames, but I couldn't bring myself to use it.

Later, a lot of people thought, "It's rough because he's using inferior equipment," but that wasn't it at all. The roughness was very hard work: I had to try and imagine how many shifts to the left and then back to the right would be feasible within a minute without the result looking just jerky. Very few, right? I had to spread each visual development out over several minutes of film running time, which was actually an hour and a half of shooting time or more.

MacDonald: Were you always looking through the camera as you did this?

Brakhage: Yes. And just to keep from going nuts—because in some cases I wanted more change than you could get if you were sitting there shooting frames constantly—I would often have a book, and be reading. I'd take a frame and would have a rough sense of how much more reading I could do, seven or eight sentences or maybe a paragraph, before exposing the next frame and creating a certain, subtle visual development. I read half a dozen books while I was making *The Text of Light,* but I was always looking when I took a frame.

MacDonald: How close was what you were seeing through the camera to what you ended up having?

Brakhage: Very close, for two reasons. First, I had real saturation because I was shooting one frame at a time, and second, I was using Kodachrome, and I had come to know Kodachrome like the back of my hand.

Anyone could get an expensive ashtray or even any drinking glass with a thick bottom and try the same thing. If you look deep into the glass, holding it where the light can come through, it will begin to reveal the world of *The Text of Light.*

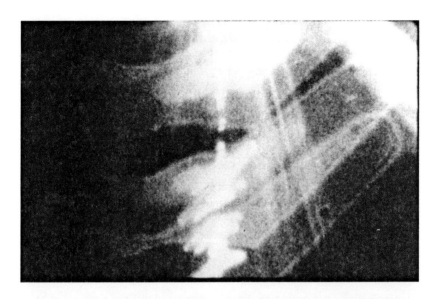

Reflections through glass in Stan Brakhage's *The Text of Light* (1974). Courtesy William C. Wees.

MacDonald: How long were you shooting in Rosenblum's office?

Brakhage: Most of a year. And then I took another year to edit. Of course, I was doing other things—flying back and forth to Chicago to teach, and doing other films—during that year. I *was* in my studio several days a week, sometimes the whole week, sometimes almost the whole space between trips. Sometimes, I'd touch home base and play with the kids and then go down to Gordon's and work. It was such an ecstasy, I can't tell you. Unhappily, the process had unhappy consequences.

It was a dangerous film to make because I was staring directly into the light. You have to be really careful that you're not burning out your eyes. You're bent over and in a great tension, trying to remember what an hour and a half's worth of shooting should look like when it comes back as a minute. I knew that I was nearly done; I had the feeling that I had really explored this world, that there was nothing more I could do. But foolishly, because my camera still had forty feet of film in it, I went on shooting, and suddenly in the midst of that final moment of shooting (which by the way gave me nothing I could use), I stood up suddenly, and my back went out and stayed out for two and one-half years. It was so bad that they said that I'd need operations; I barely got through it without being operated on.

I should have listened to myself. I know when something's done. People always ask me *how* I know. I don't know how to say how I know. How do you know when you're in love? How do you know when you have to go to the bathroom? It's very hard to say how you know the things that you really do know, but I knew, and it was blasphemy to go on with the process after I did know, and my presumption broke my back.

MacDonald: How much of what you shot ended up in the finished piece?

Brakhage: You know, I don't really remember. My rough guess is about half. Again, there was gorgeous and glorious footage which I destroyed pretty quickly after I finished editing, because I thought that the temptation would be too great to go and make *Text of Light II, Text of Light Meets the Wolfman,* whatever.

MacDonald: I was reading your little essay on Jim Davis last night [Brakhage, "Time . . . on dit," in *Jim Davis: The Flow of Energy* (edited by Robert A. Haller, New York: Anthology Film Archives, 1992), 23–30], and you draw an interesting comparison between Davis's light and yours: your light is always on some level embodied, whereas his light seems disembodied. Davis's light is *real,* but it's also almost entirely abstract, whereas the light in *The Text of Light* always seems connected with something material: it's light that's been transmogrified by bouncing off a physical reality.

Brakhage: I think that's an interesting distinction. Of course, as you know, Jim inspired *The Text of Light.* I think I might never have made it without him, and that's why I dedicated it to him.

I called Jim on the phone and told him I wanted to dedicate the film to him (in the catalogue blurb), and assured him that if he didn't like the film, I'd take the dedication back. He was very pleased—though he never saw the film.

I was pleased, too, because I had prejudices against his work when I first saw it, and some of them still remain. In fact, I was quite rude to him at a lecture. Willard Maas and I went to hear him at the New School for Social Research. He was introduced by Amos Vogel. In fairness to myself, my principal anger at him, and the cause of my rudeness during the question period, was that he declared that film had now subsumed all the other arts and there was no point of even thinking about painting anymore, or the stage, or poetry, or anything else. It was just one of the most lavish statements of filmic hubris I'd ever heard, coming from a man who ordinarily was very cautious and quiet and soft-spoken, a sweet guy. But he had had too much to drink or something. Who knows what? Or maybe he believed that with all his heart, and it may even be true—I mean, what do *I* know? But at the time I certainly didn't think so; I'm a great defender of the other arts and *do* care for them, and so I took great exception.

And I also thought his work was what I still think Francis Thompson's *New York, New York* [1957] is: a kind of cheap trickery.

In the end I came to see Jim's films as a meditation on the imagination of light.

MacDonald: I see you as more interested in incarnation and in the fact that at the edge of the actual material world, there always is this other thing, the Ineffable. I think Davis is more like Jordan Belson.

Brakhage: That's a big subject, too!

MacDonald: Yes. I'll change gears a bit. I was looking at some of Davis's work last night, and it struck me that, like Ralph Steiner, he had a tendency to put really bad soundtracks on beautiful imagery.

Brakhage: Well, a lot of people have made that mistake, including me when I was young. That's always been a tough issue for filmmakers, and more films have been ruined, and continue to be ruined, by ghastly soundtracks than by any other thing—even films made by some great sensibilities. I almost feel like there's a kind of shyness in filmmakers. They don't trust themselves; they don't trust what they've accomplished, and therefore they feel they have to lean on music, and of course, that doesn't work. Jordan Belson is a case in point. His work is so ecstatic if you can see it silently. Harry Smith also had a wacky relationship with music. When presenting the works of these people, I feel I have to present it the way they wanted it, first, and *then* I'm free to show it without the sound. At a certain point, maybe one has the right to say, "Well, *I* love this more than *he* can, so I'll do what I want with it," and see if a ghost rises in the night or whatever. *[Laughter.]*

But I have been wrong about certain things, and I know I'm extreme in my view of sound. There are sound films that I think are great, and I like some of those I've made myself, but I do believe sound really has to be necessary because you're going to pay a price for using it. Often, films age with the soundtracks. What could be more tiresomely dated than so many soundtracks for abstract work? I have that trouble with Mary Ellen Bute. Interestingly enough, I don't have it with Fischinger.

MacDonald: Fischinger is presuming that the music is crucial and important in its own right, and he works off it in a way that these others don't

Brakhage: It's also because he never synchronizes totally. Every third conjunction is off the beat. He's almost in syncopation rather than in synchronization. Then, of course, he also made the first truly silent film in the history of film when he said of *Radio Dynamics,* "Please do not play the music with this." That's the first truly silent film. So there's an intelligence in Fischinger about sound, and the same is true of Kenneth Anger, who is so deeply clear and thoughtful and sensible about music. He makes great soundtracks.

MacDonald: One of the things you talk about in your essay on Davis is your being tied to the history of Western art. It's certainly true watching *The Text of Light.* I'm always thinking, "Oh, that looks like Munch's sky above *The Scream.*"

Brakhage: Or Turner, who I think is a major inspiration on that film. As was true for *The Wold Shadow* [1972], the film that got me back into painting, *The Text of Light* is almost a history of Western painting. The second-to-last shot, for example, is almost Clyfford Still. The last shot is more ambiguous and allows the film to end. But *The Text of Light* is partly a history of Western landscape painting and means to carry that tradition on, the way *Dog Star Man* is thrashing about within the history of architecture.

MacDonald: As you edited *The Text of Light,* you had a considerable amount of material—

Brakhage: That was one of the toughest films ever to edit. Now, remember, when I'm editing it, it's already broken my back!

MacDonald: So how are you keeping this huge piece in your head? It's wonderful to watch, but to remember the specifics, moment by moment. . .

Brakhage: This may be why the seasons come to be a way of structuring music and other forms, because if you've got four seasons, that gives you something to hold on to. Certain things in *The Text of Light* look like winter, certain things look like spring. Of course, spring and summer can also look very similar, but there's a kind of a gold and a heat that's characteristic of summer and so on. So that gives you a way to distinguish footage—not all of it, but a lot of it. *The Text of Light* starts in late fall and moves into early winter; another section starts in deep summer and moves into early fall. Each movement includes the end of one season and the beginning of another. There is also a movement down from a kind of rocky prominence into more icy waterways that are melting, and finally into swamps.

These were ways to hold onto the material and keep from going totally crazy. Now I wouldn't have had to do it that way, but I think these structures are comforting to audiences; it's harder for them when you're into pure visual music.

MacDonald: Did you score it at all?

Brakhage: Oh, I always have a tendency to write quite elaborate notes on the boxes of film and to draw sketches, like you find in *Metaphors on Vision,* apropos of *Anticipation of the Night.* I haven't kept all that stuff because I feel I made that process clear in *Metaphors of Vision* [Brakhage's *Metaphors on Vision* was published in a special issue of *Film Culture* in the fall of 1963 (no. 30); sections of it are anthologized in *Essential Brakhage,* edited by Bruce McPherson; see the bibliography]. There's no point in putting people through the process over and over again, with every film. But I do need to find ways to help me hold things together. In a long work like *The Text of Light,* you're risking insanity.

I also depend upon the film to tell where it's supposed to go. A lot of the making really is just that. Something needs something else, and I'm searching, searching, searching, and suddenly, *there's* something that seems to *be* what's needed there, so I try to put it there, and it doesn't have the right rhythm. So then I go back and search and search and search and find another thing that seems like it should be there, and this one also has the right rhythm—but not the right color; it doesn't work with the melody of color that the sequence has set up. I go on searching, searching, searching, and finally all of *these* things are satisfied, but it looks like a *tree* where we haven't introduced it. More searching. You can truly go mad. And then suddenly you might find fifteen things in a row that just go together perfectly. And here's the hard part: you're holding in mind also, for a year or at least for many months, certain formal imperatives that have to be accounted for before you end, in order for the work to be entirely cohesive.

At the end of *The Text of Light* I reveal a globe—not the ashtray, just a globe that came along during the process. It's the symbol of this cohesiveness.

9/15/97

MacDonald: I've recently looked at *The Roman Numeral Series* [1979–80], *Unconscious London Strata* [1982], and *The Loom* [1986]. The more I looked at *The Loom,* the more it struck me as a major piece, loaded with thinking about the history of art and the representation of animals in art. The look of it is like a tapestry, a Navajo rug; and it seems an homage to Muybridge.

Brakhage: It *is* those things, but it's more consciously inspired by Georges Méliès.

MacDonald: You mean in its use of superimposition?

Brakhage: No. I had lived for so many years with these two windows—essentially it's two windows; there are a couple of others used here and there. I'd lived with those windows and all those animals and all that animal motion for fifteen years. They were penned in there, and that grid was put over the windows.

Over the years I came to have some sense of how the animals would move in relationship to each other. I could almost guess that if goat A and goat B were here and there, and a rabbit came in from the lower left, unless a bird flopped down suddenly to change it, everything would tend to move in certain ways and come to another composition. So being able to predict this, I felt that in a sense they were choreographing themselves, and could I but see it, predict it correctly, I could record something like the choreography of Georges Méliès, and like him, with an unmoving camera. So that was my dream.

MacDonald: Compared to other films where you work with multileveled superimpositions, this imagery feels more friezelike or tapestry-like.

Brakhage: Well, that's another way Méliès comes in. I've always felt that Méliès's sets are really carrying on the tradition of Siennese painting, as distinct from the Renaissance. As you know, Renaissance perspective has bothered me all my life, so I've been very partial to flats, which in fact is not just Méliès but the tradition of the theater, where within a very small space a series of flats can be brought up and down to create a variety of scenes.

So I wanted that flatness. I'm paying homage in every way I can to that flatness, including using telephoto lenses whenever I can get back far enough from the one window to do so. With the grid in front and the vertical logs in back, you have a great possibility for the animals being just like cardboard cutouts, until they move of course. When they move, they take on three dimensions. So that's how the loom comes into it; it relates to the grid and to the sense of everything being a series of flats and these flats moving in relationship to each other.

MacDonald: Once you get into the flatness of the image, then the whole history of flat representation of animals seems to come into play, all the way back to the cave paintings.

Brakhage: Well, you know, I have not thought of that connection consciously in relationship to this film, and it's rather amazing that I haven't because, of course, the Lascaux cave paintings have those great animals with bodies very like the goats. But I think you're right because the other film that I was making at this time was *The Dante Quartet* [1987]. I was making that by painting on IMAX film with very thick, *half-an-inch-thick* paint, belts of paint. I had no sense that it could be printed or that I'd ever be able to show what I was doing to anybody, and I *was* thinking constantly of myself in relationship to Lascaux during that process because, of course, most of the cave painters went back into the mountain and painted by themselves and sealed the caves shut, so obviously no one but them ever saw what they did. And that's why we *have* those paintings, because they sealed the caves so imperviously shut. So, unconsciously that must have been a factor in what I was doing *downstairs* when I was photographing that yard.

The other thing that must be said is that *The Loom* was shot across a period where my marriage with Jane was grinding down. I mean, I didn't know it yet, while I was photographing, but it was near the end. In fact, most of the editing was done right after the breakup with Jane, down in Boulder. In the film there's this great grief and sadness, and a tribute to Jane, and her "Peaceable Kingdom" of animals, which was alternately a burden and a joy to me. The animals were often hard to take care of and yet, of course, at the same time, I was moved by them.

I had made several films with the goats, including *Tragodia* [1976], an aesthetic study of four generations of goats, which must be one of the most peculiar and least-likely-to-be-looked-at films on earth, inasmuch as it really doesn't make it with the art crowd and *certainly* doesn't make it with the goat crowd. *Tragodia* means "goat cry." Did you know that the term "tragedy" comes from the cry of the goat?

MacDonald: Had no idea.

Brakhage: The sound they make, which of course does not occur in my film, was for the Greeks the saddest sound in the world.

Well, anyway, all that is especially relevant in *The Loom:* because when Jane is being pictured with the goat, since I've broken from her, this is tough stuff for me. At the time, I can't *imagine* how this has happened to us.

MacDonald: It's a lovely portrait of her.

Brakhage: But it must be said, after we talk about all these flattenings and all the aesthetics, that the weaving of that film was done amidst many tears and much grief and meditation, a time during which all my wishes for a Peaceable Kingdom—which includes a film I made years ago in a zoo, called *The Peaceable Kingdom* [1971], and my involvement with Edward Hicks, another inspiration on *The Loom*—have come to grief. For all the beauty of the film, I also myself, more and more, began to sense that it was filled with a kind of tragedy of constriction.

MacDonald: That *you're* penned in as well as the animals.

Brakhage: After a certain amount of being penned in, you can open a door, and people and creatures won't walk through it. But in the end I *had* to walk through, and shortly after, the whole yard was busted up and the animals were given away to different people. Homes were found for all of them, but that whole vision you see in *The Loom* is poised on the edge of being busted open into the world again. We were too much an idyll there, and it was freezing—first because it's eight months winter up there, but also in the other sense. We had come to a relationship that was no longer sustainable for Jane or me, or for the animals.

So *The Loom* is a meditation on all of that.

MacDonald: Rose Lowder did a series of films called *Scènes de la vie française* [1985–86] in which she tried to create a filmic space in which there were multiple times at once. On some level *The Loom* tries something similar. You mentioned that after all these years you knew basically what the animals would do, but there's also a sense that we're seeing three or four moments all at the same time, which I think within a long-term relationship, you *do.*

Brakhage: And I really struggled to bring that out in the little narratives going on there.

MacDonald: You mentioned Siennese painting. There's a place late in the film where there's a design along the bottom of the image—is it flowers?

Brakhage: Yes, plants and flowers.

MacDonald: It reminds me of an Italian outdoor fresco wall—

Brakhage: Oh, that's a lovely sense of it. Those plants were just there—plants in the window—so unless I'm shooting above them, I'm getting little tendrils of these plants, but I never thought of them consciously in relation to painting. Sometimes a border of flowers will be made for wall murals and tapestries even more, and illuminated books as well.

For myself, *The Loom* was a meditation piece. It made me realize—and, of course, when I put it over into language, it's far too blunt and not worthy of the film—that you cannot have heaven on Earth. That's not what Earth is for. You cannot have a Peaceable Kingdom here. I don't know why I couldn't see this at the zoo when I made *The Peaceable Kingdom*—well, I guess I *did* in a way, because I made *The Peaceable Kingdom* at the *zoo.* There's a terrible irony in the Peaceable Kingdom being where you have all these poor animals caged and trapped.

MacDonald: You've said that *Unconscious London Strata* is a favorite of yours.

Brakhage: Yes. I don't know quite why, but I've always liked it very much. It's a very long series of abstractions, and yet it seems to hold up. I'm never bored to see it, unlike some other long abstractions of mine. Partly that's because they're always just lifted directly off of real things, like Big Ben. Did you recognize Big Ben?

MacDonald: I did, yes.

Brakhage: That's the most recognizable thing, and the Thames, and some buildings.

MacDonald: You say "lifted directly off": sometimes I've not been able to distinguish whether you're unfocusing the camera and finding images in sectors of the lens that normally filmmakers don't notice, or whether you're pointing the lens at a reflective surface in such a way that you're capturing a nuance of what's reflected that normally we wouldn't be aware of.

Brakhage: Well, all different techniques are used, but one of the most pervasive in *Unconscious London Strata* is clicking frames while moving the camera. And repeating patterns of clicking, so that you have a blurred representation lifted directly off of a building or whatever is in focus, and which can at moments become referential. One day I'm shooting Big Ben on the street, and I'm clicking and moving—it must have seemed to people almost epileptic motion—and staying on the same subject for like five minutes. A crowd had gathered, and finally one of the British people asks Jane, "Would he mind if we took the picture for him?" She realized that they thought that I was desperately trying to get a picture but had some nervous disorder which caused me to twitch.

I was so excited about going to London. It was so thrilling to me that I really felt I had to bring something of it back.

MacDonald: This was your first trip?

Brakhage: Yes. In the seventies they had this great London International Film Festival. But I didn't want to bring back conventional images of London. I wanted something worthy of what London has been for me, and I'd already guessed that the London I was going to see was going to live up to the dreams I've had about London since I was a small child. Puss in Boots went there and chased a mouse under the queen's chair.

So, right from the start, I decided that this was going to be the history of the whole of London as one imagines it and that little emblems of reference would come through, but that basically it would be a tribute in visual music. I guess it's a favorite of mine because it all worked out very well, and it interests me endlessly to look at the results.

It begins when London was just a green sward with nothing on it, and there's a sense of battles and exchanges, and these are lifted off of grasses in London's central parks, which are, after all, not that distinct from the grasses that were there centuries ago when there was no London. I try to follow a kind of chronology using movements of the camera, a chronology of architectural possibilities. There are square stones on square stones, and there are movements to epitomize that, and then there are flying buttresses, and finally the delicacies of Christopher Wren. And so on. It ends with the moderns.

MacDonald: You mentioned the Houses of Parliament and the Thames. Saint Paul's is in there too, right?

Brakhage: Inside and out. But it's very hard to recognize from the outside. Actually, I don't want these exactitudes to take over. I wanted them to be there like a very few words in a piece of music. The recognizable moments help mark the chronology of the architecture, which is something I was also doing in *Dog Star Man:* as the man climbs up through those trees, I tried to use tree arrangements and movements of the camera to hint at the development of Western architecture that comes finally to the cathedrals, and finally I stick in some stained glass windows to peg it more solidly. This history in *Unconscious London Strata* is just an evolution from that, an echo of that.

MacDonald: So why *unconscious* London strata?

Brakhage: Well, because the *conscious* London strata is going to be what you're seeing as you're there. The *unconscious* London strata is all that that's been thought and felt about London, that's in the loam of your brain, but is not there before your eyes. Things before your eyes might prompt you to a remembrance, and that remembrance should be largely ineffable, which is to say unconscious. It's *there*—somehow Puss in Boots walks through *Unconscious London Strata.* I don't know exactly *where* it is, but I know it has to be in there because it's in me, as is all of Dickens and the poets and all the rest.

MacDonald: Did you start filming from the plane on the way over?

Brakhage: Yes. That was the other thing—that it should be on one level a journal of my coming into London and everything I did there. The film is laid out pretty much in chronological order, only it's trying to represent the *unconscious* things that might be being tipped off by what's before my eyes at various moments.

MacDonald: How long were you there? Did you carry the camera all the time?

Brakhage: About a week. Yes, I carried the camera constantly. I photographed originally on Super-8mm and blew it up. Already at that time, I'm knowing that Super-8mm is not really going to last. I'd made many Super-8mm films and was already beginning to worry about having to translate them into 16mm, so I'd decided that I'd shoot in Super-8 and edit the film, but that it would have to go immediately into 16mm. I did the editing with that in mind.

MacDonald: The subtlety of color and texture in the film is remarkable.

Brakhage: Well, you see, because of Western Cine, I have the great good fortune to have another way to work with color. If I shoot in Super-8mm, and edit it, and then I go down to Western Cine and we're blowing it up into 16mm, I can change the colors, shot by shot, and *did*—for all of my blowups actually. I was already calling any blowup from Super-8mm or regular 8mm to 16mm "a translation." So in that translation I have to change the colors and weight them differently because they're going to be in somewhat different films. And, of course, you're getting all that additional texture to work with because of the blowup.

Also, I put a lot of rounds in there—like "row, row, row your boat"—repeating rhythm patterns like a round; there's a lot of fugal editing.

MacDonald: The Roman Numeral Series is also exquisite. And I don't know that I can verbalize about those films very well.

Brakhage: Most of that is Super-8mm blown up to 16mm, too. Same process. All except, I think, the ninth one, which is 16mm. They were probably the first films that I shot in Super-8mm *knowing* that I would be blowing them up to 16mm. (Actually I can think of an example of a regular 8mm film that I made, knowing I would blow it up to 16mm: *Sexual Meditation: Hotel* [1972], so there may be others.) The *Arabics* [nineteen films, 1980–81] are also shot in Super-8mm and blown up, whereas the *Egyptian Series* [1983] and the *Babylon Series* [three films, 1989–90] are 16mm.

Reflected light in Brakhage's *Arabic 14* (1981). Courtesy William C. Wees.

10/6/97 [recorded at Cornell University, with Don Fredericksen's film class and several visitors, including Sarah Elder, David Gatten, and Vincent Grenier]

MacDonald: I would like to talk a bit more about the issue of domestic life. In my interviewing of filmmakers, one theme is always money. Indeed, even in cases where the family is of limited size, a child or two, and the film-maker has a decent academic job and makes a film every two years, the money for making that film is still a very big issue and causes considerable consternation. You've made tremendous numbers of films, and a fair number of children as well, so my question is, how has the financial wrestle with the domestic been for you over the years? Has it felt as though the films take resources away from the family? How have you worked with that?

Second, and again this is, I know, a very general question—how do you conceive the domestic? You were in a very long-term relationship through an era when for many people long-term relationships did not seem theoretically logical.

Brakhage: Well, the first thing I think of when you ask this question is guilt. Most of my adult life, certainly since I started having a family, has been riddled with guilt at the monies spent on films that were inevitably taking something away from what might be given to my wife or the children. And sometimes, if

I get selfish enough, I have that sense also about myself. There are monies I might have given to myself, things I might have done, places I might have seen, were it not for film.

I remember a compelling moment when I saw Orson Welles on the Tom Snyder *Tomorrow* show, back in the early seventies I think it was, being asked about film, and he said, "It has destroyed my life. It has absolutely destroyed my life." Of course, *he* had other things he *could* do, so I couldn't say exactly what he says.

I realized very early on that I was *not* a poet. I had the good fortune to live with and be a sort of housekeeper for the poet Robert Duncan, and through Duncan, who was a center of activity in San Francisco at that time, I met a whole spate of poets. And it became clear to me, in that informal school, what a poet was, and that it wasn't me. I had thought of myself as a poet making films but suddenly had the sense that I was a *filmmaker, not* a poet making a film. This took years, but anyway that understanding was the end result.

So I went from needing a pencil and a piece of paper to the comparatively enormous expenses of film. We're talking back in the fifties, when a roll of Kodachrome film through processing cost fourteen dollars. Now, with mailing and everything, we are talking at least one hundred forty dollars for about three minutes of film, before you've edited it, before you've prepared it for the labs, or anything. And then, of course, it goes to the lab, and if it becomes a sound film, it becomes ten times as expensive. Now, being a filmmaker is like being a silversmith, which in fact it *is,* in a way. And guilt is *the* major feeling.

But even earlier there were times when a kind of craziness would set in under the money pressures, and I would personalize the muse. I would speak to her as a real entity moving through me and say, Okay, the children are going to have meat three times a week at least. They are going to have new bikes as they need them. They are going to be dressed well enough at school so that they are not ashamed. And so on. And Jane is going to have money for her goats. And the roof needs to be repaired. And then you can have the rest.

I know that this has been the number one story for almost every independent filmmaker. We have at this point a tragedy, I think, that Bruce Baillie, who certainly is one of the greatest living filmmakers, hasn't been able to work with film for many years. He lives on food stamps. I don't know what he is going to do when food stamps are no longer available. The culture suffers because we are not supporting the people who are able to make beautiful films for those who are interested in the poetics of cinema.

Right now, I am under oath not to spend any money to print anything, and this means that the drawer I have at school is starting to fill up. I have sworn that I will not print anything because I cannot provide for my family. With all the illness I had last year, we are economically endangered, and I cannot even supply the children with so simple a thing as a backyard. Some grants were to come through the university, but both of them were withheld. I am fighting tooth and nail to get them back, but at a time when university administrators are trying to cut back on many things. The entire Chinese department has been done away with. I am fighting for what is a reasonable grant, a pittance in comparison to what any scientist would get at the University of Colorado, even in times like this—just a few thousand dollars to do some printing of the work I have finished, so that I can extend it into society. But if I don't get it, then that drawer will fill up, and I will send it all to the salt mine in Kansas or something, and it will sit there waiting for someone to be interested in seeing it printed.

Now, remember, *I'm* the best off of *all* the independent filmmakers, and, in fact, the target for some abuse for that reason. I fill up too many of the few slots there are for showing independent film. I know a lot of young filmmakers are enraged. I don't, of course, mean to displace anybody. My tactics are the same as always: I am *compelled* to work. So I make, and when the making is done, I feel the pressure to print, so that what I've made can be preserved, in case it is of some use to someone, and to extend it to those who *are* interested, who are a fair enough number.

My sense of the domestic was just daily life, and *before* I was married, *before* the children started coming along, I began having the sense that we mostly live at the kitchen table—or *I* do anyway—and that, while this is true, most people don't have that valorized or envisioned sufficiently to feel comfortable with it, and so they feel dissatisfied with their lives. I believe that that's one of the mainsprings of war. You feel you're not really living, so you run off to war or you go hold up a Seven-Eleven store or you go to the amusement park and ride the roller coaster—*something* to get the adrenaline going.

But there is potential in the kitchen *without* the stove blowing up. There is potential for a high-adrenaline life, or at least for a high sense of living, that was virtually untapped until what we in the West call the romantic movement. I have a variety of precedents in this: for example, painters who are important to me, like Bonnard, who paints *The Sorrow;* like Van Gogh: however wild and disorganized his kitchen table *was,* that *is* what he was painting. He was painting his daily life, and the only pity is that he was in such a psychic drama that his was the domestic life of the crazy man. But what about the domestic life of the man who isn't crazy? Manet had a deep investment with this. In fact, all the impressionists did, more or less. To paint what was before their eyes, what they were living with, what their major surroundings were. They have guided me.

Now, my daily life had family growing up in it, so *that* meant the children had to be accommodated. You ask, "Is it idealized?" Well, in some sense all art is idealized, because we are not living through it. We're not seeing all the boring moments of life. Ninety-eight percent of life is pretty boring for most people, so they stretch their nerves in order to endure. What I tried to do was to avoid the former ideals, to break through to some new ideals, and I did so with more or less success. I did not realize the extent to which my Hollywood narrative dramatic viewing still had some grip on me in making my early films, and so I feel that's where they are weaker than I thought they were, than I wanted them to be. Still, as I moved along, the films got to be less and less anything that Hollywood could use at all. And that's been an interesting thing about the whole independent film movement, or most of it, and certainly my work.

When we were young, Hollywood producers rented our films; advertising agencies rented our films, picked up bits and pieces for selling things or for weaving into the grammar of narrative dramatic cinema. I think it's been many, many years since they have been able to use *any*thing in my work, and I am proud of that.

MacDonald: I hate to depress you, but when *NYPD Blue* was first on, with its gestural camera movement, a number of us thought, "My god, Brakhage has made it to TV!"

Brakhage: This is a sharp recognition; but, in fact, *I* don't move the camera that way anymore. That's from earlier work. And, by the way, they are welcome to it. They do such a good job with it. I don't have resentment at such borrowings, except when we're in money trouble. Then I say, "Why can't I get one-tenth of 1 percent of their budget for *my* work?" But otherwise I don't have any resentment. I am really proud that the makers of *Superman* [1978] rented *The Text of Light* many times and used it to create krypton and the baby cradle of Superbaby at the North Pole. I mean, let's face it, when I was a little kid running around the block—a little fat boy with a red towel tied around his neck—had someone said, "You're going to influence the future of Superman," well, I wouldn't have needed anything more to live for! So, as long as they don't make some junky, awful thing, I'm proud and think it quite natural that the poetics of cinema feed into the ordinary daily language of cinema where people sell things.

Domesticity, however, is an issue that gets more and more crucial, even for narrative dramatic cinema. After all, what is Chekhov but domestic? What is *The Long Day's Journey into Night?* Or most of O'Neill? Or Tennessee Williams? Or Manet? Or Sam Shepherd? This *is* the drive, to expose what people ordinarily consider the boring, overlooked, uninteresting, the dirty laundry, of our daily living. I certainly favor that over "into the valley go the ten thousand"—to the glory of certain death and slaughter with puffs of multicolored smoke!

MacDonald: Let me open up another can of worms. After the screening of *Commingled Containers* last night, Sarah Elder, who is a wonderful filmmaker in her own right and not normally given either to melodrama or to exaggeration or to imprecision, leaned over to me and said, "I just saw God." I knew exactly what she meant, and it raised an interesting issue for me.

In academic life in the last generation—even though we know these two things are intimately parts of each other, and we'd be fools to pretend that they can be separated—the *political* has held sway over the *spiritual,* within academic discourse, within critiques of film. It's taken me a long time to be honest with myself that what made me commit to independent film is not primarily the political thing but the spiritual thing. Your films have always been very special to me in this regard because they are involved not just with light in the obvious sense but with "The Light," with spiritual light.

My wife, Pat, comes to the Ithaca Zen Center to sit. Sitting for two hours in a Zen meditation is something that frightens me a little, but at the same time, watching longer experimental film, and last night watching *A Child's Garden and the Serious Sea* [1991], is *my* version of sitting. It's a kind of meditation practice.

Brakhage: I am very honored to hear you say that. That would be one of my most fervent, hoped-for intentions, that humans could use my work in some spiritual way, in some meditative way. Because then you're making it your own in a way that is *freeing.* One of my problems with a lot of religions is the tendency of people to get hung up on them.

MacDonald: Could you talk a bit about the spiritual versus the political in the arts and in academe?

Brakhage: I want to jump back into the issue of the domestic a bit, because it's related to this question. When I came to divorce, which was something I never in the world would have imagined for Jane and me—we were *so* close, and we had not only the care and love of the five children growing up but an ecology in a relationship to the arts and film. But we did come to it, regardless of what either of us could do. And I really didn't expect to survive it. I didn't expect to live much longer.

In the process of finally leaving, after separating a little bit and coming back together and trying again, I moved down to Boulder to a tiny apartment and had all these films to cart down there. And as I was putting them in the locker downstairs and up on the shelves in my limited shelf space, I was coming to realize that, my god, I have represented in art, a woman and a home, an environment, more than any other artist I can think of. My dedication was *so* pervasive; I was *so* deeply involved in these very geographically and personally limited subjects, *focused* there! What would this be to me now?

For a while, I was terrified to look at any of those films. I couldn't look at still photographs of the family, and there were all kinds of objects that were so personalized by the living we all had had together that I couldn't keep them. Even certain *spoons* were charged. Well, the wonderful thing, one of the great gifts that came to me out of all this agony, was that in the end I *could* look at the films.

I had agreed to teach a course based on Marjorie Keller's book [*The Untutored Eye: Childhood in the Films of Cocteau, Cornell, and Brakhage* (Rutherford, N.J.: Associated University Presses, 1986)] where I had to face a whole lot of my own work and Joseph Cornell's and Cocteau's. So I am having to go over to school, to *show* this home life; and certain moments would tear at my throat or my stomach. But, basically, I could also meditate with them; they *were* meditative pieces. They were, yes, *of* me, had passed *through* me, were re-presentations in some sense of my life, but they'd gone enough into that enclosed form that I like to think of as art that I could bear to look at them and be inspired by them. In fact, they were curative to me, and my hope is that they will be cur-ative to others, too. I was in a spiritual crisis such as I had never experienced before in my life, and I felt at that point the perfect church that art can be.

A little footnote. In his early twenties, Ezra Pound lost a correspondence with a young girl he was writing to in New England because her parents made her break it off when he wrote to her that religion was the popularization of the arts. I will try to say it more gently than he did, because I am still filled with joy from the church service I went to yesterday morning here. If that chapel were in Boulder, I'd be going to it every Sunday. It was a beautiful service (Reinhold Niebuhr's son gave the sermon), and I was much sustained by it. I believe that when you gather together with others, there's a kind of comfort that comes from the service and from a kind of sharing of God vis-à-vis the conductor of the serv-ice or the choirmaster or the choir or whatever. *Religio* means to bind together, so it is a tougher scene in which to be unique and individual, and that is part of the *comfort* of it: you don't have that terrible loneliness that you can have with an art.

When one is getting spiritual with an *art,* one has the possibility of the rever-berating voices and envisionments and the writings and architectures of thou-sands of years of humans. That's the real *church* that all art is in relationship to, the whole history of art back to the Lascaux cave paintings at least. But with an art one *also* has the possibility of being absolutely unique and individual, which is an undeniable truth. It is the most undeniable truth that we have: sitting each in his or her chair, free from the screen, moved by it but not geared to it, not manipulated by it, but moved by it. That's the particular level of spirituality that the arts offer.

MacDonald: And politics?

Brakhage: "*Polis* is eyes," says Charles Olson, the poet: and that's why I named my police film, *Eyes.* There is the private eye, the detective, and then there is *polis.* First of all, you have to acknowledge that the human is a politi-cal animal. I'm politicking right now for what I love and believe in. Here I am talking and being as convincing as possible about what I care about. The differ-ence between me and somebody running for office is that I don't *need* to con-vince you. I don't need *your* vote. I don't want to form a cult. I've been very, very careful to avoid cults, and I live in a cult town: all you have to do is stand with your finger up testing the wind in Boulder, and a crowd will gather and form a cult around you.

I do have a sense of wanting to give to others in thanks for what's been given to me, to give back to the whole history of art in thanks for what has been given to me. I don't think I could have lived without it. And to give to God, however you want to define that word. I have my own definitions. To say the unconscious or collective unconscious, or whatever you like, is perfectly fine by me: fairies, elves. I get a little nervous with demons. But, basically, I think everyone means something similar by "God" or all the other terms for the Unknowable. That's what Samuel Beckett would have called it: the Unnamable, the Unknowable, the Ineffable.

I don't know where I was going with that. Where was I going, Scott?

MacDonald: Politics.

Brakhage: Politics? I guess I was trying to avoid politics altogether is what I was doing. Beating completely around the bush. I have been deeply moved by political events, like the death of Kennedy. I was in Custer, South Dakota, at the time, and the whole town celebrated; I was the only one not out getting drunk and enjoying the death of the president of the United States! I was horrified. I really have not understood politics very well. I vote with conscience, but I am always tortured with grief. I vote for somebody, and then I feel far too much personal involvement: when that person launches the Bay of Pigs invasion, I *hate* them; and then when they get *shot,* I feel wracked with agony.

So I'm not really very wise politically and wouldn't claim to be and wouldn't know *what* in the world to suggest. I don't know, for instance, what I *am.* I am not very happy with socialism, which is what otherwise would be the only thing I can imagine choosing, because it seems somehow dead on the arts. During my few experiences in socialist countries I couldn't feel a vital living culture going on. So I don't know what to dream for, but I have a nose that is very sharp for certain things to avoid.

I did know that during the sixties the hippies were getting fascistic. And I wasn't so dumb that I was swallowing that every man, woman, and child ought to be forcibly lined up and made to take LSD. These were statements coming out of my so-called liberal friends in the sixties. I ended up having to combat Allen Ginsberg in Boulder because he was saying that if the Trungpa Rinpoche asked for James Merrill to be killed, he would have to do it—he who had stood against the Watergate break-in so rhetorically is part of this organization that is breaking into newspaper offices and stealing material that Tom Clark is writing, and following his children to school, and scaring the family out of town. So, I've seen people swing and behave outrageously in the name of a cause—because that isn't really the way Allen Ginsberg is. I've known Allen all these years. People become completely outrageous when they have a political cause or feel that they stand for something.

Sarah Elder: I was thinking about the practice of making art and daily mindfulness. One of the questions I have is how do you get out of your own way? You have this brilliant mind. How do you put it to nap and get around it in both the shooting and the editing?

Brakhage: I work in a trance state. It used to be that I had to go work very hard for several hours, sometimes several days, to get deep enough into a trance so that I could work; and if I were called to the phone for something urgent, it took me up to thirty seconds to answer a question. The brain was coming up out of deep working concentration.

Sometimes I hesitate to use the word "trance." The Western way to put it would be "concentration," except that we've diluted the meaning of concentration and shifted it away from a spiritual accent, because *this* kind of trance is certainly one where you could hope to, expect to, meet angels and hear voices: three, six, and nine of the Muses buzzing, and you listening for your cues in an envisionment of other dimensions.

Some of the people I know in the sciences have told me that there are well over a hundred dimensions. Usually, we're just barely considering the *fourth*. In my work process it is no surprise that there are over a hundred dimensions, and that "creatures" move through these dimensions—a cartoon word for whatever these entities are who are affecting the work. I do bar certain entities from moving through me because they are not of my kind. I cannot dance with them. I bar just exactly some of those that—and I am not making a value judgment here—Kenneth Anger or Harry Smith can use very well and make a great, magnificent, powerful beauty from. *These* I don't work with, so I do have my prohibitions in the trance state. I put up my hand like that: "Don't *attack!*" There are other things that can't move through me because I am not equipped.

So I try to remain true to myself in what can move through me, that can make use of the experience of life that *I* am and be in relationship with me. I don't feel like I *make* the films, but that they are made *through* me. The work is full of errors always, but those are mine. What's good about your work is *given*. What's giving it is what gives everything: for me, it's God. I am Christian in that sense.

Vincent Grenier: In the extraordinary new piece you showed us last night *[Commingled Containers]*, I imagine that you were throwing some drops of water on the lens so that you could create a certain effect. There's something about your process that involves not doing the thing that's expected, like zooming for no apparent reason. But certain things have to happen in order for a work to suddenly uncover itself, sometimes with fantastic results obviously. I wonder if you would be willing to talk about your bag of tricks.

Brakhage: When I came to make that film, I happened to be carrying a camera with its warranty running out. I don't know why I had the damned camera. I hadn't worked with a camera for several years at that point, didn't expect to work with one again. I simply could no longer afford it; I had gone back to painting on film because it was the only way I *could* afford to make films. I was walking down by Boulder Creek. I knew I had to test the camera before the warranty ran out, and I thought, "Well, Boulder Creek is always good for something." So

I set up the camera to just take some shots, and then the trance begins; and for three hours (I won't say I don't know what I'm doing—but I *will* say that the whole point of being trained and adept with the camera and the whole point of craftsmanship is that I can *work* this camera and wring it to do extraordinary things in a trance during which I cannot remember my name) I was filming at the creek.

So during this moment, it happened that I had extension tubes that I'd carried around since my *father* bought me some movie equipment, in lieu of my trying to go back to college. He'd promised to pay a certain amount of money so that I could go to college, and I finally decided I wasn't going to and asked him if I could have some money for film equipment. Among the things we bought were some extension tubes that would permit microphotography with ordinary lenses. Well, I'd never really been able to use them. I did not make *The Text of Light* with those extension tubes; I used a macro lens. I'd carried these tubes around for thirty-five, forty years, never using them, pulling them out every now and then and looking at them, and not throwing them away. So suddenly, I don't even know why, I pulled them out and put them on and got myself macro, and then stuck that lens partway into the water on some rock. I cannot tell you what moved me to do that. I didn't worry about whether I would get a particular image, but I also can't tell you how I'd get into a state where I *wouldn't* worry about that. The tubes came with a book with all these graphs; there were a whole lot of things you were supposed to do to decide what your exact f-stop was going to be. Well, that had defeated me for twenty years. I can't face that—not when I'm being creative, anyway—so I just stuck the thing in there and started shooting.

Do you know the SILT group from San Francisco?—three young men [Keith Evans, Christin Farrell, Jeff Warrin] who go out and *bury* film in different kinds of ground, like clay, and different kinds of earth, and leave it there for a while, come back and look at it and don't like it, and put it back again until finally they get these fantastic patterns. And then they spray them, freeze them, and turn the projector sideways and run them as landscapes. They are absolutely fantastic, beautiful films. Well, Jeff Warrin came to Boulder and got so excited about *Commingled Containers* that he went down to Boulder Creek and upstaged me beautifully. He took just a Kodachrome Super-8mm cartridge, which has a little aperture that he covered with tape and then put a pinhole through it. He picked up a stick, something he could turn the film with, and stuck the whole thing under Boulder Creek and turned the film, exposing frames. Well, of course, with a pinhole camera he is getting infinite focus, so you see *all* the little bubbles in all directions and whatever little thing that is coming down that stream, every little piece of dirt and whatnot—it's a fabulous, fantastic, beautiful film. You've never seen anything like it. I don't know, maybe *he* knows why *he* did what *he* did, but *I* don't know why I did what *I* did.

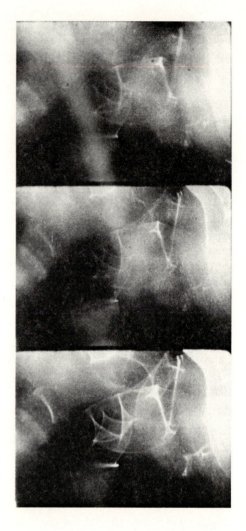

The "bubble world" underneath the
surface of Boulder Creek in Brakhage's
Commingled Containers (1997).
Courtesy Anthology Film Archives.

There are many different turns in *Commingled Containers* that I have no explanation for. Understandably, I feel I'm well trained so that under such a trance I can work and not screw up. My intuitions are good, my heart is good, and I am working hard. I'm letting myself do it. I'm risking being drowned. What more can you ask? I've worked very hard to be a large instrument and not dodge a weirdity, so that when the policewoman comes down and says, "Are you all right?" I can talk to her and say, "Yeah, I'm fine; I'm doing some experiments with water and photography." Fortunately, I can come out of the trance quickly and speak with her and deal with that, and then go on working until I'm done. I don't know quite what *Commingled Containers* means. It *is* moving. I would think every work should have something of God in it, whatever one means by "God," so that you can say you have a sense of the presence of the divine. And I think I share that just very normally with artists of all kinds. Much of what may seem strange to talk about in film is very normal to all the arts. It just seems peculiar with respect to *film*. Most people are not expecting of a film and filmmakers what they would ordinarily grant to painting and to painters or to poetry and poets.

MacDonald: Why the title?

Brakhage: "Commingled Containers" is usually what we see on trash receptacles in Boulder, meaning we can put plastic and glass and aluminum cans in this receptacle and they will be separated out later for recycling. I just spent about a year fighting to be sure our apartment complex would have this recycling. You know, you really have to struggle. The landlords aren't interested in it, and they will raise the rent a little as a result. I worked hard on that, so that term was in my mind, but I also thought it meant a lot more than recycling.

Student: Like most of your films, *Commingled Containers* is silent. I wonder if you could comment on the active role of silence in your films.

Brakhage: Well, John Cage wrote a whole book called *Silence* [*Silence: Lectures and Writings by John Cage* (Middletown, Conn.: Wesleyan University Press, 1973)], and he was one of my teachers and a friend. I think of it much more simply than John does. For the *eyes* to have it fully, silence—or quiet, anyway—is best. But on the other hand, sound is a great challenge. If a film seems to need a sound, I won't duck that. It's a challenge to add sound that does not destroy the envisionment of a film. I have made a few that I feel do this sufficiently well that I leave them in distribution. But, basically, I don't see any more reason for a film to have sound than for a painting to have sound. It's just a habit of history that we have that possibility and use it.

MacDonald: I want to end with a question that has to do with last night's screening. An artist of comparable stature in any other field would not fail to fill that auditorium last night. Announced or unannounced, the place would be packed. And so when you come in—and it's a big auditorium and there are not many people, so it's really obvious that it's not full—and you sit down in front and stay for the screening, knowing that it is a difficult film and knowing what is bound to happen, which is that periodically during the screening people are going to stand up and walk out—we *have* passed the age where people yell something on the way out—

Brakhage (laughter): Not entirely!

MacDonald: In any case, I couldn't help thinking about you down there, and I wondered, after all this time and after all this work, does it feel like an insult? It certainly proves to *me* that we in academe have failed terribly with regard to film.

Brakhage: Well, that includes me, too. I'm in academia also, plugging away at it.

MacDonald: What *is* your feeling sitting down there?

Brakhage: Well, it *is* painful, in one sense. I try to develop some techniques, and have I guess, over the years, of saying, "Well, okay, good, let them go and take the bad energy with them." I certainly don't want to trap people, because if you trap people, you get *real* bad energy. And people used to feel trapped by these events, which is why we had these riots. So in the sixties I started encouraging people to feel free to leave, and to have the *ultimate* freedom, which is to feel free to leave *and come back.* You know, go have a smoke or take a walk and come back, and see if it interests you some more—just try not to bother the rest of the audience. I even used to leave the doors open to encourage that in the sixties, because the sixties was a rough time: you had flare-ups over any-thing. I mean, I've been punched; I've been shot at; I've been threatened in the mail, and so on. And one wonders why. It isn't as if I'm doing something that really could be said to be interfering in other people's lives. But, in a way, of course, the arts *are* that. The whole *idea* of the arts is to leave people free, but to *move* them, to affect them. They are free to do what they want to do about it, but if the effect is that they are disturbed, if it touches a nerve, for a moment they may want to kill you.

I used to have a recurring nightmare that someone would stand up when I was lecturing and aim a gun at me and shoot me down. So much violent feel-ing did come across the sixties. I *did* have my life threatened very seriously, by two different people at two different times, and that's scary. I didn't know what they looked like, and (this was in Boulder) every time I went into a store, I won-dered if someone in there might be this person who said he wanted to kill me. I carry the scars of that.

So now I just say to myself, "I hope people are feeling free; I hope I have spoken well enough that they feel free to leave and take that bad energy with them."

Of course, you have to be careful not to judge too harshly; it's not *all* bad energy. I remember one time an elderly woman walked out, very angry, at a showing of *Window Water Baby Moving* in Boulder. The next day the vice-chan-cellor had a complaint that someone was showing pornographic childbirth movies—talk about an oxymoron!—to the students. And I always suspected it was this woman. Two months later, a fairly famous violinist, I forget who, was playing in Boulder, and playing rather badly—an old man and not really able to do it anymore. I was feeling sad and went out into the lobby. I couldn't quite *leave,* but at the same time couldn't stand to stay in there and listen, and *there* was this same woman. We were both there, feeling the grief of that event. She came up to me and said, "You know, I wanted to talk to you. I was *so mad* when you had your show because I had to leave and catch an airplane." That gave me something to think about the rest of my life—you never know *why* people leave, or *why* they look angry.

But, on the other hand, my happiest occasions are when there isn't any danger of this kind of contention. Every Sunday night in Boulder, for over four years now, with the help of Phil Solomon and Robert Shaler, and for a while Suranjan Ganguly, I've run a salon where I show forty-five minutes to maybe an hour and a quarter of short films, my own and those from my collection of trading and swapping films with filmmakers all my life, to what is always somewhere between twenty and thirty people. There's no advertisement; there is a little notice to announce the event—mostly it's word of mouth. People come from out of town and drop in. It's very sweet and quiet. I don't know until twenty minutes before the show what I am going to show because I leave it dependent on the events of the week, the day, or the news, or the weather, whatever, and then put together a little program. And I always make the statement, "Please feel free when the program is over to take the films out into the night or into your life or do whatever you want to do with them. I leave the doors open, so feel free to come and go." People come in late, leave early—no problem. When the show is over, those who want to talk, which is usually half that number, go down the hall to another room, where we can sit around a table, and talk about the films. I am so grateful for it. I gives me all that I need to sustain going on. I invite you all, if you come to Boulder, to join us, every Sunday night at 7:30, right through vacations, all year round. I hope to keep it going forever.

10/28/98

MacDonald: I'd like to come back to *Commingled Containers*. This was the first film in a while where you had photographically exposed imagery.

Brakhage: Yes, in at least two or three years.

MacDonald: And doing it involved baptizing the camera.

Brakhage: Yes. A nice deal had come up on a Bolex. I had worn out my old one shooting *The Mammals of Victoria* [1994]. I had announced—in that way people foolishly do—that I would never photograph again, but, I thought, "It's such a good deal, I should get it just in case."

MacDonald: Could you talk about what the film means to you?

Brakhage: As you know, I was very involved with the possibility of having cancer, and this was causing me to wonder why I would even buy a new camera or bother testing it. All of that thinking is getting translated into what I was seeing in this moment. There was the *surface* of the water, which is like all the fussiness of our daily life; then right under that surface, visible because of the play of water across these rocks, was this very organic-feeling bubble world, slowly evolving—you can't even really call them bubbles; they're

From *Ellipses, Reel 2* (1998), one of
many Brakhage films made without
photography, by using the filmstrip
as a "canvas." Courtesy Marilyn
Brakhage and Fred Camper.

such extraordinary shapes. They *are* bubbles; they're the result of some friction of air and water, but they are all these different, extraordinary shapes that look organic in their fluidity of movement. And deeper than that, there's something spiritual about them. I can't quite say what it is, but I'm certainly recognizing it, and there I am, sweating away over this stream with one foot in the water and the other knee on this rock and bent over and a long time passed—I think I was there about an hour and a half shooting very carefully.

And when the roll came back from the lab, between the exploratory surgery and the removal of the bladder, I was so moved by it, and said, "OK, this is my last film." I didn't really expect to survive. And so I sat and edited it.

I was doing another project at the same time. Joel Haertling had brought over a film of his, which he subsequently titled *Through Wounded Eyes* [1996], four strips of film of a variety of hypnogogic envisioning, which I had painted up for him, plus some footage he had made with a Grummel drill, approximating an eye aberration that he'd had since childhood. Joel had this rage against his brother, who had wounded his eye when they were tiny kids, and he couldn't get over it. I said, "Well, you're an artist, make a film of it," and so he worked and worked for years and years and—this is a beautiful thing—his brother helped him work with the drill to approximate his aberration. He brought the results to me, saying he couldn't do hypnogogic vision, so could I give him some rolls of closed-eye vision?

I had this sense that I couldn't leave Joel in the lurch. I'm the one who had engendered this project of his. I promised to see him through the film, as a kind of sacred collaboration. So with the operation upon me, here we were, desperately trying to beat the clock, and late one Sunday night we finished that film of his through the A, B, C, and D rolls. And I had the operation the next day.

So there were those two films. I laugh sometimes, thinking that it's too bad I *didn't* die, because *Commingled Containers* would be such a great final film! It somehow says it *all,* absolutely obliquely, but with *feeling.* It's a kind of an affirmation and a terror at the same time. It feels organic, *and* it feels scratched by the world, and these two play off against each other—that fussy surface and that bulbous underneath and then the light, which is very spiritual as it's captured by the water.

The camera's fine, by the way; I've made other films with it since.

MacDonald: Was your decision not to shoot film anymore entirely an economic decision?

Brakhage: That, plus the fact that, except for Kodachrome, you just can't work with reversal anymore, and Kodachrome is like one hundred forty dollars for a hundred feet by the time you've paid for all the costs. I just decided, unless I'm going to do little three-minute jewels, which I am now doing again, I can't afford to shoot film.

I've done *Self Song/Death Song* [1997], which are also photographed films, made during my chemotherapy, an attempt to hold onto the body—because chemotherapy is really like a slash-and-burn technique, and you feel that you're doing something terribly wrong to your body: you're burning everything up, hoping to starve out the enemy. It was harder on my boys and on Marilyn than on me—*I* was just sick, but *they* didn't know what was going to happen.

Anyway, one day, just to see if I could do *anything,* I was trying to get back in touch with my body, so I photographed my skin and some other things and finally made a *Self Song.* Then I made the little *Death Song*—maybe I'm going to die, and if I do, this is what it feels like.

MacDonald: Since you've returned to photographing, you've made several of my favorite Brakhage films: *Commingled Containers* and *Cat of the Worm's Green Realm* [1997]. I think the work you're doing now is as good as the best work you've ever done.

Brakhage: Thank you. I feel so, too.

Being older makes for a totally different experience. *Cat of the Worm's Green Realm* began with one of my children calling me out to look at a worm, and their favorite neighborhood wandering cat, Mag Daddy, was also there, and one thing led to another.

My newer work is complicated for people who know my earlier work. Some people have had me so tied up with the Mountain Man and with Jane and the children, and there were those who thought, as I moved on, "Well, that's the end of him." I thought so, too, at times; but I kept going, of course, and gradually there began to be a body of work that was distinct from that early work, and in fact there always had been. Even all those years when I was making those family films, about a third of my filming was involved with other things.

As you get older, something begins happening in the work process that's more natural and not as dramatic. There's a kind of making just coming out of me. A phrase I use sometimes is that I would like to leave something like a snail's trail in the moonlight. The *ellipsis series* [" . . . ", five films, 1998], which I'm working on now, are in reels that can be shown in any order. There's a loosening, a leavening some would say, in my work—and a different process. Being older makes for a totally different experience.

Jill Godmilow (and Harun Farocki)

Jill Godmilow's career as a filmmaker has always been a conscious extension of her commitment to political awareness, dialogue, and engagement. I remember, sometime during the middle to late 1970s, attending an evening of Brakhage films at Colgate University (several films in the *Sexual Meditation* series [1974] were screened) and witnessing Brakhage's discomfiture at the anger of several women who were frustrated at what they perceived as his gender-reactionary glorification of woman-as-mother and woman-as-wife. While Brakhage has always been supportive of women artists (from Gertrude Stein to Maya Deren and Marie Menken to the painter Joan Mitchell), he didn't seem to have considered the gender politics of conventional domesticity. Godmilow, on the other hand, could easily have been one of the angry feminists who confronted Brakhage at Colgate.

From the beginning, making film was Godmilow's way of contesting the politically conventional, and in fact, her arrival on the independent filmmaking scene was signaled by *Antonia: A Portrait of the Woman* (1974), one of the quintessential feminist films of the early 1970s. Produced by Judy Collins and directed by Godmilow, *Antonia* is a portrait of symphony conductor Antonia Brico, who had had early success in confronting the gender restrictions of the world of classical music during the 1930s and 1940s (in 1930 at the age of twenty-eight, Brico was the first woman to conduct the Berlin Philharmonic Orchestra), only to be marginalized as a professional musician for much of her life because of her gender. *Antonia: A Portrait of the Woman* was widely admired (it received a New York Film Critics award and an Academy Award nomination for Best Documentary [in 2003 it was added to the National Film Registry of the Library of Congress]) and was followed by two other capable, politically progressive but formally conventional documentaries: *Nevelson in Process* (1976), a portrait of sculptor Louise Nevelson at work; and *The Popovich Brothers of South Chicago* (1977), about the importance of music in a working-class, Serbian American community.

It was not until she made *Far From Poland* (1984) that Godmilow produced a film that confronted her own conventionality as a filmmaker: specifically, the approach to documentary that had informed her earlier films. Denied a visa to go to Poland to document the early months of the Solidarity movement, Godmilow began to reconsider the time-honored assumption that a documentary was valuable insofar as it recorded "reality" and conveyed to the audience a clear sense of what was happening and what it meant. Unable to function as an on-the-spot witness of Solidarity's impact on Polish politics, Godmilow worked toward a new, "postrealist" documentary aesthetic that could certainly consider the real events occurring in the Polish shipyards, but within a larger consideration of how such events can be and should be represented in film, and of how cinematic representation of real events relates to the lives of those who make such films and those who see them. *Far from Poland* is a landmark of anti-illusionist cinema that finds its closest counterpart in the films of fellow New Yorker Yvonne Rainer, especially Rainer's *Journeys from Berlin/1971* (1979)—a connection Paula Rabinowitz explores in chapter 8 of her *They Must Be Represented: The Politics of Documentary* (New York: Verso, 1994).

Far from Poland includes a variety of dramatizations. Godmilow and Mark Magill, her partner, dramatize their own debates about Godmilow's commitment to a film about Poland; and Ruth Maleczech enacts Polish labor leader Anna Walentynowicz being interviewed during the shipyard strike in Gdansk (Godmilow includes moments from the actual videotape interview with Walentynowicz so we can compare the "reality" with Godmilow's representation of it). These and other reenactments are combined with imagery of pro-Solidarity rallies in the United States, with discussions with Polish exiles, and with Godmilow's conjectures about how the ongoing events in Poland might end, into a film about the complex, elusive nature of political reality in the modern world.

Having come to the conclusion that any film that is successful in convincing viewers that they have seen and now understand "reality" is essentially a fraud, and a particularly dangerous one—since unlike conventional melodrama, a powerful realist documentary is not generally recognized, during or after the screening, *as* an illusion—Godmilow turned away from documentary altogether to work on an experimental melodramatic fiction about Gertrude Stein and Alice B. Toklas, *Waiting for the Moon* (1987). *Waiting for the Moon* uses an unusual narrative approach: Godmilow intercuts between Stein (Linda Bassett) and Toklas (Linda Hunt) proofreading a revision of one of Stein's prose works and tending to a baby during a single summer day in the country; and a narrative involving Stein, Toklas, Ernest Hemingway (Bruce McGill), Guillaume Apollinaire, and a young American committed to the Spanish civil war (Andrew McCarthy) that covers an undesignated period during which Stein discovers she is seriously ill and tries to hide her illness from Toklas. At the conclusion of this rambling narrative, we discover that the baby Gertrude and Alice are tending during the proofreading scenes is Apollinaire's child, now without a father, since Apollinaire has died from eating a poison mushroom.

Godmilow is no more interested in dramatizing a believable illusion of real events in Stein's and Toklas's life together than she was in creating a realistic illusion of current political events in *Far from Poland*. The text Stein and Toklas proofread is not a Stein text at all but an imitation by Mark Magill; and the film's narrative conflates widely disparate periods in Stein's and Toklas's lives. Apollinaire died in 1918, before Hemingway became personally acquainted with Stein and Toklas in 1923, and nearly twenty years before the beginning of the Spanish civil war. That is, Godmilow plays fast and loose with the facts of history, in an attempt to honor Stein's own iconoclastic spirit. What feels like a conventional plot is an obvious fabrication.

In the years since *Waiting for the Moon*, Godmilow has devoted herself to a series of projects honoring the creative contributions of others. The most noteworthy of these are *Roy Cohn/Jack Smith* (1995), a documentation of the late Ron Vawter's one-man show of the same name; and *What Farocki Taught* (1998), a shot-by-shot remake of Harun Farocki's early film about the making of napalm, *Inextinguishable Fire* (1969). These two films are the culmination of a tendency that has been consistently evident in Godmilow's films ever since *Antonia: A Portrait of the Woman*. Godmilow has seen filmmaking as a way of serving not just an intelligent and progressive political agenda but those particular individuals who have struggled to make intelligent and progressive contributions to their particular moments.

When Jonathan Demme failed to produce the documentation of *Roy Cohn/Jack Smith* he told Vawter he would make, Vawter turned to Godmilow. She found a way to record Vawter's performance during his final struggle with AIDS, and by doing so, to honor not only Vawter but also Jack Smith, whose remarkable performance aesthetic had been crucial for Vawter and was a revelation to Godmilow. *What Farocki Taught* was Godmilow's attempt at filmmaking *as* distribution. Furious that she had not had a chance to see Farocki's film until long after Farocki had successfully come to grips with some of the same issues regarding documentary filmmaking that Godmilow had struggled with during the early 1980s, she decided to give Farocki's film a second chance at the American audience it had always deserved, by remaking the film in a manner that would honor Farocki's work without taking its place. Within her remake Godmilow includes moments from the original film so that the viewer can compare her version of *Inextinguishable Fire* with Farocki's own, and as an implicit enticement to viewers to find their way to the original film. In my experience, I have found that critical filmmakers are not particularly generous toward the work of those with similar concerns and approaches. Indeed, Godmilow's generosity throughout her filmmaking is both salutary and moving.

Godmilow and I began our conversation in June 1999 in New York City and continued to talk during her visit to Hamilton College in December 1999 and during phone conversations (and by e-mail) during the following year. In June 2000, Harun Farocki was a guest of the Flaherty Film Seminar. When I learned that Godmilow planned to attend, I made arrangements to speak with both filmmakers during the seminar about *Inextinguishable Fire* and *What Farocki Taught.*

MacDonald: Judging from your films, I'm guessing that the worst thing you could imagine someone saying about you is, "Jill went on and on about herself."

Jill Godmilow: I'm going to surprise you!

MacDonald: I don't know anything about how you got into filmmaking.

Godmilow: Opportunities arose to make films, and I moved into them. I don't think I ever made anything stupid, but I didn't have that "I'm a filmmaker, and I'll be a great filmmaker" attitude. I've never had any compulsive relationship to film or filmmaking at all. And that was lucky for me, because I've never felt I had to have the next film ready when this one's done.

I would say mine was a very unconscious practice, until *Antonia: A Portrait of the Woman,* when I started to see myself as a filmmaker—because that film was very successful. Before that, I was a middle-class girl who was supposed to marry a dentist, and who studied Russian literature in college because she loved it and because it seemed exotic.

The summer before college, I read—it had just been republished—James Agee's *Let Us Now Praise Famous Men* [originally published in 1941], and only many years later did I realize that that book was somehow informing my ideas and my practice. I teach it now as a model for thinking about the dilemmas of documentary, because in some ways Agee is almost trying to *write* a film with those photos and discussions. *That* was the beginning of politics for me: a shocking awareness of class.

And then a year later I went to the University of Wisconsin at exactly the right time (1961–65—"the good years"). At the university I got highly politicized. I found out that politics could be a substitute for living. It was a way to feel your life could matter. I became one of the heads of SNCC [Student Non-violent Coordinating Committee] my senior year—the *full* engagement in politics, *jumping* into it.

I got out of college and came to New York, because I'd been here before and thought there was no other place to live in the world. I had this Puerto Rican boyfriend who was a painter. He didn't finish high school, and therefore was able to say one day, "Let's make a movie!"—because he didn't have any sense of inadequacy about it. I, being college educated and pretty middle-class, said, "Oh, you can't do that. You need millions of dollars and lots of know-how." Joaquin went to the public library and got a book—I don't remember what it was—that said how to make a film, and we made a feature film in Spanish.

MacDonald: That's one of the films there are no prints of.

Godmilow: Right. It was sold to Azteca Films, which was the second-largest distributor of Spanish films in the world, I think.

We knew we didn't know anything. We couldn't imagine making a Doris Day movie. But the French New Wave had arrived here in New York, and there were Truffaut and Godard running around making films that we *could* imagine making.

Joaquin's mother was a bookie; she gave us a thousand dollars. And an ex-college professor of mine, who was kind of in love with me, gave us another thousand dollars. And that was enough. We knew what was going on in Spanish-language cinema at the time: mostly Mexican fare, with beautiful blondes and handsome dark men, and lots of singing numbers in nightclubs—a very old model that no young people were interested in. We thought we had a chance to be successful if we made something that was fresh and kind of Godard-like. We mostly stole a script from a photo-novella, found Spanish-speaking actors, and on thirteen successive weekends we shot *La Nueva Vida.* Insane.

We'd rent camera equipment for Saturday shoots so we could go to get it Friday afternoon, shoot all night Friday night, all day Saturday, all day Sunday, and return it first thing Monday. And the editing—same thing: we would get a Moviola, take it apart, put it in our Volkswagen Beetle, take it downtown, carry it up five flights of stairs. Monday morning we'd do it all in reverse. I had a natural inclination toward editing, so I was the editor.

We had no technique whatsoever and made every mistake in the book. But making the film later allowed me to say I could edit, which of course wasn't true: our film wasn't synch sound, and I didn't even know that you didn't have to use every shot you filmed. My first cut of *La Nueva Vida* had *every* shot in it! I had to figure out everything for myself—we had no film community at all. I was unaware of film societies and the avant-garde. We were on our own.

When we had the film together, we said, "Now what do you do?" I think Joaquin knew somebody who knew somebody at Azteca; they bought it from us for four thousand dollars. We gave them the negative and kept one print; I never saw any of the prints they made. They redubbed the film in Spanish movie style because all our actors were speaking New York Spanglish, which was no good outside of New York. I don't know what happened to that print. We were going to use the money to buy some land in Puerto Rico, but we broke up, and my portion sat in a bank—later it allowed me to buy the loft you and I are sitting in.

I needed a job, and someone gave me the little yellow MPE book [the Motion Picture Enterprises handbook], and some obsessive part of me wrote down the names of all eighty-two editing companies in New York—I still remember the number. They were almost all on Forty-fifth Street between Fifth and Sixth. I talked to the receptionists and got nowhere, until the eighty-second, when a producer heard my rap and said, "I know an editing company that's very short on staff for the summer. Why don't you go over there?" I did and got myself hired, with lies—I said I could sync up dailies.

I spent the first night discovering how to sync sound and image, all by myself, with ten thousand feet of 35mm dailies for Quaker Oats Instant Cinnamon and Spice Cereal ads: three sixties and three thirties. There was a screening the next day at ten o'clock, and I had them ready.

I worked there for three and a half years, first as an assistant editor, then as an editor.

MacDonald: All commercials?

Godmilow: And an after-school special and a few other things. I cut a documentary on Twiggy.

During this time, *Tales* [1969, codirected with Cassandra Gerstein] happened. *Tales* was pretty radical—it was done by an all-woman crew—but also pretty unconscious. It was Cassandra's idea; she invited a bunch of friends, mostly artists—a lot of animators, because she was married to a top commercial animator—to a party and asked them to come prepared to tell some kind of story about sex. We shot it like a candid documentary, which to some extent it was.

If I'm remembering well, the men *all* told stories about sexual conquests; the women told stories about playing strip poker with their cousins when they were seven. It was *really* interesting to find out what people were able to say about sex.

We filmed all evening and through the night, and the last shot is me poking the camera out the window at the dawn. I edited what we had, and somehow—Cassandra had contacts I think—it was picked up by New Line Cinema. They were just beginning and had an odd assortment of films. *Tales* is the most antisexual film in the world, but they thought the topic would sell. It might have had three rentals. But then David Beinstock saw it, and he put it in the very first Whitney New American Filmmakers Series. Jonas Mekas also reviewed it in the *Voice* [on February 4, 1971] (I still have the review!).

So here was another whole world that I didn't know existed. I didn't even know that being part of that series might mean something to somebody. I was learning, but I was still totally unconscious about anything like a film career. Only later, when I made *Antonia: A Portrait of the Woman,* did I start dealing with those things that happen when you begin saying about yourself, "I'm a *filmmaker.*"

There were two prints of *Tales;* both are gone, and the negative is gone, too.

MacDonald: I noticed that the end credits for *Antonia* indicate that the film was directed by you and Judy Collins and produced by Collins, but your vita lists you as sole director.

Godmilow: Because *I* made the film. There are a lot of bad feelings. Judy knew *nothing* about making a film. I directed it, I edited it.

MacDonald: She put up the money?

Godmilow: Yep. She had seen *Tales* and for some reason liked it. We had a mutual friend who had introduced us. I'd moved out to California and was just back east briefly, and the phone rings, and it's Judy Collins saying, "Jill, I'm on my way to Denver in two days, to give a concert, and *Ms.* magazine has asked me to write an article about a major female role model of mine, this woman who was my piano teacher. The drummer in my band has a Bolex"—this is my life; this is how my films have happened!—"and *he* says, Why don't I take the Bolex out there and *film* the interview. Would you help me?" Then she told me about Antonia, who was a very interesting character.

Judy was assuming I was a cameraperson, which I'm not. So I said—I don't know where *this* came from—"Do you have two thousand dollars? For two thousand dollars, I could get you a cameraman; I could do sound; we could get on a plane; we could buy ten rolls of film; and we could make a real film about her." She said okay. My boyfriend at the time, Coulter Watt, was a cameraman; and I knew what a Nagra was. In two days we were on a plane to Denver.

We shot about a third of the film (the formal part of the interview in the house and the rehearsal in the church), came back, synched it up, and I thought, "There's a film here." I asked Judy if she could commit to making a film—she was at the height of her career and had plenty of money—and she got excited. We did three more shoots in Denver that year.

Making the film was a very pleasant experience, a good collaboration. I directed every scene, and every idea was mine. Of course, when the film was done and it was a big success, shockingly so—and I know it probably got the chance to *be* a success because of her name—the press wrote about it as *her* film. I had to fight her for even a codirecting credit. I kept saying, "Listen to your heart; *I* was in the editing room," but she continued to allow the press to write about it as entirely *her* film. In revenge, I list myself as sole director in my vita (I list her as producer).

When we were nominated for the Academy Award, David Geffen had just started Geffen Records and was trying to woo her; and *he* told her that we should- n't do any advertising for the film, because advertising was crude and undigni- fied and shouldn't be part of her image. In those days, and particularly in the documentary section of the Academy Awards, the people voting on films often didn't see all the films; they voted for the films they'd heard of. We were up against *Hearts and Minds,* made by a Hollywood company that put full- page ads in the *Hollywood Reporter* every day. We wanted to win; we thought by now that *Antonia* was a great film, and finally, I did convince her, and we took two full-page ads in the *Hollywood Reporter;* I can see them to this day. We didn't win, of course.

MacDonald: There's something about Antonia Brico's looks that runs so counter to how women are allowed to look in a movie.

Godmilow: Or how you're allowed to *be* as a conductor. Particularly at a time when there were no women at all conducting, here's this little, hunched-over leprechaun of a woman conducting a hundred men.

MacDonald: It's still a strong film because she's such a compelling person.

Godmilow: A very *clear* person, and also a fabulous film subject because she literally had never seen a film and she didn't have a TV. She was the only person I've ever filmed who did not have a media image of herself. We *all* perform an idea of ourselves as we've fashioned it from media. But Antonia never posed for the camera. She was completely raw that way—and anxious to tell her story.

MacDonald: How did she feel about the film?

Godmilow: I think she liked it, but she never told me as much. She did very well by the film; it got her some nice gigs—"Mostly Mozart" for the New York Philharmonic, for one—but her new career didn't last, and she was back in Denver a year later conducting local orchestras. She just died, at ninety-four [in 1989].

The reason the film got distributed was that I met Jerry Bruck, a fabulous guy from Montreal who pretty much invented self-distribution. He'd made a one-hour film [*I. F. Stone's Weekly,* 1973] about I. F. Stone, who put out this weekly newspaper. Bruck was a tough little businessman with tons of energy, and he moved that film around. He got libraries to buy it and showed it in every theater he could fight his way into. He never made a second film.

Anyway, he came to me and wanted to piggyback *Antonia* with *I. F. Stone's Weekly* for its second run. Judy and her people agreed to let me work with the film for a while, and Jerry helped me find my way into feminist screenings and feminist benefits, and I went across the country with the film. The women's movement took it up, all across the country, as did museums that were just developing film series.

MacDonald: It was the perfect role-model movie.

Godmilow: Which is just what we were all doing at that moment! Actually, John Hanhardt, who was still at the Walker, saw it at the Ann Arbor Film Festival, where it won some sort of special jury prize (I still have a soft spot in my heart for the Ann Arbor Film Festival—I wouldn't make a film without sending it there), and called me. He'd just been hired as the curator of film at the Whitney, and he said, "I'm moving to New York; can I have it for the opening film?" The Whitney had a great press team, and since it was the opening film of his series, every New York critic wrote about it; there was even a review in the *New Yorker!* And they were raves. Then it played sixteen weeks in Boston

Antonia Brico in Jill Godmilow's *Antonia: A Portrait of the Woman* (1974). Courtesy Jill Godmilow.

and ten weeks in Chicago, and in San Diego, and L.A., and about thirty other cities. I did self-distribution for a year and a half. I didn't get rich, but I made some money, a salary of about three hundred dollars a week.

Then Judy's people realized that the film had gotten hot, and Rocky Mountain Films sold it to Phoenix Films, who exploited it like mad, sold 250 prints; it was in every public library in America. I got 11 percent of Judy's profits (the real profits went to other people).

But *Antonia* made me a fundable filmmaker, and suddenly there was the New York State Council on the Arts [NYSCA], and the NEA, and I could apply and sometimes get money to make films. I went almost twenty years without having to do anything but work on my films, except for a bit of editing from time to time. That was a good run.

But by the early nineties, when I got to be fifty, I looked around and said, "Well, I don't think I want to be a bag lady, I'd better get a job where there's a pension plan and a health plan"—NYSCA was now funding primarily multicultural work, and I could no longer get a grant—and so I ended up at Notre

Dame, with what turned out to be a very good job, teaching film production and film criticism.

MacDonald: I remember seeing the *Far from Poland* script come through the NYSCA funding panel and thinking, "What the hell is *this?*" When I finally saw the film, not long ago, it seemed *so* inventive. I'm a great admirer of Yvonne Rainer's films, and a lot of what she's doing in her films is also there in *Far from Poland.* I'm thinking especially of the use of current political issues and events, surrounded by your personal relationship, which you're dramatizing—I assume on the basis of real personal struggles you were going through or had gone through.

Godmilow: My partner at the time, Mark Magill, was tremendously helpful—more than just helpful. He wasn't a theorist, but he was in a world that was already postmodern and thinking about representation. He helped me find the freedom to take all those chances, some of which were scary, particularly playing myself. We were from different generations; he was younger, a member of the generation that felt that anybody who was still politically involved was lost. All that shit he says to me in the opening section, the soap opera part of the film, comes directly from our conversations.

I had come out of this heroic, feminist moment of documentary, where one was ready to do *anything* to get the film you wanted: we actually *planned* to make Antonia cry, and pushed her and pushed her, because we hadn't seen *rage.* She was a pretty spiritually evolved person, had found her way to Yogananda, and really *didn't* live in anger. Though I didn't realize it then, I can see now that she already knew exactly how to live—no hopes, no fears. But we were young filmmakers and feminists, and we wanted rage (we called it "wanting her to get in touch with her anger"), and we provoked it. Finally, she flowed for twenty minutes.

Obviously, I wouldn't do that today.

When *Far from Poland* was finished and I had decided to like it, and not be embarrassed by it (*even* in spite of Jim Hoberman calling me an asshole in print for having made the film), I could look back at *Antonia* and see that, despite the fact that it was beautifully put together, it was *bullshit* in its creation of a pat heroism in Antonia. At the very end, after the final sequence, I end the film with twenty-three frames that were exposed when the camera was being taken off the tripod, twenty-three frames of nothing; I see now—and I don't think I'm mythologizing myself—that that was a tiny act of resistance to my own part in producing what was a kind of bullshit heroic film moment.

MacDonald: How did *Far from Poland* develop?

Godmilow: It was invented, piece by piece, with a couple of very important people in my life sitting behind me saying, "Just keep trying; it'll become something." At that point, I certainly didn't have a clear picture of what I call now a "post-realist nonfiction film."

MacDonald: When I think of *Antonia, Far from Poland,* and *What Farocki Taught*—the films I'm most familiar with—

Godmilow: Those are my only good ones! I got nervous when you said you wanted to see the others!

MacDonald: For me the drama of your work, both the work you like and the work you're embarrassed about now, is that you're trying to be intelligent about what you're doing *without giving up the idea of serving.*

Godmilow: And teaching.

MacDonald: Your redoing the Anna Walentynowicz interview (and also the William Raymond performance of the censor, K-62) is very similar to what you did later in *What Farocki Taught:* you have somebody reenact an interview and declare that it *is* a reenactment by showing parts of the original interview.

Godmilow: You're right, and I've never noticed that.

MacDonald: The paradox is that you hate heroic *portraits,* but you still love heroism. That's the argument between you and Mark Magill in *Far from Poland:* he wants you to give up the bullshit of representing people in a certain way, but you hold on to the idea that some people sometimes *do* heroic things.

Godmilow: In fact, in *Far from Poland* I tell the story about how much of a pain in the ass Anna *was* during the martial law period, with her little hunger strike, *just* as she's being lifted by the crane up over the sixteen thousand workers. The original interview was set up to make her *so* heroic that I wanted to interrupt or complicate it, bring it back to something real.

The two things come together: you can't have progressive change without annoying people. But it's true: I *do* fall in love with the Annas of the world.

MacDonald: You described *Far from Poland* as a kind of assemblage; I'd like to hear about that process.

Godmilow: Well, I'm in Poland doing these tapes about Jerzy Grotowski, the theater director [Godmilow's *With Grotowski, at Nienadowka,* an hour-long documentary about Grotowski, was finished in 1979], because Andre and Chiquita Gregory have asked me to go film with them, when the strikes start in the shipyards. My reaction is, "Oh, wow, we have to go to Gdansk; I have to go shoot it!"—the old impulse, to shoot the "real thing" as it's happening—but we couldn't go because we were Grotowski's guests. Nobody knew how this Solidarity thing was going to play out, and he could have ended up in jail if someone invited to Poland under his auspices got involved with the workers. So, with great restraint, we finished shooting with him, and then I rushed back to New York, found some quick money—pretty easily—and got ready to go back to Poland to shoot a documentary about what was happening there. I thought it was going to be the most important thing that happened in the twentieth century. I wasn't so far wrong.

I wanted to go watch these people, who had spent fifty years talking in *code,* suddenly able to speak. That's why so much of *Far from Poland* is about speaking and texts that get published and what it *means* to communicate like that—horizontally. I put a crew together, applied for the visas, but I was just a bit late: the Polish government had decided they couldn't give one more visa to a journalist because Warsaw was full of journalists. I tried everything. I pulled a lot of strings with some State Department connections. But I couldn't go.

I was depressed, because it never happens that you *have* the money and can't shoot the film! This friend of mine, a composer, Michael Sahl, who didn't know any better, said, "Well, that shouldn't be any reason why you can't make a film! Just start collecting stuff about being *here* while that's going on *there*." I argued; I bitched; I didn't want to hear it. I *wanted* to be miserable, but somehow he got through to me, and when he left at about four in the morning, I decided I *would* find some way to document those events here, and wait and see what happened next.

I got going, piece by piece. I had met Andrzej Tymowski, an anarchist who came out of the Polish community in Michigan, a Polish American who spoke good Polish, when I was looking for a translator to go to Poland with me and had asked him if he'd go. He'd said, "In a minute!" He knew a lot of the intellectuals who were helping the workers in Gdansk, including two, Irina and Jan Gross, who I interviewed in New Haven. They'd been part of the 1969 generation in Poland but were Jews and had had to get out of there, because the Poles—after a big political movement—always blame Jews.

But Irina and Jan were still connected—it was their generation of university students who were advising the workers. That was what got me the most excited about Solidarity: the serious collaboration between intellectuals, who do have certain skills, and the workers, which was part of Solidarity from the beginning. I thought it could be the model for every country, and that *that's* what needed to get documented. I thought the Left was *fucked* in this country, but that the Poles had found the way out.

Then, I found Marty Lucas, an itinerant videographer. I was still, and still am, very much a filmmaker. I've done some tapes, but if I *possibly* can, I'll shoot on film; I like the authority and weight of the film image, and the attention it can get. I've seen people get attention with video, but *I* don't know how to do it. Film and video are *not* the same thing. The order of meaning in video is different. People call everything filmmaking now, and it drives me crazy.

I started out shooting tape instead of film because I didn't know what I was getting into and tape was a lot cheaper. Marty became a kind of collaborator, and we went to this rally—there had begun to be rallies—and there's Barbara Garson doing her sixties speeches, and Michael Harrington calling the Solidarity movement a Socialist movement. We collected all that. Andy also translated the Anna Walentynowicz interview and showed it to me. It was stunning.

That same week I saw Mabou Mines' production of *Dead End Kids* (which is about science and nuclear energy and the whole fascination with "the secret

Ruth Maleczech as welder and Solidarity union activist Anna Walentynowicz in
Godmilow's *Far from Poland* (1984). Courtesy Jill Godmilow.

element," all the way from the alchemists to Hiroshima). Ruth Maleczech did
a performance of Madame Curie, based on her diaries, in a perfect Polish-French
accent—one of the most amazing performances I've ever seen. When I saw her
do Curie, I knew I could reenact some of the Solidarity material. And that's
when I jumped into the film with some confidence. Ruth seemed perfect to play
Anna Walentynowicz and was willing to work with us.

In *Far from Poland* she's both reading a text and performing, what I call, for
lack of a better term, "a reader's performance." She's not trying to *become*
Walentynowicz; she's respeaking, reperforming her words. It's hard to describe.
I shot it on tape first to see if my theory was right: whether you could take texts
from Poland and reenact them and make a film that was really *about* Poland,
without the "*I* can represent Poland because I was *there* and I shot this footage
and here it is, and therefore you can believe me" pedigree—which I've come
to believe is a deeply corrupt dimension of documentary. It seemed like a
delicious way to go.

And then there was this terrible problem of making a film about something
that was still happening and wouldn't stop—*not* something I'm anxious to try
again. *Impossible!* But it was a fascinating dilemma: the question of when

documentaries stop, and how they usually try and close things that shouldn't be closed, and all that comes with that. So how *do* you end a film about ongoing events? My solution was to go way up ahead of events and to dramatize something that couldn't possibly have happened yet, something that would happen in the late eighties. I still like that ending, but I think by the end of the film, most people are just too exhausted to take it in. Finally, martial law was declared in Poland, and my beautiful movement was shut down.

I struggled with all those wonderful issues. I did feel that for once *I* was deciding what was important to speak about—instead of letting what was possible to *film* tell me what I could speak about—and that was a great gift, and the reason why I don't think I could ever go back to a classic realist documentary practice.

I still like *Far from Poland* a lot. But it's too long.

MacDonald: Let me go back to two films you made before *Far from Poland: The Popovich Brothers of South Chicago* and *Nevelson in Process.* Both are pretty conventional docs, just the kind of thing you moved away from. The Nevelson piece seems to go back to *Antonia,* especially in the sense that what seems to fascinate you about her is her physicality as a person doing something.

Godmilow: Yes. Well, given the stuff she was working on then, it seemed that the thing to do *was* to watch process. I agree that the film is conventional—it does her bio, roughly, and all that, but there's Louise running around that foundry: you could *see* her ideas at work.

MacDonald: What's with those eyelashes, by the way?

Godmilow: Well, she didn't have much in the way of real eyelashes, and like most women wanted more. And this is what I love about her: she couldn't just put on fake eyelashes as if they were her own. She glued five sets together and put them on, so they would be obviously artificial.

MacDonald: Self-reflexive eyelashes!

Godmilow: Exactly! Those eyelashes also account for the fact that there are no on-camera interviews in the film, which is pretty unusual for a portrait of an artist. We had planned to do an interview but ended up deciding to use just her voice; you could not see her eyes from any camera position. I'm glad, because she's been interviewed so many times and has so many stock lines about who she is and how she became that way—she sounds full of shit. So we got her a little loose with some wine and used just a tape recorder, and she told us lots of stuff she had never before told in public—some of it so personal we didn't feel it should be in a public document like a film.

MacDonald: She's certainly learned how to get the guys she's working with do what she needs them to do.

Godmilow: She does a kind of Jewish mother shtick. For all her strength, she still needs to use classic female communication techniques to get what she wants and to make everybody feel they're part of what's going on. It took me a while to give up hating her for this. As she explains in the film, to be a female painter was one thing, but to say, "I'm going to sculpt, and I'm going to work big" was *really* male terrain. I ended up with tremendous respect for her. It wasn't that hard, in 1967, for a woman to say, "I'm going to make a film." It was a lot easier than for Louise in 1930 to say, "I'm going to make sculpture." She was tough.

MacDonald: The Popovich Brothers is a capable film, and in some ways I like it, but in the wake of the recent wars in the Balkans, the film has a different read. One has to question their focus on their ethnicity.

Godmilow: I understand what you mean, and at times that's made me self-conscious, but in the end I decided it's a false question. The Serbian American community—the grandfather came here in 1905 or 1910—deeply feels its Serbianness and is very interested in maintaining it just to have a community, and the music is the key. I'm embarrassed for them to have the word "Serb" mean monstrous ethnocentric rapist. *These* people are, in fact, salt of the earth, very generous, very democratic, and not ethnocentric at all. They are in no way supporters of Milosovic and his gang.

The Popovich brothers are second generation; they're shop stewards, union guys. The film was criticized at the Flaherty [the Flaherty Film Seminar]: somebody said, "Yeah, but what about racism; you don't deal with racism! Those workers hate blacks." Another of those documentary dilemmas. Can you make a loving portrait of working-class people, without dealing with *all* the issues that surround them? I understood the questioning at the Flaherty, and I've probably asked other filmmakers the same question, but in *this* instance it was completely inappropriate! *[Laughter.]*

The film was in some way *about* the issue of cultural ethnicity. How is it that four generations later, kids in South Chicago proudly call themselves Serbian Americans? What's the mechanism? For Serbians it's clearly music. These guys are deeply involved in the musical life, which is their social life as well. They really *have* joyous shared traditions.

It's also true that I couldn't make *Popovich* today—after *Far from Poland* and the transformation in my thinking that that film represents. I couldn't make it *because* it excludes important questions about representation. *Popovich* seems to assume that there are no questions about that ethnic community, except how long will it last?

If I made *The Popovich Brothers* now, it's not just that I'd just ask additional questions, about racism in their community and whatever. I'd give up *the whole form of the film,* the whole conceit that if I work hard enough I can *deliver* this community to you in my one-hour documentary. In other words, I wouldn't use the conventional form that implicitly says, "Because this is unscripted and unrehearsed material, it's the Truth, and all you really need to know."

If I did a film about them now, it would still be as loving, because I did end up loving this family, and wishing it were mine; and I still respect their music. The film just wouldn't take the same shape. And that's a *big* difference. I don't even know if the brothers would participate in *that* film, though they probably would, because while you could say that in some ways they are parochial and unsophisticated, they were also highly intelligent and capable of trust.

MacDonald: Now that you mention family, it occurs to me that I don't know anything about yours.

Godmilow: I'm an assimilated Jew with second-generation parents who went to university and became dentists. I grew up in the suburbs of Philadelphia, part of suburban culture in the fifties—detestable!

MacDonald (laughter): So you're on the run from your *own* heritage.

Godmilow: I've been running as fast as I can all my life. The politics of the sixties gave me the chance to get out. I feel blessed to have come into adult consciousness at a moment when there was something to give yourself to, because I had no real community.

My sister and I were the only Jews in our high school. I had to ask a junior to my senior prom so I could go, because I would never have been asked. I did go, but spent most of the prom smoking cigarettes in the parking lot in resistance against the whole thing, and was punished for smoking. It was very subtle discrimination; nobody ever called me a "dirty Jew," or anything like that, but I was miserable.

I went to a Quaker work camp the summer before my senior year, which was really the beginning of my life. My mother always had a feeling for Quakers and was sick of watching us hang around at the local swimming pool all summer. She found the American Friends Service Committee workshops, and my sister went off to Great Barrington, Massachusetts, to build a grease pit for a halfway house; and I went off to spend a whole summer in Lilleborn, Missouri, to put tin roofs on sharecroppers' houses. The other kids at the workshop were from progressive schools in New York and were way ahead of me politically and socially. They'd picketed Woolworth's and had been to Paris and had sat where de Beauvoir and Sartre had sat, and so on. I sucked up an education that summer, because it was the first time I saw a life that wasn't about whether you were pretty enough to attract a guy and get a friendship ring.

Then I had to tolerate my senior year in high school! But I *knew* now that there *was* a world and that there were things to do. So I was saved by the Quakers, and every year I contribute money to them. I fiercely reinvented myself in about six months.

On the other hand, I consider myself completely a Jew, culturally. *That* you don't escape. Talking about medical problems at the dinner table—I'm *constantly* reminded that I do that. Other people are horrified. So I certainly *am* Jewish. But I'm also a badly practicing Buddhist. When I got this job at Notre Dame and had to fill out the forms—and only at Notre Dame would they ask you what religion you are—I wrote "Born Jew, practicing Buddhist: can you handle that?" I guess they could.

MacDonald: Following on the heels of *Far from Poland, Waiting for the Moon* is an interesting project, because here you take a set of historical realities and fictionalize dimensions of them.

Godmilow: Right.

MacDonald: Let's talk first about the collaboration that resulted in the film. The third draft of the script says "story by Jill Godmilow and Mark Magill"; the film itself says "written by Mark Magill, directed by Jill Godmilow." This is a film about a couple and a certain tension between them, which I'm tempted to read as partly about you and Magill, a follow-up to the tensions in *Far from Poland.*

Godmilow: You'd be overreading. Mark and I developed the story together. But Mark *was* the writer, and he was the one who could write in "Stein-ese." So he did the writing, and I directed the film.

MacDonald: He does Stein very well.

Godmilow: I adored it. I'd say, "We need a scene that does so and so," and we'd talk about it, and he'd come back with a draft. We would *re*write it together; but he was the one who could look at a blank page and come up with something.

That film started at the very first moment when filmmakers realized that you could make a dramatic feature outside of Hollywood. Everybody was saying, "You just do it for a hundred thousand dollars." With *Far from Poland* I had pretty much burned my bridges on documentary. I thought I'd said everything I had to say about it, and that was that.

Mark and I were sitting around, goofing, at the kitchen table, and I said, "Let's make a feature for a hundred thousand dollars." And nobody remembers who exactly said what, but one of us said, "It would have to take place all in one room"—meaning that's not much money. And the other said, "What room would that be?" We were both crazy for Gertrude Stein, and so one of us said, "the salon room at 27 rue de Fleurus [Gertrude Stein and Alice B. Toklas's Paris home]," which to me was the most exciting room in all the history that I knew, because of what went on there and who passed through there: Gertrude and Alice themselves, plus everybody else that was important in art during the first half of the twentieth century, plus the paintings covering the walls. An incredible room.

So that was where the idea came from, and then we set out to write a script that we could shoot for one hundred thousand dollars. What we actually wrote in that first draft must not have looked much like what we ended up with (I don't remember too much about it), because in the end, *Waiting for the Moon* cost nine hundred fifty thousand dollars.

Our idea was to make a film about famous historical characters but refuse the burden of historical accuracy—in fact, to flaunt inaccuracy. It seemed like an absolutely *Stein* idea. We did *not* want to do a film that aped her writing style but something that caught her spirit of not being interested in facts. We wanted to present Hemingway and Apollinaire, but to confound the possibility that these

Godmilow (*in middle*) and crew, shooting café scene for *Waiting for the Moon* (1987). Courtesy Jill Godmilow.

events were in any way what actually happened, the Truth. This idea comes right out of *Far from Poland.*

MacDonald: Of course, the more you know about the period, the more you recognize the fabrications. I'm sure some people think it's pretty close to the reality.

Godmilow: Oh, I've gotten letters saying, "I didn't realize Gertrude was that ill!"

It never occurred to us that anyone would be fooled. We both assumed that we were writing for the most sophisticated audience we could imagine. I'm not a believer at all in talking down. We assumed our audience would know that Apollinaire was dead in 1918, and that Hemingway wasn't on the scene until 1923, and that Gertrude and Alice never raised a child, and so on. And yet we wanted to have all those people *in* the film because they were so much a part of her life and had become so much a part of Stein lore.

One of the things that kicked the film off was that my mother sent me, for my birthday, *The Encyclopedia of Literature.* I opened it and looked up Stein, and it said, as probably many books do, "famous writer, da da da da, many famous friends, she lived with her secretary Alice B. Toklas." One goal for the film was to correct that notion of their relationship. I always believed that Alice could write (and in *The Autobiography of Alice B. Toklas* Gertrude lets us know this is true). We wanted to have Alice be as smart as Gertrude and to suggest that writing is a dialogue with the world and very often a dialogue with a partner.

Also, of course, Gertrude and Alice were a couple in every sense of the word. The idea of them having a personal, domestic problem, a classic couple problem, which was also linked to Gertrude's attitude about what's important and what's not, was the way that we thought we could *insist* they were a couple. But, of course, because I didn't do the sex scene, because I didn't want to feel obliged to provide "proof" that they were lesbians (and I was fully conscious about my decision *not* to do that), some people thought I was representing them as just two friends. The gay community attacked the film and said, "Where's the sex!"

I knew that I wouldn't have had to do much: if I'd had a double bed and arranged the sheets so that it was clear that Alice also slept in the bed, *that* would do it. But I wasn't even willing to do that much. I took some shit for it, but I would make the same decision today.

MacDonald: The film seems to recognize that when you're a couple for a certain period of time, and they were a couple for a *long* time, sex ceases to be this big thing: it's *not* the focus of the relationship anymore; work is, or the experience of sharing a life.

Godmilow: But in that moment, with hardly any gay feature films out in the world, I guess the gay community felt I had stolen a major lesbian literary figure, probably the most important one, and turned her into a heterosexual. I was completely aware that that criticism would come, but I couldn't change my mind. Besides I don't like sex scenes in films.

MacDonald: I hate sex scenes.

Godmilow: I don't want to be where two people I don't know are screwing. I wouldn't be there in life, and I don't understand why the cinema has this special dispensation to show you things that you wouldn't know about your closest friends. I've always resisted it. I don't think those scenes work. They're never erotic. (Well, there are a few exceptions, like Harvey Keitel and Holly Hunter in *The Piano* [1993]: very hot, but I hate the politics of the sex, so let's rule even that out.)

When the film was done, they sent me off on a press junket to fifteen cities in thirteen days. Every interviewer would sooner or later say, "Well, *were* they?" And I'd say, "Of course!" And they'd say, "Well, how come we don't *see* it!?" Men were angry about this, even though we were talking about two old ladies. To feel obliged to prove that they love each other by showing them having sex—*that* would have been a sexist thing to do; you wouldn't have to prove a heterosexual couple was heterosexual by showing sex. And Gertrude and Alice never talked or wrote about sex, so showing their sex wouldn't have been true to them.

Also it was partly a response to the Hemingway scene in *A Moveable Feast* where he *forces* you to conjure up some idea of Alice and Gertrude in a sexual relationship.

MacDonald: Well, he's focusing on his youthful shock about their having a more complex relationship than he had imagined. We feel the embarrassment we always feel on coming upon the sexual goings-on of friends or family.

Another possibility: couldn't they be lesbians but not have sex?

Godmilow: Or not be having it anymore. I wanted all those questions open.

I did not set out to make a lesbian movie, or to prove that Gertrude was a lesbian. I set out to make a film about Stein and about a relationship, and about where work comes from. Of course, Gertrude would be *impossible* as a partner, not because she was nasty but because of her ideas, which I so love and respect. I think she's the most important writer in English in the twentieth century. I know you admire Hemingway, so I'm sure you'll disagree.

MacDonald: I'd certainly agree she's one of them.

Godmilow: She and Joyce are my two.

MacDonald: I'd say she, Joyce, Hemingway, Faulkner. Unlike the others, Stein has had incredible influence on film (on Brakhage and Frampton, for example) and on art, and also on writing: the history of visual poetry, or "concrete poetry," is full of Stein references. But Hemingway is the crucial figure in transforming what Americans understand correct prose to be.

Godmilow: I'll give you that. But on the level of *ideas* about *art,* she's unbelievable.

MacDonald: On the version of the script I have, the title is "On the Trail of the Lonesome Pine," which makes sense because that was Stein's favorite song. How did the title end up being "Waiting for the Moon"?

Godmilow: I *hate* that title. We fought for "On the Trail of the Lonesome Pine." It made a lot of sense to us, because the song is full of *June, moon, spoon*—the language thing. Lindsay Law of American Playhouse said that the title was too long for the marquee, that we had to change it, that it didn't make any sense and sounded like a cowboy movie. Sandra Schulburg, our producer, agreed with Lindsay. We fought them tooth and nail, and finally won—down to the day when the titles had to be ordered, at which point the insurance company that was giving us the "errors and omissions" policy (that's an insurance policy that all films have to have, so that if a film is sued for any reason, a broadcaster or an exhibitor isn't liable for a lawsuit) got squeamish. Just at that moment, MCA was reissuing a Laurel and Hardy film based on the Broadway show *The Trail of the Lonesome Pine.* The insurer said they wouldn't give us the policy unless we changed the title. So we had to come up with a new title almost overnight, and all the ideas, including the one we ended up using, sucked.

MacDonald: How did you decide on the structure? It's a very formal structure for a narrative piece: intercutting between the day of the proofreading and the movement through an ongoing historical time.

Godmilow: It was just an experiment to see if you could represent two kinds of time happening in different registers. One reason to do that is to set up questions about the narrative. We thought that because there's a baby in the proofreading scenes, one of the games of the film—and I don't think it was all that successful—would be the audience wondering, "Whose baby *is* this?" Of course, the idea of Gertrude Stein with a baby is ridiculous. Actually, we thought two questions would hold the film together: Is Gertrude ever going to tell Alice about the illness? And how did Alice and Gertrude get a baby?

MacDonald: By making proofreading the activity that, ultimately, the narrative must be delivered *to* (by means of the baby arriving), you privilege the fact of their working together on their life's work. After all, the *only* reason we care about Stein and Toklas is not because they're lesbians (or not lesbians) but because of the work that came out of their partnership.

Godmilow: Absolutely! The other shit just doesn't matter.

MacDonald: How did Linda Hunt get involved in the film?

Godmilow: I was so interested in being antihistorical that when we started casting, I tried to countercast, refusing to use an actress who looked like Stein. So I sent Linda Hunt the script and asked if she would play *Stein,* and I'll never forget this moment. She comes to the casting session, and as she marches across my loft toward where we're sitting, says she adores the script and wants to do the film, but there's a problem: "I'm here. I can play Gertrude Stein with my hands tied behind my back, but I *will* not. I *will* play Alice."

I said, "Of course, you *could* play Alice, but why?"

And she said, "Because I'm *always* cast as the Other, and what I'm interested in learning how to play is the normal, the wife." And I said, "Well, you can play Alice, but who can play Gertrude against *you?*"

In the end it forced us into a more traditional, "realistic" casting, but I was willing to do it to have Linda in the film—not for publicity reasons, marquee value, but just because she's so wonderful. And I dug her attitude. I'll tell you, Scott, I could have had any woman in the country for Gertrude—it was unbelievable. Tyne Daily. Angelica Houston. Colleen Dewhurst.

I even asked Eva Mattes, the brilliant German actress (she plays Fassbinder in *A Man Called Eva* [1984, directed by Radu Gabrea] and Celeste in Percy Adlon's film of the same name). Eva wanted to do it but couldn't get close to an American accent. There was good *language* in the film and a great character that every powerful woman in the film business wanted to play. But to countercast—that was fundamental in my thinking.

Linda Hunt found us Linda Bassett, who is a wonderful actress but had never been in a movie before. Linda Hunt took responsibility to work with her, and she did just fine—but in the end it was not what I wanted.

MacDonald: Given how much you and I have argued about Hemingway, I'm surprised at how kind you are to him in this film. I don't know whether you *mean* it as kind, but I like the character.

Godmilow: Tell me why.

Linda Bassett as Gertrude Stein and Andrew McCarthy as a young American traveling through France in Godmilow's *Waiting for the Moon* (1987). Photograph by Maryse Alberti. Courtesy Jill Godmilow.

MacDonald: He has a sense of humor; he certainly gives and takes with Alice and Gertrude. He's who he is; he's warm with the child, and he's a riot during the scene where they're staging the play.

The achievement of the film is to do this clearly fictional treatment of historical reality and yet bring through some real sense of who these people probably were.

Godmilow: Thank you so much. That *was* the idea. We wanted to see if we could get at the truth, not because we studied their diaries and had all the details correct but in some deeper, artistic sense.

MacDonald: What was the impetus for *Roy Cohn/Jack Smith?* Did you know Smith? I'm sure, knowing you, that you followed Roy Cohn's career.

Godmilow: Roy Cohn I followed, but didn't know much about Jack Smith. I missed being part of that underground scene that knew to go to Jack Smith's loft at two o'clock in the morning to see him make a performance. I have few regrets in my life, but that's one. I only knew *Flaming Creatures* [1963], which I thought was one of the most astounding films I'd ever seen. But I did not know Smith's performance work at all.

I *was* a close friend of Ron Vawter, and I saw the dress rehearsal before he opened *Roy Cohn/Jack Smith,* and it was a revelatory evening for me. The Roy

Cohn part not so much, except that Ron was such a superior performer that he could *do* Roy Cohn that fast and that well. But the *Smith* part was stunning, because Ron made it so hard to get to Smith. His chaise lounge was so aggressively deep downstage: you had to stare as hard as you could—and wait through the pauses and delays. And there was this slide show going on all the time that you couldn't quite read. I *hated* Jack Smith through the whole thing—the way that middle-class society can't stand someone *that* affected—but somehow by hanging in there to the end (and because Jack was a genius, and I'm a sucker for smarts), I began to see how Ron's performance was working to honor Jack's outrageous performance, and I felt that it was one of the most important things that had ever happened to me in the theater. Somehow by the end of it I felt that I had understood for the first time what all the affect of gay style was about. *Ron's* performance helped me realize that Jack was the daddy of all of what came to be called performance art, and even of what performance art was about.

As far as I know, there's very little documentation of Smith's performances (I found only one little film by Midi Onodera where you can't really see what Jack is doing). Ron was determined to do justice to Jack. He's actually wearing a bug in his ear during the performance, so he can hear an audiotape of Jack's performance of *What's Underground about Marshmallows.* For Ron, who talks very fast—more like Cohn—to perform Jack Smith's glacial speech, he had to wear a bug. Timewise, the piece is absolutely Jack Smith. Ron knew Jack very well and studied his performances. Ron wasn't *close* to Smith, who he said was the most frightening man he'd ever met, but he loved what he did in the theater.

Ron said he made the piece because when he was young and coming to terms with being gay, the two models he could identify were Jack Smith and Roy Cohn, and they *both* terrified him. Were *these* the possibilities?

The night after I saw Ron do the performance, I approached him and said, "There *has* to be some record of this. Can I film it?" I'd never wanted to film a performance, so I knew this would bring a new set of challenges. And Ron said yes. So I started fund-raising—and found absolutely nothing. The project was put on hold. Meanwhile, *Roy Cohn/Jack Smith* was a huge success touring Europe, and won Best New Play in London. Maybe two years later—I had just come out to South Bend to teach—I got a phone call from Ron: "Jill, Jonathan Demme has asked if he can make a film of *Roy Cohn/Jack Smith.* Would you give it up?"

MacDonald: I was going to ask how Demme's name got on the film. Because his *Swimming to Cambodia* [1987] is, for me, the great performance film.

Godmilow: It's not a pretty story. Of course, the reason Ron was asking me to give up the project was that if Demme did it, there would be some money in it for him—Ron, sick with AIDS, wasn't able to pay his medical bills. I immediately said, "Absolutely." My original instinct had not been *my next film,* but *this should be recorded,* and Ron was not going to be around forever. So

I forgot about it, and three years after *that,* Demme had not even begun to produce his film, and Ron was now *very* ill and called me again. Demme had just made *Silence of the Lambs* [1991], which had been attacked by the gay community for the portrait of "Buffalo Bill" as a gay killer—

MacDonald: I've never seen him as gay, just confused about what his gender *is.* But I've heard that in some audiences some people yelled, "Kill the faggot!"

Godmilow: Well, he read as gay to the gay community. Did *Demme* want us to read him as gay? I don't know. I do think you have to control meaning when you're messing around with that kind of stuff. I don't think Demme was worried about it and should have been.

But anyway, Demme had got so caught up in getting *Philadelphia* [1993] made that he hadn't gotten around to Ron's piece. Ron wasn't sure how much longer he'd be able to do the performance. Dates had been set to remount the piece at the Kitchen, where Demme was supposed to shoot it, but he was going to have to reshoot scenes from *Philadelphia* and couldn't do Ron's piece.

So Ron is now asking if I can still do it, and if I can shoot on the dates that had been set up for Demme—in a month. And no money. I said, "I'll try."

I was close with the Good Machine people (Hal Hartley's producer, and Ang Lee's) because we had tried to get a feature project of mine going and I had taken Ted Hope to Ron's piece the night I first saw it. They were a young and spunky company and said, "Let's do it!"

That fall I ended up in the hospital with a blown appendix, misdiagnosed, and almost died—twenty-five days in the hospital! I was out of my classes so long that Notre Dame gave me a medical leave for the semester, so once I was on the mend, I was able to go to New York and shoot the film and cut it. We raised just enough money for hard costs, and Ellen Kuras, a fabulous cinematographer, lent her crew to us, no salaries paid; and on the money Good Machine had been able to raise, we shot two performances with three cameras.

Vawter was then quite sick with AIDS; originally his performances of Cohn were much faster, mind-bogglingly fast—you had to listen with such intensity. After the shooting, Ron went off to Holland to be in a play (Heiner Müller was directing), but he died before the piece got up. It's a miracle we were able to make the film.

In that month of prep time, I'm lying in a hospital bed, trying to figure out what *is* a film of a performance? Can it be more than that? Can it go *beyond* the performance, and how? I don't want to make a film that produces an audience as if they're *there* at the Kitchen, as if it's being done *for them*—that's a lie I'm not interested in telling. I'd come up with a few ideas of what a *film* of the performance should be. At that point, cross-cutting the two performances had never occurred to me.

MacDonald: I assume the original performance was Vawter coming out and talking a bit, then the Roy Cohn section, then the Jack Smith.

Godmilow: Right. It ends with Jack Smith, on the tape, saying "Good-bye!" Ron was pretty sentimental about Jack and wanted to give him the last word. Penny Arcade was given Jack's ashes, and she gave half of them to Ron. Every time Ron did the performance, he put some of Jack's ashes on his eyelids.

MacDonald: So why that opening credit, "Jonathan Demme Presents"?

Godmilow: I guess this can go into print; I don't give a fuck. I was furious at Demme for putting Ron into a situation where he was about to die with no record of the piece except Lincoln Center's one-camera video, which is awful. I said to Ron, "See what you can get out of him; he's got money; maybe he'll give us the budget." Demme had gone around during this press tour for *Philadelphia* announcing in interviews that his next film was of Ron Vawter doing *Roy Cohn/Jack Smith,* so to save *his* ass *and* try to get some money for our production, we asked if he would be executive producer.

In the end we never got a penny. I would have taken his name off—it galls me that it's there—but Good Machine was in the movie business, and I guess they thought it would help the film circulate. I don't think so. In certain gay quarters it was a negative, but I don't think it had much impact either way. It just bothers *me* personally; I'm the only one bothered, I guess.

MacDonald: How did you decide on the intercutting?

Godmilow: What I did not foresee, and it was a big lesson, is that when you see someone portraying a historical figure in the theater, the only way to take it in is as if *that's* the guy. What the film gave you was Roy Cohn for forty minutes. I could not find a way to produce *Ron Vawter performing* Roy Cohn. All you got was Roy Cohn. So the Roy Cohn footage wasn't interesting at all; it was just like somebody giving a speech on television—and Ron got lost in Cohn.

But the Smith worked completely and was so much more interesting. You're involved in trying to figure out what Jack Smith *is,* is this for *real?* That process on film was as interesting as it was in the theater.

The intercutting was an attempt to save the film. The challenge was not to destroy the time sense of either of the two pieces. I needed to work with very large hunks of the material.

MacDonald: At first there seem to be just subtle ironies at the points where you switch from one to the other, but later on, when you cut to Smith, it's as if he's been listening to Cohn.

Godmilow: That's right. It wasn't a plan; it's what came out of working with the material over and over. I came to see it as two performances of self. I came to see that being a homosexual—at least in that generation—meant you had to perform yourself, whether you were *in* the closet *or* out. If you're *in,* you have to perform antigay, or at least heterosexual; but if you're *out*—and Jack Smith was as out as you could get—there was another kind of performance you had to do, which of course Smith exploited and exploded and turned into his art.

Of course, another dimension to all this is that Ron and Jack and Roy Cohn all died of AIDS around the same time.

So I found parallels. They're subtle and I hope not too insisted on, but many, many things about the two performances began to come together. It was not interesting to me to simply perform Cohn as an asshole and Smith as a saint. I had to find other things.

Another dilemma was that the audience for the film was not the Downtown Wooster Group set, who are totally confident in laughing at *Roy Cohn/Jack Smith*. Homophobia reigns in this country to this day, and it would have been a false thing to produce the film just for an audience of people confident that homophobia doesn't affect *their* lives or *their* thinking.

MacDonald: The film is dedicated to Alf Bold.

Godmilow: Ron's idea. He called me at one point and said that's what he wanted. I'd met Alf a couple of times but didn't really know him. Alf meant a lot to Ron because he had done a lot of gay programming at the Arsenal in Berlin, very early on. Then the question became where to do the dedication. If you do it at the end, you create this love and sadness emotion that blocks out the other, more complex emotions I hope the film creates out of all the contradictions in watching these two performances. You'd just weep, for Alf, for Ron. So I did it another way.

MacDonald: You mentioned to me one time that when you saw Ken Jacobs come out of *Roy Cohn/Jack Smith,* he seemed negative about the film.

Godmilow: I can only guess what he thought, but I think he was telling me I did a terrible thing. Ask him sometime; I'm frightened to ask him! I know he knew and loved Jack Smith and may have felt that Ron performing Jack and then me making a film of Ron performing Jack was some sort of apostasy. [In January 2002, I spoke with Jacobs about this incident. He explained that whatever feelings he had at the premiere of *Roy Cohn/Jack Smith* were a response to the pain of Smith's and Vawter's early deaths, and to reservations about Vawter's performance—not about Godmilow's film.]

Hoberman, who really loved Smith too and understood him and wrote well about him, refused to review my film. Somewhere he says something like, "There's even a film that commodifies Jack Smith!" He's no friend of the film. He may feel it's Jack Smith lite—the way van Gogh can be wallpaper. *Roy Cohn/Jack Smith* was a horrible failure in terms of reviews—the worst trip I've ever had. Very painful. Taubin started it. She felt you shouldn't even be in a room where the film is showing—that you should wait in the lobby and then go in at the end for Ken Kobland's credit sequence!

Peggy Phelan, a wonderful author and performance studies professor, wrote a paper about the reception of *Roy Cohn/Jack Smith,* theorizing that my film showed up too soon after Jack's death, and all the people who knew Jack, and loved him and felt that they owned him, couldn't handle it. They wanted to be insiders at the private funeral, and my film was like funeral crashing.

But my film was about *Ron's* work, not about his (or Jack's) passing. My film is not about being an insider, and it's not a mourning vehicle. Certainly Ron is *there,* and I loved him as much as anyone in the world and think about him every day. But the film is not *Free Fall* [1993, by Gea Kalthegener and Douglas Ferguson], which records Ron's last days. If you want to *die* with Ron and *be* Greg Merton losing his lover and all that shit, you can see *that* film. My film is about work.

MacDonald: There are a lot of paradoxes around Smith. Supposedly Smith hated Jonas Mekas because Jonas wouldn't return *Flaming Creatures,* but it's only because of that, that most of us even know who Smith was.

Godmilow: I had to ask Jonas if I could four-wall *Roy Cohn/Jack Smith* at Anthology. I could *not* find a place in New York that would show it. And Jonas, "Uncle Fishhook" to Jack, was grand about it, I must say. I have a lot of bones to pick with Jonas, but I love him for that—he's obviously way past those petty jealousies and embarrassments.

The young gay community hated the film, too. They did not want to see these old, fucked-up, weirdo farts, Cohn and Smith, and learn anything about *them.* I'd watch the other films in the gay film festivals, and they were all about beautiful young men and their lovers and their problems. For a year all I did was go to gay film festivals with this film; and it was a horrible discovery to realize that anything like an avant-garde gay audience is pretty much gone, or at least that the people going to gay festivals definitely didn't want to know about Jack Smith. I'm no expert about gay cinema, but at these festivals, the audiences seemed totally without patience or serious interest. At the Castro in San Francisco, an eight-hundred-seat theater, five hundred walked out—though those who stayed were very supportive.

MacDonald: Lawrence Brose told me he emptied the Eastman House with *De Profundis* [1997]!

Godmilow: I'm so glad I'm not alone! *[Laughter.]* Well, I have no regrets. I thought the film was a gift to audiences, but it seems to be something for the archive. I'm just glad it got made. It's very hard to explain what Jack Smith did, so it's nice to have Ron's take on it.

Ron was difficult in some ways. We had huge confrontations about the music. In the theater Ron would actually play music from Jack Smith's collection all through the performance. We had a month to clear the rights (and no budget), and we didn't even know what half the songs were, but Ron said, "I *have* to use that music, *have to.*" Ron didn't understand that, unlike downtown theater, films get sued for copyright infringement. I figured we'd need to get the rights for some of the music, but we could do soundalikes for the rest of the music, which is what we ended up doing: about three clips are the original music; the rest are brilliant soundalikes, written by Michael Sahl, my friend from *Far from Poland.* Ron fought it. In the end he forgave us, but he made me feel very bad during the whole preproduction.

The best experience I had in connection with the film was in Torino, where they showed *Roy Cohn/Jack Smith* in the afternoon and then had Kenneth Anger show a brand-new print of *Scorpio Rising* [1964], along with Jack Smith's *Normal Love* [1964]. In the midst of tons of terrible films by gay filmmakers, here were the fathers, and still to this day nobody comes near them. What was so striking was to see how much territory they had laid out, *way* back. Everything that's smart about the gay aesthetic was in those two films. And there was Anger, telling wonderful stories about looking for props with Jack. He was generous and highly intelligent and still very attractive.

There are some films that just must be seen, including *Scorpio Rising* and *Flaming Creatures*. I feel the same way about Buñuel's *Land without Bread* [1932]—Buñuel defined the documentary for me, and for forty years, everybody has been running from what he taught, as if that film never happened, making endless films that "give you the word" about homeless people and welfare mothers and nuclear explosions.

MacDonald: You've clearly decided that one of the things that needs to be done is to honor people who have done important work. When I saw *What Farocki Taught*—and I feel similarly about *Roy Cohn/Jack Smith*—I realized that that tendency is evident in your work all the way back to *Antonia*.

Godmilow: That's not a conscious idea for me at all!

MacDonald: Really?

Godmilow: Things have just fallen that way. I think probably it has to do with the fact that I've never seen *myself* as an original, but I do feel I *can* be original in this other mode. I do want a real subject. There's a big impulse in me to say, "Look at this!! This is *amazing!* This changes everything! Wow!" Teaching is good for me because I get to do that, day in and day out. I'm not someone who could write scripts, and I'm not Tony Conrad, who would realize that there's something to say about how projectors work and could make a film like *The Flicker* [1966]. Tony's film is great, but I think what I do is fine, too.

The other thing is that after *Far from Poland,* the dilemmas of documentary were *so* evident to me, and each of my homages is an opportunity to take another shot at rethinking what it *means* to document something. How can a film that documents be stronger than awe or respect? Think of what PBS has done with the documentary. It's produced *just* awe. "Here's Georgia O'Keefe; she was amazing! Isn't it beautiful?! Don't you wish you could be that talented and that tough?!" The audience position promoted by PBS is "Geez, I'm glad there are people like that in the world, but I can't empower myself to do such things. I can hardly even speak about them, much less *do* anything myself. I'm just glad I live in a world where I can *know* about people like this." It's very self-satisfying *and* very debilitating. I want my films to be *useful*—how can watching Ron Vawter perform be of some *use?*

In some ways I'm still the little suburban girl who was supposed to marry a dentist but got lucky. It's like I'm still saying to my buddies at Springfield High School, "Hey, there's other shit besides the basketball game and buying clothes and friendship rings!"

MacDonald: I first heard about *Inextinguishable Fire* from James Benning, who admires it, about a week before Ruth Bradley brought *What Farocki Taught* to the Athens Film Festival. When I finally saw Farocki's film, I was underwhelmed and realized that had I seen it without the context of your film and Benning's interest, it wouldn't have struck me at all. I'm wondering why it hit you strongly enough that you would conceive a remake.

I *was* struck by *your* film, because the idea of an avant-garde filmmaker suppressing a certain dimension of herself so completely as to allow another filmmaker a total say in *her* film seemed entirely novel.

Godmilow: I *never* thought you'd wonder why I was drawn to *Inextinguishable Fire!* It seems *so* brilliant to me. I figured that whatever anyone thought of my usurping the film, they'd forgive me because they would see how important Farocki's film *is.* It's at least one solution to what I consider the essential dilemma of documentary—the same dilemma Resnais is talking about in *Night and Fog:* how do you talk about the Holocaust without producing a pornography of horror and mourning? How can you talk about napalm without showing that little girl running down the road on fire? And how can you talk about it so that you're actually *learning* something, so that you don't produce an audience of "totally innocent" people watching and caring about the horror *that somebody else made.*

So, first, I realized immediately that Farocki had pulled that off. Second, I was shocked to see that he had done it way back in 1969 and angry that I didn't know the film, because in 1981, I was trying to solve those same problems for myself with *Far from Poland.* Third, there was the tremendous generosity of the film: we Americans *had* to make antiwar films, *had to.* But that a *German* would take up that subject and gently address an audience of middle-class professionals and say, "This is how *you* make napalm and other horrible things" was one of *the* discoveries of my life, the first film since *Land without Bread* that I thought was able to create a fascinating, sober document about an extremely difficult subject and produce not just information and feeling but intelligence.

During that first screening of *Inextinguishable Fire* at Anthology Film Archives, I thought to myself, "How can I get everybody to see this!?" I could become a distributor, but who's going to rent this twenty-two-minute, crudely made black-and-white film that's twenty-five years old, about a war that's been buried by other wars?" Then the idea came: I'd *distribute* it by *remaking* it, and *some* people would see my film and wonder why I would remake his and find their way to the original. I went up to Harun after the screening and asked if we could have lunch the next day because I had a proposition to make. He came and agreed to let me do something with his film.

My film was successful in that it helped get Facets [see the filmography] interested—four of his films are now available on tape—and MoMA has four 16mm prints. Until then, you couldn't see Farocki's work in this country. So my idea of filmmaking *as* distribution was successful.

6/00 [At the Flaherty Seminar with Farocki and Godmilow]

MacDonald (to Farocki): Did *Inextinguishable Fire* have an American life when it came out?

Farocki: No, none.

MacDonald: I know very little about the film, other than having seen it several times. I don't know much about the European context the film came out of, and I don't know what *you* thought you were doing. Or who you made the film for.

Farocki: At the time when I made the film, I'd just been thrown out of the German film academy.

MacDonald: Why?

Farocki: It's not really worth telling anymore. Students still experienced this authoritarian behavior in European universities, and we were struggling against that. Although we were right to struggle, it all became very ridiculous, a kind of regression. In the end I was thrown out of school.

Some of us had ideas about an independent film that would go beyond the independence of men like Godard or Pasolini. We hoped that, following the Russian example, we could travel through Germany with VW buses and show films especially made for specific political opportunities—the kind of stuff that Chris Marker has documented about the Red Train. So, in the spirit of all that, I thought I should focus on technical intelligence, because the revolution in the academy was only in the humanities, and I wondered why nobody was looking at the engineers; they're so much more influential.

I had had a very strong education in the work of Bertolt Brecht, and so I always tried to find a structure of distanciation. And suddenly there was an opportunity to make a film; a woman TV producer I knew called me around Christmas and said, "There's still some money in the budget, and it will be lost if we don't spend it this year." So I made a proposal. The film was finished within six weeks or so—and to my surprise was relatively well received: festivals were interested in it and also audiences in the student community, especially the rising political clientele coming together in those days. It got a prize and, as a result, was shown several times on TV.

MacDonald: No kidding!

Farocki: Yes! It was actually made *for* TV. And the director, or president or whatever, at the TV company, after learning that it had won a prize, said, "We should show it again!" *[Laughter.]* I don't think many people saw it.

Of our class of Berlin filmmakers, some later became members of the Red Army and died; others like Wolfgang Petersen are now very well known, but nearly all gave up Brechtian distanciation and metatheoretical approaches. I tried to stick to Brechtian style and in the early eighties made a film with a Brechtian approach to acting. And even when I tried to make a so-called normal feature film, I still tried to have something of the distance that you sometimes find in American movies from the fifties. I wanted to get rid of the big scenario, and actors standing around representing points of view. If you use actors, you have to work continually with them, and I wasn't interested in doing that.

Godmilow: An interesting detail: when I was remaking *Inextinguishable Fire,* I asked Harun if he intended from the beginning to dub his actors' voices. He said, "No, but in the acting, there wasn't nearly enough distance, and so I dubbed them later." When I made my film, I thought I could get the performance from my nonprofessional actors that he got as a result of the dubbing, but I was completely wrong. I recorded them sync and, like him, ended up dubbing them later.

Farocki (to Godmilow): Your film also got a lot of attention, or both of them did, because of this act of the shot-by-shot remake, which is very rare.

MacDonald: At least in film. In the other arts there is a tradition of respectful copying.

Godmilow: There *is* another independent film that perfectly replicates a film made in 1969: Elizabeth Subrin's *Shulie* [1997]. Both films were at Rotterdam, and of course, the critics wrote about them together and picked sides: Subrin's is more pure; but Jill's has a subject, while Subrin's doesn't. Actually, I can't figure her film out, and she doesn't like mine.

MacDonald: There's also Van Sant's remake of *Psycho* [1998], which I think was underrated.

Farocki: I feel that way, too.

MacDonald: Of course, the new *Psycho* wasn't scary (and I wasn't crazy about the casting), but I enjoyed seeing how Van Sant's remake foregrounded the gap between 1960 and 1998, and how Van Sant replaced the kind of shock Hitchcock's film created with the postmodern "shock" of departing from his shot-by-shot strategy, and homage, at crucial moments.

Godmilow: An ex-student of mine saw an announcement that Van Sant was going to remake *Psycho* and sent it to me, outraged that Van Sant didn't know *I* was making *my* film. But I thought, "Good for him—I understand completely." He had bought himself the space to do something he loved, by making *Good Will Hunting* [1997]. Of course, I'm not a *Psycho* fan; I'm not even a Hitchcock fan—I've always hated being scared at the movies; I was always *too* scared.

Farocki: But still, the shot-by-shot remake is rare in film, though, as Scott says, not in painting or in music.

In the medieval era, writing *was* copying, and even in my lifetime, people used to learn about poetry by memorizing poems by great poets. It's puzzling that there's so little of this tradition in film history.

Godmilow: But what matters is more than the fact of the remake. Harun's film is a reminder of what a political film *can* be, a film that actually has an *analysis* of something and shows it to you in an interesting way. The kinds of cinema we're making endlessly now are ways of running away from the political, ways of *not* dealing with the economy, with power relationships, of not dealing with *any*thing.

What I found amazingly generous was your ability to make a film about napalm, without expressing anger at Americans.

MacDonald: Actually, I do see *Inextinguishable Fire* as an angry film—just not a self-righteous angry film. I don't think Americans in the sixties would have accepted self-righteousness from Germans. We were still processing the reality of the Holocaust.

Farocki: It sounds great for Jill to say my film is generous, but actually I'm ashamed that in my film I use the examples of Hiroshima and Vietnam, and *don't* say Auschwitz.

Godmilow: How can *Americans* say Auschwitz and not talk about Hiroshima— ever, ever, ever?! We *love* Auschwitz; it allows us to forgive ourselves anything.

MacDonald: One of the most direct moments in *Inextinguishable Fire* is when Harun burns his arm with the cigarette. It declares that *this* film is the opposite of the kinds of film Jill is talking about, which try to *relieve* stress, trauma, bad memories—

Godmilow: They're doing therapy!

MacDonald: This is not therapy. It's, "OK, we're for real. This is all I'm going to show you, but I am hurting: this issue causes pain."

Godmilow: Right. It's a dramatic gesture that's also antidramatic. Compared with napalm, it's antidramatic. That's the genius of the film, the way that it can operate without producing horror, but calls horror up, and then is *intelligent* about how the horror is produced *and* about how media helps produce it. I think *Inextinguishable Fire* is very much about cinema—at least within the context of today, it is, and that's another important thing about it. All we talk about now is cinema, cinema, cinema—but this film is a demonstration of how cinema can speak about very difficult, complex things without producing a pornography of violence and misery, *and* without getting the CEO of Dow Chemical on camera and making him the singular enemy and proving that *you're* heroic because you went all the way to Michigan for an interview and he turned you down six times, but *you* stayed—which has become the tradition of American radical cinema. *This* film flies in the face of that and proposes alternatives to it.

Burning laboratory rat in Godmilow's *What Farocki Taught* (1998), her remake of Harun Farocki's *Inextinguishable Fire* (1969). Courtesy of Jill Godmilow.

It also represents a part of film history—people *made* films like this then—so *Inextinguishable Fire* is a lot of things to me. Who knows if it will be influential again? Probably not, but I can hope.

MacDonald (to Farocki): What exactly are you taking apart with the forceps?

Farocki: A guinea pig.

MacDonald: Like the cigarette burn, it's a scary and disgusting moment that stands in for giant atrocities.

Godmilow: That use of models has its roots in Brecht.

Farocki: Yes. There's a Brecht line, "The fly's death can be a drama comparable to the end of the Napoleonic army in Russia"—it was done in that spirit.

Godmilow: I'd love to hear you talk about how you actually thought the film out. I can't yet think like that.

Farocki: It's very difficult to reconstruct, but I'll try. A cinematic critique of capitalism in those days was always about a general feeling of alienation—Monica Vitti chewing her fingernails and so on. In this case the alienation is literal: people watch horrible things on television in the evening which they have produced during the day—at least in a metaphoric sense. As a child, I heard a joke about a man who makes machine parts: he sneaks a part out of the factory every evening with the idea of building the machine at home. He wants to produce a vacuum cleaner, but it turns out to be a submachine gun. I tried to recycle this story in a different context.

I must ask you, Jill, did you ever consider burning yourself in your film?

Godmilow: Sure I did.

Farocki: Why didn't you?

Godmilow: When I was trying to decide whether to copy all of your film or just some of it, a good friend, who I trust, said, "Make sure, whatever you do, that you don't *displace* Farocki's film." I was afraid that to take your place in that shot might look like some kind of feminist gesture. All kinds of meanings threatened to come in that I thought were inappropriate and that I wouldn't be able to undo or repress.

Then the interesting problem was, who *can* perform Farocki? At the time, I thought you were Egyptian. I went through the photo book of the faculty at my university; and Mario DeAnda, a Mexican American who worked in the admissions program, looked the part. I found him and showed him the film—I didn't think I had a chance: would you be in my film and burn your arm please!—but he was very taken with *Inextinguishable Fire* and wanted to do it.

By the way, Harun, where *are* you from?

Farocki: My father was a Muslim from India, and my mother was German. I lived in Indonesia for a while, but that has nothing to do with my genes. I'm a German.

MacDonald: It's a generous gesture on *your* part, Jill, to superimpose Harun's film every once in a while *in* your film, so that we can actually measure the difference between them.

Godmilow: I was proud of my copy, and I wanted to show everybody! I'm kidding, of course.

Farocki: Those moments in Jill's film remind me of a moment in *Lion's Love,* where Agnes Varda asks Shirley Clarke to say a certain line. Shirley Clarke tries and says, "I can't say it," and Varda, who is wearing the same clothes, says, "OK, I'll replace you." She moves into the image, performs this line, moves out again, and the film continues. That was a great idea.

MacDonald (to Farocki): I'm not clear as to what the two "models" are in *Inextinguishable Fire.*

Godmilow: I had to ask him that myself. The first time just the project director and the CEO are watching the newsreel, and that's introduced with a title that says, "Model 1," and the second time, it's the whole group, and that's introduced as "Model 2." I *think* the first model is, "Oh, look what we're doing! Isn't what we're doing awful!"; and the second one is, "I don't want to look at what we're doing; I'll leave that at work!"—the two ways that the engineers and scientists distance themselves from what they're doing.

Farocki: That's exactly what I meant.

Godmilow: When I was making *What Farocki Taught,* the *one* thing I considered changing was the part about making submachine guns for Portugal. I was thinking that since the generation that might know about the African struggles against the Portuguese is gone, that reference might not make sense. But I finally thought, "Naaah, leave it as it is."

Farocki: I've been married to *Inextinguishable Fire* for thirty years, but when I see *your* film, I see *my* film behind it, and I see it more clearly than I do when I watch my own film!

Peter Kubelka

On *Unsere Afrikareise (Our Trip to Africa)*

Since so much of alternative cinema is devoted to a critique of commercial media, those of us who are committed to exposing others to this complex history are often faced with the challenge of demonstrating that the alternative films we admire do more than refuse to offer audiences what conventional films offer them; that, in fact, they provide experiences that are at least as valuable in their own right as those they critique. Most alternative films are, to say the least, slowly acquired tastes, and films that are immediately recognizable as accomplished and powerful and interesting by most of those who see them are the exceptions: there's Stan Brakhage's *Window Water Baby Moving* (1959), of course, and Bruce Conner's *Cosmic Ray* (1962) and Su Friedrich's *Sink or Swim* (1990). But the film that makes the single most powerful case for the accomplishment of alternative film is probably Peter Kubelka's *Unsere Afrikareise* (*Our Trip to Africa,* 1966).

Nearly half a century after it was completed, *Unsere Afrikareise* not only remains as powerful for first-time viewers as it has ever been but also recently has begun to be recognized by those who have little interest in its avant-garde status: a new generation of scholars-teachers reconsidering the history of documentary, and of ethnographic documentary especially, have correctly understood Kubelka's short (12½-minute) film as a significant contribution to our thinking about the cinematic representation of nonindustrialized peoples and of Africa in particular. This new audience has discovered what audiences for avant-garde film have always recognized: that *Unsere Afrikareise* numbers among the most powerful and insightful cinematic exposés of the brutalities of colonialism.

When Kubelka has discussed *Unsere Afrikareise* with audiences and when he has written about it (see his "The Theory of Metrical Film," in P. Adams Sitney's *The Avant-Garde Film: A Reader of Theory and Criticism* [New York: Anthology Film Archives/New York University Press, 1978], 157–58), his focus has been his formal strategy for interpreting the experience of traveling in Africa with the group of Austrian businessmen who hired him to document their safari in 1961. Having spent years studying the imagery and sound he recorded during the trip, Kubelka edited selected images and sounds into a montage so that, to use Sergei Eisenstein's terminology, each image "collides" with the image that follows, each sound collides with the sound that follows, and each image collides with the sound that accompanies it. For Kubelka, the particular "essential" quality of cinema is its allowing the sound-image synchronization of real experience (when we drop a hammer, it makes a sound as it hits the floor) to be overcome: because sound and image are recorded by different systems, the filmmaker has the option of reconstituting an illusion of the original synch event from the filmed image and the taped sound *or* of using artistry to explore the myriad possibilities of combining images with sounds that would not accompany them in reality.

Kubelka's commitment to using the essential formal options of cinema to fashion a cinematic art that can compete with the artistic accomplishments of music, painting, and literature has, from time to time, led commentators to wonder how fully aware he was and is of the implications of the subject matter of his films. Recently, for example, Catherine Russell has argued that *Unsere Afrikareise* "produces only . . . traces of guilt without a legible morality": "In the complete absence of voice-over or any other form of explanation, the imagery is radically decontextualized" (*Experimental Ethnography: The Work of Film in the Age of Video* [Durham, N.C.: Duke University Press, 1999], 132, 129). I would argue that Kubelka's precise editing strategy recontextualizes the imagery he uses in the film so that we can hardly fail to read his indictment of the system of colonial exploitation the Austrians on safari unwittingly represent (exploitation in which Kubelka and his viewers are complicit: it is "our" African journey, after all). It is true, of course, that Kubelka's refusal of voice-over, and of any textual form of explanation or interpretation of what we see, places the onus and pleasure of interpreting the film fully with viewers, but it is partly Kubelka's faith in viewers that makes *Unsere Afrikareise* so impressive.

The fact that the audience for *Unsere Afrikareise* has continued to grow suggested to me some years ago that an extended discussion with Kubelka about the experiences that led to the film, about his understanding of the film itself, and about the importance of this particular film for his career and life might be of use both to those who already know *Unsere Afrikareise* and to those who are just beginning to explore it. I had an opportunity to talk with Kubelka in

October 1999, when he was a visiting lecturer at Bard College. Since then, Kubelka and I have been in communication, fashioning our discussion into the interview that follows. We are grateful to P. Adams Sitney, who worked with Kubelka in Vienna during the summer of 2002, making final corrections.

MacDonald: I'm curious about the circumstances within which the original material for *Unsere Afrikareise* was recorded. Could you talk about the specific route of the trip?

Kubelka: We went through Yugoslavia in the Volkswagen bus that you see in the film. Originally, we left from Wels, which is the town where the Austrians who hired me to make the film lived.

MacDonald: How many people were there on the trip altogether?

Kubelka: I'm wondering how much I should say about who they really were, because I don't want to bring them personally into play. I have often said that this film should not be thought of as a personal account of these special people. They represent a whole class.

They were wealthy people who lived in a small town. They were not passionate hunters. Among Austrian businesspeople, to be a hunter brings a certain prestige. You might start by paying to shoot deer in Austrian hunting reserves. Then you might upgrade and go to Poland, maybe, and shoot a bear. To upgrade from that, you would go to Africa or somewhere equally exotic. This is exactly what they did. Theirs was not really a trip of desire but a reflection of a certain social structure, which makes it understandable that they didn't really want to travel. They didn't really want to see people different from themselves.

As soon as we got into Yugoslavia, they were already afraid of experiencing anything new. For example, they had brought packaged food with them, cans of horrible Knorr brand soups—because they were afraid of ordering good, interesting, local food, even when it was available. They would rather open a can.

The participants were the couple who had hired me; a friend of theirs, an architect, and his wife (the blonde one with the big breasts you see in the boat); a person from a lower social class who had hunting experience; and me. The architect and his wife were paying members, but this other man, seen in the shot where two men are in the water washing themselves (the one in front is the wealthy person; the one behind him is the hunter), and I were hired by the couple.

In Africa two more German people, who had been in the army during the Second World War and then had emigrated to Africa, maybe for political reasons, joined us. They were two of those Europeans who keep the colonies running. One of these two was the chief of electricity and chief of the mint in Sudan. When you hear me saying, "Goethe was an asshole," he's the one who says to me, "No!" and begins lecturing to me in a patronizing high-school-teacher, know-it-all voice.

As to the trip, we went through Yugoslavia into Greece by bus, and in Athens we took a boat to Cairo. The bus was on the boat.

MacDonald: Were you filming the whole way?

Kubelka: I was filming, but not very much. Already in Yugoslavia I did make the very important shot at the end of the film where a woman walks through a snowy landscape, part of the coda of the film, which consists of three shots. There is the naked indigenous man, with a spear and a piece of raw meat in his hands, who walks though the image. Then you hear a motor noise and somebody says, in broken English, "I like to visit your country." Then I cut and, in silence, there *is* "my country" (in reality not Austria but Yugoslavia, but it doesn't matter because it's the same landscape and weather). Then you see the peasant woman looking just like the women in the country place where I grew up. "My country" is shown silent; then I cut again, and the indigenous man walks out of the image as we hear, "If I find chance." This gives the whole film a complete turn, because you start to imagine what would happen if he had the chance and the means to come and do to *us* what *we* did to *them!*

MacDonald: My reaction is always that since he is naked, he would never be allowed to be himself in a European country.

Kubelka: But you could also imagine that Europe might fall into the kind of powerless state many indigenous Africans are in now. They can't keep us from going there. They can't say no. What I imagine is that he would have the power to come naked and impose *his* views on *us,* and be himself and hunt the chickens in our yard, and we would have to endure it. This is what "I'd like to visit your country" means to me.

Back to the route of the trip. We went through Egypt by boat from Cairo up the Nile to Aswan.

MacDonald: Where are the two minarets we see?

Kubelka: In Cairo, where we stayed several days. Then there was the trip on the Nile, and in Aswan we stopped again and then continued by bus to Khartoum, where the two German government employees joined us. The hunters hired a big Mercedes truck with a Sudanese owner-chauffeur to carry all the trophies that they hoped they would shoot. In fact they did load the whole truck with dead animals, but since they hadn't prepared them in time, the bodies started to rot, and all of it was discarded, the whole stinking load.

In my film, I didn't *show* the worst things they did—for several reasons. I didn't want to make simply an antisafari film or a direct, obvious accusation. My method was to suggest ideas through the *editing.*

With the same material I could have made a travelogue that they would have liked.

MacDonald: How long did it take you to get from Austria to Khartoum?

Kubelka: Roughly ten days. I don't recall exactly. We stayed in Athens; we stayed in Cairo; then there was the trip on the Nile—two days, I think. After that we took the Sudanese railway into the Sudan.

That was an interesting train. It had five classes. The first class was for Europeans only. The second class was for less high-class Europeans and for the highest officials of the Sudan. The third class was for upper-class Sudanese people. The fourth class was the best, in fact. It had no windows but a double roof over the wagons and open slits for the air to come in. In the fourth class you sat in the shadow, the second roof protecting you, with the air circulating. All the more expensive classes were horrible because there was no air-conditioning, so we were sweating and suffering. The fifth class was a sheer platform and nothing else, where the low-class Sudanese would sit with their animals and their families, roasting in the sun. The price was one hundred times more expensive for the first class than for the fifth class. The social structure of this train was amazing.

Once we stopped, and out of nowhere came these people selling special teas. The Islamic people went out to pee, but there was nowhere to hide, and they were extremely shy. They walked far into the desert until they could hardly be seen anymore, and they squatted down and, covering everything with this white cloth they wore, did their business. We sat and sweated in the train.

MacDonald: What else was filmed on the way to the hunting grounds?

Kubelka: Going down, I filmed only once in a while. I made some shots they ordered me to shoot. I was penniless, so I could not do just anything I wished to do. I was dependent on them to pay for my food.

MacDonald: They bought the film?

Kubelka: They bought the film *and* the camera. I had nothing. Of course, they let me feel this every day, and by the time we arrived in the Sudan, the relationship was already unpleasant. I was disgusted with the way they behaved. We were having all these new experiences, and I was very excited to be there. I admired all these things that *they* despised, patronized. I had to suppress my feelings.

MacDonald: So by the time you are getting ready to film the hunting, you already know how you feel about this enterprise.

Kubelka: Very much so. But on the other hand, I had agreed to make their film. At first, I didn't even think of making a film for myself. I filmed not having any idea how the film would look when it was finished. I had absolutely no plan, no script. I filmed bits and pieces as they came along. I was already a filmmaker; I knew what film *was,* but in this case, I was not really conscious, and did not at first think of this as *my* work.

On the other hand, when I was shooting, it had to be something I felt that I wanted to do. Even when they said, "Make this shot with this tall black guy, and we'll make fun of him," I *wanted* to do this because of what it showed about *them*. I often let myself be ordered to make certain shots.

MacDonald: Especially in the hunting scenes, there are unusual tonalities to the color. As you were making imagery, how conscious were you of how you wanted it to look?

Kubelka: I did not manipulate anything, technically. I manipulated where I put myself and how the light should fall, but I did not do anything artificial. You could say I used unsophisticated postcard compositions, where the important thing is right in the middle.

I knew from the moment I became involved with film that I didn't want to work with a second-rate medium. I wanted film to be as strong as other media and even stronger than other media for what it alone can do. I've always seen a competition between media, which if you examine art history, is actually there. Starting in the Baroque, there is a competition between painting and music. Music eventually becomes the leading medium with the advent of the Viennese classic: Haydn, Mozart, Beethoven, et al.

I feel that even Eisenstein, who was and is praised for his composition, and tried so hard to create rhymes between aspects of his shots, cannot compare with painters, in terms of composition. When it comes to composition, film is a second-rate medium, and painting shames you every time.

I was concerned with composition while filming *Mosaik im Vertrauen* [1955]. I was still working with composition in *Adebar* [1957] but in a different way: *after* filming. I looked for compositions that fit what I wanted. In *Schwechater* [1958], I did not look at composition anymore. I didn't even look through the aperture. And in *Afrikareise* I made simple postcard compositions, which, as it turned out, were very useful for editing and for creating the metaphors I was interested in.

You asked about my manipulation of light. There was none. Sometimes I slightly underexposed, because this was color-positive Gevaert stock, which if overexposed, even a little, gets very ugly. I did want an African temperature. I wanted the film to look hot or at least warm. Afterward, I printed on Kodak stock, on purpose: I didn't want the look of my film to be completely dictated by the Gevaert color system. I didn't want it to be all Kodak either. By mixing the stocks, I got a special kind of color.

MacDonald: How long did the hunting go on?

Kubelka: Several weeks. The whole trip took maybe six weeks.

MacDonald: And there were also professional hunters capturing animals for a zoo? When you said that last night, I realized that it's obvious, though I had never made myself conscious of it. There's the giraffe with the truck following it.

Kubelka: Yes. They use a long wooden pole with a lasso.

We were introduced to these people; it was one of the scheduled adventures. I asked to be on one of the jeeps during the giraffe hunt. It was quite adventurous because at times the car would actually leave the ground. I had to hold the camera but couldn't use both hands to get a firm grip.

MacDonald: One idea that I've heard about you and *Unsere Afrikareise*—for me a preposterous idea—is that your care in your lecturing to be sure that the audience looks at the way sound meets sound, the way sound meets image, the way image meets image, reveals that you care only about form and have no concern for the actual colonialist politics of the situation depicted in the film.

Kubelka: No, it's quite the contrary. I do not *speak* about the politics because I want *the film* to speak about this. My lectures are an attempt to teach the viewers my cinematic language, *not* to translate into spoken language what the film says.

In any case, I believe that there is no translation when it comes to the essential content, the "hard core," of a medium. For example, if you had two sculptures, a bad one and a good one, it would be almost impossible to describe in words what makes the good one good and the bad one bad. You'd have to see the sculptures, touch them, directly confront them. And the same thing goes for film. I don't want to verbally interpret what I say in a film. I want the people themselves to *experience* the film's meaning, its political content.

MacDonald: I understand each intersection of shot and shot, sound and sound, image and sound as a nexus of idea. I was thinking last night about the cut from the two snorkels to the two minarets. On the most obvious level, there are, in both cases, two things sticking up, but the juxtaposition is complicated in its implications. On the one hand, somebody is looking down; and on the other hand, the towers are reaching to the sky. The one is a material quest, the other suggests spiritual aspiration—

Kubelka: There's also the theme of what in Italian is called *cornuto.* When you are betrayed by your wife, you are a cuckold: you have horns. I, so to speak, cuckold this whole trip. In another image one of the men stands in front of a fire, and a tree seems to come out of his head, making "horns."

There is, of course, another important layer, the language that is spoken. You lose this layer if you don't speak German and Sudanese. I'm very happy that the film is so successful in America, even though people don't understand what is said. Which, of course, proves my belief that when you record sound, you have incredible information on many levels, not just the meaning of the words said. All this other information is there, even if you *don't* speak German or Austrian dialect or Sudanese.

MacDonald: You hear information in the woman's smoker's cough.

Kubelka: Right. And you can understand the mood of the moment. You can understand a level of education. You understand different *kinds* of laughter, the vulgarity of some laughter and the embarrassment of other laughter—all that incredible richness of information that sound brings.

MacDonald: Is it fair to say that the film was a way for you to confront both the revulsion you had at what you were seeing and your recognition that you were not separate from the trip or what it represents? We're all complicit in the history that these rich Austrians are acting out: all modern, industrial nations have thrived on the exploitation of other peoples; and films, even independent forms of film, are a product of industrialization. Is it fair to say that you were horrified by the trip and at the same time understood that you are part of that system?

Kubelka: Of course. This is reflected in the title: the fact that I say, "*Our* trip to Africa," which includes me.

MacDonald: It also includes us, as viewers.

Kubelka: Of course. It includes everybody—except the Africans, if they were to see the film.

MacDonald: Because they didn't travel to Africa; they're already there.

Kubelka: Yes. And this travel was done *to* them, so to speak. But it *would* include the Europeans, Americans—modern civilization in general. But mainly the title says, *I,* the filmmaker, was with this trip, and although I didn't kill and shoot, I was there.

MacDonald: And you were shooting on a different level.

Kubelka: Yes, I also "shot" them.

I *was* horrified by what happened—that is true. But on the other hand, I do not see life in a simple black-and-white manner. That such and such a thing is bad, even horrible, doesn't mean there is only one experience of it. You can be horrified by *and* laugh at the same thing. I'd like to bring up the term "heredi-tary sin" (*Erbsünde*), as it is taught in the Catholic religion. As a child, I was raised Catholic. I was born in Vienna, then spent a lot of time in a small village in the country, which was very important for me. In the summers I was a cowherd. I lived with my grandmother and my grandaunt because my father, who was a musician, was on tour a lot. My grandmother and grandaunt were *very* Catholic, churchgoers, and I was indoctrinated with a Catholic upbringing. Of course, from the beginning, I never really believed everything they taught me. What I could not deal with at all was the idea of "hereditary sin." They tell you that when you are born, although you have done *nothing* wrong, you bear inher-ited sin, which you need the Redeemer to get rid of.

Only later on did I realize what this means. It means that, living in a civiliza-tion, you bear the consequences of what your ancestors did. For example, liv-ing today in America, you pay for what your ancestors did to the slaves. They imported slaves to America; these slaves had children; and you now have a black population with all these difficulties because your ancestors didn't educate the slaves. Now, even if *you* have been born completely innocent, as an American you have to deal with this. And *that* is "hereditary sin."

In my youth my religion teacher was not able to explain this to me, and I broke with Catholicism and became a free thinker, an atheist, when I was ten years old. When I was fifteen, I tried to come back and couldn't do it, and I then slowly freed myself of all this part of my education. When I realized that there was no essential difference between the prophet Isaiah and, for example, poets such as Emily Dickinson and James Joyce, and I was able to look at religious revelations in the same way I would look at poetry, I experienced the joy of being able not to hate religion but to enjoy its poetry just as I would let myself be guided by the revelations received from Joyce or Dickinson. Today, poetry or the other arts—film, for example—perform the functions the prophets had three thousand years ago.

Another thing, when I was twenty years old, I could no longer stand to be a member of mankind. I wrote a declaration: "Herewith I declare my resignation from mankind. Sincerely, Peter Kubelka." But I could not implement the consequences, because if I step out of mankind, where do I step *to?* There *is* nowhere else. I do feel like I wouldn't like to be a member of this civilization, or of my community. But there is no way out. You can kill yourself, but that doesn't change anything. At a certain point, it was very important for me to have at least said that maybe if one *could* resign, I would have resigned. But in the end, participating in the civilization in which we live means that you carry the heredity consequences of everything that has been done before you. You can be of an opposite opinion. You can mildly change maybe your own course of life. But nobody can claim that they are not part of their civilization. Everybody carries guilt.

And *therefore,* you are *also* able to laugh about things that are tragic.

Yesterday, I said that *Unsere Afrikareise* should not be seen as *just* tragic, or as *just* horror. You may also laugh about what you experience in the film. My desire, when everything ends, is to go out with a laugh—Ha-ha!—not whining about the world but seeing clearly what it is.

I had a teacher, not an official teacher but a man whom I admired very much, and who had respect for my films: Friedrich Heer, a great historian who wrote *Europe, Mother of Revolutions* [London: Weidenfeld and Nicolson, 1971] and several other important books. He was much older than I, and is long dead now. When I was still in my formative years in Vienna, in the fifties, we used to drink and talk. He was the first one I heard talk in terms of the next ten thousand years. He opened me up to not think of just today, this afternoon, or tomorrow, or this year, but to envisage a depth of perspective, to become conscious that our contemporary lives are embedded in something which has already been going on for thousands of years and will continue to go on. There are developments now which will not be complete for a thousand years.

This is how I see the artist. The artist is not somebody whose prophecies are implemented tomorrow. The *politician* is somebody who has only one chance to implement things. When he's gone, after his term ends, his chance is over. What he cannot do now, is not done. But for artists it's different. Some of them dream up things that perhaps will be useful in a thousand years, if mankind lasts that long.

Of course, this is an attitude that can encourage you to go on, even if something you do seems to be going nowhere.

MacDonald: It might also relate to your body of work. One of the things that puzzles some people in this country—I don't know how it is in Europe— is that you made this very small body of work (in terms of time: all your films together add up to only sixty minutes) and then seemed to stop. The question is why you're not still producing films. It occurs to me that one answer might be that the minute you would produce more, you would create less attention to the work you've already made. *Unsere Afrikareise* continues to energize us: I've seen it at least once every semester for twenty years, and I'm still finding things that I haven't noticed or thought about before. If you had made twenty more films, I would probably move on to those other films and dilute my attention to *Afrikareise.*

Kubelka: Yes, that's true, but actually it was not a tactical decision. I consider myself lazy (although people say I work a lot). I don't want to do something if I don't really feel a burning need to do it. I could have made many films on the model of *Mosaik,* many films on the model of *Adebar,* many films on the model of *Schwechater,* and many films on the model of *Arnulf Rainer* [1960]. *Arnulf Rainer* uses only black and white, but I could have gone on, into color flicker, and that would have taken me in the direction of Paul Sharits's work. He implemented many things I had *thought* about but didn't feel I needed to *do.* In a way, each of my films is a prototype and postulates a certain *way* of making films, and each film was a step to the next phase. Actually, after I finished *Schwechater,* I made a number of painted filmstrips that would have produced what is now called color flicker, but I went on to reduce the material for the next film, *Arnulf Rainer,* to the four essential elements of cinema: light, nonlight, sound, and silence. The white light, of course, contains all colors, and white sound, which I used for the soundtrack, all pitches.

The other thing is that in the seventies, I started to despecialize. I consciously thought, "I don't want to see myself limited by being an artist. I want to be just a human being, an unspecialized human being." I do possess several specializations. "Filmmaker" is my deepest specialization, and I did not really stop making films, because all those years when I was teaching in Frankfurt, I worked with students who were making many things I wanted to see and which I might have made myself. I just didn't need to be the producer.

I do feel I have done my share as a filmmaker. I have done something which is still not completely received by the public and, as you suggest, is still radiating. But, being conscious that life is unique and short, I tried to step out of narrow forms of denomination, like "filmmaker." I was first a "musician"; for example, I sang with the Vienna Boys' Choir. After fifteen years, I completely left music for cinema. Then, slowly, I got my music back again. I started to study old music, old wind instruments, regained playing ability, and founded Spatium Musicum, an ensemble with which I might perform modern music (Schoenberg, Webern), Baroque music, pre-Baroque music, back to the eleventh century. We also sing folk and classical music and Gregorian chant.

This gave me the opportunity to research what I called "independent music," all through the evolution of European musical history. My concert programs are structured like the montage in a film. The various pieces appear in an order that makes them react, each one with the next and the one before so the whole concert can express my opinion of the essence of music.

America started me on my theoretical work: when I first came here, I never thought I would lecture about anything, but then I was encouraged to become a theorist of cinema. When I studied various other art forms in order to find criteria which might help me establish cinema as an absolutely autonomous art form with its own hard core that could not be reached by any other medium, I came upon "cooking." By "cooking" I mean the process of giving form to the edible sculptures of which our food really consists. I look at the preparation of food as it has evolved since even before the Stone Age, from the position of an art theoretician and not from the position of nutritive science. In the last decades I have expanded my activity as a lecturer, transcending film theory toward a general theory of cultural evolution. I recommend seeing cooking as the oldest art form. To prepare living matter and make it edible was perhaps the first human activity that involved changing the material world. If we contemplate and analyze cooking as cultural communication, then I believe we discover a new understanding of the earliest developments of mankind.

I also founded a museum [Oestereichisches Filmmuseum/the Austrian Film Museum], so I am also "founder." But in the end, I'm a curious, general human being. My specializations are just my working tools.

Some people used to say, "You're a philosopher," but I have great difficulty with philosophy because I think the philosophers expect too much from language. They stick to language as the only tool. Language cannot bear that.

When I lecture, I don't use a specific, prepared text. This is quite on purpose. But I always prepare very carefully. As you know, I don't drink before I lecture, and I like to drink. People may say, "He shows his films for the two thousandth time, so what's the big deal?" But every time I do it, it *is* a big deal for me, because I don't believe in recycling a verbal presentation that I know by heart. Every time, I do it differently. I don't believe in the stability of a formulation, either. In a way you could compare me with a sculptor who works on the same theme again and again and again. Yesterday, I said some things that I had never said in that way before. You could call these lectures works of art—not in the sense that they are so *good* but in the sense that they are my creations. They exist as works.

And they are not narrowed into the meaning of the words. There are gestures; there are demonstrations—I don't want to put myself in the hands of language alone. I work a lot in nonverbal communication, in nonverbal thought. Actually, I don't believe in thought as such. There is sculptural thought; there is musical thought, which you can absolutely *not* translate into words. Of course, a language for *describing* music has been developed. There are descriptions of symphonies, which if you have studied the matter and know the language, tell you something. But they can never really *translate* the musical work.

There is also a fight between the modes of thinking: language often invades and substitutes for other disciplines.

MacDonald: In American academe we're in a battle right now between language and image. At least in relation to film, language is trying to take back what image is successful at. Some scholars, committed primarily to language, seem to try to reduce film to language, and in effect are helping to force the *experience* of film out of the academy altogether, so that only language is left.

Kubelka: This battle between forms of thought/language is demonstrated in feature films which are based on novels. I like to go to Hollywood films. It amuses me, for example, to go to a film where, for commercial reasons, the wrong types of actors play the leading roles. *Eyes Wide Shut* [1999], the last Kubrick film, is totally ruined by the two leading actors. In the script, the doctor is a normal doctor who is a bit provincial, but in the film he's played by Tom Cruise, a most beautiful, elegant, well-dressed actor. Nobody believes he's a provincial doctor. And his wife should be a plain family woman, focused on children; and *she* is played by Nicole Kidman! There's a fight between the script and the realization. When you watch, it's like a superimposition of two different kinds of experience.

MacDonald: Let's return to *Afrikareise.* I'm wondering to what extent, as you lived through the weeks you were in Africa, you made contact with people other than the Austrians you were traveling with? One of the things that has struck me the last few times I've seen the film is the African woman who, while dancing, looks at the camera. Her look is very penetrating, a totally intelligent look and, for me, one of the most powerful things in the film.

Kubelka: This was a special relationship, a kind of love affair that was never consummated.

I tried to get away from the expedition, whenever I could. In Khartoum I went to the market and met a young man there who was selling things. He spoke a little English, and we talked and got to know each other, and he invited me to a marriage at his house. His brother was getting married. I managed to get permission to leave for a day but stayed away three days. At this marriage, I was able to observe the traditions of Islam as it was lived in that Sudanese society, where boys and girls were not allowed to mingle on an everyday basis but saw each other on festive occasions.

Successive images of African "trophies," from Kubelka's *Unsere Afrikareise* (*Our Trip to Africa*, 1966). Courtesy Anthology Film Archives.

The marriages there take as long as the family can afford. An aristocratic marriage might last a month. A marriage in a well-to-do family might last a week to ten days. And during these days the hospitality is overwhelming. When I arrived, they gave me a huge metal bed to take my siesta in. The bed was in the shadow when I lay down. I fell asleep, and suddenly I felt a swimming sensation. I woke up and saw that four people were carrying my bed into the shadow, so that the sun would not hit me. Several times they came and moved my bed.

There were these dancing events where the boys and the girls would meet. The girls, starting with the very young ones, four years, six years, eight years, ten years, twelve years, fifteen years, which was maybe marrying age, would all dance. First the very youngest, then the next group, and so on. The boys, who would be in similar age-groups, would watch them. I learned that this happened several times each year, as they grew up, so that when a boy reached the age of marriage, he knew exactly which girl he wanted and would tell his parents to make negotiations.

The girls also had the possibility of making their sympathy public. A girl would dance and at a certain moment would let her head fall back, in abandonment, so that her tresses would hang down. A man could indicate his intention toward this girl by going to her and making a kind of whipping noise with his fingers. Then he would bend his head near where her head was. If the girl liked this man, she would move her hair like a whip and all her tresses would hit him in the face, an incredible moment of eroticism, accentuated, acoustically, by old women, standing nearby, who made a cry when the tresses hit the face. Incredible. If the girl did not like the man, she would do nothing. It's amazing, this traditionally regulated way of communication: one knew exactly who liked whom and which pairings were building toward marriage.

There was this one girl who liked me, and she must have told somebody—somehow I found out. So as she was dancing, I went and did this gesture and she hit me with her tresses. But, of course, we could not continue the relationship. But she did consent to dance for me. The man who had invited me helped arrange the whole thing. We met in a place where no one could see, so that I could film her and she danced for me, in daylight. By European standards this would have been like a woman showing herself naked, or even something more—an extreme trespassing on tradition. All that, of course, is in the film, in how she looks at me.

MacDonald: I'm glad I asked!

Kubelka: I don't think I've ever told this story publicly before.

After three days I had to go, which was sad—and very impolite. It's rude to leave a marriage celebration in the middle, but the celebration was to go on for ten days. I had to do lots of explaining. Of course, they understood.

I had other interesting experiences, which are not in the film at all.

MacDonald: Tell me another.

Kubelka: One happened when I spent the night alone on the Nile, waiting for a hippopotamus to be swept ashore. When a hippopotamus dies and sinks in a river, the indigenes know exactly where it will surface again: it will float down the river and will be swept ashore at a particular place. The Austrian hunters had shot a hippopotamus but, of course, didn't want to stay for the unpleasant part. They preferred to leave all the unpleasant things to me. I was happy because normally they were jealous about what I would see and they wouldn't. But in this case they were afraid to stay the whole night alone and wait for the hippopotamus to float ashore, so they left me there. I sat the whole night on a little folding bed which they had brought with them. I had a rifle, canned food, and my tape recorder and camera. It was there that I shot those images where it's very dark and you see many black people huddling and then dividing the meat of the hippopotamus.

During that long night, two young boys would come and sit with me, and they would speak with their night voices. This was something that moved me incredibly because it's something we've lost in our civilization. We light up the night; we destroy the night. And we talk as loud at night as during the day. When the sun is down, *these* people talk softly. They have a day speech and a night speech. These boys talked this night speech. I put in that quiet sound as a contrast to the violence you see during the catching of the giraffe.

There was a tribe living in this region. The tribe had a chief, and during the night the chief came, and I greeted the chief. We had no common language, but I decided I would talk to him in Viennese, because he wouldn't understand English anyway. I was hoping that he would understand my intentions from the nonliterary qualities that spoken language has. If you listen to somebody, you know if he likes you or not. You know if the person is angry. You have an idea what his intentions are. So I addressed the chief as if he were another Viennese, just like I'm speaking to you now. And he spoke in *his* language.

He was sitting on his mat; I was sitting on my folding bed. During the conversation, I realized he wanted to explain something, and he pointed to me and to himself and indicated big and small. After a time I realized he wanted to sit with me on my "throne," because he saw this folding bed as an instrument of heightened personal prestige.

MacDonald: Because, on some level, it was.

Kubelka: Of course it was! I found out much later that ethnologically the chair is not simply a utility instrument, it *is* a throne. It was conceived as such. In Africa you can still see this in many places. Normal people sit on the floor, and only the king sits on the throne. Sometimes the king sits on a crouched human. Sometimes the throne has an anthropomorphic form, like a human being crouched. We don't know how to sit on the floor anymore.

In the sixties, the hippie culture reintroduced sitting on the floor, but I'm not comfortable, anymore, sitting on the floor.

Anyway, when I realized what he meant, I said, "I'm very happy to have you sit with me on this throne. Would you please take a seat?" Speaking normally, you automatically make the right gestures. You don't discriminate. He understood perfectly and, ceremonially, sat himself next to me, and we stayed the rest of the night without speaking a word. He was completely content, and we waited for the morning. In the morning his other subjects arrived.

What followed was very interesting, and very complicated, because the level of organization in his tribe was such that they themselves did not have the economic means to hunt a hippopotamus, which is an expensive venture. You need canoes, a certain number of warriors, and so on. This tribe wanted access to the hippopotamus shot by the expedition.

And there was a mutiny going on. One of the warriors wanted to dethrone the chief. The chief was wearing a sort of nightgown that just covered his private parts. Just an old shabby nightgown. But the others had nothing. Toward morning, when the first of his warriors arrived, he ordered them to bring me something. They said they didn't have anything. He got angry, and they went away and came back bringing buffalo milk in a container that evidently had held gasoline—out of prestige because they were proud of this metal container. Then there was a long drinking ceremony. The chief offered me the milk, so I drank. Then I had to give it to the chief, and the chief drank. Then I had to drink again. I wanted to hand the container, with the drink, to somebody else because there were people around. Then I realized I couldn't do this. This was a hierarchical ritual in which I always had to drink before one of the warriors could take a sip.

By this time it was day, and the hippopotamus had floated into this place. The warriors were waiting to take action. The insurgent warrior started to insult the chief, who was old and bodily weak. One could see that he had no physical authority. So I thought I would help him. I had with me some cheap glass necklaces that the Austrians hoped to use for barter. I stood up, took one of these necklaces, and said to the king, "Would you please accept this necklace." I put it over his head, around his neck, and formally endorsed him. It had an incredible effect upon the others. Then the insurgent came up to me very close and said, "I want something too! What about *me!* Give one to *me!*" And I said, "No! You get nothing! *This* is the chief." And it worked. It may not have worked for very long, but it worked for this moment. One could feel the chief's power grow.

I had the order from the Austrians that the Africans could have the carcass of the hippopotamus, but I had to save the head with the teeth, which was regarded as a trophy. So I stood by and watched the body cut up and saw that the head was saved.

Do you want one more story?

MacDonald: Sure.

Kubelka: This one was very important for me. I was fascinated by African music, with what might be called ethnic music. This was one of the main reasons why I accepted the commission to go and make this travelogue. I wanted to have an occasion to actually hear indigenes making music.

I should tell you that there is nothing in the film that was not recorded during the trip. This is true of both image and sound. There was no mixing of sound, which means that when you hear music and spoken words at the same time, that was the way it was recorded. The music you hear in the film comes either from the car radio or was recorded live in the various locations. For example, the music played when the lion is hoisted up onto the car was recorded in Yugoslavia, at a marriage in a very small town in the country, where the musicians walked with the instruments and played. The Frank Sinatra piece was recorded in a kind of pub in Malakal, run by Italians.

In the hill country, toward Ethiopia, we were in a town that has a big market where many tribes meet. We were staying in a colonial hotel, which the English had built. One night, in the distance, I heard African music and was so eager to get closer to it, I risked my life. The hotel was behind barbed wire, protected because this was a dangerous region. I just walked out, in the darkness, toward the music. I came into an assemblage of huts, to the astonishment of the people there. I had my tape recorder with me, and that music is in the film. It's the music you hear when you see the Arab man go behind the white lady and there are these yellow columns. The music is similar to a jackass's braying.

MacDonald: That's what I thought it was.

Kubelka: Well, there *is* a jackass braying; then I continue with the *music,* which imitates the jackass braying. The music is also very erotic, like the jackass's braying, which is an expression of its desire for a female. The music takes a parallel form.

So there was the music. It turned out that I had chanced into a brothel. There were musicians and there were whores and there were heavily drinking men. They asked me what I was doing there, and I tried to explain that I wanted to hear the music and wanted to be allowed to stay. (This is all without any common language.) They gave me a seat, and I sat there for a while, taping and watching what was going on.

Then several things occurred. One of the men, who was very drunk, started to heckle me. He started to make obscene gestures and flick his hand in front of my face. He wanted to fight. It was very difficult for me to decide what I should do. I tried to say I didn't want to fight, I just wanted to listen to the music; and I stayed friendly. Then one of the girls decided she wanted me to come with her and pay and be her guest. I really didn't dare to do it, since this was the girl the heckler had his eye on.

The whole thing built up and became very dangerous. They all had knives, and this was a place where you really had to know how to defend your honor. I had seen people with slices in their bodies from knife fights, and I started to be afraid, but I was still taping—this music meant so much to me. In *Adebar* I use pygmy music, but from a recording. This was one of those moments when you say, "You only live once." But then the girl came and threw her hair around my head and danced in front of me, and the man became more and more aggressive. Finally some of the older men, who were not so drunk, came to my aid but wanted me out. I tried to say, "I would like to stay a little more," but they made sure I left. I walked back in the dark to the hotel.

Whenever I could I tried to step out away from the safari, but most of this is not in the film.

MacDonald: When you got back to Austria after the trip, you thought you were going to do two films: their film and your film. What happened between you and the Austrians as you slowly discovered they weren't going to get their film?

Kubelka: We had had a falling-out already in Africa. They were saying I wasn't a good comrade because I didn't laugh at their jokes—things like that. So when we came back, the climate was already rather cool. They thought that now I would make the film and that they would have it within four to six weeks, so that they could show it to their business friends.

MacDonald: A cine-trophy.

Kubelka: Yes, yes! *[Laughter.]*

I have suppressed some of these memories because they are so awful. Anyway, once we were back, of course, they weren't paying me anything, and I was penniless again.

I had no work print for *Afrikareise;* I couldn't afford to make a work print. I had color-positive stock, so I made a black-and-white negative, of very low quality, and used that black-and-white negative as a work print to edit the film. In order to know what colors I had, I cut frames from every shot, either from the beginning or the end, and made a catalogue: I numbered every shot and pasted it on a piece of cardboard so that there were two frames that I could look through. These cards were approximately ten inches long, and each had approximately ten different color images on it. Altogether, there were about fourteen hundred shots.

My working process required lots of imagination. My limitations turned out to be very important; my limited economic situation has always helped me. Not having money and not having machines at my disposal forced me to make the film in my head instead of following the suggestions of a Moviola. The editing table is a very dangerous instrument because it provides you immediately with an easily palatable product. It suggests harmless solutions.

I started working on the film in the work space of a foreign news service correspondent (later I worked at Listofilm, a lab in Vienna). He let me edit the film on his table but only during off-hours when other people weren't working. I

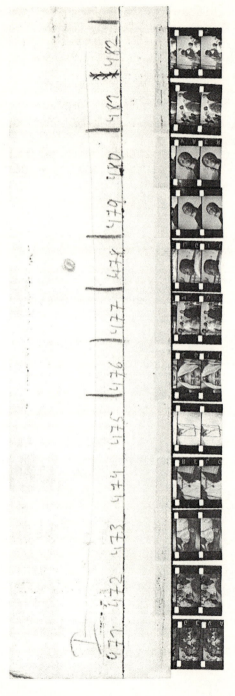

From Kubelka's "Dictionaries" for the *Unsere Afrikareise* project: pairs of frames from the individual, numbered shots used during the editing of the film. Courtesy Peter Kubelka.

could go there, work a little bit, then go home again and work in my imagination, which, by the way, is what I also had done with the metric films
[Adebar, Schwechater, Arnulf Rainer]. The metric films were all made without
projector, without Moviola, by hand. I always carried pieces of those early
films in my pocket to look at, to touch and compare. The fact that I touched
the film strips continuously led me to the essence of cinema. The *material*
taught me what to do.

So I started to work on what became *Afrikareise,* with the people who had
commissioned it exercising constant pressure. At some point, when they realized I was *only* making *my* film, there were lawyers involved, and we reached
a compromise that I would give them all the material which is not in *my* film,
the bulk of the material.

MacDonald: Image and sound?

Kubelka: Yes. They thought they would edit it themselves, which they
never did.

This all went on for five years, and all these five years, I lived like somebody
pursued by the law. It was a horrible situation, and my worst years, economically.

When, finally, the film was finished, I did what I had done with my earlier
films. I made one public premiere for everybody: for friends, for other artists,
and for the people who had commissioned the film. For *them* it was a scandal,
and after the screening they tried to beat me up in the corridor—which they
couldn't do because I was a judo fighter, and it was easy for me to defend myself.

Then they were determined to destroy the film. There were lawyers again,
and they wanted me to hand over the film.

MacDonald: So they read the film quite correctly!

Kubelka: Generally, yes, they did, though they didn't really understand what
I was doing. For example, in the scene where you see the elephant lying wounded,
there are two hunters to the left side, still shooting at him. And I have synchronized, with these gunshots, this man who says, "Elephant" and taps his finger on the table. So you have a sound which is very harmless, the fingers tapping,
synchronized with the rifle going off. *They* read this as a defect: "You were not
even capable of recording the shots correctly! You do not have good shots, so
you make *us* look ridiculous." They found it embarrassing. In the end I made
an agreement never to show *Unsere Afrikareise* in their hometown, which I have
not done to this day. I don't know if they're still alive or not.

At the time of the premiere in Vienna, I had just come back from my first
trip to America. When I was almost finished with the film, it turned out that at
that time, 1966, Listofilm, which was then my lab, could not make optical sound
in 16mm. I didn't want magnetic sound; I wanted good optical sound.

My American filmmaker friends, whom I had been getting to know since
1958—Stan Brakhage and, since 1963, Jonas Mekas and P. Adams Sitney—had
constantly been saying, "Come to America!" Jonas had even gotten me a

grant from Jerome Hill, who was giving very small grants so that filmmakers could finish films. I was the only non-American who got one of twelve grants: ten dollars per week, forty dollars per month. I got this grant in 1964, and during the last two years of making *Afrikareise,* I was sustained by it. It was my only income, but it raised my spirits tremendously.

Then Jonas made arrangements for a New York premiere, and Brakhage invited me to give a lecture in Denver and to come and stay with him. He said I should print *Afrikareise* in his lab, Western Cine, in Denver, that they could do good optical sound.

After fourteen years of barely surviving—from 1952 to 1966, I had not earned a cent from my own work—this flight to Denver was actually paid for by a lecture fee, and for me this was a flight in heaven. After fourteen years of never having acknowledgment, never receiving pay for what I did, my *work* paid my way. I will never forget that moment. It was a beautiful day, no clouds, and I saw America gliding under me. And there was Brakhage waiting in his Land Rover.

The first thing we did was go to a steak house, a wonderful event because there was the blazing Denver sun around noon, and we entered this steak house, which was completely dark, and ate these *huge* steaks, unlike anything I had seen before. Then we went to Brakhage's home. He had moved out of his studio and left it to me so I could finish the cutting of the original negative. I had come with the work print and the sound and had not yet cut the original. I edited the film, and we printed it in Denver, and, in fact, Brakhage was the first to see *Afrikareise,* other than the technicians.

Then I went back and premiered the film in New York. It was a huge success. Many filmmakers and also nonfilm artists (Rauschenberg, Oldenburg, Warhol . . .) came. I was invited to do a lecture at Harvard, in a very distinguished lecture program. I told them I didn't do lectures and they said, "Either you do a lecture or we cannot pay you to come, because this is a lecture series." I hesitated, but everybody said, "Do it! Do it!" So I did this talk at Harvard, and from then on there was a constant demand until 1978, when I got my professorship in Frankfurt.

Later Brakhage said to me, "When you came to America, you always had your eyes on the floor; you walked with your head bowed. Now, your head is up."

I will never forget what America did for me. For the first time people wanted to ask me questions. In Austria, you could only speak ironically about what you did. Questions were either traps or jokes. Here, I encountered a completely different approach to my work and to myself. I gained a new life.

Jim McBride

On *David Holzman's Diary*

Jim McBride's *David Holzman's Diary* (1967) remains one of the quintessential films of the sixties. As fully as any of the commercial and independent films that encapsulate dimensions of the complex spirit of that tumultuous decade—Jordan Belson's *Allures* (1961), Kenneth Anger's *Scorpio Rising* (1963), Robert Nelson's *Oh Dem Watermelons* (1965), Andy Warhol's *The Chelsea Girls* (1966), Yoko Ono's *No. 4 (Bottoms)* (1966), Michael Snow's *Wavelength* (1967), Mike Nichols's *The Graduate* (1967), William Greaves's *Symbiopsychotaxiplasm: Take One* (1971), Dennis Hopper's *Easy Rider* (1969), John Lennon and Yoko Ono's *Bed-In* (aka *Bed Peace*, 1969), D. A. Pennebaker's *Monterey Pop* (1969)—McBride's portrait of a young filmmaker trying to make a film out of his own life reveals the many intersecting social and aesthetic currents that made the sixties so unusual. Within the context of an expanding Vietnamese war and domestic racial turmoil, David Holzman (L. M. Kit Carson) pursues his ever-more-frustrating attempt to be a voyeur of his own experience. When he films his girlfriend, Penny, as she sleeps in the nude, despite her forbidding him to do so, she leaves him; and David relentlessly records her departure and his attempts to get back together with her once she's moved out—until he is stopped by a policeman while he is covertly filming Penny in her apartment.

Throughout *David Holzman's Diary*, David's—and McBride's—fascination with film equipment and with film history is obvious. David talks to his "friends," his Eclair camera and his Nagra tape recorder, while sitting in front of an editing table in a room decorated with a poster for Orson Welles's *Touch of Evil* (1958), stills from Godard's *Contempt* (1964) and *A Married Woman* (1963), and photographs of Richard Leacock, D. A. Pennebaker, and Godard. David

David Holzman interacting with the camera in his apartment/studio in Jim McBride's *David Holzman's Diary* (1967). Courtesy Direct Cinema and Mitchell Block.

often quotes Godard's famous line, "What is film? Film is Truth, twenty-four-times-a-second." We journey out onto the street with David and his camera rig as he explores his Upper West Side neighborhood and when he is testing his new fish-eye lens. Indeed, it is David's downfall that his equipment and his determination to use it to document his own experience lead him into a cul-de-sac: the film apparatus becomes a wall that imprisons him, leaving him, in the end, with nothing.

For most of those who see *David Holzman's Diary* without knowing anything about the film (when I use it in college courses, I am always careful to avoid revealing that there were a director and actors), David's adventure with his camera and his losing Penny are intimate and gripping. McBride creates a remarkably credible illusion that we are watching real life as it happens. As a result, when the final credits reveal that what they have seen is an enacted melodrama, and that there is no David Holzman except in their imagination, audiences are usually frustrated and disappointed, *and* astonished both at their own gullibility and at McBride's skill in fooling them. The lesson of *David Holzman's Diary*—that film is *not* Truth, twenty-four-times-a-second, at least not in the sense we might think—has always been and remains a powerful one.

The audience's disappointment that the narrative about David is fabricated is also ironic, in that so much of what we see in the film *is* an effective documentation of what it felt like to be in New York City in 1967. "David's" various experiments with his camera—his recording of an evening's television viewing, one frame per shot, for example—create a sense of everyday life, as do his walks along New York streets. Further, McBride's narrative about David was based largely on his own experiences and fascinations, and partly on avant-garde filmmaker Andrew Noren, whose early films were remarkable for their intimacy and sexual openness (most of Noren's early films are lost; I am judging from *Kodak Ghost Poems—Part I, The Adventures of the Exquisite Corpse* [1968], which David Holzman would love to have made). The connection between David Holzman and Noren is clear in L. M. Kit Carson's introduction to the published screenplay of *David Holzman's Diary* (New York: Farrar, Straus and Giroux, 1970): "And Noren made movies just like this, confronting himself at random hours: the camera squatting on its tripod coldly grinding along watching Andrew and his girlfriend drink coffee, fuck, etc. . . . And when Jim talked to Noren now, Noren kept kicking Jim's imagination in the ass" (viii, ix).

For those of us who love the broadest range of American independent cinema and revere its landmark achievements, the past twenty-five years have rendered *David Holzman's Diary* poignant in a sense McBride never intended. While McBride's breakthrough film was seen in a few theaters, and in colleges and universities nationwide, it was by no means a commercial success. For a moment, it might have seemed to McBride that his inventive feature would provide him with ongoing opportunities to make films, but in fact, this was not the case. After *Glen and Randa* (1971), McBride stepped into obscurity and spent more than a decade struggling to make ends meet and to find a place for himself in the film industry. Finally, in 1983 he reemerged with a remake of Godard's *Breathless* (1959), starring Richard Gere; and he has continued to work in Hollywood, sometimes with a modicum of success—*The Big Easy* (1987), *Great Balls of Fire!* (1989)—but usually on more obscure projects. He has finally achieved something like a secure place in the industry, but it is his first film, more than any other he has made, a movie that until very recently he seems to have had little interest in and which he made for a cash outlay of around $2,500, that will keep his name and reputation as a serious filmmaker alive. *David Holzman's Diary* was admitted to the Library of Congress's National Film Registry in 1991.

I spoke with McBride in New York City in December 1996. When McBride sent me corrections for the interview (in June 2003), he explained, "In a funny irony, I decided, about a year and a half ago, to go back to my roots, so to speak, and make a sequel to *David Holzman's Diary,* revisiting the now-aging filmmaker some thirty-odd years later. This time, I've written a script and have been trying to raise a relatively small amount of money ($2 to $3 million) to do it in high-definition video. So far, no takers, and I may end up doing it for far less money with a bunch of my students [at the American Film Institute Conservatory's Narrative Workshop]."

MacDonald: I've often started my Introduction to Film classes with *David Holzman's Diary,* and it continues to take students by surprise. For all the talk about how younger people are more tuned in to the media, they have the same reaction that audiences have always had: they're shocked and disappointed that they weren't actually looking at real events. I'm wondering how you feel about the film now.

McBride: I haven't seen it or talked about it in many a year. In Hollywood you don't have a past.

MacDonald: Has there been a lot of academic interest in the film?

McBride: There's always been some, but honestly I just haven't been aware of the film for quite some time. There was a period when I was constantly getting invited to film festivals and conferences to talk about *David Holzman's Diary,* and it showed up in university courses, and that may still be true, but I haven't had contact with the people who use the film. *David Holzman's Diary* does have a unique place in movie history, but it's not that widely shown or seen. The truth is, I don't even have a print. Seven or eight years ago I used to have prints of all my early stuff, but I moved from one house to another, and somehow those prints got lost in the transition, and I've never been able to recover them.

The point is: no, I haven't been keeping track of this stuff. There was a time when I just assumed that somebody else would, and they did. But suddenly these things have become less relevant, and the Good Samaritans are gone. When *David Holzman* was accepted by the National Film Registry at the Library of Congress, even they couldn't dig up a print for a long time.

MacDonald: You were pretty young when you made *David Holzman.*

McBride: Twenty-five.

MacDonald: Had you always been a film person?

McBride: No, I was just a liberal arts student. I think I wanted to be a writer. I started out at Kenyon College in Ohio. In my second year I got friendly with a Brazilian exchange student who told me about a program they were starting up for people to do their junior year in Brazil. I had wanderlust and jumped at that chance and spent most of 1959–60 in São Paulo. While I was there, I often got bored and went to the movies a lot. It was real cheap. The memorable experience for me was *La Dolce Vita* [1961]. I thought it was incredible, but mine was still an amateur's interest.

When I came back to the States, the only school that would accept my Brazilian credits was NYU so I ended up finishing at NYU. And while I was there, I took an elective in film history, just because somebody told me you watched movies all day and it was easy to get a good grade. I saw all these great movies that I hadn't known existed, like *Potemkin* [1925] and *Citizen Kane* [1941], and began to realize that the people in my class were planning to have careers in movies. It had never occurred to me that ordinary people could go into the movies. And as soon as it did, it sounded great to me, and I became a passionate movie buff, and I started to major in film.

MacDonald: I assume that *David Holzman* was not your first film.

McBride: I did make one other film. I was working for the radio station of the Riverside Church—I can't remember what they called it—reviewing films and doing other stuff for them. They had done a series of audio documentaries about civil rights that had won a lot of awards. In one they'd actually snuck into a Klan meeting and recorded. I was asked to do a little film based on the recordings. I did a ten-minute promo using still photographs and a soundtrack made up of excerpts from their recordings. That was my first film.

MacDonald: Nothing before that?

McBride: No. When I was at NYU, I participated in the making of a couple of films, but in those days one out of five students actually got to direct a film; the other four helped, so I helped this guy, Lewis Teague, make his film. Lewis works in Hollywood now. He did *The Jewel of the Nile* [1985], *Navy SEALS* [1990], *Alligator* [1980]. . . I did camera, editing, sound; but I didn't have the opportunity to do my own thing. So that's as far as I got. And I don't know what I would have done even if I had had the opportunity to direct. It was a gestation period for me.

MacDonald: You mentioned that you became a big film buff in the midsixties. At that time, New York was certainly a great place to be a film buff.

McBride: It was, yeah.

MacDonald: Do you remember particular films or kinds of films that had a lot of impact on you?

McBride: Well, *Breathless* was the first one. That was an extraordinary eye-opener for me. In those days I was particularly interested in film language; and the way Godard approached film language, breaking all the rules and reinventing them, was tremendously exciting.

MacDonald: I still remember my surprise, early in *Breathless,* when Michel turns to the camera and speaks directly to us. Was that direct engagement of the viewer an influence on David's direct engagement of us?

McBride: Probably, yes. I remember being impassioned about three, or maybe four, parallel historical tracks which didn't really have much to do with each other—although in those days, they all seemed to be related. One was the French New Wave. Another was the classic American movies of the thirties and forties.

MacDonald: *Rear Window* [1954] seems important to *David Holzman,* and there's a *Touch of Evil* poster on the wall—

McBride (laughter): You're right, the fifties, too. I guess classic American film in general, though I think at some point the thirties and forties became the key decades for me. But that doesn't mean I wasn't interested in what came before and after.

But *Rear Window was* something. It's interesting that you mention it, because it made a huge impression on me when I first saw it, which was long before I ever had any interest in movies. And by the time I did have an interest, that film was no longer available. You couldn't see it. For years you couldn't see any of Hitchcock's films, at least the ones he owned himself, until they began to rerelease them.

MacDonald: Right. You couldn't even show them in film history classes. So those are two tracks: the French New Wave and classic Hollywood . . .

McBride: A third was cinéma vérité: Leacock and Pennebaker and the Maysles brothers, and the rest. And the fourth was the American Underground, which was very, very active and various and interesting.

MacDonald: Where did you go to see Underground film?

McBride: It was always shown at holes-in-the-wall in the East Village or in somebody's loft. I remember going to see Andy Warhol films in lofts. Somebody would announce a showing and set up some chairs, and we'd sit and watch *Eat* [1963], or whatever, for four hours.

MacDonald: Did you go to Cinema 16?

McBride: I was a member for a couple of years, I think. When I was at NYU, Brian De Palma, whom I knew from the neighborhood, was making these little 16mm movies and getting them shown at Cinema 16, which I thought was kind of amazing. I remember going to see *Woton's Wake* [1962]. We did see some interesting stuff at Cinema 16. Certainly Maya Deren, but I'm not sure what else. In those days anything you could see was a plus.

MacDonald: David Holzman's Diary is a film lover's film, full of all kinds of allusions to other kinds of work. There seem to be a set of allusions to experimental underground film. Even something as simple as David's filming Penny sleeping is reminiscent of Warhol's *Sleep* [1964].

And David's getting a fish-eye lens and playing around with it out on the street suggests the use of the fish-eye lens in experimental film, beginning with Sidney Peterson in the forties. Your use of autobiography also seems to come partly out of the Underground—though some of the vérité makers also did autobiographical films.

McBride: Yes, I think what we did reflected everything we had experienced, including *Sleep.*

MacDonald: In his introduction to the *David Holzman* book Kit Carson mentions Andrew Noren as one of the people whose work was seminal in this project. How did you meet Noren? What of his work had you seen?

McBride: Well, Kit Carson and I collaborated on a monograph for the Museum of Modern Art about cinéma vérité, which never was finished. The part of it that we did accomplish was going around talking to filmmakers about their process.

MacDonald: How did you get this commission?

McBride: Kit got it. Kit is very good at hustling gigs. Willard Van Dyke had just recently taken over the museum film department, and Kit knew Willard somehow and wangled this project. Cinéma vérité was a passion of both of ours.

David Holzman came out of that project. The whole idea of truth in cinema seemed interesting at that point in life.

So we went around and talked to Ricky Leacock, Pennebaker, Bob Drew, the whole bunch. But we also decided to include people like Warhol and Andy Noren. When we went to interview Warhol, both Andy and Gerard Malanga were there, and Gerard answered all the questions we put to Andy. Andy just sat there and smiled.

Andy Noren had done this one film that had knocked me out. It was an interview with a girl.

MacDonald: Say Nothing [1965]?

McBride: That was it. It impressed the hell out of me, and we sought him out. He turned out to be a really interesting guy, and we hit it off and became friends.

MacDonald: So how did all those experiences lead to the *David Holzman* project?

McBride: I can't remember the chronology.

MacDonald: In the *David Holzman* book, Kit Carson's dates are a little bizarre. He mentions that in late 1967 you and he were having coffee somewhere, and you showed him this outline for this film about a character like David Holzman, but it has to have been earlier than that. Some of this stuff that you record from the TV for the film was recorded in July 1967.

McBride: It *was* earlier. I made this film twice. Are you aware of that?

MacDonald: No.

McBride: Well, before I knew Kit (I'm trying to remember how this all happened because I guess it did start before we did this interview project—this is all *so* long ago), I was working at a company that produced films used to sell land in Florida. It was an interesting learning experience about how to make movies for a particular purpose. There were only three people in the whole company, so I got to do a lot of different things. I got to shoot, to cut. This was my real training, more than school was. I had a good relationship with the guy who ran the place, and he would let me borrow equipment on weekends, and I started making this film with the actor Alan Rachins, who later went on to do the TV series *L.A. Law.*

MacDonald: When was this?

McBride: Nineteen sixty-five, I would guess. So I'm producing this film and had all my friends involved. Every weekend we'd go out and shoot something. Then I got fired from the job—it had nothing to do with the film I was doing—but I packed up all the film I'd shot, stuffed it into a cardboard box, and put it in the trunk of my beat-up old VW and left it there for a couple of weeks while I was looking for a cutting room I could use to edit the film. When I finally found a place, I went to the car, opened the trunk, and the film was gone.

I think in those days when people saw raw film on reels, they thought immediately of porno. At least that's my guess: someone took it thinking it was porn.

But I never did find it. It was a totally demoralizing experience, and I went for more than a year not even thinking about making a film.

Meanwhile, I had started working with Michael Wadleigh, a very accomplished vérité cameraman. I began to work with him as a sound man and sometimes as an editor. At some point, I told him about my film, and he got all excited and said, "Let's make it!" He had a whole setup: access to equipment and a little editing space with a Moviola. So we shot the film, using leftover film stock. We were constantly working on other projects where we'd end up with a lot of short ends, and you could send pieces of your film to be developed along with whatever job you were doing. So it really didn't cost much.

But it was Michael's involvement that allowed us to remake the film, and it was at that point that I got Kit involved in the project.

MacDonald: How fully was the story fleshed out when you began? The film is about the character David Holzman, but interspersed with what happens to him are many other kinds of material that create a general context for his story. I'd imagine that you went into the film with a fairly sketchy sense of what was going to happen.

McBride: Well, you're exactly right. It was part planned and part totally unplanned. We were impassioned by this vérité idea at the same time that we were picking it apart and making fun of it, but we also wanted to be open to whatever might happen in the course of things. There was a rough plan, but never a written script.

We did things in blocks, and most of the stuff of David in his apartment talking to the camera was done over one long weekend. I had spent the previous week sitting in the room with Kit and a tape recorder, saying, "Now in this scene, you're going to say this," and he'd sort of put it into his own words; and then I'd say, "Well, this part was good and that part wasn't so good." We were writing it out, without putting it down on paper. By the time we had done it a few times with the tape recorder, we knew exactly what it was going to be.

MacDonald: He's very good.

McBride: He's terrific, yeah. Kit contributed a lot of the language, but some ideas, too.

Then there was all the going-out-into-the-street-and-filming-life stuff, which we did piecemeal. I guess the most memorable thing, at least for me, is the encounter with the woman in the car who talks so frankly about sex. This was totally unplanned and happened just the way you see it in the film.

MacDonald: I read somewhere that he/she was in the midst of a sex change operation.

McBride: Yes, she was a man becoming a woman. We just ran into her one day and did the interview with her. I don't think Kit was even there. It was me and Mike Wadleigh asking those questions. And then she disappeared.

David Holzman (L. M. Kit Carson) in close-up, in McBride's *David Holzman's Diary* (1967). Courtesy Anthology Film Archives.

Whenever we'd get film back from the lab, we'd gather friends and look at it. One particular friend of mine happened to be there when we were looking at that material, and a week later he called me up and said, "I have to talk to you. I just had this really disturbing experience." He had been walking down the street, and she had driven up and thrown open the passenger door, inviting him to get in (it was three or four o'clock in the morning). He'd recognized her and hopped in, only to discover a little later on that she was a transsexual. He'd never had an experience like that, and it was very upsetting to him. I remember him saying, "I don't know whether I fucked a man or a woman!"

A year later, when we finally got a distributor, we had to track her down to get a release. She was apparently famous in the neighborhood.

MacDonald: I've been doing some writing recently on senses of place in independent film, and when I was writing about city symphonies, it struck me that on a certain level *David Holzman* is unusually good as a document of the Upper West Side at a certain point in time. This sense of place comes partly from several little experiments that echo avant-garde approaches of the era, like that long continuous shot where you move past the old people on the benches, or the sequence where "David" makes one frame of every image he sees on TV on a particular night.

McBride: Well, I lived on Seventy-first Street between Columbus and Central Park West and went by that little park every day, and I was fascinated by the place; it was such a weird combination of old people and junkies and kids. I had had the idea for that shot for a long time before we actually made it.

MacDonald: There was this vogue at the end of the sixties, in the wake of the Warhol films, of extremely long, continuous takes. Noren's *Say Nothing* is a continuous, thirty-minute shot.

McBride: Which is what was so compelling about it. The idea of real time was a big issue in those days, at least to me and to other filmmakers I knew.

I had the idea for the shot, but it was actually Mike who executed it, and he did it in a way that I wouldn't have thought of: he had the camera cradled in his arms and shot in slightly slow motion.

But a lot of the other stuff was just, "Well, let's go out and see what we find." We'd go out in the street with the idea of just picking up flavor. A lot of it was architectural. The Ansonia Hotel, and the house William Randolph Hearst built for Marion Davies, and the Dakota—they were all familiar landmarks to me because I'd spent my whole life on the Upper West Side. That's where I'm from. So there was a little bit of just wanting to get the local flavor into the movie. I think I was also impressed by some Alain Resnais films that used architectural tracking shots.

MacDonald: My students are so disappointed at the end that the film has been a ruse, but what's interesting is that only about half of the film is a narrative fabrication. Everything else is actually *more* real than what we're used to seeing. There's a paradox: on one level, *David Holzman is* less real than they thought; but on another level, it's *more* real than they realize, at least during their initial disappointment. And that *other* level of reality is what gives the story its power.

McBride: Yes. I think that's what's exciting. It *is* real in spite of the fact that it's a made-up story. It's a real place and a real time and, in fact, most of the events—even though they might have been fabricated—did come out of my own experience. There's a shot where David sees a girl on a subway train and follows her out of the train and onto the street. In the film she was played my wife. But I had had a similar experience where I followed somebody and she turned on me. I *was* a kind of voyeuristic person, watching other people on the street, looking in their windows, and vicariously living their lives.

MacDonald: Where did you shoot? Was it actually your apartment?

McBride: David's apartment belonged to my friend Lorenzo Mans, the guy in front of the mural, which was actually not in his apartment. David's apartment was in the Seventies, between West End and Riverside.

MacDonald: When the film was finished—

McBride: Well, it didn't *get* finished for a long time. It was just a lot of pieces. I mean, it never *felt* finished. Of course, I was constantly working on other things, too, and I think for a long time I was avoiding putting it together.

David Holzman filming himself, in *David Holzman's Diary* (1967). Courtesy Direct
Cinema and Mitchell Block.

Marty Scorsese was a classmate of mine at NYU, and after I left, Marty and
Mike were still there. Maybe Marty was teaching—I can't remember exactly—
but they had become friends. And at around the time we were making *David
Holzman's Diary,* Marty was doing his graduate thesis, or a redo of the master's
thesis film he had done [*I Call First,* 1968] with Harvey Keitel; ultimately it
became *Who's That Knocking at My Door?* [1968], which was semisuccess-
ful. Mike was helping Marty reshoot some stuff for this new film, and they were
editing it at Mike and his partner's place on Eighty-sixth Street, and I would see
Marty there all the time. It was inspiring to me that he was actually putting a
film together, and so I started putting mine together.

As we assembled *David Holzman,* it became clear what was there and what
was missing, and it turned out that what was missing wasn't all that much, and I
began to fill in the holes. But there was something about watching Marty that
made me want to finish the film. I don't know whether he's aware of that or not.

So all I'm saying is that it was a kind of piecemeal, organic process that
finally ended up being a film. *David Holzman's Diary* was finished in 1967.
After I had edited the film, I had David say, "This is July 1967" in his final
monologue, but we shot most of it earlier.

MacDonald: Did *David Holzman* really cost twenty-five hundred dollars?

McBride: That was the cash outlay. We always used borrowed equipment, and we got lab processing through other jobs. The only real costs were the finishing in the lab and the mixing, which added up to about twenty-five hundred dollars.

MacDonald: So how did the film work its way into the world?

McBride: We had one screening at the Film-makers' Cinematheque, then the film was shown at the Flaherty Film Seminar, and that fall it was at the Mannheim Film Festival.

MacDonald: What was the reception at the Cinematheque?

McBride: Well, the screening wasn't for the Anthology people. I just paid to use the facility and invited friends. That was the scariest moment of my life, I think, because I had *no* idea what I had done, and nobody had seen it, and I didn't know whether it was stupid or good.

It was very well received. I remember that Andy Noren was there, and for some reason his opinion was very important to me. He didn't come up to me like other people did to say they liked it or didn't like it. I saw him hanging around in the background and later found him in the bathroom. He liked the film but thought I should have gone further, and he wondered why did I have to make it fiction?

MacDonald: Now, the assumption is that it's the ultimate trick film. But I can imagine that the kind of people you brought together to see it, especially those who knew something about the project, would not have seen it that way at all. They would have seen it as a fiction about a character, and being fooled would probably not have been part of the experience for them.

McBride: Yes, I think you're right. That wasn't what was important to me at the time, either. It wasn't until we started showing it in foreign venues that the deception aspect of the film became an issue, both positively and negatively.

I want to say something about an early film and filmmaker of whom you may not be aware. Stanton Kaye did a film called *Georg* [1964]. It was made before *David Holzman's Diary* and dealt with a lot of the same issues as *David Holzman's Diary.* Sometimes when people interview me, it sounds like I invented this form or something, but I didn't really. I don't really remember *Georg* all that well—I certainly couldn't describe it to you at this moment—but it was a very interesting diary movie where the guy set up the camera and walked in front of it, and talked to the camera. It influenced me a lot. I think it gave me the idea for *David.* I want to give credit where credit is due.

MacDonald: I think the fact that Kit Carson is such a good actor and that you're in so close with him makes the reality of your film more compelling.

McBride: Yes. *Georg* has a certain distance.

Anyway, we had met Willard Van Dyke at the Flaherty Seminar, which was also the first place that *David Holzman* was invited to be shown.

MacDonald: What do you remember about that Flaherty Seminar [*David Holzman* was shown at the 1968 Flaherty Seminar, held at Windham College in Putney, Vermont, and programmed by D. Marie Grieco]?

McBride: I remember the beautiful setting and some wonderful films, including, I think, my first experience of *Louisiana Story* [1948]. The fun part was running into Bruce Conner, Bob Nelson, and other West Coast filmmakers whose films, particularly Bruce Conner's, I knew and loved. We were all young, and everybody else seemed to us to be older and more serious, so we did things like exchange name tags to goof on the "straight" folks.

MacDonald: In a recent issue of *Wide Angle* about the history of the Flaherty Film Seminar [Erik Barnouw and Patricia R. Zimmermann, eds., *The Flaherty: Four Decades in the Cause of Independent Cinema* 17, nos. 1–4 (1995)], somebody says that *David Holzman's Diary* destroyed documentary.

McBride: I don't remember anybody saying that, but if they did, it was only a theoretical conceit. Those days were a golden age of documentary filmmaking. And still today there's plenty of fine work around. And we've got mockumentaries and reality TV, too!

MacDonald: So *David* goes to the Flaherty and to Europe. What kind of experience did you have with it after those initial screenings?

McBride: All that I remember is my own incompetence in getting the film out—maybe that's not a fair way of putting it. There certainly *was* a lot of interest in it. You have to remember the context of the times—this was 1967, 1968, 1969—the hippie years, the time of alternative everything; and I had strong political feelings about independent film versus Hollywood movies. On the basis of *David,* I even got a couple of feelers from studios that I summarily rejected.

What I did was associate myself with several alternative distribution efforts. One was Leacock/Pennebaker. Another was something Mike Wadleigh and several of his cronies were trying to put together. Each time I would sign up with one of these groups, they would make all these elaborate plans and then go out of business. I began to think that I was the jinx, since it happened with such regularity. This was a three- or four-year process, and so the time passed when the film could have had some kind of a theatrical life, and in the end it just never did.

The best thing about that process was my getting involved with some people that Wadleigh knew, who were a little more professional than the people I knew. These guys came to me and said, "Well, you've made a movie that's a little on the short side—*David* is only seventy-four minutes long—and we're finding it hard to sell it as a package, but if we gave you ten thousand dollars, would you make a ten-minute film to go with it that would make it a salable package?" I jumped at the chance.

I ended up making a film that was closer to an hour long, *My Girlfriend's Wedding* [1969], which you may never get to see. *My Girlfriend's Wedding* was completely off-the-cuff. I had met this wonderful English girl and had fallen in love. She'd already made arrangements to marry somebody she'd never met, in order to get a green card and stay in the country. He was going to do it as a political statement. When this group made the offer to me, I'd just met this girl and knew this was happening, so I said, "Let's film her wedding." And that's what we did. I asked Mike Wadleigh to shoot; it was all the same bunch that had worked on *David Holzman.* We got back together and made this little movie all in one day.

MacDonald: And *did* they get released together at any point?

McBride: No. Because these people went out of business, too. Neither film got released—period! *David Holzman* had a small theatrical release in France. It had a lot of activity in other countries; but here, it only got semireleased in colleges and universities. I went through several different distributors over the years and never got a penny for the film.

MacDonald: Is *My Girlfriend's Wedding* available anywhere?

McBride: My Girlfriend's Wedding still languishes in obscurity.

MacDonald: So next you go through this period where you make *Glen and Randa, Pictures from Life's Other Side* [1972], and *Hot Times, A Hard Day For Archie* [1974]. Then there's a gap of almost ten years before *Breathless,* with which you reemerge. What happened? You'd made a name for yourself as an independent filmmaker, then you seem to disappear.

McBride: It was a period of great despair. I wasn't not working because I didn't *want* to. It may seem to you that there was a lot of activity before the nonactive period, but most of *that* time was, for me, pretty inactive also. I was desperately trying to find ways to make movies, and occasionally I'd get the chance to do something. *My Girlfriend's Wedding* happened a good couple of years after *David Holzman's Diary* was finished, and *Glen and Randa* was a couple years after that.

When the AFI started, I was one of the first people they contacted. They said, "We're going to make features. We want you to make our first feature," and gave me a grant to write a screenplay—my friend Lorenzo and I wrote it—which became *Glen and Randa.* The AFI dicked around with the screenplay for over a year. They had this grand plan where they were going to get financing from the studios, and it never happened. So they felt guilty and said, "If you ever want a small grant, we'll give you one."

I ended up getting to make *Glen and Randa* through more or less commercial channels. And then afterward, when nothing came my way again, I called up the AFI and said, "About that grant you promised me . . ." And they gave me about fifteen thousand dollars, which I used to make *Pictures from Life's Other Side.*

There was a lot of coming and going. I had a child. I moved to northern California and lived in the woods—my hippie period. Then I got involved with some Hollywood hippies, the people who made *Easy Rider,* and they said they wanted to make a movie with me, and I spent the better part of a year, again with Lorenzo, writing this very odd, interesting script about mountain men in the Rocky Mountains in the 1840s. That's a whole long story in itself, but basically we spent more than a year on this project, and it fell through.

So I went from the heights of being discovered by Hollywood and thinking I was getting a chance to make a big feature film (and to finally make a living), to the depths of despair. I moved back to New York with my family and couldn't get anything going. I ended up driving a cab.

In New York, I ran into this guy I'd gone to junior high school with, who was making porn films with his father. To make a long story short, he said, "We're about to make a new movie, and if you can come up with a script for a sex comedy about teenagers, where in every scene they're either doing it or talking about it, then you can have the job." That's the beginning of what became *Hot Times, A Hard Time for Archie*—it had many different titles.

Anyway, it wasn't like I had a great run of filmmaking. I was constantly scrambling and most of the time idle, or if not idle, at least not gainfully making movies. I got involved with dozens of projects that didn't come to fruition. Part of it just had to do with the times. When I made *David Holzman* in those early days, there was a tremendous amount of excitement about independent films and this terrific economic boom. Independent filmmaking existed on the fringe, where people with a little extra money who wanted to get into the world of the arts could, for a small investment, be part of something. But that all fell apart in the early to middle seventies. Suddenly people couldn't throw money away anymore, which was what investing in independent movies generally was. The whole scene just dried up.

By about 1975, I began to feel like it was never going to happen in New York, and that if I wanted to keep making movies, I had to go where they made movies. I went to L.A. I had written a script that I thought would be a surefire entrée into Hollywood, a salacious script about the sexual revolution, about underground life in New York City. It turned out to be something that people in Hollywood didn't want to know about. Instead of it being my calling card, it had the opposite effect and pretty much put me out of the running for a long time. So I spent a long time there without getting anywhere.

MacDonald: How did you stay alive?

McBride: Well, I did get involved in a couple of development deals. And at one point, through a friend, I got a job to write the narration for a Sam Fuller movie, *The Big Red One* [1980]. It was my first real *Hollywood* experience, in the sense that I felt I was selling out.

The Big Red One was an autobiographical film about Fuller's experiences in World War II; it was his personal movie. It had taken him a million years to get financing for it, and he turned in a four-hour movie. They wouldn't accept it at that length. He refused to cut it, so they fired him and hired an editor to cut it down to two hours. That's where I came in. I did try to be very faithful to his intentions. I was very scrupulous about it. Fuller had written the story as a novel before he had written the screenplay. I got hold of the manuscript (it had never been published) and wrote the narration using his words.

So, anyway, I did all kinds of stuff like that. I was a single father with a young boy. It was tough, and I had to do what I could.

MacDonald: Had you divorced?

McBride: We'd never been married, but we had split up.

MacDonald: What interested you in doing a remake of *Breathless?* The idea of remaking a film was unusual at a certain point. I mean nowadays everybody is remaking everything.

McBride: It's funny. I didn't know what the fuck I was doing in Hollywood, and I didn't know how to fit in there. The ideas that I kept coming up with were just dopey in the context of commercial filmmaking, and it took me a long time to get the point and figure out what I *could* do that would interest *me,* but would also interest *them.* For the longest time, I just kept drawing blanks. And I don't really know exactly what the gestation of the *Breathless* project was. The thought just came to me one day: well, this is something that they might go for because here's a movie that has a lot of cachet; it's famous but nobody's seen it; and in a funny way, it's a good old American story because it's Godard's homage to American B movies.

I don't know, it seemed as if maybe this could work; but also I thought, "God, how embarrassing! What a stupid idea this is!"

Somehow, I mentioned the idea to Tom Luddy, who used to run the Pacific Film Archive. And he said, "Well, let's call Jean-Luc"—because he was a friend of Godard's—and we did and Godard said, "Okay, sure."

MacDonald: Did Godard know *David Holzman?*

McBride: He knew *about* it, and so I seemed like a legitimate person to him. He was very gracious about my idea and gave me a free option. At some point he came to L.A. trying to get one of his own projects off the ground, and I chauffeured him around for a couple of days. It was the thrill of my life, hanging out with Jean-Luc Godard.

We signed a contract, and with that and with Kit Carson's help—Kit got excited about the idea—we got it under way. Kit knew this girl who worked for Marty Erlichman, a producer who was known for managing Barbra Streisand; and Marty thought this was an interesting idea, though he'd never seen the original movie. We got a print and rented a little screening room and screened it for him, and Kit and I are sitting nervously in the back, and Marty is sitting up in front, and in the middle of the movie we hear snoring. Marty is fast asleep. We didn't know what to do. Finally, the film ended and the lights went up, and he said, "Okay, let's do it." But that was just the beginning of a five-year process. We did get a little money from Universal to write a script, and then came the process of trying to get a star involved—an endless, demoralizing process that finally, five years later, produced Richard Gere.

But I was embarrassed about the project from the very beginning, about the whole idea of trying to remake one of the great movies of all time. It was dopey, really. But I swallowed my pride and just made a movie, and I was happy with the movie. I did go out of my way not to imitate the way Godard had made it, and to just try and make it a very American, very Hollywood kind of story.

I was right to an extent; it did have the cachet to make me legitimate in Hollywood. But it was a painful process. The whole transition from independent to Hollywood filmmaker was painful.

Abigail Child

Those of us who work at chronicling what we see as crucial dimensions of cultural history can hardly fail to recognize that we are prisoners of our personal taste. This is as true in what I have been calling "critical cinema" as it is with the most popular movies. My own experience with cinematic alternatives to pop cinema has involved a range of short-term and long-term responses. There have been instances where I have immediately admired and enjoyed, even understood, films that would obviously not appeal to conventional viewers. I was fascinated and enthralled by *Barn Rushes* (1971), the first Larry Gottheim film I ever saw, at its premiere in Binghamton, New York. As different from my conventional film experiences as seeing *Barn Rushes* was, I understood that Gottheim was using cinema as a way of extending and rethinking Monet's explorations of light. Similarly, I was enthralled by the first three sections of Hollis Frampton's *Hapax Legomena* (1971–72) and especially with *Poetic Justice* (1972, the second part of the seven-part suite of films)—in which the viewer reads a 240-page screenplay, page by page during 31½ minutes—when I saw it at Hampshire College in 1974, despite the continual distraction of furious viewers noisily stomping out of the auditorium. That *Poetic Justice* may have been poetic justice for these particular viewers would in no way have ameliorated their frustration with Frampton. But I was up half the night, writing notes about the Frampton films.

In many other instances I have been frustrated with films that seemed to have nothing to offer me, at least nothing I wanted, despite the fact that others clearly admired these films and had no doubt about their accomplishments and value. For nearly twenty years I could not fathom the widespread admiration of Yvonne

Rainer's films, especially once Babette Mangolte was no longer providing her highly formal cinematography (Mangolte shot Rainer's *Lives of Performers* [1972] and *Film about a Woman Who . . .* [1974]). In fact, by the late 1980s, I was so aggravated by the combination of my resistance to Rainer's films and the near-unanimous admiration of them by nearly all the colleagues I respected that I sometimes found myself practicing a wholesale denunciation of Rainer's work: "Yvonne Rainer is the most overrated filmmaker in the history of avant-garde film," I would announce to myself while driving my car or walking the dog. And then, in 1990, I saw *Privilege* and not only thoroughly enjoyed, understood, and admired it but realized that it delivered Rainer's entire oeuvre to me—I became an enthusiastic (and relieved!) convert.

My experience with Abigail Child's work is much closer to my wrestle with Rainer than to my experiences with Gottheim and Frampton, though to some degree this is a function of the Child films I saw first. I began to be aware of Child's work during the 1980s, when she was engaged with a set of explorations of image-sound relationship that extend the montage of Peter Kubelka's *Unsere Afrikareise* (*Our Trip to Africa,* 1966) into wildly staccato experiences that feel particularly elusive because of their density of image, sound, and idea. For many years, I have been particularly passionate about films that defy the acceleration of contemporary, commercial culture by slowing things down, and so it is not surprising that I made my first inroad into Child's work by way of *B/Side* (1996), her evocation/documentation/interpretation of her experience of living in a section of New York City that, during the 1990s, had been colonized by legions of the homeless. In its mixture of methods and sources—Child dramatizes moments in the life of a young homeless woman of Caribbean heritage; she contextualizes these fragments of story with black-and-white film documentation of New York City street scenes, and especially of sectors of the city where the homeless lived and conducted marginal businesses, and with color video footage of the construction, then destruction, of a homeless encampment across the street from her apartment, in June and October 1991—*B/Side* helped me to come to grips with the intricacies of image and sound in the higher-velocity Child films that had frustrated me for so long.

The seven films that constitute *Is This What You Were Born For?*—*Prefaces* (1981), *Both* (1988), *Mutiny* (1983), *Covert Action* (1984), *Perils* (1986), *Mayhem* (1987), and *Mercy* (1989)—are an exploration of cinematic possibility. Child works with found footage and imagery she shoots herself in various amalgams that allow her to reflect on a wide variety of dimensions of film history, including the commercial cinema (*Perils* evokes early film narrative; indeed, it was shot on the site of an early D. W. Griffith studio; *Mayhem* is Child's rumination on film noir); home movies (in *Covert Action,* Child means to lay bare the gender politics evident in a collection of home movies she had found); educational films and industrials (like Bruce Conner, Child inventively recontextualizes imagery taken from straightforward informational films so that this imagery speaks well beyond its original intent); and even her own outtakes (*Mutiny* and the recent video, *Where the Girls Are* [2002], use outtakes from Child's early documentary projects). Throughout this work, Child's fascination with the possibilities of the soundtrack in relation to montages of visual image is obvious. Indeed, her films are some of the few in the history of critical cinema that articulate sound with the same complexity and precision as they articulate visual imagery.

A general review of Child's approach cannot convey the particular challenges of her work. Indeed, few film artists more dramatically reveal the limitations of academic film study, which often seems far more interested in developing intricate arguments about texts *about* film than in exploring intricate films. Child's montages are often astonishingly intricate and require precisely the sort of careful, detailed study that those who analyze poetry or the structure of cells assume they must bring to their efforts. There is no space in a brief introduction to even begin to unpack one of Child's films, but perhaps a rough review of the opening seconds of *Prefaces* will be useful. During the first thirteen seconds of the film, we see about eighteen images (in some instances it is difficult to know if a particular image includes more than one shot) and hear at least nine sounds. The longest shots in the minisequence are the first, a black-and-white image of a waterfall, 3½ seconds long, and the thirteenth, a black-and-white negative shot of a woman having her ear examined, about 2 seconds long. In between these two shots we see (and in several instances almost see) a double-layered image of what is, judging from what occurs later in *Prefaces,* an African landscape; then a moment of darkness with a touch of blue; then a steel foundry furnace at work; then a black-and-white romantic landscape with what looks to be a distant standing figure; then two black-and-white abstract images in black, white, and gray; two unidentifiable color images with touches of gold; and two color street scenes, the second with a bright orange wall.

The variety of sounds is comparable to the variety in the imagery. Actually, the sound begins before the imagery, with a moment of orchestrated music that suggests a soundtrack from an adventure movie. This orchestral moment is followed immediately by a second orchestral phrase, from a more romantic film or moment; then by a brief moment of a woman singing opera; then by an unidentifiable rhythmic phrase; then by a man speaking a foreign word—it sounds like *wasabi;* then by a momentary continuation of that very first orchestral phrase; and, finally, by one male voice saying, "No, this isn't for me; this isn't for me," and a second, saying, "Ho ho!"

As one examines this tiny passage, the precision with which the image/image, sound/sound, and image/sound juxtapositions are articulated becomes obvious. Of course, the very relentlessness of Child's montage and the continual interruptions of one kind of image or sound by another are themselves a

Image in negative of woman apparently
undergoing an ear exam, followed by a single
frame of a second woman lying down (dead?),
then one of two frames of the first woman,
reversed—these final frames are virtually
invisible when the film is run at normal speed—
near the beginning of Abigail Child's *Prefaces*
(1981). Courtesy Abigail Child.

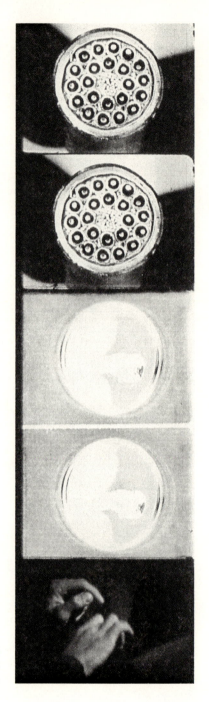

Successive frames of biological experiments
(?) and hands typing, from early in Child's
Prefaces (1981). Courtesy Abigail Child.

comment both on the nature of modern life in a consumer society and on the many concerns competing for one's attention and engagement. At first—and later, too—we can feel overwhelmed by the sheer number of images and sounds and by Child's implicit assumption that we will recognize her care in presenting them to us; but as the film proceeds, we slowly recognize what some of the more difficult-to-identify images are, and how they contribute to a variety of metaphors for Child's filmmaking process and to the particular concerns of this particular film.

In the passage I have roughly described, the waterfall suggests the relentless flow of image and sound in *Prefaces;* the shot of steel fabrication suggests the construction of the montage we are watching; the ear examination references both Child's commitment to the soundtrack as an equal partner with the image track and her interest—clear throughout *Is This What You Were Born For?*—in how women have been represented within film history and how they function within modern industrialized, technological culture. And, of course, the man's saying, "No, this isn't for me; this isn't for me," is Child's wry comment on what she (correctly) assumed would be the response of the largely male film studies establishment of 1981 to her work. Like the poetry of Ezra Pound and John Ashbery (a Child favorite) and the prose of Faulkner and Joyce, Child's films require a sustained effort. In fact, they probably require access to a Moviola or some device that can allow for a full examination of the details of their construction, second by second. Though Child is widely recognized as an important contributor to avant-garde film—her work is routinely included in the annual "Views from the Avant-Garde" section of the New York Film Festival; P. Adams Sitney's new edition of *Visionary Film* includes a brief discussion of Child—no one has yet stepped forward to provide anything like a thorough investigation of her films. Like Hollis Frampton, Child imagines an audience far more deeply committed to film culture than is common these days, even in academe—an audience comparable to those that have formed, over time, around the work of Pound, Proust, Joyce, Faulkner, and other challenging major figures in the literary arts.

When one sees Child's films from the late 1970s on, it is difficult to imagine that she began her career as a documentarian for NBC television in New York City, making relatively conventional films about prostitution and street gangs. But early on she realized that, despite their successes, her NBC projects were not providing her with the aesthetic challenges she needed, and once she moved to San Francisco in 1976, she reinvented herself. Her formative influences, once she had begun to make films again, were experimental poetry and experimental sound work—as well as a variety of filmmakers: Peter Kubelka and Frampton, in particular. In recent years her early involvement with documentary has reemerged, first in *B/Side* and in *8 Million* (1992), a documentation/interpretation of Ikue Mori's sound compositions; and more recently in *Below the New: A Russian Chronicle* (1999), her response to a visit to Russia.

Child is a poet, as well as a filmmaker (see the bibliography for details). She teaches at the School of the Museum of Fine Arts in Boston. I spoke with Child in her New York apartment—a sixth-floor walk-up on Avenue B—in January 2002 and subsequently by phone and e-mail.

MacDonald: I know you didn't start out to be a filmmaker.

Child: No. I started as a photographer and became a filmmaker by moving toward the broadest, multiple synesthesias—the *maximal* voices, rather than the most specialized. As an undergraduate at Harvard, I majored in history and literature. Each year I took one art course, and at the end of four years, I realized that they were the courses I enjoyed the most—the ones where I would start work at eight in the evening and it would be midnight the next time I looked up—so I applied to graduate schools in art. I went to Yale because they didn't require you to specialize. Architecture, film, photography were all together.

Harvard did play a role in my development as a filmmaker: Derek Lamb, the animator from Canada, showed me my first experimental films. I was a suburban kid who had never seen anything non-Hollywood, other than *Sundays and Cybele* [1962, directed by Serge Bourguinon] and a couple of Godards, in an art-movie house in East Orange, New Jersey.

I grew up in West Orange, home of Edison's famed Black Maria, to which we went on a field trip in the first grade. I remember being astonished at the walls that moved. West Orange is close to where Nick Dorsky grew up. He's older than me, but we're from the same suburban, North Jersey world; on the weekends you'd drive your car up to the South Mountain Reservation to see the sparkling fall leaves and gun your engines, then go to the sweet shop.

As I remember, Derek Lamb showed us three experimental films: part of Brakhage's *Dog Star Man* [1961–64]; and Len Lye's *Trade Tattoo* [1937], which I thought was *fabulous;* and an Arthur Lipsett: *Very Nice, Very Nice* [1961]. I remember thinking, "interesting, very interesting, but I want to reach the People"—I was eighteen, and to the extent that I was thinking about filmmaking, my intention was to become a documentary filmmaker. I took anthropology at Harvard, in a program that took you to Chiapas. That was an important experience for me, and for a while I thought I would become an ethnographic filmmaker. I never did take a course with Robert Gardner, who was already at Harvard—he scared me—but I did take an animation class with Derek Lamb and sat next to Caroline Leaf, who discovered sand animation. She brought sand in from the Boston coast and did her fantastic sweet stuff.

At Yale, there were really no film classes, except for a history of film course. But there was a weeknight program where I saw *Fuses* [1967, by Carolee

Schneemann] and thought it was great; and there was another program that showed classic commercial stuff. We'd go from anti-Vietnam protests to see John Ford westerns, which seemed to make a crazy kind of sense. In my second year of graduate school somebody donated money to Yale to support filmmaking, and I got eight hundred dollars to make my first film.

By this time, I was engaged to Jon Child, whom I'd met at Harvard. Jon was a musician in New York; we later married (Nadelson is my real name).

Jon was a jack-of-all-trades and a great technician. He played in a band and was a recording engineer. He can do anything technical, and I learned a lot from him. We did our first film together.

MacDonald: This is *Except the People* [1970]?

Child: Yes. For the editing Jon was able to get a "freebie" through a friend at an advertising house: I could go in at 9:00 P.M. and work until 8:00 A.M. on an upright Moviola, the kind with foot pedals, and I remember thinking one night, "I *love* this! This is what I want to do for the rest of my life." Editing film let me think about music, sound, image, language—the *multiplicity* of the thing is what drew me. At that point, I still thought I would become an ethnographer, in South America (I spoke Spanish); and in some ways I *do* still think of myself as an ethnographer, but of urban spaces. So that was it—that moment was decisive. I knew I was going to be a filmmaker, and editing was my calling. I finished the film and showed it to my professors at Yale, and they liked it; and it was shown all over the country, including at the Whitney and at Film Forum, which was still uptown on the West Side [Film Forum, founded by Peter Feinstein in 1970 and directed since the early 1970s by Karen Cooper, moved from the Upper West Side to SoHo in 1975].

At the time, I was living in a tiny apartment in the East Village with Jon; and at some point I said, "OK, let's do a second film." In doing *Except the People,* we had met a guy who had been involved in the Jewish theater on Second Avenue during the thirties. He would go on and on about the neighborhood then—because by now the neighborhood was falling apart. *Now,* we learned, he went to whores.

I was coming out of the feminist movement and thought, "Ah, this is my next subject!" So *Game* [1972] was about a prostitute and the whore "stroll" that existed at that time on Second Avenue below Fourteenth Street. That film also went to the Whitney, and to a Swiss festival and Swiss TV, and to the Flaherty.

MacDonald: What was the Flaherty experience like?

Child: It was important, largely because I got to see a great number of films, and because Amos Vogel curated a program that included Georges Franju's *The Blood of the Beasts* [1949], some Chinese documents of operations with acupuncture, and *Night and Fog* [1955, Alain Resnais]. What a show!

I met Ruby Rich [author of *Chick Flicks: Theories and Memories of the Feminist Film Movement* (Durham, N.C.: Duke University Press, 1998)] at the Flaherty. She was a skinny girl, with curls down to here, a lime green jumper, beautiful, very excited, very energetic—lovely. The Flaherty was at Harriman House that year—a really nice place in the woods where the deer hadn't been hunted, so they came right up to the pool.

Game was attacked, I guess because it's an ambivalent documentary. All the inconsistencies and ambiguities and cross-genre material that were to appear in my work later on were already there—in a kind of naive form. Marcel Ophuls defended *Game.* There was a crowd who had some "pure" idea of "documentary," and Marcel is going, "No! This film is great!"

After that, I took my two films to NBC television, to an executive producer who had been a reporter in Israel during the 1948 war. He saw *Game,* looked at my résumé, and said, "Okay, you're hired." It was a freelance gig. The other freelancers told me, "You'll have to work too fast, but if you do enough of them, one will click." I met a lot of Left documentarians on the job. We were all doing city stories, and because I had done *Game,* I was assigned "dangerous" women projects, street crime subjects. By the midseventies I had a job as a female director-producer for NBC, earning enough so that I could take a half year off for my own projects. So it was good training, and allowed me to stay on in New York.

The first film I did for NBC was about single mothers. I focused on three single mothers, in a classic TV documentary format. You had to do these pieces within five weeks, which meant that on a Monday you were given your assignment; you called people Tuesday, Wednesday, Thursday; you went out and shot Friday, Monday, Tuesday, Wednesday; you edited for two weeks; you had one week in the lab; and then it went on the air. I was working with these incredible union editors at NBC, almost all Italian. They were cutting sync sound films on rewinds—they had rigged this great system. By the time I left that job, they were working on flatbeds, Moviolas.

The second piece I did for NBC was *Savage Streets* [1973], an amazing assignment about the South Bronx. It was due in November, but they gave me the assignment in July, so I went up there early. That was the only time I was scared. One day I went with cops. Another day I met up with a reporter who had been with the *Chicago Sun Times* and was now with *Newsday,* a black man who became a mentor for me, because he had had a lot of experience—just what I didn't have.

This was when there were areas in the South Bronx where even the cops and the firemen wouldn't go—because if they went in, they'd be attacked. Buildings were allowed to burn to the ground. It was intense. Through various people I knew, I found three different gangs. Roberta Cantrow was working up there with a theater group, and she gave me some names.

I found a gang called Savage Skulls, and what interested me about them was that a twelve-year-old member had died, and his brother, who was eleven, was still in the gang. The mother was trying to keep the eleven-year-old away from the gang and had moved to Queens. They had photos of the funeral of the first brother, so I could start the piece with the photos and then bring in the younger kid saying, "I want to die just like my brother did." Then you could speak with the mother. You could build a story around the situation, with multiple perspectives: the cops, the kids, the moms.

I had Julianna Wang as cinematographer, one of two women in the union at that time. Julianna is really strong, right on top of the action, and a great camerawoman, so the film is beautifully shot. But it was difficult because all these big Italian and Irish union guys were saying, "You?—*you're* giving directions?" Particularly on the South Bronx street-gang piece, it seemed like the union guys quit every night. If you look at the credits, there are like six gaffers. These guys hated the project; they hated these people; they hated that we were giving them attention.

And the gangs were lying to me. We did stay on the streets long enough so that things happened: we were rolling during a fight where somebody's neck is cut. Much later, some of that material ended up in *Mutiny.*

The South Bronx experience taught me something about ghetto kids. It seems to me that a third have been mentally and physically damaged. They've either been hit too hard or seen too much violence, and they're going to be dead before they're eighteen: they don't particularly *want* to live and will try anything. Another third have been damaged but not quite as badly, or at least they're smarter, and run the system; they become successful criminals, but they'll be lucky if they're not in jail by the time they're twenty-one. Then there's a third group who have grandmothers or *somebody* who ropes them back in time, and they'll get out.

I met kids who could slit someone's throat, but were *so* vulnerable, because they were so desperate for some adult to be kind to them, to listen to them; and they were telling me these incredible stories. This one guy said, "I saw my father shot in the head." His father was killed in front of his eyes while he was holding his hand. How do you ever get over the anger and the pain? It was a war zone, and they were war-zone kids.

One time, somebody pulled a gun on me and cocked it, and I'm flippantly responding, "Oh, what could *this* be?" Ignorance is a kind of courage, or courage is ignorance—in any case, the kids were knocked out that I didn't freak, so they put the gun away, and that was the end of that.

What *was* horrific was going into the apartments where these gang guys lived with their girls, who seemed to be about fourteen. There was dog shit all over the floor. It was wild, and it was sad.

MacDonald: Do you think of yourself as a person drawn to danger?

Child: No, not at all, why?

MacDonald: I used to think of you living over here in Alphabet-land [Avenues A, B, C, on the east side of Lower Manhattan] when it wasn't at all a safe neighborhood.

Child: I wasn't living here because I was loving danger but because it was where I could afford space. So many artists lived on First Avenue or eastward.

Basically, I was a protected suburban kid who'd lived in the same house for eighteen years. Maybe if you *are* that protected and safe, you can do risky things, especially in your work. Maybe when there isn't security in your life, it's harder to be risky aesthetically? In any case, to go back to your question, *I* didn't think of myself as drawn to danger.

I spoke to Charles Musser recently, and he said that he'd heard that I carried a switchblade. *[Laughter.]*

I *was* living with Jon, a rock and roll musician, and I was hanging out with him in recording studios. I was a groupie in a way that I wouldn't have admitted at the time. I was in the studio with Jimi Hendrix. Through Jon, I also met Jerry Ragavoy, who started the Hit Factory and wrote "Take a Piece of My Heart," which was recorded by Janice Joplin. Jerry is a white guy from Philadelphia who connected to black music and wrote great Motown songs. He'd have the studio musicians come in and do a new song, and then the next week Stevie Winwood and Traffic would come in and do their version. And it would be like two different songs. Jon would mix for them and for the Band, and I would get to attend *those* sessions. I learned so much, hearing things repeated and looped, and gone back over, and layered, and mixed, and rerecorded, or recorded in different styles. I know it's had a big effect on my filmmaking.

MacDonald: It's interesting that of the three avant-garde films you saw at Harvard, you liked Lipsett and Lye the most—both are sound filmmakers.

Child: Sound and humor.

Actually, all this about the recording studio was initiated by your question, was I drawn to danger? No, I was drawn to *excitement, intensity,* and cultural resonance. I had a healthy level of fear, but also a lot of energy. Those street documentaries put me in touch with social ambiguities and a larger, more political life. To be out on the street, to be with the *real,* felt alive (however naive I might have been in defining that "real").

Savage Streets turned out to be the only time I was censored in my TV work. I came back with the footage and said, "Let's do a woman's voice-over—*I'll* do the voice-over"—I thought it would be amazing to hear a woman over the harsh world we were seeing. My producer said, "No, no. We're going to get Piri Thomas to do the narration" (Piri's the writer who wrote *Down These Mean Streets;* presumably, Scorsese paid him for the title). Piri's a nice enough guy, and a real romantic, so there's a highly emotional, lavishly Latin voice-over on the finished film. I thought, and still think, it's wrong and pushes the film into a different, completely crazy space. *Savage Streets* went on TV, and people loved it. The president of NBC saw it and thought it was the best thing he had ever seen, blah, blah, blah. So they put me on *The Today Show* with Piri, who totally dominated the conversation. I'd never even seen *The Today Show,* but there I was at seven o'clock in the morning, being interviewed. They showed six and three-quarter minutes of the film, because if they showed seven minutes, they would have had to pay me. The stinkers. Later, my producer said, "Did you real-ize you had a hole in your pants?" *[Laughter.]* I guess I wasn't thinking about how I looked.

My last piece for NBC was on radical nuns. The outtakes became *Some Exterior Presence* [1977]. By that time, I was unhappy with television—especially with the fact that time, or really the lack of it, was effectively another kind of censorship. And with documentaries in general I felt that at best I was only preaching to the converted.

In the early days, I was part of New York Newsreel (before it became Black Newsreel). I'd go to the meetings and knew many of the filmmakers, including Geri Ashur and, from a greater distance, John Douglas and Robert Kramer. I particularly respected the Maysles brothers as filmmakers, and Charlotte Zwerin, who edited *Straight, No Chaser: Thelonious Monk* [1989].

I was also finding my way into a very different world. I had met Andrew Noren through *Game,* at the International Festival of Women's Films (organ-ized by Christina Nordstrom) in 1972. There he was, lurking in the shadows. I hung out with him from 1972 to 1974.

I also met David Liu, who became the head of ITVS; his wife, Margot, had taken me to my first Richard Foreman play. I was introduced to the Wooster Group and Anthology Film Archives. I remember a Richard Foreman piece where Aline Mayer and Sheila McLaughlin were two nude pillars. I was intrigued. I became part of this fledgling community.

So, from about 1974 to 1976, I'm doing documentaries for NBC, but I'm also getting involved in the downtown art world. In 1973 I received an AFI grant, and for the first time I didn't have to work for a living. Since I had more time, I volunteered for a Bob Wilson piece—he had an ad in the *Voice* for someone to be an ostrich. In high school I'd heard about Happenings, and when I saw Bob Wilson perform during a visit to New York (I was still at Yale), I thought, "Whoa, *that's* really it!" And so, when I got this six months off, I became an ostrich in *The Life and Times of Joseph Stalin* [1975]. And I started improvisa-tion classes with Meredith Monk, Trisha Brown, and Simone Forti. It was an exciting time—and all of this was pushing me away from documentary, telling me there was something else.

And then, I saw Hollis Frampton at Anthology. My work doesn't look like Frampton's at all, but *Zorns Lemma* [1970] was important. In part this was because Hollis was working with language. I remember watching *Zorns Lemma* and thinking, "You can do anything you want, and you can make whatever you want!" It was very freeing—even transformative.

In the summer of 1975 I went to Hampshire College, to the University Film Study Center summer event, and there I saw films by George Landow, Peter

Hutton, and Robert Breer. I took an optical printing workshop with Stan Lawder and John Rubin and did little films, and met a lot of people. I particularly remember seeing Peter Hutton's work—it was so relaxed; and then Peter comes onstage, chain-smoking and charmingly nervous, the opposite of the films.

I came back from that summer, completely exploded, but I had to do one last job for TV. I'd gotten a commission for a half-hour program, part of a new ten-program PBS series, *Women Alive,* and made *Between Times* [1975] with some Minneapolis suburban girls—some of that material ended up in *Mutiny.* Actually, *Mutiny* contains outtakes from several of my documentaries rolled up together with some new material; it's a kind of revenge against TV.

MacDonald: It seems to me that in the late seventies you go through a period where you're experimenting with approaches you'd become aware of by going to avant-garde film events. I'm thinking of *Some Exterior Presence, Peripeteia 1* [1977], *Peripeteia 2* [1978], and of *Pacific Far East Line* [1979] and *Ornamentals* [1979], which, for me, are your first really good experimental films.

Child: They are my first experimental films altogether. Just before I went to Hampshire, the apartment I was living in (which I got from Abbie Hoffman—that's another story) was robbed, and then robbed a second time (the thief came back to get what wasn't taken the first time). I lost everything I had of value, except my 16mm Beaulieu, which was in the shop at the time. Afterward I just couldn't stay in the apartment anymore, so for a while, I was moving into another sublet every three months. I think I had a nervous breakdown.

I did an independent shoot for a July 4, 1976, project, got paid a few hundred dollars (I never saw the footage), and left New York with my Beaulieu and a suitcase. I went west, first to the Naropa Institute for the summer, and then to San Francisco, and didn't come back to New York until 1980.

Naropa—the Buddhist center in Boulder, Colorado, which supports dance, music, and poetry classes—was great for me. I saw readings by Burroughs and Creeley and Ginsberg, and took classes with Meredith Monk. And I met Yani Novick, a dancer-performer who was willing to provide me with loft space in San Francisco and, amazingly, with an editing bench and a hot splicer and rewinds. In San Francisco I pulled out material from the last year and started over, as an experimental, "back-to-zero" filmmaker. That's when the films you mentioned were made.

Some Exterior Presence, the first of them, is based on Feynman diagrams of electrons, in that the film imagery goes forward, backward, or is flipped, all of which are analogous to the three movements electrons can make (at that time, I liked to read physics, not because I understood it all the time but because the ideas were provocative). I needed to optically print to finish the piece, and somebody told me that Henry Hills had an optical printer, so that's how I met Henry.

I also got involved with the San Francisco poetry scene. I'd always kept a notebook, and during those last years in New York, I'd begun to read poetry again. Between 1975 and 1976, I read much of the English poetry of the last fifty years. When I encountered the short poems of Louis Zukofsky, I remember my exhilaration.

I met Ron Silliman, a major figure in the Language Poetry circles—then an unnamed, loose, energetic bunch of poets from all over the country. Ron was on unemployment, living in a hippie coven (the last?) in Pacific Heights, and totally interesting. I'd been doing some dancing, which was very healthy, but I was hungry for language. Ron invited me to a reading group where we read Barthes and Sartre and Fredric Jameson and Walter Benjamin—my introduction to Western cultural critique, which helped me make better sense of my experience at NBC, among other things.

MacDonald: Forgive me if I do a mini-psychoanalytical read of the films after *Some Exterior Presence.* In *Peripeteia 1* and *2,* you're dealing with a shattered frame and with a gestural camera, which could be read as a hysterical use of the camera—it's as if the shape of that film is your attempt to regain control of yourself after that breakdown in New York. By the time you get into *Pacific Far East Line,* you've pulled yourself back together and you're *building* something.

Child: When I'm making a film, it is like constructing a building. I was interested in architecture early on. Spatial relations are important to me. In fact, it's possible to think of some of my work as a spiral shape; there is continuity, but it's "bent"—it's around the corner. The spiral is used to shape *Ornamentals, Prefaces,* and *Covert Action.*

In any case, those four years in San Francisco were incredible; San Francisco was good to me. It was cheap. I lived on food stamps and unemployment, worked as a film shipper, a Berkeley gardener, in a law office, in an illegal bakery, as a census-taker, and as a dancer and trapeze artist. I was living in a sublet, fifteen-hundred-square foot loft, and I had film equipment. I was two blocks from Gasser's, on Third and Folsom Streets, where, years earlier, Kerouac would drink. I could get my film to the lab five minutes after rolling out of bed.

I was able to do a lot of film and be a participant with both the community of filmmakers *and* the community of poets. There were readings every week at Grand Piano; there were talks and Poets' Theater. The poets' community was *very* satisfying. Poets remain my community; they've been an important part of my filmmaking and of my thinking about filmmaking.

MacDonald: Ornamentals is like your Ph.D. thesis in experimental film. It's a compendium of Robert Breer, Marie Menken, Bruce Conner, Landow, Frampton—*Lemon* [1969] is in there—Kenneth Anger, Peter Kubelka. It's as if you're saying, "Okay, here's what I've learned in this graduate school of San Francisco." It's also an exquisite film.

Child: Thank you.

I'd seen most of the filmmakers you name in New York. San Francisco was more about a supportive community and having time and space to explore.

I had been reading Foucault on order and power, and that was important for this project. I wanted to make a film based on the color spectrum, to undermine expectations and genre. I took these emotional images (when I look at them now, I'm less sure I would categorize them that way), fragments, that come partially from New York and partially from San Francisco—the passage from New York to San Francisco is imaged in the content itself—and structured it according to the color spectrum. I cut it on rewinds.

MacDonald: Was Marie Menken an important filmmaker for you?

Child: I remember seeing her work before I went to San Francisco. It has a wit that I relate to. I remember the girls graduating in *Go! Go! Go!* [1964]. I also love Joyce Wieland's *Hand Tinting* [1967].

MacDonald: A specific connection I make between your work and Menken's is your use of "light writing"—I don't know what else to call it. In *Peripeteia* you do lovely work with a gestural camera, causing colored lights to "write" on the filmstrip. Menken does that in *Go! Go! Go!*

Child: I didn't think of that. That *could* be a connection: women, the body, filmically embodying gesture. But I think Frampton is the one who inspired me, with his mental figurations and his language orientation (he wanted to be a poet). He was also into structure, complexity, and programs for construction, and that fascinated me.

It was also during those San Francisco years that I met Warren Sonbert, Nick Dorsky, and Jerry Hiler, and we became friends. We'd have Thanksgiving dinner and go to the opera, and there were great dinner parties, walks—another community, and another set of influences.

MacDonald: In both *Pacific Far East Line* and *Ornamentals,* you use the motif structure so characteristic of your later work, where you start with one type of image, bring in a new one, then bring back the first, then add another, then bring *that* back in, so that they become threads in the weave of the film.

Child: That's true. The *Peripeteias* are *camera* explorations, not editing explorations at all. In fact, *Peripeteia 2* is a work print. I've lost the original.

MacDonald: About another aspect of the San Francisco scene: at a certain point, you and Henry Hills become editors of the *Canyon Cinemanews;* it seems very clear to me that you and he set out consciously to change the journal.

Child: Actually I think *Henry* may have set out to change the journal; I wasn't aware of its history at that point. Originally, I was an assistant, and later became, at times, the editor.

I wanted to help create a lively journal. I remember only slowly being aware that many people in America and Canada were reading what we did. I had thought it was a more local endeavor. And we got these crazy letters back—furious at us or at an article, or whatever.

MacDonald: One of the things that's interesting about the *Cinemanews* issues you were involved with, and I wonder if you were the instigator, is the kind of poetry that the journal printed. The *Cinemanews* had always included poetry, but the kind of experimental writing that the journal was printing was suddenly very different.

Child: I had met the Language Poets before I met Henry. And it fed into the *Cinemanews*.

MacDonald: Were you involved in the distribution arm of Canyon?

Child: I worked at Canyon Cinema, as a shipper, part-time, for several years in the late seventies. That was great because it meant I could look at films five nights a week. We were young and crazy and energetic enough to say, "OK, we're getting together tonight to look at three new Paul Sharits films!"

Henry was very close to Carmen Vigil, so we got to attend gatherings at Carmen's house, with Frampton and whomever; we'd go for drinks or mushrooms or whatever was cooking. There was an intimacy there.

MacDonald: Another thing that changes when you and Henry become involved is the percentage of interviews with filmmakers.

Child: We both thought that what the artists say is the most interesting, so we pushed that. Also, we wanted to bring in more theory. Malcolm LeGrice had arrived in San Francisco, and he was very interested in ideas. He influenced all of us.

MacDonald: Did you live in the same place in San Francisco the whole time you were there?

Child: Yes.

MacDonald: The place from where you shot *Pacific Far East Line?*

Child: Exactly. I would have stayed in San Francisco, but that loft was in the downtown area where they were building the Moscone Center. It got too expensive. At one point, I was going to move into a building Nick and Jerry lived in, but I ended up following Henry Hills back to New York. Love. *[Laughter.]*

I left San Francisco, feeling that with *Ornamentals* I'd learned something about color, light, and structure. And on the way back to New York, I wrote out a script for a seven-part film.

MacDonald: Is This What You Were Born For?

Child: Yes. The script was different from what the film ended up being, but not *so* different. I had conceived from the start that each of the films would have a different sound-image relationship.

Ron Silliman used to talk about the field of poetry as a matrix with full and empty spaces, and I'd been thinking of film as a matrix and wondering where the empty spaces were, where I could make discoveries. I decided the emptiest space was the area of sound/image. There was Kubelka; obviously, Kubelka's *Unsere Afrikareise* was, and is, really important to me. And there was Len Lye, and Lipsett. And Frampton. But almost no one else was investigating sound and image. I was sure this was an area where I could contribute something new.

The first section, *Prefaces,* was going to be wild sound. I was living in downtown Manhattan, on Ludlow Street, and I did some shooting there and used a little found footage. Then that summer I went back to San Francisco and on hand rewinds edited the imagery and then the sound and developed a kind of Cageian organization of industrial sound, human voice, city traffic.

I began *Mutiny* with the outtakes from *Between Times.* I made a three-minute piece and hated it. I thought, "I'm stuck in high school, and I'm never going to get away from these girls!" Rafik, who rented equipment and editing, sold supplies, and had screenings in the back of his loft, named "OP Screen," had a single-system sound camera that he rented, an Auricon, the kind that Warhol used.

I filmed local artists in local environments: Sally Silvers dancing at NYU, Shelley Hirsch singing at the Italian street festival, Polly Bradfield playing violin in Chinatown—those are the three main contemporary performers. I went back to *Game* and *Savage Streets* for additional material, edited it together, and that was *Mutiny.*

MacDonald: Both *Prefaces* and *Mutiny* have a very similar color palette. It's very distinctive in your work, actually, all the way up to *B/Side.*

Child: Hmmm. I think *Prefaces* and *Mutiny* use many colors.

MacDonald: They use many colors, but there are certain oranges and golds that seem to be motifs, and there are a lot of colors that aren't there.

Child: Those are city films, and there's not much green because of that. Also, and importantly, they use reversal film and, in these cases, are one-light prints.

I did, and do, edit for color. In *Surface Noise* [2000] the lab had a lot of trouble. They would say, "But this is really weird color." And I would say, "Yep, I want that really strange pink next to that weird turquoise blue."

MacDonald: I guess what makes me conscious of this is the difference in color between these films and *Ornamentals.*

Child: Ornamentals is 16mm Kodachrome, which I never had access to again. I did seven prints at the time with the last of the Kodachrome stock.

MacDonald: Tell me more about the seven-part structure of *Is This What You Were Born For?*

Child (joking): Well, I like the number seven . . .

MacDonald: You were saying that the fundamental differences between the sections are distinctions in sound-image relationship?

Child: Yes, but, you know, everything gets skewed in the process of actually making work. The first film used wild sound; the second was sync; the third was going to be voice-over; the fourth and the fifth were originally going to involve de Sade's *Justine:* one would be silent; another structured off music.

After *Prefaces* and *Mutiny* came *Covert Action,* which used voice-over. I had already shot two poets doing an improvisational dialogue, but the imagery was so dull that I got rid of it and used the sound improvisation as a score. The imagery was all home-movie material.

Couples in home movies recycled
in Child's *Covert Action* (1984).
Courtesy Abigail Child.

In home movies, I realized, there *is* partially a real dimension, but what I
was interested in was not the surface reality but the Henry Jamesian aspect to
that imagery: "What's going on *underneath* the picture?" That's why *Covert
Action* has such a layered soundtrack. There's an inner monologue that does-
n't jibe with the outer world. I think that's true about presentations of families
in general, maybe particularly about the presentation of women. In the home
movies in *Covert Action* the women are collaborating in implicit violence

and are revealing how women have to present a front when a whole other experience is happening inside them.

MacDonald: Alan Berliner, whose work parallels yours at a certain moment, plays with that idea in *The Family Album* [1986]: the home-movie imagery gives you one dimension of family life—nearly all home movies are about trying to make the family look wonderful—but the soundtrack reveals the distance between the way the family *looks* in home movies and what those people in the movies are really feeling. You do it differently.

Child: Actually, some of the *Covert Action* material comes from the same source as the footage Alan used in *The Family Album.* There was an ad at the Collective for Living Cinema for a collection of home movies, and Alan got there first and bought most of it. By the time I arrived, just an hour of it was left.

The real difference between his work and mine has to do with compression and density and confrontational humor. *Covert Action* is more direct, and as a result, it remains a contemporary viewing experience, I think.

To get back to the scoring of the film, I usually do a rough cut of the images first, but in certain films the score is something distinct, the *plot,* if you will, that threads through the piece and determines its direction. In *Covert Action,* the score is the voices of the two poets, Carla Harryman and Steve Benson, talking back to the image and against the image and to each other.

MacDonald: You say talk back to the image. Did they see your imagery?

Child: No. But I cut them *as if* they were talking back to the imagery; you'll hear, "What were they thinking?" as you're looking at certain faces. I was playing with these kinds of connections.

Prefaces and *Mutiny* had been single-track compositions. Then with *Covert Action,* I thought, "Well, I have two tracks, how can I make the sound be more like a chord?" You get the image and not just one sound, but a whole set of sounds that continually change the way the image reads. With *Covert Action* I had two tracks and the film was about male-female relations: a man and a woman were talking; and the images were about men and women.

MacDonald: Let me get clear on this. The man and the woman talk on the same track, and the other track includes all these other sounds?

Child: In the final mix, I had a track that was the woman; another, the man; and many—six to ten—other tracks with several different kinds of sound. But working on the Steenbeck, I had only two tracks and had to bounce these voices and sounds back and forth. The paradigmatic moment in *Covert Action,* for me, is the hula dancer. I put a piece of music on one track that goes like this [waving her hand like a snake], and on the other, I'm cutting in all these other sounds. It's a double rhythm. I was interested in a beat that would fight against the other beat, and I wanted *both* to work against the image.

I dislike it when people say, "Oh, it's like sampling." No, it's not like sampling *at all.* Because if you just randomly put sound up against that imagery, it won't do what I want it to do. My sound and image are precisely articulated, to the microsecond, which doesn't mean I'm not discovering things, just that the sound is not random in its connection to image. For example, the sound over the woman doing the hula is, on one track, the soundtrack from *Cobra Woman* [1944, by Robert Siodmak]; on the other, it's Nina Hagen, John Zorn, John Cage, and some country rock music.

The country rock is in there because you're seeing home movies and a domestic world. Country music is great *music,* but if you actually listen to what the lyrics say—"He's hitting me, and I'm still here" or "She was great, but I'm leaving her"—it's full of pain. If you live the life of most country lyrics, you're in trouble. In other words, country music is ambivalent and contradictory—multivalent—paralleling the way we experience interiority.

I felt that *Covert Action* was the beginning of my narrative work. It's about the human body and sexual relations.

MacDonald: The imagery in *Covert Action* is from home movies, but there are also intertitles: "In our society, flesh is gummed with sentiment," and so on. Whose texts are those?

Child: Mine. I felt I needed another set of images of some kind.

MacDonald: They look like they're from old movies.

Child: This was coming out of writing poetry and a sense that I needed something to counteract the voice-over. Originally I did the intertitles on a typewriter for cheap and just shot them on some kind of reversal, so it was white on black. I had a selection, and it took time to figure out which ones worked. Then I redid the ones I chose.

"My aim is to disarm my movie," says one of the intertitles—*because* I was looking at this footage and found it so emotionally laden and so prescriptive, with these men pulling the women up onto their laps and mauling them. I remember Margie Keller saying about the imagery, "It's so violent."

At night when I was editing, I'd think, "If I make this so that the men look terrible, that'll be didactic; and if I make it so that everything seems just happy-go-lucky, *that's* denial." I wanted you to be able to look at it once and laugh and look at it the second time and sort of gasp.

MacDonald: I thought that perhaps the intertitles were quotes from theory.

Child: I said earlier that reading Foucault helped inspire *Ornamentals,* but I don't put theory *on* my work, and I don't quote from theory in the work. I don't love those late seventies' films that did: *Riddles of the Sphinx* [1977, by Laura Mulvey and Peter Wollen], *Sigmund Freud's Dora . . .* [1979, by Anthony McCall, Claire Pajaczkowska, Andrew Tyndall, and Jane Weinstock]—simply not my favorite use of theory or of film.

The theory that appeals to me is a theory that changes, a theory that breaks, a theory that incorporates breaks, a theory that is *not* prescriptive, a theory that allows for improvisation, that actually responds to the world. I read theory, and it feeds the work, but it doesn't prescribe the work. I *do* think my work can give rise to a lot of theoretical speech—usually not the currently popular theoretical speech, however. Hopefully, the work is ahead of theory, not quoting it.

I *am* interested in pleasure. I *love* movies, and I love eclectic movies. I agree with Ellington, "All music is good music." I feel that about films, which is also why I use all different kinds of material in my films. They're all equally relevant.

When I finished *Covert Action* in 1984, I thought, for the first time, "This is unique. It doesn't look and sound like anybody else's work." For *me, Covert Action* was my first real success.

MacDonald: The middle sections of *Is This What You Were Born For?* are more involved with narrative.

Child: Yes. I wanted to explore narrative. I had read Barthes's critique of *Justine,* and I was fascinated by the structural elements he describes: the repetition, the pyramidal structure. Actually, I shot the material that's in *Perils* for *Mayhem,* but because I was shooting with a print stock with ASA 6—a print stock that's used for titles—it had such a different look that in the end I couldn't use it in *Mayhem.* It became its own film. That wasn't in the original plan, but it became part of the work, and *Perils* has its own position within *Is This What You Were Born For?*

The sound in *Perils* is all music. I used cartoon soundtracks and in the process learned more about music composition. At one point, the track was heavily layered with cartoon soundtracks, *too* layered, and I realized that you have to open up and have space—silence—in order to have music.

That was also the first time I brought in musicians. I had the film almost finished, so I split it from a five-minute piece into three or four sections, and had the musicians lay down tracks and also provide some wild beats. I picked the best take and did the mix. I had known something about mixing from those early days, but this was another level of learning.

And then, in *Mayhem,* I took on melodrama. The score for *Mayhem* began with fragments from Mexican melodramas that I recorded off Channel 49. Also, I had done interviews with people in different languages, and I included some of that material, because I was thinking of all those European fiction films that I watched as a kid, with the subtitles.

MacDonald: Perils seems to be about the process of making *Mayhem.*

Child: You could think of it that way, but it's not. *Perils* is an homage to silent film. It does have a lot of referentiality: I was shooting it against this Rivington Street wall where Griffith's original studio was, and with open-air lighting. If a cloud came over, we had to stop shooting. In fact, we shot for three days and, because of the clouds, only got about two minutes each day.

I was interested in fiction, and *Mayhem* continues my explorations, investigating film noir. I love noir lighting. I love the fact that noir women are really powerful. I realized that their power in noir is why they're always punished, so I decided that in my film they *wouldn't* be punished. They'd get what they wanted, which is why at the end they get to have sex with each other and with the robber.

But all of that came slowly. When I was still thinking of de Sade and *Justine,* I shot for a year and threw out everything I shot; it wasn't right. Then, finally, I started to shoot material that began to work. I did a lot of work with photographs. I had people imitate positions from Mexican comic books. And there was a lot of theatricality.

Then, at the end, I knew I needed nudity or I'd be doing the same thing as noir does, which is bring up sexuality but never deliver. What I shot of my friends didn't work, so I put out a call to Mr. E. He supplied the porno footage for the end of *Mayhem.* He gave me two kinds. One was just a guy and a girl going at it—very sexy. And he had this other material, which I think is French, with two women in a courtyard; and that's what I chose because it had all these references to what I considered the beginning of fiction—the Garden of Eden, for example—and an incredible reflexive moment where the guy peeking at the women having sex gestures to the audience in collaboration. I thought, "*That's* what *my* film is about: how to construct a story that you are aware of at every moment *as* a construction, but that you also love as a movie, a movie that gives the kinds of pleasure movies can give."

Mayhem is also an indirect response to Laura Mulvey's writing, which is what I think got me in such hot water, because at that point in the 1980s Laura Mulvey was the dominant precept under which women looked at film. I wasn't allowed to look at women the way *I* looked at women. My work was rejected by feminist communities on both coasts, either not included in conferences, or featured and attacked.

Because *Mayhem* is about sexuality, it made people crazy, just crazy. It was taken off the projector at the gay festival in San Francisco, and in the Toronto Experimental Film Congress catalogue, it has the only negative write-up, of the many films shown—a distressing experience in the end, if exciting in the short term.

It was censored from PBS, probably the first art film to be censored after the change in FCC rulings in the late eighties. And somebody who had been on a NYSCA [New York State Council on the Arts] panel told me, "You'll never get a grant if you use *Mayhem* as your work sample." It was frustrating, though now the whole thing seems kind of silly.

No one could deal with *Mayhem.* I suppose it was too ambiguous and felt unsafe.

MacDonald: I didn't know what to do with it, didn't know how to think about it. I found the male actors pretty repulsive. And the film made me feel stupid.

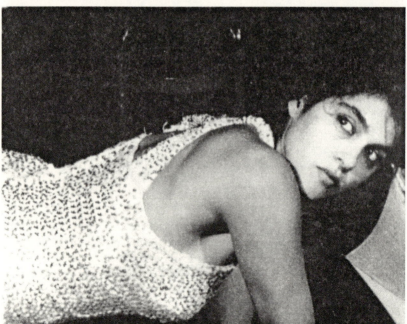

Diana Torr *(above)* and Ela Troyano in *Mayhem* (1987), Child's evocation of film noir. Courtesy Abigail Child.

Child: But aren't you interested in work that has intentions you *don't* fully understand? And the male actors are beautiful! Elion Sacker, who was with the Performing Garage; Plauto, a bisexual Brazilian photographer; and Rex, also bisexual. Perhaps you're simply more comfortable with the male gaze?

MacDonald: I don't have a problem looking at men—I'm just telling you what I felt about these men in this film.

Child: Well, I think that "repulsive" is a pretty strong word here.

About stupidity—mmm—my films are demanding. I don't aim to be difficult, but there's a level of mental liveliness that I'm interested in. Su Friedrich was presenting yesterday and said something like, "If the audience is confused, I've failed." I was surprised, and realized I disagreed. I don't think my job is to clarify everything. I don't think the world is clarifiable. There's the banality of evil *and* the unspeakable, the unapproachable, the unabateable. Trying to have everything make sense all the time would seem repressive and oppressive to me. Also arrogant, since I see/feel the need for Keats's "negative capability"—the idea of proceeding through *not* knowing.

But I do think that a lot of the negative response to my work has to do with that—that rather than "going with it," people feel they're missing something, feeling, as you say, "stupid."

MacDonald: I don't think the sexuality has much to do with the reception of the film; in fact, sexually, the film isn't all that wild. There is porn at the end, but it's nice porn.

Child: Well, lesbians attacked it: they said my use of that porn diminished sexual relationships between women! I think you underestimate the sexual critique in the film and how that was received by audiences.

What struck me in the eighties was that in hip-hop, what I was doing was clearly acceptable. I would read reviews of hip-hop and could have used the reviews to describe my work.

MacDonald: The same people who would hate your film would hate hip-hop.

Child: You think?

MacDonald: Your work came at a moment when much of the culture was trying to recover from the over-the-top period of the sixties and seventies, to get control again. And here you come, going *further.* You were willing to be abrasive in a way that people were no longer willing to handle.

Child: Whoa! I don't consider my work "abrasive." "Beauty will be convulsive or it will not be" seems relevant still. If anything, I think my work shares in a musical, mental, and physical ecstasy, which *has* traditionally been seen as "disorderly" and threatening to a static social realm. In any case, the eighties were particularly focused on autobiography—not only in experimental film but in the kind of video that was dominating most funding and curating. People reverted to what I consider an outdated approach—psychological analysis of the author—rather than *looking* at the work, perceiving the work as material for examining social meaning, social history.

MacDonald: How does *Both* fit into *Is This What You Were Born For?*

Child: Both came later and is a silent piece. I added it as a way to stop the flow of the series, to slow it down. It's a study of the female body, of female nudes.

MacDonald: Silence is an important use of sound.

Child: That's how I felt.

Mercy was the last in the series. Originally, *Mercy* was going to be made from the outtakes of the other six films. But when I started to do that, I decided, no, those shots are out because they were meant to be out. So I shot some new material and used some found footage Gail Camhi had given me.

For *Mayhem* I had brought in musicians after I had about 90 percent of the sound. One of the musicians was Shelley Hirsch, who did vocals, but I had cut out most of her vocals for that film. I did leave in "No! No!" and a few other little things. However, I had a lot of outtakes of her, and they were so excellent that I decided to use her voice as the score for *Mercy.*

Mercy is the first time in the series that the sound goes across a cut and doesn't always punch against the image; sometimes it goes with it and *then* punches. I think I was feeling the staccato rhythms of the first part of *Is This What You Were Born For?,* and I wanted a wider grasp of rhythms. I wanted to try soft sounds, as well as loud sounds. I didn't want everything on the same register.

MacDonald: Were you conscious that *Mercy* was going to conclude this particular investigation? *Mercy* and *Prefaces* seem very close.

Child: Yes. That *was* absolutely conscious. They're both encyclopedic in structure, and neither goes into a specific topic. I meant them as bookends.

When I say "encyclopedic," I mean that they were panoplies of world images, and colors, and topics—visual cavalcades of images, flows. Although having said that, it's also true that *Prefaces* has this trope of the ear and hearing and communication within a colonialized setting that I critique. There's that centerpiece image of colonialism, where black Africans approach the European administrators. "Unfortunately," says the narrator, "there's no room for all of them"—the height of colonialist, imperialist insanity.

On the other end of the series, *Mercy* got its structure when I decided to focus on the male body shivering, the body of a scientist, the body lying down. If much of my work in the earlier films had been about what enforces or reinforces femininity or femaleness, *Mercy* is largely about what reinforces maleness. There *is* a powerful moment in *Mercy* involving a female body—the woman in some kind of machine where they are going to do an X ray; she's strapped down, and this machine is coming down—terrifying.

Well, after I finished the series, I was exhausted. I'd spent eight years on an hour and ten minutes of film!

MacDonald: I had a very hard time with that work when I was first seeing it. I just didn't know what to do with it. It seemed *so* over-the-top. I still struggle with it. *Our Trip to Africa,* although heavily edited and complex, is a comparatively easy film, partly because it makes such a clear point about colonialism. Your work goes further into ambiguity.

Child: Do you listen to Sun Ra?

MacDonald: I don't.

Child: Music—especially Sun Ra, "Ascension" by Coltrane, some of the Cecil Taylor solo pianos—these kinds of experimental music relate to *Is This What You Were Born For?,* as does John Zorn, and a lot of hip-hop. The people in those worlds, and poets—people who are used to speed, density, complication, ambiguity—*they've* always been an enthusiastic and comprehending audience.

On the other hand, Alf Bold—a wonderful soul—looked at *Covert Action* at the Collective in 1986 and said, "You can't do this." I looked at Alf and said, "I *did* it, and I stand by what I did!" And more and more, that film and the others do reach people.

MacDonald: Let's jump to *B/Side,* which *was* accessible to a lot of people, though I'd guess that it also created problems, but for different people and for different reasons than *Is This What You Were Born For?*

Child: Yes. By 1988, 1989, 1990, the homeless situation in this area of New York City was immense. Here I was, living in a wonderful space, with the homeless all around me, and I felt I had to deal with the issue in some way. I didn't want to do a "straight" documentary; one had just been done by Scott Sinkler and Sachiko Hamada [*Inside Life Outside,* 1988]. I was writing a script that had fiction *and* documentary elements, and then suddenly, events were happening right outside my window, and I began to record them with a video camera. The script and the video record of the homeless encampment came together.

I had a sense that I'd use narrative to get you to attend to the film, and that would deliver you to the document; I'd seduce you in, then pull out the carpet—a related process to what I had done with *Mayhem,* or at least what I had had in mind. I got some money and shot the fiction part of *B/Side* in 1992, went to Russia for a couple of months in 1993 on a Fulbright grant, came back and shot more documentary material, and started to edit.

I knew immediately that I couldn't use irony and speed in the way I had in my other work.

MacDonald: Can you articulate why?

Child: I felt that irony alone couldn't approach what was going on here. I remember standing out in front of the homeless encampment with another guy in the building who's also Jewish, and we both said, simultaneously, "I think I can understand something of what happened in Germany." I don't want to diminish the Holocaust, and I know this was *not* the same; we weren't exterminating these people. But they *were* all black or Latino, and we would walk by, and that "walking by" someone in need was similar, *emotionally,* to the public abandonment of the Jews to their "fate" during the Holocaust.

So I didn't feel that irony was the right response. Also, I was interested in opening up my rhythms. I had been doing "string quartets" in *Is This What You Were Born For?* Now, I wanted to do a symphony piece. I wanted to keep people's minds going, and knew I needed to use a new rhythm. *B/Side* took two years of editing, and it was a struggle because there were *such* divergent materials.

It was especially hard to find how to go to that color video material and come back to the black-and-white fiction. The video material had an authenticity that the fiction didn't have. At one time, I had the video scattered throughout, but finally figured out that I could begin with it and end with it. I was amused and intrigued by the fact that the video, which was kind of greasy and hard to look at, was *real;* and the black-and-white, which *looked* real, *wasn't* real.

Also, I did a lot of research with found footage.

MacDonald: One attack on the film, a predictable one, was that the home-less don't have a voice. And I remember thinking, "This is not a film about the homeless, it's a film about *your* attempt to deal with the complexity of liv-ing where the homeless *are.*"

Child: No. *B/Side* is not just about *me* living next to all this. It was a ques-tion of how I could show you how the city exists, its anomalies and anomie, how *you* are living next to the homeless and walking by them. I wanted to make their lives more present and more local, less avoidable.

But . . . giving voice to the homeless—did I not think of it? Of course! I tried voice-overs, the voice-over of Sheila, the voice-over of random homeless men and women, *my* voice-over. Nothing worked. I've read that Scorsese and his editor did twenty-three or fifty-three voice-overs, whatever, for *Taxi Driver* [1976]. So maybe I gave up too soon.

But I also felt that when you do hear voice-overs with material like this, it always turns out to be information you already know. You *do* know the story. There were moments when I was going to interview some homeless guys I knew, and they'd say, "Don't talk to *him,* he already talked to ABC." I even had some material from ABC-TV where a woman who is in the background of my movie is *on* ABC talking about the situation. I was going to use that, but it took away from the "reality" of the film in a strange way; it became "press." I was trying to capture the voyeurism and "outsideness" of my space, but also something of what it was like to be *in* that space, and how that space is multiple and variously defined: squat, shelter, homeless, lot, Dinkinsville.

People liked *B/Side* who I'm sure wouldn't like my other work: Latino organ-izers in the Bronx, architects, urban planners. *B/Side* expanded my audience.

MacDonald: Another attack on the film must have been that it aestheti-cizes a horrific situation.

Child: Right.

MacDonald: I understand that objection but wonder whether making a horrific film about a horrific situation would somehow be better.

Child: B/Side started as a fiction, and it includes fantastical elements: the lots of rubble made into gardens next to the lots of rubble made into houses. There's also this Latin American/Caribbean space happening. And I wanted to give credence to the fact that this was the third world a mile from Wall Street. It *wasn't* the world the way the TV people discussed it; it was people who were mentally damaged, often suffering economically as a result of mental disorders, as well as housing disorders.

On the other hand, and I don't want to romanticize a desperate world, but if you actually *looked* at this world, you saw things that could surprise you. I consulted with Nick Dorsky during the editing of the film, and I remember him saying, "You look at these guys in this hopeless situation, sweeping the dirt, and they all have beautiful muscles; they're gorgeous." Partially, that was from being in jail and working out in the gym; partly it was from living outside. There was so much of the *body* there. Dealing with the body was a lot of what was happening: getting dressed, where do you wash? where do you eat?

MacDonald: Often during *B/Side,* we're tempted to read scenes as the woman protagonist's memories of the past, but we don't know if they *are* memories or if they're fantasies of another possibility.

Child: Right. I had learned that many of these people had moved to America with a hope of something better and then found themselves dislocated again. I saw a double displacement: first, from the homeland, and then, from the American Dream. The homeless are the failure of our own colonialist policies *and* of the American Dream.

MacDonald: At first the woman seems to be dressing up, maybe to go to work or look for jobs, and then slowly that comes apart. And at one point she goes and buries something under the bridge. Another woman follows her.

Child: I had a complex plot that, during the editing, kept getting peeled away. What you are left with are parts of a plot that doesn't necessarily cohere. In my initial scenario the woman is living in the garden and still has a job. She somehow loses the job and ends up more and more on the street, more fully homeless, and at one point she's got a lover.

The only things going on in my neighborhood at the time were people fixing cars, selling odds and ends, looking for food, and doing drug deals. One of the early subplots involved a drug deal—people leaving money, picking up dope.

MacDonald: How do you see your films functioning in the world, and in relation to your audience? In a general sense, what do you think you're doing as a filmmaker? We could talk about this in connection with *Surface Noise,* which seems to revisit the world of *Is This What You Were Born For?*

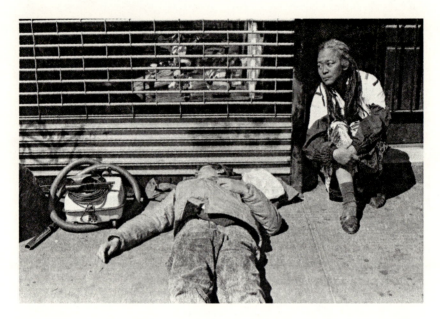

Sheila Dabney (*right*) as homeless woman in Child's *B/Side* (1996). Courtesy Abigail Child.

Child: Just to clarify—I think of *Surface Noise not* as an evocation of *Is This What You Were Born For?* but perhaps of *Prefaces* and *Mercy,* the two bookends of *Is This?* Those two films, like *Surface Noise,* are in color, and they're encyclopedic: they allow for an endless proliferation of images that are then structured into some kind of coherence. By "encyclopedic," I don't mean that they include everything, just that they're very open—I gave myself permission to include what I saw as a vocabulary of the media world.

The films in *Is This What You Were Born For?* have different degrees of focus. *Prefaces* and *Mercy* have very large themes—themes of industrialization versus the body, marketplace values versus more individual values, external space versus internal space. The black-and-white trilogy *inside Is This What You Were Born For?—Covert Action, Perils, Mayhem*—is about the internalized space that's affected by popular culture. These films have a more precise focus, and they're also structured differently, more in chapters or, in the case of *Mayhem,* in terms of the emotional values of certain soap opera songs and twists of narrative. In *Prefaces, Mercy,* and *Surface Noise* the footage is drawn from such a broad field that the structure is more overall.

What am I doing as a filmmaker? I see my work as an exploration of how to make meaning. A deconstruction of the "gluey givens," say, but not through an-art-for-art's-sake reflexivity or a desiccated modernism but rather through

a proliferation of vivid world icons, images, popular templates that are recon-
structed so that they can both critique and enliven. To cause an audience to
interact, to finish the work with their experience and speculations, to take that
audience to a new place which becomes then familiar, to expand the known—
all that, and to laugh.

MacDonald: You dedicate *Surface Noise* to Warren Sonbert, which seems to
have to do with the structure of that film—not just with the fact that this was
the film you were working on when he died.

Child: I *was* thinking about Warren's work from the beginning of *Surface
Noise.* He had died before I started it.

MacDonald: Most of your films are very different from Sonbert's, but *Surface Noise* is closer, in part because, like so many of Sonbert's films, it's a kind
of travel film.

Child: If *Surface Noise* is similar to Warren's film, it is both in its content
and in the values that underlie our choices of imagery—I mean in terms of color
values, movement values, cultural reflections. Warren talked unceasingly about
being influenced by music, and *Surface Noise* uses a kind of translated, bas-
tardized sonata form.

Yes, *Surface Noise* is in conversation with Warren.

Of course, Warren would shoot all his imagery, and *Surface Noise* is not all
shot by me—in fact I shot very little of that material (*Prefaces* and *Mercy* include
more of my own material). But I thought that by looking at images for their
color, their action, for their world-travel look, and structuring them musically,
I was evoking Warren. There is a shot in *The Carriage Trade* [1972], and only
Warren could get this, where he goes into the Plaza Hotel, and there are all these
twenty-year-old white boys, very privileged, boys who might ultimately rule
the country; then he goes into the bathroom, and we see an older black man
whisking dust off the shoulders of a young white guy. A brief but very painful
shot. Warren was complicit with upper-class values in ways that allowed him
access to that kind of imagery, but Warren was completely aware of the implications of and his responsibility to that moment.

I'm standing in a different position: in my work I have a somewhat different
angle on class.

MacDonald: Several specific shots in *Surface Noise* remind me of Warren.
One is the shot that looks like it's below an elevated train.

Child: Actually, that's a shot in a Moroccan market, and yes, that directly
alludes to *The Carriage Trade.*

MacDonald: I think of your work as, at least in part, a reaction to personal
filmmaking, in all its manifestations over the past years. When I try to think
of what "personal" might mean to you as an artist, it seems to me that it
would be the "music" you make with/within a set of cultural influences and patterns that you recognize you are a part of, that you're working from inside of.

Is "personal cinema" in its various manifestations one of the things you most dislike?

Child: I was just at a show, and my friend was explaining her disappointment with the work—"Well, it's just not personal!" And *I* was saying, "No, it *is* personal; this woman *loves* her childhood, but the work has no meaning outside of her nostalgia." For me the failure was not that something was not personally passionate or intense, but that it had no mental activity. I *don't* like psychodrama, even though I play off drama, and trauma, in my work. When I first saw Maya Deren, the psychodrama was the part of her work that I didn't like. It put me off, even as a young twenty-year-old. Only later did I look at Maya Deren and think that she's pretty amazing, *despite* the psychodrama.

The big testing ground in the 1980s was *your* family: everybody was doing work on their grandfather, their grandmother, their father, their mother, their sister, their brother. *[Laughter.]* That kind of focus on the personal was a classic first-film motor. It's like that first novel: it's gotta be all about yourself, and sometimes it's really strong and sometimes it's not.

Of course, I do believe in internal lives and internal imagination and private space, but I believe we are *strongly* formed by our outer space, and by who we dialogue with. The idea of community, the idea of the politics of the world we exist in, has always been important for me. Now, I grew up across the sixties and early seventies, with the feminist movement, with an awareness of civil rights issues, with antiwar protest, so it's no surprise that I understand that the external world is part of our internal life, that we live as people in the midst of other people.

MacDonald: This certainly makes sense in connection with *Surface Noise.* In that film, we see a number of nationalistic demonstrations, a lot of industrial imagery, a lot of science and technology imagery—all these areas that flow around us as we develop. There's a lot of childhood in there, too—kids growing up—but it's almost all kids in bunches with each other, playing, and even the girl alone on the roof is listening to music. It's all about influences coming from outside in.

Child: "Surface Noise" refers to the noise that's around us all the time, the annoying surface noise *and* the delightful surface noise: the birds twittering and the garbage truck.

I think everybody has a personal voice, but, in my filmmaking and in my poetry, I'm not interested in the "I-went-out-on-the-street-and-saw-my-first-daffodil-and-the-drunken-bum" voice. I'm much more interested in the fact that as I walk across Tompkins Square Park and see that daffodil and a destitute man, that the economics of the city have changed, that there's this semi-omnipresent feeling that we're a target in a war that's beyond our power.

I'm always looking for the placement of the body within the culture. My idea of a "personal cinema" is not cinema about my private life so much as a handmade cinema, or a cinema that approaches the world outside the normative mainstream modes. My work comes out of "the personal is the political."

I would say that *Perils* and *Mayhem* and *Covert Action* are intensely personal to *me*. *Covert Action* is about how, as a woman, one cooperates with the powers of oppression. The women nod and smile as they're being pushed and shoved around like loaves of bread. For me that movie is still very intense.

There's an intensity of feeling that I bring to the films and that I hope they evoke, but I don't want them to be just about Abby. Of course, you make a film, and no matter how much you think you know about it, it surprises you and reflects back what you're thinking. Burroughs is relevant: "You make a cut in the present and the future leaks out." It is exciting during the process of making a film to realize, "Oh, *this* is what you're thinking!"

MacDonald: You quote from many forms of film, but you rarely quote from well-known films, popular or independent.

Child: I've nearly always used found material, but you're right, I've almost never used famous material. In *Surface Noise* I do quote Dziga Vertov—the woman on the roof with the earphones is a subtle quote of Vertov's *Enthusiasm* [1931].

The problem is that if you take a shot from Hitchcock, *of course,* it's going to look good and be interesting. There's no challenge. I'm interested in a quote that's not Hollywood. I ask art to be transformative, both to me and to my audience. I've seen some fantastic conceptual work, but it's got to resonate in ways that bring in the world. Also, I'm not somebody who loves work that's about other people's work—how thin is your life if all you can talk about is the art world?

I do think the personal is a very interesting issue. There are some great films made out of this very personal space, but that just isn't what I do—even though I think the intensity and the drive of my films *is* very personal and motivated by intimate spaces in my own psyche.

MacDonald: You were talking earlier about how *Surface Noise* relates more to the films that frame *Is This What You Were Born For?; Dark Dark* [2001] seems to return to that central black-and-white trilogy.

Child: The more I edited it, the more it looked like *Mayhem. Dark Dark* continues my exploration of how we make meaning out of narrative: what are our expectations, how do our expectations get decided, reversed, or fulfilled, how is it that we make meaning out of almost anything.

So *Dark Dark* does extend my interest in narrative and narrative issues, and what I really like about the film is that, strangely enough, it's something like what my dream was for *B/Side*. For *B/Side* I wanted to intercut three or four narratives, and in some very unpristine way, *Dark Dark* does this. It was an exciting, fun film to make, and a relatively quick project.

MacDonald: I like the gesture of the un-clapstick—the clapstick in reverse: it fits with your career-long interest in breaking from sync, in *un*-synching film.

Child: *I* love that after a while you don't know whether the shots are upside down or not because of the way your eye adjusts. Of course, we actually see upside down: the images come into our eyeballs upside down and get flipped in our brain.

I've always been interested in gesture: the gesture of the body, which is language before speech, meaning without text, without words. *Dark Dark* is full of all these little bits of gesture that make you aware of the presentational mode we're usually engaged in.

MacDonald: Do you know the sources of the three narratives—the western, the love story, and the film noir? The love story is a version of O. Henry's "The Gift of the Magi," right?

Child: Yes. I don't know where the others come from.

Dark Dark is my cutting-room-floor film. It's also a love letter to all the people who make films—to all the bad actors, and all those clapboard people, and all the crews that are endlessly involved. I've always had a fantasy of filming the extras in the background of a Hollywood film while a feature is being shot. There are all these other stories happening that create a poly-universe. The Bill Greaves film *Symbiopsychotaxiplasm* [1971; see *A Critical Cinema 3*], does something like that. What's going on in the *making* of the film is more interesting than whatever script is being filmed.

MacDonald: What are you working on now?

Child: I'm working more with the computer. I did all the sound effects in *Dark Dark* with Pro-Tools on my little computer, and I'm doing more and more digital stuff, which has been interesting and frustrating and exciting at the same time. I'm just finishing up a little trailer called *Subtalk,* a response to 9/11, but also part of a bigger Web project.

Two other projects are films. One is *Where the Girls Are* [2002], which is ideally both a single-channel work and a multiscreen installation, focusing on post–World War II American suburbs. This may be my most personal film, in that it's exploring the world where I grew up, seen through the twin lenses of colonialism and immigration.

MacDonald: This is a world that as a filmmaker you've tended to avoid.

Child: Exactly. Nick Dorsky teases me about it; he says, "Abby, this is going to be *A/Side!*" *[Laughter.]*

Chuck Workman

Chuck Workman's filmmaking career has taken a variety of twists and turns. During the late 1960s and early 1970s, he made a living doing ads for whoever would hire him, and for a time worked as an editor for the Argentine director Leopoldo Torre-Nilsson. Then he found his way into producing trailers for low-budget commercial productions and, later, for major studio releases: *Star Wars* (1977), *The Wiz* (1978), *1941* (1979), *Paris, Texas* (1983). In more recent years, he has produced and directed feature-length documentaries: *Superstar: The Life and Times of Andy Warhol* (1990) and *The Source* (1999), about the Beat generation; and he has made feature-length compilation histories: *The First Hundred Years* (1996) for HBO, tracing the history of cinema; and *The Story of X* (1998) for the Playboy Channel, a history of pornographic film. And he has written, directed, and produced several fiction features, most recently *A House on a Hill* (2001).

Workman's forte is making films from other films. This ability is obvious in his documentaries and feature compilation films but is most noteworthy in a considerable series of films he has made for particular occasions. The most widely seen of these are the brief compilation pieces he has produced for the Academy Awards shows over the past two decades. Two of the compilation pieces—*Precious Images* (1986), which honors the Academy of Motion Picture Arts and Sciences (it won an Academy Award for best live-action short); and *Pieces of Silver* (1989), made for Eastman Kodak on the occasion of the hundredth anniversary of George Eastman's development of flexible-roll film—have been released as 16mm films; but the others, including a history of comedy, a history of the world as told in the movies, a history of children in film, were seen on the annual awards shows and then placed in the Academy archives.

In the best of his compilation pieces, Workman reveals his mastery of editing. His strategy is not just to provide a succession of moments of nostalgia and humor for film-loving audiences but to create distinctive films that make a variety of implicit comments on the nature of commercial production and the ways in which it has been understood. Workman recycles clips from earlier films using a variety of classic editing strategies to provide energy, humor, and insight. At times, he will present clusters of recycled shots that reveal an obvious similarity within equally obvious differences (people slapping other people in a wide range of Hollywood commercial features, for example); at other times, he will build meta-continuities from bits of the continuities of other films and send them crashing into images that take the film in an entirely new direction. While his goal is entertainment—"I *love* the audience!"—from time to time, his montages achieve something well beyond the kinds of entertainment provided by Academy Awards shows.

The climax of *Pieces of Silver* is a particularly good example. It begins when Workman cuts from an audio clip of music from *Out of Africa* (1985) to an excerpt of the Talking Heads doing a rousing version of "Life during Wartime" in Jonathan Demme's *Stop Making Sense* (1984). As is true throughout *Pieces of Silver,* Workman's recycled images come in a rush—more than a shot per second—energized by the rhythm of the music and arranged so as to create an evolving set of experiences. Early in the montage, Workman provides a cluster of close-ups of characters within narrative features, looking directly at the camera, and he plays with particular juxtapositions of images (a shot of Bogart in *Casablanca* [1942] lifting a cigarette to his lips is followed by a shot of James Dean in *Giant* [1956] lowering a cigarette); or surprises us, either by returning to a particular image over and over (a man repeatedly trying to break a bottle of champagne over the prow of a ship) or with a series of shots of remarkable diversity: a close-up of the woman robot in *Metropolis* [1926] winking at the camera is followed by a long shot of a huge explosion in the jungle, from *Apocalypse Now* [1979], then by a long shot of an amazing stunt where a man jumps out of a helicopter; then by a time-lapsed, close-up of a rose blooming. The overall impact of this sequence, at least for me, and for many of those I have shown the film to, is a rare form of exhilaration (I remember feeling the same way as a child seeing the original *King Kong* [1933] for the first time, and I have felt it more recently watching Bruce Conner's *Cosmic Ray* [1962], Martin Arnold's *Pièce Touchée* [1989], and Tom Tykwer's *Run, Lola, Run* [1999]).

Workman's homage to the opening century of film and television history in *Pieces of Silver*—and much the same is true for his other compilation films— serves, on one level, as a meta-advertisement for the general experiences of moviegoing and television watching. Like many viewers, I am excited by the number of clips I can identify, and frustrated and intrigued by those I do not recognize: the film fanatic in me wants to make *all* the identifications. On another

Rose and "flower" in Busby Berkeley routine, in Chuck Workman's *Pieces of Silver* (1989). Courtesy Anthology Film Archives.

Successive shots of a diver in Leni Riefenstahl's *Olympia* and of newsreel footage of the *Hindenburg* exploding, in Workman's *Pieces of Silver* (1989). Courtesy Anthology Film Archives.

level, *Pieces of Silver* is frustrating because of its omissions. The film focuses on American commercial filmmaking, with at most periodic honorific nods to European and Asian classics, and it ignores nearly all forms of critical filmmaking. This latter omission is particularly aggravating, since Workman's method in *Pieces of Silver,* and in most of his occasional films, originates in the tradition of "recycled cinema" or "found-footage filmmaking"—Esther Shub, Joseph Cornell, Bruce Conner, Ken Jacobs, Abigail Child, Peter Forgács, Alan Berliner, et al.—and in experiments with montage editing by Slavko Vorkapich, Stan Brakhage, Peter Kubelka, and others. When I mentioned my frustration to Workman, I got a surprisingly candid answer.

While Workman works in the heart of Hollywood and has an access to the history of Hollywood cinema most independent filmmakers can only dream of, he continues to demonstrate a considerable range of interests and abilities, and to take chances with his reputation and his finances. The interesting and engaging new feature, *A House on a Hill,* can easily be read as his artistic credo. The focus of the film is Harry Mayfield (Philip Baker Hall), an aging architect who returns to work on a house he abandoned decades earlier after the house burned down, killing his only son. When a Los Angeles couple becomes intrigued with the hilltop site of the house, Mayfield's ex-wife (Shirley Knight) offers to sell them the land, with the understanding that Harry will design the home they plan to build. As Harry begins the project, a young filmmaker friend of the couple (Laura San Giacomo) decides to document the process. Later, when the couple abandons the project, and the documentary is put on hold, Harry decides to finish the house on his own.

Workman's contemplation of his own career is evident throughout *A House on a Hill.* Harry's struggle with the couple's assumption that they know how this house should be designed clearly echoes the struggles of so many filmmakers working in the industry with those who have financial control of their projects. The San Giacomo character's excitement about documenting the life of a creative person echoes Workman's own documentary projects. And Harry's final decision to build the house in his own way reflects Workman's commitment to this unusual narrative feature, and to his inventive experiments with the size and shape of the movie image throughout this film. Like both creators in the film, Workman is simultaneously recognizing his personal and artistic limits *and* honoring his ongoing capacity to surprise any attempt to underestimate or compartmentalize him.

I spoke with Workman in Beverly Hills in April 2000; we have corresponded via e-mail since then.

MacDonald: You seem almost obsessively busy, and you make a *lot* of work.
Chuck Workman: I *am* always busy. And luckily. If I'm not busy, I get nervous. It's not because I'm afraid I can't feed my family—although that might

be part of it—I just feel that if you're not making work, you're wasting time. It's very easy to get caught up in the Hollywood pattern of just enjoying yourself while waiting for the next project. That makes me nervous, and in any case, I always have something else I want to try, so I've managed over the years to get a lot of work done, both commercial work and work that's less commercial. If I'm not doing commercial work, I try to do something that's just for me. One year, I did a video installation for the Hollywood Entertainment Museum; I was asked to do it by a friend at Paramount. That wasn't a commercial job, but I enjoyed it.

MacDonald: One of the themes of *A Critical Cinema 4* is intersections between avant-garde film and commercial film. And the minute I had that idea as a theme for the book, you came to mind. You make a certain kind of documentary, and you do it well enough that it could certainly be your career—a career that many filmmakers might envy. But in addition you've created an unusual niche for yourself where you make occasional films, in the sense of "occasional poetry": you make compilation films for particular occasions. Every year at the Academy Awards they announce a new Chuck Workman compilation piece, and recently there's enough applause to show that people have come to recognize a certain kind of work as yours.

Workman: They've not only started to recognize me; they're starting to say, "Oh, no! *Another* Chuck Workman film?"

For me there are two kinds of art making. There's art making for an audience, and there's art making for the art itself. You're making movies for the audience, or you're making something about the medium. I try to do both. The Hollywood world is interested in the audience. When they say "making money," that means the audience likes what they did, and everything is set up for that; the idea is to interest and delight the audience either in a routine way, by giving them something good in a form they're used to, or by doing something different. If you're interested in *just* the image or *just* the medium itself, or just trying to get certain thematic ideas into the medium, you'll have a very difficult time in Hollywood.

I came out here with a script with a lot of scenes in it and a lot of characters. A former head of Columbia, who was the producer I was talking to at the time, said, "Oh, that's very *Nashville*-ian." And I said, "Oh, great!" I took it as a positive, not knowing he meant it as a negative. His bottom line was that *Nashville* [1975] didn't make any money.

This year for the Oscars I did a little two-minute piece on children in film. And I included *Lolita* [1962], just as a joke, just before the last shot, of the Yellow Brick Road! *[Laughter.]* I put it in for the obvious ironic reasons. And it made the producers nervous; they were trying to make a fairly clean show, and there was Sue Lyon twirling a hula hoop.

MacDonald: That kind of irony is typical of you.

Workman: Yes it is, but in the end I took the shot out. One of the producers said to me, "By the way, *Lolita* never made any money"—forgetting that this was a great director's film of a great novel.

Those things happen constantly. The success of your work has to do with the number of people who like it and the number of people who pay to see it. Luckily they don't care too much about the critics, but they do care very much about the audience. I *love* the audience, but I also try to think about the image and how I can manipulate it. People don't give the audience enough credit.

I've always thought about style and content in what I feel is a fairly sophisticated and interesting and hopefully artistic way. But the work that I was hired to do for years was very commercial work. I started on low-end commercials.

MacDonald: Did you go to film school?

Workman: No. I was an English major, first at Cornell, then at Rutgers. I came from a Jewish middle-class background where unless you went to law school, you'd better find a job. This was in the midsixties when there were a lot of interesting films coming from Europe, and I said, "I'd like to do *that,*" never thinking about making *commercial* movies. I wanted to be a writer or a film artist like Godard, or Truffaut, who was an artist for a time. Or Eisenstein. That was the stream I wanted to swim in. But that stream doesn't flow through Hollywood.

I had to find a job, and in time my work brought me here. Luckily, whatever style it is that I've developed works in the Hollywood context. I try not to pull myself back and say, "Well, I have to make this a little easier for the rest of the audience to understand," but I guess I do that automatically sometimes. And I *do* suit the material for the context that it's in. But most people who like my Oscar films like my documentaries and even the more obscure stuff that I've done.

MacDonald: On one level, the documentaries and the occasional compilation pieces are very similar: they're both assemblage work. You've done other kinds of films, too, but in *Superstar* and *The Source* and in *Precious Images* and *Pieces of Silver,* you generally take pieces from other films and bring them together.

Workman: Exactly. It's nice to create your own images, too, and I was able to do that in *Superstar* and *The Source.* But that takes a while. When you work with images of the quality that I've worked with, it's hard to feel *your* imagery looks good! I'm used to working with John Ford and Hitchcock material! That can be daunting and can hold you back. I'm just beginning to understand what *my* style is when I'm actually creating the images myself. But up until now, I've had a bumpy career in directing original material, and it's only in the documentaries and in some commercials that I've really made that work, and I think now in my new dramatic film, *A House on a Hill.*

MacDonald: You *have* found a way to use material made by other people so that it becomes yours. I got fooled by the Billy Crystal introduction at the beginning of the 2000 Academy Awards show because he used some of "your material," which isn't *your* material, of course, but material you've used enough so that I think, "That must be Chuck Workman because I know that image."

Workman: I said to Billy Crystal, "You're using all my shots!" And he laughed because he got the joke. He did use my style, in a wonderful way. More power to him. So, yes, you *do* use that material and you try to make it your own, but of course it's *not* your own. There's a nice phrase, "transformative art," that I think has come out of deconstruction theory. And that's basically what I'm trying to do. I'm not saying that that John Ford shot is *mine.* But I am taking the iconography and using it in a way that takes into account its many levels of impact and meaning. Even when I did *Precious Images,* which was probably the first film of mine that did this in a complete way, I was relying on the iconography of that imagery, on whatever resonance that imagery has, on all the various levels. It's more than sampling and less than original poetry.

MacDonald: During the last ten, maybe fifteen years the most pervasive approach to avant-garde filmmaking has been what tends to be called "recycled cinema": recycling material from other films into your own film.

Workman: Don't you like "transformative" better? *[Laughter.]*

MacDonald: Well, sometimes it's transformative; sometimes it's just recycling! Recycling is a way of being in a dialogue with history.

Workman: I never thought of it that way. I have to respect the material I work with *and* at the same time have a little bit of, not exactly contempt, but distance.

MacDonald: You mentioned that you started with low-end commercials. So how do you go from there to doing trailers for major films? That's a pretty big jump.

Workman: I did low-end ads for toy companies, for whoever would hire me, and I also did low-end trailers. I would do the horror film for MGM, while someone else was doing the big movie with Steve McQueen. I was getting B movies or C movies that they knew were no good, but had to sell. These companies have a bunch of vendors; and early on they probably said, "Well, let's give that one to Chuck, but of course we can't send *him* into a meeting with Sydney Pollack." But I was happy to do whatever they gave me. I was trying to make a living. I *was* very interested in doing more artistic work, but the artistic pretensions got pushed aside in the effort to try to please the client and have him call you again. I did find a niche in sales-oriented material where I could experiment a little and grow. I worked for salesmen who didn't care what the commercials looked like, as long as they sold the product.

MacDonald: This is the late sixties, early seventies?

Workman: Yes, when I started my company, Calliope Films.

MacDonald: Why "Calliope"? Calliope was the Greek muse of epic poetry.

Workman: Yes, and there's the musical instrument, but I think it was just that it sounded kind of pop, kind of *Yellow Submarine*-y, which I liked at the time.

Anyway, I found that if the record or the toy or the movie was selling, I'd get another commission. Early on, I did lots and lots of trailers for movies you've never heard of.

MacDonald: Name a few.

Workman: Drive-in [1976]. Ever hear of that?

MacDonald: Nope.

Workman: Traveling Executioner [1971]. *Fun with Dick and Jane* [1977]— actually a pretty good movie. I would win an award every once in a while for a trailer. I worked mostly for MGM and UA.

MacDonald: Who gives awards for trailers?

Workman: There's always been a group that gives the Key Art Awards— "Key" being the image that the studio picks. My son just got nominated for the *Sleepy Hollow* [1999] television spots. In those early days, I never got near a movie like *Sleepy Hollow.* The biggest project I did was *Goodbye, Mr. Chips* [1969] with Petula Clark. At the time, I wished I could do "the Pepsi commercials," as I used to call them—the better commercials. But, of course, I also learned that, if I *were* doing Pepsi commercials, I'd be dealing with art directors. The one or two times I had that experience, it didn't go well. I used to do featurettes—eight- or ten-minute fillers about the making of films, that would go on network television. They were quite popular. You see them now on the movie channels. I remember doing one for *Burn!* [1970], the Marlon Brando film. They gave me that because they thought I was kind of artsy. I made a little seven-minute film, and an art director came in and started giving me ideas. It wasn't that I was a stubborn artist; I just disagreed with him. I didn't know one was *supposed* to agree on a creative level. I wasn't looking for advice about how to put it all together. I had had my own insecurities about how to put things together, and once I licked those, I didn't feel like listening to somebody else. I'm still that way.

Well, I learned to do a lot of things. I learned to shoot. I would go out and do these small commercials, and I'd say, I think I'll operate the camera today, or I think I'll do it all with a moving camera, or I think I'll light this one, or I'll be the sound man today. It didn't matter; they didn't care, as long as they were selling their product. But it was a wonderful education for me for ten years. I learned to be a strong editor, and if I wasn't that great at shooting, I got to be okay.

My first little Hollywood hit was a nice behind-the-scenes portrait of George C. Scott working on *The Last Run* [1971] that the eleven people that cared about it at the time liked. So that part of my Hollywood career kept going. One day, a friend, Paul Hirsch, one of three editors who was cutting an obscure movie called *Star Wars,* called me up and said, "I'm working on this movie, and they don't like the trailer. I know you do trailers. You've never done these big ones, but do you want to do it?" I said, "Sure." And I did it, and they used it. In fact, the movie was such an amazing phenomenon in those days that being "the person who did the *Star Wars* trailer" still follows me twenty years later. It was actually the third of the *Star Wars* trailers, but it was the one they used. And it was a good trailer; I liked it.

As a result of that, I got involved with Steven Spielberg. George Lucas recommended me. Spielberg wasn't happy with the trailer he had for *1941.* There was a lot of secrecy about *1941.* I assume George told Steven, "Chuck will keep things to himself, and he'll do a good job." After that, I started getting a few big pictures. For a time, I became the person who did interesting, stylish trailers for serious filmmakers' movies.

When you do a trailer for a movie, even if it's a good movie, you have to be emotionally involved in the movie to understand what works in the movie, *and* you need to stand away from the movie and look at it in a very cold, clear way. Which makes it very difficult to do your *own* trailers.

The trailer for *Paris, Texas* was my last. I remember thinking, "This movie's so good that I'm doing an homage, not a trailer!" A trailer is a promotional tool to sell tickets. After some years of doing them, I found I either *hated* the movie and thought, "What *is* this piece of garbage I have to sell!" or I *loved* the movie—*Paris, Texas* was a wonderful, wonderful movie—and didn't want to do just a trailer. So I had to stop. My career was ready to move on anyway.

And luckily about the same time, *Precious Images* came out, and I was able to get more interesting work.

MacDonald: How long were you working on *Precious Images?*

Workman: Not very long. Two or three months. The Directors Guild was having a seventy-fifth anniversary, and they wanted to do a film. I'd been active in the Directors Guild, in what they call "Special Projects," and I had made two documentaries for them called *The Director and the Image* [1984] and *The Director and the Actor* [1984]. I won a Cine Golden Eagle. (Anybody who wins a Cine Golden Eagle knows that it's a wonderful award, but they do give a *lot* of them, fifty to a hundred a year.) Anyway, I thought, "This is great: you don't just make movies to advance yourself in Hollywood; you've won an *award!*" It was as if a whole world opened up to me. It sounds very naive, I know.

As a result, I had the confidence to say, "Let's not do a documentary for the Directors Guild anniversary; let's do a little trailer of everything that members of the guild have done." "How long is it going to be?" "Well, under ten minutes." They said, "Well, they'll never run it if it's more than five or six minutes; we want it to run in *theaters.*" Of course, I had so many movies I wanted to include that the time constraint forced me to compress the film more and more. The cutting got faster and faster, but I realized that the film was still working. And I was moving things around, and it was *still* working. I started finding these wonderful little combinations of shots, the kind of edits that I'd been doing for years in other things, but suddenly in this film I wasn't *selling* anything. It was a wonderful moment for me. I *very much* got into the freedom of working that way.

MacDonald: The music in that film works particularly well with the visuals. I assume that's also something you had worked on for years, in the ads and the trailers.

Workman: Yes, for years. I was very interested in music. The piece I mentioned on *Burn!* had had music by Ennio Morricone, *big* music with Brando riding around these hills in the Dominican Republic, or wherever the hell they shot the movie, with the fire in the background. I remember the woman from UA, who was in charge of featurettes, looking at what I did, and saying, "Oh, that's wonderful, Chuck; of course, we can't use it, because it won't sell the movie."

Well, this time I didn't *have* anybody telling me, "We can't use it." I was only concerned that people would like *Precious Images* because it was so different from anything they had seen before. It *wasn't* so different from *Koyaanisqatsi* [1984, directed by Godfrey Reggio], which had been successful with audiences. I thought to myself, I know that *that* works, and I can make this work in the same way. Of course, the Stan Brakhage films and other films that I had seen in my years in New York used this kind of cumulative editing—but no one had done that before in mainstream Hollywood, with the exception of Slavko Vorkapich.

MacDonald: You know, the irony of it is that *Precious Images is* a fantastic selling film on a more general level: it sells the idea of a thorough awareness of commercial cinema. When I show *Precious Images* to students, they want to run out and see all the films they don't recognize, so that they get all the jokes. And *I* still feel that way when I see the film.

Workman: I think one of the reasons I was successful with *Precious Images* was because I was *allowed* to be successful. All I had to do was honor the American cinema in an interesting way (and have Robert Wise, the head of the committee, like it). Robert Wise had been an editor; he looked at *Precious Images* and said, "This works." I was lucky. A lot of people do a good piece of work, and then somebody messes it all up, probably more in film and architecture than anywhere else, and probably more in film than in architecture.

MacDonald: Given what you said about having had to suppress your own urges in order to get stuff sold for all those years, your framing the film within shots from *Citizen Kane* [1941] is like a declaration of independence.

Workman: Yes, that's true, though I don't think I was conscious of that.

MacDonald: How did you develop the structure of *Precious Images?*

Workman: I certainly didn't have a structure going into it. Toward the end of my doing trailers, *they* had a structure. During the mideighties, when I was in New York and had a larger company, I would get calls to do trailers, and I would generally have somebody who worked for me cut them, and I'd articulate a structure. I might say, "Okay, give it a three-act structure, and edit to make sure two or three interesting things happen." That was the kind of structure I was looking for in *Precious Images.*

In the early eighties, I also spent a lot of time working in the theater and at one point was in a playwriting workshop with Joseph Kierland, where you'd read your play and everybody would discuss it. Joe was very involved in structure, and he didn't care too much about content, so they were some of the strangest plays you can imagine (there were some good ones, too). It didn't really matter as long as it made sense in terms of structure. I got very interested in structure as a result of that experience, and I still am. Not just how something begins and ends, but the overall arc, as they say these days. *Now,* Hollywood is obsessed with structure—there are books about it—but at that time people didn't talk about three-act structure and that sort of thing.

Anyway, I said to myself, "What *is* the structure of *Precious Images?*" And I thought, "It's a sprint. You take a breath and you *go.*" But still it needed a shape.

MacDonald: You move through a series of genres.

Workman: Exactly right. I went with genre. I decided finally that I wasn't going to arrange the film chronologically. I'd arrange it by genre, so in one section I'd have all the westerns.

MacDonald: Of course, once the viewer thinks you're into a particular genre, like the western, all of a sudden there's *All the President's Men* [1978], which is not a western but also *is* kind of a western.

Workman: Exactly. A lot of the sequencing had to do with the movement in the frame and how it worked visually, but I was playing with genre assumptions.

MacDonald: You define genres, while simultaneously questioning what genre is, and how a given genre is defined at any moment.

Workman: Actually, I don't believe in genre theory, Scott. I think genre criticism is bogus. It adds to the Hollywood categorization of movies. It's a great way for Hollywood to sell movies to fifteen-year-old kids, but that's no art form. Genre paintings are not the greatest paintings either. Genre pulls you down. I was questioning genre because I didn't believe in it. Visually I was saying, "I know you think these are all action movies, but in *Boy's Town* [1938], Spencer Tracy slapping Mickey Rooney is also a piece of action, even though that's a soppy, sentimental movie. So these *slaps* go together. It wasn't, let's put all the kisses together and all the slapstick, so much as, let's cut a kiss from the animation *Lady and the Tramp* [1955] into the middle of these very romantic movies, so you can see the surprising resonance of an image from one genre to another.

This again comes back to being able to distance oneself from the material and not romanticize it too much. Of course, in *Precious Images* it's all happening at high speed, but people are getting it. That's was what was so fulfilling for me: people *got* it—not just film critics or the *Koyaanisqatsi* audience but people who just like movies.

So, *part* of the structure worked off genre. Then I had a more free-form section with all the movies that I couldn't find a place for in that earlier section. The overall structure—"genre" in the beginning, free-form in the middle, and then a big ending—evolved as I was doing the film. It took a lot of discipline, and still does when I do that kind of film now, to save good scenes for the end. Even in the history montage I did this year for the Oscars, I ended with a little bit of a recap, and I had to have the discipline to save good scenes for the recap.

MacDonald: Are you going to release the one you did this year as a separate piece, like *Pieces of Silver* or *Precious Images?*

Workman: I don't think anybody would clear the rights. The whole trick of *Pieces of Silver* and *Precious Images,* or things I've done for Universal or for anybody else, is that there's an institution behind it that will clear the finished piece for other uses. To get the new piece out would require a lot of lawyers going through a lot of material, even if we got it for free. The only way to do this kind of film is with some sort of nonprofit institution. So the Academy *could* do it if they wanted to, but the Academy wouldn't do it because then every person that ever did a tribute for the Oscars would want to do the same thing. I think this kind of work is almost over, at least for me.

MacDonald: What I found interesting, even disconcerting, about the history piece is that while you trace the history of the world, as imaged in film, from the beginning of the world up to the present, the *film history* time line is totally scrambled.

Workman: Exactly right.

MacDonald: To go back and forth between a modern film and an old film adds an edge to the world history you trace.

Workman: By now, I've done enough of this kind of work that I'm allowed to experiment, so I wanted to try that. It's not really fair to the people who produce the Oscars—they're nice people—to fool around *too much,* but they've been wanting me to fool around for ten years, so I fooled around one more time. This time, some people said, "Oh, I wasn't crazy about the Chuck Workman film, but I loved that other one about the kids." Well, I did the kids one, too, so it's not that I feel bad about it and, in general, the history piece went over well; but afterward, for the very first time, one or two critics were saying, "Well, do we really want still another long tribute in the middle of the show?"

What you said about the approach is interesting because I did think about that. I had done simpler chronological films earlier: a little three-minute montage for Universal of their films, beginning with the silents and ending with *Schindler's List* [1993]. I got several jobs after *Precious Images.* Somebody called me from Paramount and said let's do a film. And then somebody called me from the Writers Guild and said let's do the film that became *Words* [1988]. *Words* I like a lot. And then came *Pieces of Silver*. I also did one for the Academy, called *And the Winner Is* [1989]. Those films often used a chronological approach. So this time, in the history film, I decided to try a more complex kind of chronology, but I didn't think the general audience would be thrown by the result, though maybe some were.

MacDonald: The structure goes through the history of the world, then there's the short recap, and right at the end of the recap there's *Gandhi* [1982] and *Schindler's List*—

Workman: And the Spike Lee movie *Do the Right Thing* [1989]. The baby at the end of *2001* [1968] is the last image.

MacDonald: Did you end there because you particularly admire *Gandhi* and *Schindler's List* or Gandhi or Schindler?

Workman: Far from it. I don't like *Gandhi,* and I'm not crazy about *Schindler.* No, not at all—they were just very dynamic images. I'm thinking about *images* in *movies;* I'm not really giving you what *I* think about history, or about movie history, at all.

You know, I use imagery from *Braveheart* [1995], but I only saw the beginning of it. And I've never gotten to the end of *Dances with Wolves* [1990] either. Sometimes I use things I've never really seen all the way through and sometimes have to cut things I *am* interested in. For example, I had *Chaplin* [1992] in there. I love Robert Downey Jr. as an actor. *Chaplin* wasn't a very interesting movie, but Robert Downey Jr. was great. I had a shot when Chaplin arrives in Hollywood in a sequence about the rise of Hollywood, and a little sequence of *Singin' in the Rain* [1952] about talkies arriving. Neither made the final cut. *Jurassic Park* [1993] is far from my favorite movie, but I open with it. I *do* try to include a few movies that I really like. I wanted to include an image from Orson Welles's *Chimes at Midnight* [1967], his Shakespeare adaptation, of the famous fight scene in the mud and the wonderful end line, from Shakespeare, "Jesus, the things that we have seen!" I love that line, but I couldn't get permission to use the word "Jesus"—it's easier to say "Fuck Canada" on the Oscars than to use "Jesus"!—so I felt bad about that.

I'm going through a period in my own little stylistic mind where I'm playing with the shape of the screen and with boxes inside the screen. I did that in the Oscar piece this year, and I'm doing it in *A House on a Hill.* I sometimes call it "the *Thomas Crown Affair* effect," because the first *Thomas Crown Affair* [1968] did that.

You know better than me, there's very little new. Most of the stuff I'm doing, I'm sure I saw in a class at NYU. When I was in New York, I used to go to an extension class, taught by Amos Vogel. When I went into film, I didn't know anything about Stan Brakhage, and a lot of filmmakers, so I took his course and watched all those experiments.

I even wrote a parody—you can get it on the Internet; my *daughter* found it—called "50 Terrific Movies and How to Make Them," for the *Peter Max* magazine. It was basically a parody of what I'd been seeing in that class—although that work certainly did affect me in interesting ways.

I always thought experimental film was important. I knew that there had to be more than Hollywood melodrama and conventional documentary. I knew that filmmakers were checking out the alternatives, and that that had to be incredibly important. Except for that world, American cinema is almost totally bereft of experimentation. There's more in the European cinema, because there's less at stake in terms of money and mass-audience approval. They can be more interested in the work itself. You never get a Tarkovsky or a Kieślowski in the United States. Impossible. You get somebody like Martin Scorsese, who's working in genre; or Ford, also working with genre.

MacDonald: I agree with you completely that on some level experimental film is very important—I'm spending my *life* on this stuff! But one of the tragedies right now is that the last two generations of this work are very precarious.

Workman: Why *is* that?

MacDonald: There's so little financial support for it right now. The one totally dependable distributor, Canyon Cinema in San Francisco, has a hard time keeping their staff because they have so little money. And how much of this stuff will actually get preserved? Anthology Film Archives is hand-to-mouth. We're coming to a moment where something has to happen.

Workman: That's amazing, because in any other art form, the more abstract, more experimental material is what everyone is interested in. Think about architecture and painting. Experimental work is admired and rewarded. In movies this doesn't happen. I think about this all the time, and I'm sure you do, too. Why *is* this? What happens in the movies that makes melodrama the overwhelming approach? It's not just that there's no *funding* for experimental film; there's no interest in it in American theaters. None. Zero.

MacDonald: The irony is that there *is* among directors, even great directors. They seem to know about it; they talk about it.

Workman: A *few* directors know about it. The *strangest* directors know about it! Woody Allen is on the board of Anthology. Of course, Scorsese. Scorsese is a great source of knowledge now. Bresson died recently, and I had to tell the people involved with the obituary section at the Oscars that Bresson had to be in there. "Who's he?" a lot of them said. And then they called Marty up to find a clip; he personally took the phone and helped find the clip. And Coppola does it, too. They *do* get behind experimentation, especially by foreign directors. But there really isn't any broad interest.

But how can there *not* be interest? How can *every* director not be watching the stuff over and over again, trying to figure it out! They'd rather study *There's Something about Mary* [1998], or whatever the current movie is. They want to see *that* three times! It *is* interesting how the Farrelly brothers made that film into a success, but it represents such a limited part of this huge art form where you can take reality and record it and move it around and adjust it. There's no other art form that does that.

MacDonald: There's a moment in *The First Hundred Years* where Scorsese is talking about film experimentation in the sixties, and he says, "And the most important of all is Cassavetes." Cassavetes *is* terrific, but I thought, "Oh shit, you have to narrow it down to this *one* guy?"

Workman: I don't remember where I got the clip, but it wasn't my interview. It could've been a film about Cassavetes. But I let it happen. So blame me.

MacDonald: When I first saw it, I thought he was going to say Kenneth Anger.

Workman: No. He's not going to say Kenneth Anger. People in Hollywood *like* Kenneth Anger, and know about him, because of *Hollywood Babylon* [Anger's history of Hollywood scandal (San Francisco: Straight Arrow Press, 1975)].

I'm sure all those guys feel overlooked. If you were Stan Brakhage, you'd feel, "Wait a minute, I'm Stan Brakhage. I've got people saying I'm God's gift to cinema, but I can't get a reservation in a good restaurant in San Francisco, let alone pay for it." It's a shame.

MacDonald: A complaint I have with *Pieces of Silver,* which for me is the best of your films, is that it goes through the various areas of film history starting with precinema, early cinema, news, advertisements, but never really gets to experimental film. Now you *do* do a little of that in *The First Hundred Years;* there's some Brakhage imagery, a little Mekas, a little Warhol. But it seems paradoxical since your *method* is closer to experimental cinema than to almost anything else—especially to Bruce Connor's films and to the heavy editing of other films from the late fifties and the sixties that you probably saw in Vogel's class.

Workman: Yes. Also, I got to know Jonas and hung out a little at Anthology. And I knew other filmmakers—Bob Downey Sr. was a friend of mine. I sort of got into the scene a little bit. I never made any of those films. I wanted to, but I never did.

MacDonald: I assume that Eastman Kodak wouldn't have cared to have a section on experimental film in your homage—

Workman: They wouldn't have cared at all, one way or the other. They were always supportive.

Why *didn't* I do that? I'm trying to figure out why. There's no reason why. I used experimental animation, and maybe I felt that was sufficient. And then I finally came to my senses a year or two later. I certainly put in Brakhage's

baby from *Dog Star Man* [1961–64] in *The First Hundred Years*. I cut from that
to *Raging Bull* [1980].

MacDonald: And there's *Chelsea Girls* [1966]. And there's Jonas Mekas
dancing around—

Workman: From *Hallelujah, the Hills* [1963, by Adolfas Mekas]. *The Brig*
[1964, by Jonas Mekas] is in *The Source*. And Bruce Conner is in *The Source*,
because he was very involved with the Beats.

I try to be as inclusive as possible, but yours is a very good criticism, I
have to admit. I wish somebody would ask me to do a film about experimental film. I'd need to redo my editing style—what would I do with Snow's *Wavelength* [1967]! How could I slow things down? *[Laughter.]* I guess I could use
Back and Forth [1969]! I would find a way; actually I'd *love* to do it. I would-
n't parody those films; I would do an homage, but still I would fool around, and
it would be fun and really interesting. Actually, I don't know if I have the necessary contempt for experimental films. I don't know if I could make fun of
some of those movies. They're done with such seriousness.

MacDonald: I was watching a film this morning, and there was a Slavko
Vorkapich moment in it. Was he important for you?

Workman: He probably influenced my work a lot. I went to a retrospective
of his work in the late sixties and got interested in the outsider artist in Hollywood. Pablo Ferro was another, and Saul Bass. I think Hollywood sees me as
another Saul Bass type, which for me is a great compliment.

Saul made some wonderful films. And Vorkapich was always a very interesting filmmaker to me. Amazing, really. I've looked at those scenes for *San
Francisco* [1936] and some of his other montages, frame by frame.

MacDonald: My favorite passage in *Pieces of Silver* is when the music from
Stop Making Sense comes on. That moment with the Marx Brothers and the sky-
diver, the moment that ends with the woman robot's wink from *Metropolis* [1926]
and the explosion from *Apocalypse Now* is exhilarating.

Workman: Oh, I felt very secure when I was doing that. I felt like I was
putting everything in just the right place. And finding that music helped a lot.
Stop Making Sense was such a good movie. Robert Haller [director of Anthology Film Archives in New York] likes *Pieces of Silver,* too. He wrote a wonderful discussion of it for an Anthology program. He absolutely caught it at a level
I didn't realize was there.

MacDonald: Are you going to continue making the short occasional pieces?

Workman: I don't know. I was just telling someone I'm not going to do them
anymore. But I've said that every year. I don't think that they're good for me.
I do take my filmmaking seriously, and I think these pieces are starting to invade
my more serious work.

MacDonald: Is it that you feel you've got a form that you're good at, but
can't do what you want with it?

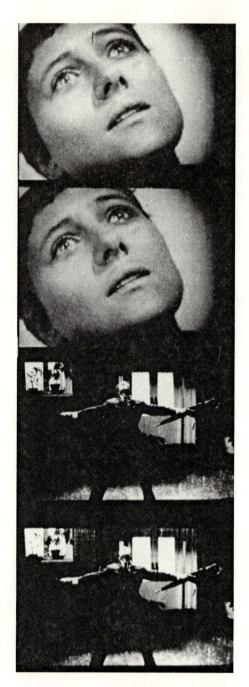

Successive shots from Carl Theodor Dreyer's *Passion of Joan of Arc* and Stanley Donen's *Singin' in the Rain,* in Chuck Workman's *Pieces of Silver* (1989). Courtesy Anthology Film Archives.

Successive shots from Arthur Penn's
Bonnie and Clyde and Sergei
Eisenstein's *Potemkin,* in Workman's
Pieces of Silver (1989). Courtesy
Anthology Film Archives.

Workman: No. I think I've *done* almost everything that I wanted to do with it. I'll probably continue to do it some because that work does support me. But I'm more interested in longer work, and feel like I haven't really explored *that* in a way I might have. I wish I were twenty years younger.

On the other hand, these short pieces *are* fascinating to do, and I get great feedback from them, and I do learn things about my own work when I do them. I just don't know how many more I can do—that's all. I did enjoy my Warren Beatty tribute.

For the past ten years, a lot of my creativity has gone into longer films: *Superstar, The Source,* and *The First Hundred Years.*

The First Hundred Years was pretty glossy. Every time I would try to do something offbeat or witty, HBO would stop me. The version I wanted had an edgier feel to it; it wasn't as saccharine. I had a wonderful section where I intercut Fred Zinnemann and Robert Altman and used the *High Noon* [1952] music. Zinnemann is saying, "You have to take your time and know *exactly* what you're doing beforehand"; then I cut to Altman saying, "I don't want to know *anything* when I walk onto a set." I loved it. Altman said, "HBO's going to make you cut me out of it." I said, "Get out of here!" but HBO had a problem with Robert Altman at the time and kept suggesting that I take this sequence out of the film, for all these weird reasons: "Well, it's not chronological; *High Noon* is the fifties and Altman is the seventies; it'll throw the viewer off." In the end, I took it out, but I really liked that section. Altman *is* in that film, but somewhere else.

The First Hundred Years led to a curious project. HBO and Warner Video released the film in a limited way, and Hugh Hefner happened to run it in his screening room. He sent me a nice note, and I called him and was invited to visit the Playboy Mansion. We talked about doing a film together—he had just helped Rob Epstein with the financing of his film about gay images in cinema [*The Celluloid Closet,* 1996]—and for some reason I told him I was interested in doing a history of dirty movies. And I didn't mean Jean Harlow or May West. I meant the use of cinema as erotica or pornography or whatever you want to call it. I hadn't seen too many of these movies, and had never even rented an X-rated video. I remember that the movies I was interested in during the early sixties—foreign and independent films—played at the same theaters as *The Immoral Mr. Teas* [1959, directed by Russ Meyer] and the like.

But I loved the idea that there was a whole unexplored genre that got along fine without any Hollywood support in production or distribution, that had its own look and style, however crude. So I made *The Story of X* for Playboy. It was fun and at first interesting, but got a little boring after a while. I *was* able to sneak in an interview with Bertolucci and even a scene from *Weekend* [1968] with Bardot. It may be the first and only time Godard has played on the Playboy Channel. We shot Buck Henry on the set of a porn film narrating the whole thing. I think it has some interesting sequences, especially the montages we did of stag films, nudist films, fifties soft-core exploitation, adult video, and a bunch of other categories. A lot of these montages were cut by my son Jeremy, who maybe related to the material better than his middle-aged father.

MacDonald: So are *Superstar* and *The Source* the kinds of projects where you most get to do what you really want to do?

Workman: More than anything else, yes. Those are *my* movies. Any compromise I make, I make with myself. I'm not saying I've taken no prisoners. There are *many* compromises, in both movies, in terms of trying to make them theatrical. But basically their funders don't get in the way at all.

In the case of *The Source,* the executive producer was Japanese, and the only thing he asked me was not to have too much Buddhism in the material. He's probably Buddhist and sensitive to that. But that was all. In the case of the Warhol film, the woman who funded it had just seen *Roger and Me* [1989, directed by Michael Moore], which includes a cute sequence during the credits, so she wanted to make sure that *I* had a good scene at the end like that, because *Roger and Me* had made all this money. So I put a scene over the end credits that I kind of liked: the amateur painters talking about Andy Warhol.

MacDonald: How did *Superstar* come about? That's your first longer documentary.

Workman: It *wasn't* my first one. I had done other documentaries, but they hadn't worked, in the same way that I've done shorts that haven't worked.

MacDonald: When you say they "didn't work," you mean you finished them, but—

Workman: Almost. I didn't finish them with the polish that they should have had, or solve all the problems. As an editor, I can fix most things and make a film audience friendly. It may not be very good—but it won't look bad. Sometimes I make a film, and if there's no commercial reason for it to be finished properly, I just say, "OK, I've got what I wanted out of that"—and move on.

In the late eighties, during the Intifada, I made a documentary about Israel. Before that, I had made only promotional documentaries, the behind-the-scenes-making-of-a-movie documentaries I mentioned earlier. So I decided to go make this film in Israel. I was very interested, still am, in places where there is a revolutionary, radical foment going on within an established institution: Ireland, Israel, parts of Latin America. I spent some of my early career in Argentina.

MacDonald: Argentina?

Workman: I worked as an editor for Leopoldo Torre-Nilsson. When I was twenty-two years old, just starting out, I worked as an editor cutting toy commercials. And the Mexican owner of this toy company wanted to make a feature, and he got Torre-Nilsson—with the exception of Buñuel, the leading Spanish-language director in the world at that time—to direct. Torre-Nilsson wanted to make an American film, so the film got made [*Monday's Child,* 1967]. Anyway, the toy company owner suggested me as an editor. Torre-Nilsson said,

"I have my own Argentine editors, thank you very much." "Yeah, but Chuck is *American,* and you need an English-speaking editor; work with him, and then you can fix things up with your Argentine editors"; "OK." And it turned out that Torre-Nilsson liked me and took me to Argentina for a second film [*The Traitors of San Angel,* 1967].

MacDonald: Do you speak Spanish?

Workman: I do now; I didn't at the time. Both films were in English—very good but obscure films. I was lucky to have this exposure. The Argentines wanted me to make a film about democracy in Argentina, and *I* wanted to make a documentary on Evita Peron (this was after those years of oppressive dictatorship). So I went back there again.

But at that same time, my son was about to be bar mitzvahed, and I got very Jewish for those five minutes, and went to Israel, and I discovered I *loved* Israel. I felt it *was* a blessed place. I'm not religious at all. At this point I probably don't even believe in God, but at the time, ten or fifteen years ago, I was into it. And I wanted to make a film about what was happening in Israel, called *Keeper of the Light.* And I did make it. No money. I just went on my own. I brought a great cameraman, Burleigh Wartes. I was the sound man.

MacDonald: It was shot in 16mm?

Workman: Yeah. There was another big institutional film about Israel being made abut the same time, and I got some of that crew. I just shot whatever I wanted. I followed some tourists around. It didn't really come together as a film: it was formless and sloppy. But I didn't care. I took it to a couple of festivals and then forgot about it. It allowed me to learn about myself and about making documentaries. Everything I've ever done has been that way: I've done one or two things that don't quite work, learning how that sort of thing should work, or at least what works for me.

Superstar worked because I had done the Israel film which didn't quite work.

MacDonald: What I enjoy most about *Superstar* is Warhol's relatives in Pittsburgh. Here's this guy who's the epitome of the sophisticated New York artist, and you reveal that, ironically, what seems most New York about him is actually a kind of working-class Pittsburgh take on things.

Workman: Yes, and that seems obvious now, doesn't it? Why wouldn't anybody else shoot that? I had no idea what these people *looked* like! *[Laughter.]* But if you know anything about life, you *know* that that's going to be true. This guy wasn't *born* that weird; he came from somewhere.

Of course, another thing that happens when you're making a film is that you exploit—I use the word in a broad way—you exploit the material that works well. So the minute I saw the Warhol *family,* I said, "Oh, let these ladies who like to sing together, sing; let's have them talk about Andy; let's get the scrapbook." When I showed up at his farm to do the interview, one of the brothers was wearing overalls and these big, Hollywood-looking sunglasses. He says,

Publicity still for Chuck Workman's *Superstar: The Life and Times of Andy Warhol* (1991). Photograph courtesy of *Love Boat* and Chuck Workman.

"Wait, I'll take my sunglasses off," but I said, "No, no, leave them on." Those are the dumb little things that you do as a director to push an idea a little bit. The documentaries I make *are* directed—no question. Not that they're manipulated in terms of reality, but they're certainly pushed in a certain direction, sometimes based on decisions I've made in advance.

In *Superstar,* for instance, there are a lot of handheld shots of the artwork. No good documentary cameraman would ever shoot those handheld. They might shoot the interviews handheld, but they're not even comfortable with *that.* I said, "No, no, do it handheld." "But it'll shake!" "I know, but they're edgy people!" It's a visual metaphor that I try and take through the film.

I also worked hard in *Superstar* and *The Source* to show different generations responding to a particular phenomenon. There are things in the thirties that I take seriously that people in the forties didn't, because to them these things were too avant-garde. I take avant-garde filmmakers very seriously now, but in the sixties the people I knew did *not* take them seriously because they seemed to be strange, incompetent people running around with 16mm cameras.

MacDonald: When you decided to do *The Source,* at what point did you make the decision to have the well-known actors play the Beats? For me, that doesn't quite work.

Workman: For some people it doesn't; for other people that's the part that works best.

When I made *Superstar,* I had tons of images to work with. But now I was making a movie about three *writers.* Once I show all the beatnik jokes, and do the interviews, what *visuals* do I have? How do I *show* what they were writing and integrate it into the movie so that it's really the stuff of the movie? Or *half* the stuff: the other half is their influence on the times.

MacDonald: Did you yourself read the Beats in the fifties and sixties?

Workman: Only Kerouac. I didn't read any Burroughs. I remember a girl I was going out with having a copy of *Junkie,* which was forbidden, in a drawer. And Ginsberg—I bought *Howl,* and some Ferlinghetti, but I was nothing like the people interviewed who say, "I read such and such and it changed my life," or "I went to New York in pursuit of Ginsberg and poetry."

So to get back to your question, I had to deal with the *word.* How do I *show* the writing? I do show a lot of imagery of people typing, and scenes where you actually see the text. More than necessary, frankly. But that still wasn't enough. So I decided to have pieces of these texts performed. But we all hate bad re-creations. I decided to have actors play the personae of particular works. In other words, I decided to take advantage of the fact that many of the Beats' writings were personal memoirs, or *felt* like personal memoirs. I could have used very obscure actors, but I thought, "Why not get good actors? I'm using good music." Of course, it was also strategic. It's much more interesting for somebody to watch Johnny Depp read Kerouac than to watch an actor that *reminds* you of Jack Kerouac. But it *was* important to me that Johnny Depp, Dennis Hopper, and John Turturro are very good actors, and they seemed the right actors with the right sensibilities.

MacDonald: To look at the end credits and see how many places you went to for the bits that end up in *The Source* suggests how much work goes into this kind of compilation work.

Workman: Well, *you* just asked me, where's the experimental film in *Pieces of Silver?*! I feel I have an obligation to the material to be inclusive. I don't want to leave anything out. If you're going to do the story of the Beats, you'd better try to get as much as possible. It was the same with Andy Warhol. We chased his art all over the world. He had just died, and the estate was nervous, and museums were afraid of offending the estate, and the estate didn't seem to want us to make the movie. We finally got permission to shoot art at a small museum in London, and at the same time they were showing some of his films, so we shot them off the screen, because the Museum of Modern Art wouldn't give us any of the films, even though they weren't copyrighted.

MacDonald: Why not?

Workman: After he died, it was a very ugly mess for several years. There was a lot of money involved. But I try not to take no for an answer. I try to chase the material as much as possible. I will take no eventually, but not at first. My budgets are a little better than some, so I'm able to push a little bit, but I could never have bought the Rolling Stones song I use four minutes of, except that Mick Jagger liked the piece I wanted to use it with. Yoko Ono liked Andy Warhol, so I was able to get a John Lennon song.

MacDonald: How much of this do you do yourself? It doesn't look like you have a big staff.

Workman: When I make a movie, I have about five people. Sometimes, only two. I generally have a coordinator, but often you have to call people yourself. I do have a staff and need to work with lots of lawyers. The Oscar show is very well staffed because there's a lot of paperwork, and every image that I use has to be cleared with a big fat contract, and there are a lot of questions. "Does Clint Eastwood know you're using this?" "Can you shoot a copy over to Meryl Streep so she can see what you're doing?"

MacDonald: I just went through getting images for a book, which is like small potatoes compared to what you do. And *that* was exhausting.

Workman: Oh, but stills are the worst. Because many still photographers feel they are the most demeaned people in the world.

Years ago, when I made *Precious Images,* David Shepard, head of the Directors Guild Special Projects, made four phone calls. There are more than four studios! But he only made four calls. A year later Warner Brothers sent David a letter, "What is this movie *Precious Images?*" I mean there was no concept of reusing material in those days. Who would ever want a one-second clip of early Charlie Chaplin? Somebody in the legal department would handle it if it ever came up. Now, there are departments in every studio, at every network. Every network has people selling material. I don't mean stock footage houses and news libraries—there were always those.

Disney was the first studio that really understood about reuse. They made enormous amounts of money re-releasing *Pinocchio* [1939], or whatever, every ten years. They were and are very protective of their images. But MGM was never going to re-release *Singin' in the Rain;* they sold it to television, and that was the end of it. They never expected there'd be people interested in showing a clip of Gene Kelly jumping around in the rain.

Actually, I think it's better for the movies in the end, that these images get out. People going into filmmaking now are seeing so many images. Even if you're not that excited about old images, you're seeing so many that they're going to affect you. And I find that nothing but positive for the future, because if we can constantly see all this stuff, we'll get to see that the junk *is* junk. We'll get to recognize junk. Yes, we may still want a McDonald's hamburger on a rare occasion; but if we're used to eating *good* food, we'll say, "Hey, let's go to a good restaurant tonight," and after a while, you're dealing with a generation of people that know about sushi bars. So all these channels and all this interest is

Chuck Workman (in center) and crew on set of *A House on a Hill* (2001). Courtesy Chuck Workman.

certainly making people more conscious about *all* imagery. It allows me as a filmmaker to make more sophisticated movies that more people will understand.

MacDonald: I read your new feature, *A House on a Hill,* as a kind of Workman artistic credo. Both Harry and the filmmaker documenting him seem to represent dimensions of your career: you're dealing, like most of us older guys, with the process of aging and the construction of a career, a body of work; and like the filmmaker in the film, you've made documentaries about creative people. Was this project, for you, an expression of your current thinking about your life as a filmmaker? And is the film personal in other ways? Forgive my asking, but have you lost a child?

Workman: Frankly, the film isn't as autobiographical as it might appear to be. I'm lucky enough to have had two children who are still flourishing, although I did lose a brother-in-law to AIDS in 1988 and watched my wife and my mother-in-law react to that tragedy, and felt its sadness closely and still do. But that's the extent of any early loss in my immediate family. Still, this kind of traumatic occurrence must be important for me, maybe in some subconscious way: the risk of a child's welfare, if not the loss of a child, comes up in my earlier film *The Money* [1975]. Of course, losing a child is a potent symbol of unrecoverable loss, of someone who is usually innocent, and of all the guilt carried from then on by the survivors who were in charge.

In *A House on a Hill,* I meant the accident to the child to show the extent that everyday experience impinges on the life of an artist, the main character Harry, and the possible consequences of that. I'm something of a stubborn guy myself, like Harry, so I understood that part pretty well. The guilt of the mother, who inadvertently got the whole tragedy started, is the guilt of the well-meaning parent who tries for some happiness for herself and accidentally causes harm to her children. As a child of divorced parents, I saw a bit of that, although never to this extreme. But in terms of career and recognition, I've been luckier than Harry, and can't really identify with his frustrations—although I understand them—or with his purity, which I envy.

I wrote the genesis of this script more than fifteen years ago, when I did feel pretty frustrated, when I was ready to give up film and devote my career to theater. It wasn't until I had given up the commercial track I was on that I was ready to return to film and got to work on some of the things I felt strongly about artistically. In the original script, the character of Harry Mayfield was older, about eighty, and the idea for the film then was that he would go back and finish his career, and his life, by creating his last "monument." The title then was "Mayfield's Monument." The current film ends differently. The emphasis is not on the monument but on Mayfield; not on artistic legacy, but on the artistic process. I suppose I've learned that just doing something in the present should be as important as what the future will think of the work—but this is a difficult idea to live your life by and takes some courage. Harry has that courage.

MacDonald: Your exploration of the possibilities of shaping the image is both unusual and effective, in the sense that while viewers (at least this viewer) are aware of the experiment—surprised by it, aware of how you "sync" sound and the movement of the changing frame, etcetera, they aren't thrown out of the narrative. Indeed, the device confirms the idea of the film as your artistic credo, since your shaping space is analogous to Harry's.

Was the idea of working with the shape of the screen always a part of your thinking about this project?

Workman: I've been thinking about the shape of the screen for some time; and reshaping the screen has been part of film history since the beginning. Why not change the screen shape if it's integral to some overall vision? The idea of a story about an architect who shapes space gives a narrative-based excuse for reshaping the screen, but I would hope the technique does more than that. The shape of the screen contracts as Harry works, when he concentrates on his designs. The screen is very wide when we see characters who are part of the world outside of Harry, and these wider frames are comparatively busy. All I can say is that I did try to work out when to work with the device and when not to, but my "rules" were flexible. Sometimes the screen shape changes because it's a design element that seemed "right" at that moment. It does distance the viewer—a bit in a Brechtian way, I hope. It makes you aware that this is a little different than a traditional narrative you'd lose yourself in, and might make you watch more carefully.

MacDonald: This film takes some chances. It's a film about an aging man with no romantic life—hardly a typical Hollywood topic!—and it's obviously experimental in form. How well will the film need to do for you to be satisfied with it? Who do you see as the audience for the film?

Workman: The film will be released in various media in a small way in late 2002 and will be out there in some form. I hope people will find their way to it. There certainly were moments when I thought to myself that certain fixes might make the film more audience-friendly, more accessible, less experimental-looking. It could be more traditionally scored and edited, for example. With some judicious editing, the aging main character could be changed into a sentimental old codger up against the world. But I thought, "Why do that? This is a chance, maybe one of the few chances I'll have, to make a film the way I see it." It may sound arrogant, but that was more important to me than making the film mass-audience-friendly. I'm the one who's always running around saying that films ought to be more adventurous, and that the art of film should be farther along after more than a century, that it shouldn't be so commercially oriented—so I might as well try to follow these ideas in my own work. At the same time, I like to think I have this unspoken dialogue with an audience—some audience, somewhere—and that my films are made to connect with that audience, however obscure or different the work may be.

Of course, not all our films work or turn out the way they should. So we try again.

Shaped, multilayered images in Workman's *A House on a Hill* (2001). Courtesy Chuck Workman.

Chantal Akerman

On *D'Est, Sud,* and *De l'autre côté*

There are filmmakers who find a particular cinematic niche and explore it relentlessly throughout their careers. Hitchcock, Keaton, and Flaherty are obvious instances, and in *A Critical Cinema 4,* Peter Forgács. And there are filmmakers who are driven to explore a wide variety of approaches: Howard Hawks is a good example, as, more recently, is Jonathan Demme. In this volume an obvious instance of this tendency is the Belgian-French director Chantal Akerman. During the early 1970s, when she was living in New York City, exploring what was then called Underground Film and/or the New American Cinema and, especially, what P. Adams Sitney called "structural film" and related approaches, Akerman completed *Hôtel Monterey* (1972) and, later, *News from Home* (1976), impressive, evocative, highly formal ruminations on New York City. In 1975 came *Jeanne Dielman, 23 Quai du Commerce, 1080 Bruxelles,* the film that established her, at least in the United States, as a major contributor to critical cinema.

This three-hour-twenty-minute, 35mm depiction of the daily life of a single mother (and prostitute), played brilliantly by Delphine Seyrig and captured with rigorously formal cinematography by Babette Mangolte, reveals the obsessive-compulsive dimensions of everyday, mundane experience. By midway through *Jeanne Dielman,* Akerman has transformed the screening room: the audience becomes as obsessive-compulsive as Dielman herself is, in their awareness of Dielman's domestic rituals. Like Gertrude Stein, Akerman reminds us that we are what we repeat, and more: that in our relentless attempts to create secure lives within an ever-changing world, we are always in danger of destroying the very life we hope to protect. And she reveals that the life of a very particular woman living at a quite specific address in a European capital has a good bit in common with the everyday lives of people everywhere. *Jeanne Dielman* is as deeply embedded in *place* as are Akerman's New York films. Like Flannery O'Connor, Akerman is aware of "all those concrete details of life that make actual the mystery of our position on earth" (O'Connor, *Mystery and Manners* [New York: Noonday, 1961], 68).

In the nearly thirty years since she finished *Jeanne Dielman,* Akerman has made many kinds of film, but she has consistently located whatever kinds of action she has depicted within carefully wrought, identifiable places. Indeed, in recent years, she has at times made place itself her subject, as she does in a recent trilogy of films: *D'Est* (*From the East,* 1993), *Sud* (*South,* 2000), and *De l'autre côté* (*From the Other Side,* 2002). While these films were not conceived as a trilogy, their focus on particular geographic regions—Russia and Eastern Europe at the end of the Soviet era in *From the East;* the American Deep South, and in particular the horrific murder of James Byrd in Jasper, Texas, in 1998, in *South;* and the U.S.-Mexican border, now in a process of transformation as the Bush administration builds a literal wall between Sonora and Arizona in an effort to minimize illegal immigration, in *From the Other Side*—and Akerman's visual style (her rigidly formal compositions and her tendency toward long, continuous takes) make the films feel so much of a piece that it is difficult, even for Akerman, not to think of them as a trilogy.

My longtime interest in Akerman's work, and my particular fascination with cinematic depictions of place, led me to meet with Akerman in New York City in December 2002, when she presented the Place trilogy at the Museum of Modern Art. We discussed the trilogy and refined the resulting interview by e-mail. My particular thanks to Sally Berger for assistance in arranging these events and this interview.

MacDonald: At least in terms of the nature of your involvement in place, your recent films seem different from your earlier films. This is not to say that your earlier films weren't involved with place: *News from Home* certainly was—and is the closest of the earlier films to these. But I'm wondering how new *From the East, South,* and *From the Other Side* feel to you.

Akerman: Well, if there *is* something new, and this is more true in *From the East* and *South* than in *From the Other Side,* it's in how the films relate to different layers of history, how we look at the events now and see other moments of history in them. When I made it, *News from Home* did not have that dimension. Of course, *now,* if you see *News from Home,* it *is* about history: it was shot in 1976, and the subway has changed; the clothes have changed; the whole city has changed. *News from Home* has become a historical documentary about New York in 1976.

But *From the East* and *South* are about layers of history; they don't have to wait to develop a historical dimension. In *South,* for example, the story of the murder of James Byrd in Jasper, Texas, taints everything in the movie, so that when you see a tree, you might think that that tree could have been used fifty or seventy years ago to lynch somebody.

A similar thing happens in *From the East.* When you see all those queues of people in the train stations in Moscow in 1992, those scenes also remind you—or at least remind *me*—of images of the Second World War, and especially of the concentration camps. Even the people just standing there waiting for their buses, and the people carrying packages through the snow, remind me of the Jews waiting to go to the camps. I didn't see many images of the camps. My mother was in Auschwitz, but she didn't talk about it much. But I do know that every morning the Nazis were saying, "This one can stay and work; this one cannot." So people were waiting to know their fate. When I saw *From the East* finished, I thought, "Well, I did something related to the camps without even knowing it." So both *South* and *From the East* were and are political movies, without being obviously so.

MacDonald: They're meditations on political situations.

Akerman: You could say that.

From the Other Side is more directly about a political situation, not just in the sense of what's happening *there,* at the border between Mexico and America, but in a more general sense: it's about any society dealing with the foreign, the Other. I mean the film to be political, but in a philosophical way. So it's philosophical and political in the same way as—maybe even more than—*Je tu il elle* [1974] or even *Jeanne Dielman . . .*

Jeanne Dielman was considered a feminist film, but that was not my goal when I made it. My goal at the time was to show someone who organizes her life so that there is no hole in her time, because when there *is* a hole, there is also anxiety. I could have done that same film about a man, except that I was more interested in showing a woman's everyday gestures. I don't think it was feminist in the sense that many people have said—at least, a film about alienation because of gender was not my goal. Maybe the film *became* that, but for me *Jeanne Dielman . . .* was more about letting everyday gestures exist in a film, which at the time was rare. Usually the everyday aspects of life were cut out or not written at all. *Jeanne Dielman . . .* was an act of love for those gestures that you see when you're a child, that you are surrounded by as a child. In a way, the repetition of those gestures is very good for a child.

MacDonald: Those gestures are "home."

Akerman: Exactly. They're home.

MacDonald: When you started on *From the East,* how fully had you preconceived the project?

Akerman: All I knew was that I was going to start in the summer and that I was going to end with the winter. And I knew I was going to start in Eastern Europe and end in Moscow. But I didn't know anything about what was going to come in between. Really, I *found* the movie. We made three trips, and at the end of the second trip, I realized what I wanted to do.

At the beginning I didn't know where exactly I was going to go. I didn't know what I was going to shoot. We had the map, and I would say, "OK, take this road. Take that road." I was just looking around, I didn't know exactly for what, but as soon as something was telling me something—I don't mean with words, just when I was *feeling* something—I would say, "Stop! Put the camera here, and shoot." But why I was making those choices, I couldn't have told you.

MacDonald: One of the problems I have looking at *From the East*—and I assume this is largely because I'm an American—is that I never know where I am in that film. I guess I know when I'm in Moscow, at least sometimes, but almost the whole film seems to be taking place in Russia.

Akerman: It has nothing to do with your being American. *Nobody* knows where the various images were shot.

In fact, I started in Eastern Europe—in East Germany—then went to Poland, then to Lithuania, Belarus, Moldavia, the Ukraine, and then Moscow.

MacDonald: I did finally begin to wonder whether *not* knowing is part of the point, that during the cold war, all the countries in the Soviet bloc had the feel of Russia.

Akerman: Yes, that's true.

I like that film. Making it was a strong experience.

MacDonald: From the East creates an amazing sense of life at the end of Soviet domination of that part of the world. I don't know Eastern Europe at all—I've been to Latvia once, and to East Germany, during the eighties—but when I was there it seemed a painful period in many ways.

Akerman: It still is. It's different than it was, but things are still difficult.

MacDonald: It's amazing how little interaction there is between you and the people you film—except in those instances when people seem to be angry with you for shooting.

Akerman: At the bus stop they were angry at me, but just because I was slowing their bus down. We were moving so slowly in the car that the bus had to wait for us. That's all.

MacDonald: I was thinking that the people you film don't trust the camera at all; they seem afraid of the camera, which I take to be a vestige of the oppressive society they've been living in.

Akerman: I think that's really about being in a big city. In Moscow, people are very tough when they're outside of their homes. At least they were when we

Women at work in Chantal Akerman's *D'Est* (1993). Courtesy Chantal Akerman.

were shooting; I don't know if that's still the case. They pushed you and they didn't *see* you.

In New York in 1973 or 1975 or 1976, it was exactly the same, maybe because city life in New York was dangerous at the time. That's not true any more. New York feels very safe. When I was doing *Hôtel Monterey* in 1972, I was in a small elevator in a hotel with my camera: people entered, and there was no response to me or the camera at all, *nothing*. I had the same experience when I was shooting *News from Home*. The people in Moscow in *From the East* reacted to me in the same way that the people in New York did in the seventies.

I don't know if the passivity you see in *From the East* was related to seventy years of communism or Stalin, but it's certainly there.

MacDonald: About the interior shots—are they directed? Did you need to set them up and light them? And how did you find those people?

Akerman: They were a bit directed—a bit. And, yes, I lit them, with a single light. During the making of the film, we were helped by a documentary studio in Moscow, and I told them I wanted to meet people, and was able to. I talked with the people and made arrangements to film those I liked and thought were interesting, in their apartments. When I *felt* something, I shot.

MacDonald: Did you ask them to do specific things?

Akerman: In the case of the woman who plays piano, I said, "Please sit there at the piano," but I did not ask the little boy to play with his little car the way he does in that scene, which I loved. I asked the woman with the record player, "Let's listen to a song; you choose one," and she did. The little girl with the lipstick?—no I didn't ask her to do that. I asked the woman who you see with her son, "What will you do when you go to see your son?" And I asked her to do what she usually did.

So, yes, I asked people to do a few things, but I didn't contrive what they had to do. The film was directed slightly, with their complicity, and taking into account what they thought they could bring to the shooting.

MacDonald: What was the editing process for *From the East?*

Akerman: Generally it was organized in the order in which we shot it. That is, it starts in Eastern Europe and ends in Moscow; it starts in the summer, then it's autumn, then winter.

The editing of the successive shots was done by trial and error. We'd say, "What about those three shots together?" We'd try that, and then we'd try something else. As to the length of the shots, that's very complicated. I have to be very relaxed, very close to myself, so that I can really feel each shot. I'd be sitting next to my editor, watching a shot, and when I felt that the shot had gone for just the right length, so that something came through, but not too much, I'd say, "Here!" So in the end *D'Est* was made by screening the shots over and over and over. It took us a while, because we looked at every shot many times. Deciding the right length for the shots was really a nightmare.

MacDonald: There *are* some incredibly long tracking shots.

Akerman: I hope people can stand them!

I had not seen *From the East* for a long time until this weekend, but every time I see the film, I see more and more of the details on the faces of the people. There is so much to see in one face, and there are hundreds of faces in the film. I was surprised at how absorbed I became in all those faces. I don't mean to give myself flowers, but *From the East* is still striking, I think.

MacDonald: Yes, it is.

When I first saw *From the East,* I had been reading a lot about moving panoramas—a nineteenth-century entertainment form where a long, narrative painting would be unrolled in front of the audience; it was a predecessor of the movies. Sitting and watching your panoramic shots of people and places evokes that earlier form. Did you have moving panoramas in mind when you made *From the East?*

Akerman: No. I don't know anything about moving panoramas.

MacDonald: Is there only one version of *From the East?* I know you made it into an installation. Could you talk about that process?

Akerman: There is only one version of the film. The installation is something else, and there is only one version of the installation, too.

I had wanted to make that film about Eastern Europe for twenty years, and at one point I was approached about the possibility of doing an installation. I didn't care so much about doing an installation, but I thought it might be a way to get money for the film. I said maybe I could do something about Eastern Europe. I was asked to write a proposal. I had no ideas—just a desire to make the movie. But in the end they didn't find the money anyway.

Later, *I* found the money in Europe to make the film, and did make it, and two years later, Bruce Jenkins called from the Walker Art Center to say, "We have some money for you to make an installation." I said, "Fine."

I didn't know how to do an installation, so I just said, "Well, let's have three monitors and three tape decks, each with a different bit of the film. We were looking and looking and looking at the three monitors, and suddenly I said, "Look! There's something happening there." We saw that something *was* working, so we had a triptych. Then we did the same procedure again and again, but with different material, ten times; and then we had ten triptychs. The first eight were the best, so we ended up with twenty-four monitors, eight triptychs. And then I put the last monitor on the floor with my text.

That was my first installation, and of course, when you do something for the first time, you are usually lucky, and I was lucky with that one. Now I'm starting to think of installation in a more specific way and in a more serious way, and it's more difficult.

But if nobody had asked me to do an installation, I would have never done one.

MacDonald: South was your first American film in quite a while. What drew you to the Byrd case, in particular? It *was* a horrifying story.

Akerman: I read about it in a newspaper. It was a very strange, terrible story. But I had wanted to make a film about the American South before the Byrd case happened.

MacDonald: Did you start it before the Byrd case?

Akerman: No, but I had had the idea at the end of April, and the Byrd case happened in June—I don't remember the exact day [Byrd was murdered on June 14, 1998]. I read a blurb in the newspaper, and I said, "I'm going to make the movie about the South and about what happened in Jasper, Texas." I made plans to go to America and went to Jasper at the end of my trip.

MacDonald: How long after the crime did you shoot the film?

Akerman: Three months.

MacDonald: Many of us who grew up in the sixties still have a fear of the South.

Akerman: I know, but, of course, that's why I went there. I had read a book by James Baldwin—in French, I think it was called *Harlem Quartet;* in that book Baldwin conveys so well the fear and the silence of the South. That and the Faulkner books drove me to do that movie.

MacDonald: Any particular Faulkner books?

Akerman: I've read most of them. I mix them up. But probably *Light in August* [1932] was important.

So when the Byrd murder happened, I said, "I have to go there," and I was lucky enough to get to Jasper just before that memorial service in the church, because that's an incredible scene.

MacDonald: How did you get to be present for that?

Akerman: I just called the minister, to have an interview with him—he was Byrd's minister—and he said, "There's a memorial in two days; you can come," so we went and we shot.

MacDonald: Did anyone announce to the congregation that you were doing the film?

Akerman: I don't know. But we were very welcome, as you can see. We were totally welcome.

MacDonald: Why are the kids hiding in the pews during the church scene?

Akerman: It's part of the church ritual, I think. I don't know.

MacDonald: Did you consider filming any of Byrd's family?

Akerman: No. I did not need that. I think it would have been awful to go and say, "Hey, your father died. What do you think about it?"—after only three months.

Someone asked me how I made the decision not to use any of the news footage of the murder. I think that evoking an event is usually stronger than showing news coverage of it. But people who want to make a film about an atrocity always face the question of how much of the event to show. Claude Lanzmann found his own way in *Shoah* [1985], and other people have found their own ways. There's always a question of what to show and what not to show, and how to make people feel the event.

MacDonald: South reminds me of several of James Benning's films, especially his *Landscape Suicide* [1986] and *Four Corners* [1997], in both the formality and length of the shots, and in the subject matter.

Akerman (laughter): Well, I don't know his movies, but I know *him.* I met him at CalArts [Benning teaches at California Institute of the Arts in Valencia, California]. He's a great guy.

MacDonald: Also, your last shot, that almost seven-minute tracking shot down the road, along the route where Byrd was dragged, reminds me of *Shoah.*

Akerman: Well, as you know, one of my obsessions is the concentration camps and what happened there. But I've never seen *Shoah;* I've been afraid to see it, so I don't think Lanzmann has had any influence on me.

When James Baldwin writes about the silence of the South and how he doesn't know what's hidden behind the silence, that behind the silence can be someone who wants to kill you—well, again, I was thinking of the camps.

MacDonald: There are strange markings on that road.

Akerman: The marks were made by the police. That's where they found bits of Byrd's flesh and blood. The marks are fading away as the cars drive over them. We drove over them, too.

By using that very long shot, I was trying to capture maybe a very, very, very, very tiny bit of what Byrd went through.

MacDonald: Altogether, how long were you in the South?

Akerman: We didn't stay long—three weeks.

MacDonald: What was your general sense of the South?

Akerman: Everything is so isolated there! One home is here, and the next home is far away; and of course, I was thinking, if you're in the middle, you can be in danger.

Of course, I had read a little before I went, and knew about the civil rights movement. It's strange to go to those cities where you know those things happened—Birmingham and Selma. Even if you don't see anything happening when you're there, those places are very charged with that awful history. That's what I tried to show. When I show an empty cotton field, empty because now they use machines to pick the cotton, you still imagine those fields with slaves in them.

MacDonald: Even going to Jasper takes you back in time. It looks like a town in the fifties, except for the cars.

Akerman: Right.

Also, I visited schools there, and even though there is no legal segregation anymore, there was very little mixing: the kids were either white or black.

MacDonald: That separation comes across in the film, because the people, especially the white people, talk about how well everybody gets along, but we never see whites and blacks together in the imagery.

Akerman: They don't live in the same neighborhoods. They don't go to the same schools. They don't even go to the same churches! Well, some of the richest blacks and whites go to some of the same churches, but that's unusual.

Sometimes they make sports together.

MacDonald: Actually, I think, at least in the United States, sports is the only place where race really gets worked on.

Akerman: I don't want to be harsh against the Christians in Jasper, but I had an interview with the minister, and he was defending the American way of life and complaining that "the young people don't believe in the American way of life anymore." I said, "Maybe they have reasons!" He didn't think so. Maybe he didn't want to speak to *me,* but I tried to push him, but he wouldn't show any anger over the Byrd murder. All the Christians tended to say, "Maybe the murder will help the community to get better." I don't understand that.

The only ones who showed any anger were the Islamic blacks. Christianity doesn't let you show your anger. Anger is not part of the religion. But in Islam, there is a space for anger—at least from what I've heard; I'm no expert. The one guy in the film who says "It shouldn't have happened" is from the Fruit of Islam.

I think that at one point the churches were very good for the blacks, because that's where they could meet and sing together, and they did important political work in the churches, as we all know. But that's not true anymore. Now the church is really working against the blacks.

MacDonald: You balance the scene in the church with the white guy talking about how the Aryan Nation people are taking over churches.

Akerman: Well, *those* people are the really extreme Right, and very frightening.

That guy, John Craig, spent years working as an FBI agent, infiltrating those groups. I met him at the memorial service at the church; he was in the back. He explained to me that there are a lot of crazy people in the South, and that there is still a lot of Ku Klux Klan activity in that area; it's just that they don't express themselves openly. You don't know; you can meet someone who looks awfully nice, and he can be a member of the KKK.

Craig explained to me that the people who have the power in Jasper are the whites, and some of them are members of the KKK, and everybody knows it. The mayor of Jasper is black, but according to Craig, he's just a token. He also told me that the Jasper case was one everybody knew about, from the TV coverage, but that there are other cases that are called "accidents" but are not accidents. The guy said he had tons of stories to tell me.

I have been in America a lot, and I have lots of feelings about racism in America; but, you know, racism is racism. I know plenty about racism myself from my experiences in Europe. Racism is all over, everywhere: on the other side of the town, on the other side of the ocean, on the other side of the family—everywhere. Of course, here in America it's about black and white. In other parts of the world it's about other things.

MacDonald: How did you decide to make *From the Other Side?*

Akerman: I wanted to go to the Mexican-American border because I read an article in the newspaper and was struck by the words used by one of the Americans who was quoted in the article: one word he used was "dirt"—"We don't want that dirt"; "They're going to bring dirt." That made me think of other times in history when the word "dirt" was used: for example, for the Jews—"dirty Jews."

I went to Mexico to see what was happening, with no conception of what kind of film, if any, I would do. I didn't want to have any conception; I wanted to be totally open. I went there to have an adventure and, of course, when you don't have a conception and when you don't know what to do, you can be at peace and be in contact with yourself and with the world, and in the end, you may be able to do something. The concept for a film grows from the experience.

MacDonald: One of the differences between *From the East, South,* and *From the Other Side*—a small difference, but it has a strong effect—is that, in the new film, we hear you asking questions. There's a connection between you and the people you're talking with that we don't feel so clearly in the earlier two films.

Akerman: That's right.

MacDonald: I assume this was a conscious choice, at least in the editing.

Akerman: Mmmm, in fact, no. In the South people tended to make long speeches. I'd ask one question, and off they'd go. The sheriff, for example, knew his part by heart. He had said what he said many times before, and was ready to talk. Many of the people from Jasper wanted to save face and were happy to talk at length.

It was not the same in Mexico, so I had to ask questions. Stylistically, I prefer not to ask questions, but when that's impossible, I accept the fact.

I think that, in a way, *From the Other Side* is less "pure" than the other two films, which is funny because it's also a movie about the Other, who is "impure." Even the elements of the film are mixed: there is Super-16 material, and DVD, and I use some archival footage. I usually don't mix media.

MacDonald: Which is the archival material?

Akerman: The negative imagery, when you see what look like phantoms, and the shots of the Border Patrol working at night.

MacDonald: Over the last few years, there's been a lot of discussion about the separation between the filmmaker and the subject in documentary, and how the camera often becomes a kind of wall between these two realities. Here, it's almost as if you can't stand to be that separate from these people, especially in a film that's meditating on the problems of separation. Even the line we hear you say to the sheriff near the end—"She was never hungry"—works this way.

Akerman: But, you know, it's very instinctive. After the film is made, it can look like this is what I meant to do, but it's just what happened during the process.

MacDonald: Another difference in *From the Other Side,* compared with *From the East* and *South,* is the music you bring in at the beginning and near the end.

Akerman: Monteverdi. In a documentary about the Mexican-American border you would normally use Mexican music or American music. I think the Monteverdi makes the film less naturalistic and more emblematic—less about this particular place than about the larger issue of how people deal with the Other.

MacDonald: Did you spend a lot of time in Mexico?

Akerman: No. I went, and came back, and went, and came back. Not so much time. Altogether less than two months.

MacDonald: When you went to Agua Prieta, did you fly to Tucson, then cross over at Douglas, Arizona?

Akerman: No. I went to Mexico City, then I took a flight to Hermosillo, and then we drove to Agua Prieta, and I crossed to Douglas from there. I wanted to get to the border the way the Mexicans did.

I loved Mexico; I felt like I could have shot ten movies there. Of course, I was not looking for trouble. One of my Mexican assistants liked to go to the bars; he was fascinated with the underlife. But I was not interested in that. I was in a hotel where people were very nice, and I felt great.

The first day after we arrived in Hermosillo, I went with a friend of mine, Minda Martin, to look for a city where I could shoot a film about the border. First, we went to Nogales and had a nice breakfast there. Then we went to Agua Prieta, and immediately I said, "This is where I want to shoot." It was perfect.

Then later, I went back to Mexico, and on that trip we drove to the little village where I shot the material of the old man and woman and the young boy, who are still suffering over the lost of a loved one who tried to cross the border.

MacDonald: James Benning told me that when he did his *Utopia* [1998], which is about the California-Mexico border, the minute he got over into Mexico, he was nervous about walking around with his camera, and he stayed very briefly.

Akerman: He was alone?

MacDonald: Yes.

Akerman: We were four people: myself, the cameraman, a sound man, and an assistant. I was not afraid, except during the night when we found that group where the man reads the letter. We were far away from the city, and the landscape there is like the moon. If I had been alone there, I would have freaked out.

MacDonald: How *did* you find that group of people?

Akerman: We were driving along the border. I knew there were a lot of Mexican gangsters around, and my cameraman was not feeling great. He kept saying to me, "Let's go back." But I said, "No, keep going." I felt that something was going to happen, and that's when we found that group. They had been led by a "coyote" to a place where they were robbed by the Mexican police. When we met them, they had nothing. We asked them what they wanted. They said that they could not go to America anymore, and I couldn't take them there, so I ended up taking them back to Naco, about twenty-five miles west along the border.

Before we left them, the one guy said, "I wrote a letter about our situation. Can I read it to you?" I said, "Can I shoot it?" (I hadn't been shooting before—they were in a bad state.) And so he read the letter, which is about what it's like to be an illegal immigrant, and to have nothing when others have everything. It's a very moving text.

MacDonald: A particular question: in the landscape shot where the guy is working in what looks to be a garden in the foreground, are we seeing the wall in the distance?

Akerman: Not everyone sees that; it's difficult to see—but yes.

They're building a wall in Israel now, too. Well, maybe there it's for the best—a way to separate two populations who are joined together in such a horrible dance.

The wall between Arizona and Sonora, in Akerman's *De l'autre côté* (2000). Courtesy AMIP Multimedia, France.

MacDonald: Did you cross the border into Douglas to get the interview with the people in the luncheonette?

Akerman: That was between Palominas and Douglas. I shot many more interviews in the luncheonette, and many were terrible. People said terrible things. I didn't use them because I didn't want people to say, "Hey, *they*—the Americans—are freaks; *we* are not like that!"

Last night, one person, and maybe others, thought I was attacking America in the film, but I'm not, you know. We have all the same problems in Europe. The problem is not the Americans; the problem is humanity, and the people who always want to say, "You are not one of *us*. You are the Other. You bring dirt and disease." In fact, that's probably *more* European than American. I mean Americans do it, too, but I would say it's more a European problem.

MacDonald: That's generous of you, maybe overly generous.

Akerman: Well, during the last century and before, America was bringing people in from all over. That was never the case in Europe. European countries have tended to protect their borders, and even communities within these countries have struggled terribly: the Jews obviously, but not just the Jews.

Of course, now there is Bush. But you know, in Europe, in France, there is also an extreme right wing—maybe a little bit less a caricature than Bush, but only a little bit less. I don't think that in France a political guy would speak about "The Evil" and "The Good." For me that kind of talk is unbearable, but we have a very right-wing government in France.

I think we—all of us—are in a very bad situation right now; it's probably the worst things have been since the Second World War. What's going to happen with Korea and North Korea, with Yemen, and with the Americans in Iraq; and in Israel; and what's going to happen in Turkey if the European Community doesn't accept them? The guy who is at the head of Russia is totally crazy, too, an ex-KGB guy; and Bush, another crazy guy, is the son of the ex-CIA head. Bush is dangerous. And Putin, too: what he did in that theater a month ago was incredible, and nobody said *anything* in Russia! There's that passivity again.

So I'm afraid for the world.

MacDonald: The final shot of *From the Other Side,* the shot from within the car driving along a Los Angeles freeway, is very powerful because it's so different from the rest of the film—both in the kind of action filmed and in the location. Also, that's the only shot in any of these films that has narration.

Akerman: In a way it's the coda of the movie. My narration tells the story of a guy who is looking for his mother, who has disappeared. She has crossed the border into the United States in order to make money and send it back to the family; but the money hasn't come, and the family is not sure what has happened to her. The son crosses over to try and find his mother and does find the landlady where the mother lived when she first arrived. It's clear from what the landlady says that the mother was not understanding this new world, and that the world was not understanding her.

The story of immigration is not just whether you get across but also how, if you *do* get across, you begin to have a life in the new place. It's not enough just to survive. What kind of life do you have, and I don't mean just in terms of whether you make money. In a way, you've lost contact with yourself. You've alienated yourself from yourself. You are in a place where the people don't get you. Yes, after a few generations people adapt to the new country, but for the first generation things are very hard—not only here in America but everywhere.

The French are awful with immigrants. For generations there have been lots of Algerians working as cheap labor in France. The Germans brought people in, too, but only for six months or a year, but in France the men who have come to work have been able to stay. They have children, and then grandchildren—and many of those grandchildren are angry about how France exploited their grandfathers and fathers. I live in a neighborhood in the middle of Arabs and blacks, and you can see some of the kids—not all of them—totally refusing to do what the French do. They have two options: they can become religious, by which I mean Muslim, or be acculturated as French. There's nothing in between.

In France there are five million Muslim men who didn't assimilate at all and don't want to assimilate, and that's going to be very complicated. I'm not judging anyone; I'm certainly not judging the ex-immigrant—you can't call them immigrants anymore because legally they have French citizenship—because I can understand why they feel as they do, why they feel that the laws of the French are not *their* laws. But it's very problematic, because in one country, there should be the same law for everyone. It's like we are sitting on a bomb.

And, you know, that's why I did *From the Other Side* in Mexico. When something is too close, you just can't *see* it; and I thought that at the Mexican-American border I would be able to have a better look at the whole European situation, the whole world situation.

I'm not anti-American, like a lot of French people are; I have been here a lot.

MacDonald: Are these recent films instances where you shoot a lot and then you use a little?

Akerman: Well, in *From the East,* I didn't shoot so much because it was in 16mm and more expensive, but for *South* and *From the Other Side,* yes, we shot a lot. We built the movies, structured them, during the editing. When I teach (I'm not teaching at the moment), I always tell my students to try and not shoot too much. Since I have shot in video, I know there's a tendency to do that.

I started with film, so when I say "a lot," I mean much less than most of the people who are now using video. They can shoot a hundred hours for a film, while for *South* and *From the Other Side* "a lot" was only twenty or thirty hours. But for *From the East* we shot only ten hours, and the film is 107 minutes long—a ratio of seven to one. Not much.

MacDonald: Do you think of the three films as a trilogy, or was that MoMA's idea for marketing this set of events?

Akerman: No, I proposed them as a trilogy. I didn't think about a trilogy when I was making the films, but after the three were finished, I decided they *were* a trilogy.

MacDonald: Will these new films be in distribution in the United States?

Akerman: Well, First Run has *From the Other Side,* but for noncommercial distribution.

MacDonald: But not *South?*

Akerman: Nobody has that one.

MacDonald: That's a film that has a lot of relevance, not just for people interested in film history but for people teaching southern literature, teaching about place.

Also, to my knowledge, there's not another film about the Byrd murder—nothing but press coverage.

Akerman: Yes, it's incredible. Some black people were happy that I made the movie, but some others were saying, "Well, a black person should have made the film." I said, "But it was *not* done, so I did it."

MacDonald: Are you going to do more of these kinds of films? Do you have another place subject in mind?

Akerman: No. Not yet. But, yes, I hope to do more of these films. My next film is supposed to be a comedy. I always like to go from one kind of film to another.

MacDonald: What are some of the main differences between making a fiction film and a documentary?

Akerman: When you're making a fiction film, you always have the script to follow. Sometimes what you do can be better than the script, but at worst, you always have the script to work from. There is no script for a documentary, at least not for the documentaries I make. I go out into the world and hope to find a film, and sometimes I do find a film. So on that level, documentaries are more difficult.

There are also many similarities between my fiction films and my documentaries. My framing and cutting are similar; I'm trying to do many of the same things. This is obvious in *Jeanne Dielman . . . ,* which uses the same kind of long shots as these recent documentaries do, and which is framed in much the same way.

And I'm the same person, so the same interests are evident in both forms.

MacDonald: Are there particular documentarians whose work you follow?

Akerman: I have to admit I almost never go to see anything. It's not because I don't like what I do see; it's just that I'm busy and often I'm tired, and just don't have the time and energy to go out. Sometimes I agree to be on a film festival jury—then I see a lot of films in a week or two. But, otherwise, I rarely go out. I'm ashamed to admit it. It shouldn't be that way. I'm sure there are many interesting films to see.

Lawrence Brose

On *De Profundis*

Lawrence Brose's films, and *De Profundis* (1997) in particular, represent an intersection of two subhistories of critical cinema, usually understood as distinct from
one another: the history of working directly on the filmstrip and the history of
what has come to be called "Queer cinema." Using the filmstrip as a base for
painting and for other manipulations has a long history that includes Man Ray's
"rayogram" technique (laying objects on an unexposed strip of film and then
exposing it to light, so that the objects make a direct imprint on the filmstrip);
Len Lye's coordination of painted imagery and music; Harry Smith's early
"batiked" animations in which colors were layered onto the filmstrip using "Come
Clean Gum Dots" and Vaseline; Stan Brakhage's *Mothlight* (1963), in which
moth wings, blades of grass, and tiny flowers were collaged along the filmstrip, which was then printed; and *Fuses* (1967), in which Carolee Schneemann used a variety of techniques—painting and scratching on top of photographed
imagery, exposing the filmstrip to various natural processes—to express the emotional and spiritual dimensions of her sex life with James Tenney.

In recent decades a good many filmmakers have worked with these and related
techniques, in some cases because of their fascination with them, and often
because working directly on the filmstrip has become a less expensive way of
making film art than shooting and developing photographic imagery. During
his final years, when his finances were particularly stressed, Stan Brakhage
returned to painting on film and produced dozens of films. And generations of
younger makers have found new ways, and have revived old ones, of producing direct imagery: David Gatten unrolled unexposed film into a crab trap, threw
the trap into the South Carolina surf, and allowed the ocean to inscribe imagery

onto the filmstrip (*What the Water Said, Nos. 1–3,* 1997–98); for *Flight* (1996), Greta Snider used hand processing and the rayogram technique to evoke her relationship with her deceased father; for the epic *Regarding Penelope's Wake* (2002), Michelle Smith used what she has described as "frame-by-frame collage/montage/hand-painted/ripped/cut/etched found footage" (program notes for the film's premiere at the 2002 New York Film Festival); and Brose used a painstaking process of hand processing to alter a variety of photographed and found imagery—old home movies, early gay pornography, and his own documentation of a Radical Fairy gathering in Tennessee and of several drag performances—to create his first long film (sixty-five minutes).

Unlike nearly all the filmmakers who have used the techniques just described, however, Brose has used the formal manipulations of his imagery as a means to an overtly political end: a new sense of gay rights that does not involve the suppression of "queerness." Brose's exploration of hand processing creates an always changing, frequently gorgeous cinematic ground within which he can consider the implications of Oscar Wilde's aphorisms ("The only way to get rid of a temptation is to yield to it"; "I'd rather have fifty unnatural vices than one unnatural virtue"); his prison letter, "De Profundis," and his dandyism, for radical gays and for more conventional communities. The resulting experience is something of a phantasmagoria of image and sound that, on one level, "queers" the history of film as visual music (Oscar Fischinger, Len Lye, Norman McLaren, et al.) and, on another level, formalizes—cinematically *materializes*—the widespread fascination among gay men with drag, a fascination that has a history that both transcends film history and has regularly contributed to it. The critical cinema has produced a considerable number of landmark explorations of drag, including Jack Smith's *Flaming Creatures* (1963), Kenneth Anger's *Inauguration of the Pleasure Dome* (in various versions since the mid-1950s), and John Waters's *Multiple Maniacs* (1970), *Pink Flamingos* (1972), and *Female Trouble* (1974), to name just a few. Like these earlier films, *De Profundis* confronts cinematic convention by combining an aggressive awareness of gay desire and some of its radical manifestations in a repressive society, with an unusual approach to generating imagery—a combination that creates considerable challenges for viewers.

I spoke with Brose in Utica, New York, in November 1999; we refined the interview on-line.

MacDonald: Last night, when you were talking at Hamilton College about the personal background of *De Profundis,* the catastrophe of that period of your life—your business going under; your previous boyfriend and current boyfriend *both* dealing with AIDS—I thought of one of Winslow Homer's great paintings, *Lifeline* [1884]: making *De Profundis* must have been a lifeline for you.

Brose: What's interesting is that I didn't work directly on the film (I had done research and other back-burner stuff) until I had severed *everything,* until my partner and I had split up, and my former lover had passed away. Then I thought, "I've got to take control of my life—this is about *me* now." I moved back to Buffalo from Rochester, found a studio right below the gallery here [Brose is executive director of the Center for Exploratory and Perceptual Art (CEPA) Gallery in Buffalo], and went to work. The energy and focus it took to make *De Profundis* were provided by all those experiences that I was now moving away from. It was a violent closure, psychically. I remember telling my therapist that I had two choices: to get pushed off the bridge or jump. I decided to jump. I did wind up landing on my feet, and *De Profundis* was a big part of that.

Making the film was an important, almost alchemical, experience in my life. Before, I was pushing myself; now, I was compelled. The film *had* to be made, and it needed to be its *own* journey, its *own* immersion in experience. And in the end, the experience *of* the film, of *viewing* it, is an immersion experience also. The conditions surrounding the making of the film helped to shape its intensity, its visual and sonic concentration.

MacDonald: What was your goal for the project, insofar as Wilde was concerned?

Brose: There were so many things going on simultaneously with the film, including my anger with the gay community. My research on Wilde showed me that all the biographies looked at the "De Profundis" letter, which Wilde wrote when he was imprisoned, as this defining moment of maturity in Wilde's writing. I thought, "No, that's not where maturity exists, at all. In fact, his language becomes imprisoned within the prison letter."

I wanted to refocus on the other aspects of Wilde—especially his idea of transgressive aesthetics. It took a long time for me to find the right scholarship. It was really Eve Kosofsky Sedgwick's book, *Epistemology of the Closet* [Berkeley: University of California Press, 1992], and then Jonathan Dollimore's *Sexual Dissidence: Augustine to Wilde, Freud to Foucault* [New York: Oxford University Press, 1991], which took Wilde's writing apart and set up a whole series of ways of looking at it, that helped me the most.

At the time, I was full of anger about what was happening in 1993—at the Washington March, for example—and the way in which gay radicalism was being consolidated and silenced for political expedience, to help get laws changed. I'm certainly not against reforming the law. What I am against is the way that the gay voices that get heard are *not* representative of the majority of the gay community. They're mostly the voices of white, middle-class men who are so scared of losing what they have available to them—privilege, of course, and access to money and power—just because of this minor "flaw" in their lives. In 1993 the gay community *should have been* consolidated around the idea of universal health care, so that *everyone* could benefit, and around the idea of defining family and domestic partnership not just as the traditional idea of a couple but in recognition that families exist in various forms. There were, and are, many things that need attention.

So I had a lot of personal anger. People sometimes sense it in *De Profundis,* though I don't know if it comes across in general in the film.

MacDonald: It's not *only* anger, though, which is why it's an interesting film.

Brose: Definitely.

I'm beginning to work on a new film, *Crossing.* I have an idea of the ideological arena in which I want the film to function, but I can't force things into that. I do believe in being informed about social critique and visual culture, about ideology, but ideology needs to be buried in the work; it should be something that holds the work up—the fact that you *have* a position—but it shouldn't be the driving *surface* of the work. We've all seen work where the maker seems to say, *"Here's* my philosophy; now I'm gonna cram it down your throat!" I think you have to be much more subversive than that. There are openly polemical works that are effective, but not many.

MacDonald: De Profundis is made up of a variety of kinds of materials, most of which I don't recognize. Could you talk about what you used and where it came from?

Brose: There's "documentary footage," home movies, and vintage gay porn. I documented the May Day ritual at a Radical Fairy gathering, an annual event in Short Mountain, Tennessee. The trick there was not only to get permission to film but to find a way of making people comfortable with me, so that I wasn't just a detached intruder, documenting something. The Fairies have had some problems with people who have gone to Short Mountain to film. I was fortunate to have close friends who are Fairies. But even so, it took a while. In the end, I made two trips, over a two-year period—to get to the point where everyone was okay with my filming.

MacDonald: How long did you stay?

Brose: A week at a time, twice, around the time of the May Day celebration, which is what you see in the footage. The first time I went, I did shoot, but it felt awkward, and some footage didn't come out. It was a mess. Going back the second time, I could tell that people already had a sense that they could trust me, which meant I could trust myself.

There are also the performances that I set up for the film and shot: Mark Miller in the leather harness; Agnes de Garron in drag, on the Promenade in Brooklyn, and in trench coat and fedora.

MacDonald: Looking just like William Burroughs.

Brose: Yes, amazing.

MacDonald: You also use found home-movie footage.

Brose: Right—16mm home movies from the twenties and thirties.

MacDonald: And the porn material.

Brose: Some of that I was able to get from a couple of videos of the history of gay porn. I also got old, 8mm porn at shops in New York that deal in vintage material. I was interested in the idea that for the community of gay men making it and then seeing it, early gay porn was a kind of home-movie experience.

MacDonald: What's the image with the swimmer?

Brose: The swimmer is stolen from a John Ford film—*The Hurricane* [1937]—where someone (I think it's Jon Hall, but I'm not sure) dives off a ship. Everything in *De Profundis* is appropriated, but this is really a stolen image—and I love the fact that I stole it. I shot it off the television monitor.

MacDonald: Did the structure of *De Profundis*—there's a prelude, and a main central section, surrounded by two sections of equal length (each exactly one half the length of the center section)—precede your generation of the material?

Brose: This film comes out of *Film for Music for Film,* a series of films where the musical composition comes first, so I that I begin with something rock-solid that I don't touch. I become a slave to it, as opposed to the usual way in which music and sound in general are used to support film imagery.

What I'm doing there is not new, obviously; animators do it all the time: Oskar Fischinger and Len Lye, for example. So there *is* that tradition. Of course, working that way is a real pain in the ass, too. I am coming to appreciate it, but I hated doing it for *De Profundis*. Of course, now that I'm making a film where I've given myself total freedom, I find myself longing for the anchor that music provides. So it cuts both ways.

My film started with the musical composition *De Profundis* [1991] (Oscar Wilde's prison letter set to music for vocalizing pianist, composed and performed by the American Frederic Rzewski) and my decision to work *against* it, in a sense, by creating these other sections to surround it. I also used images and scenes that undermine or provide an alternative to the romantic existentialism of the text.

The prelude and the first part, with the loops of the nineteen Wilde aphorisms, was edited in two days. I was *burning* through it, and it was brilliant. I went back and made a couple slight revisions, and it was done.

MacDonald: But you had worked for a long time on the material you edited so quickly, right?

Brose: I usually don't talk about my process all that much, but, yes, by the time I'm editing, all of the material has been optically printed, processed, colorized, and hand manipulated, which takes a long time. I had two rooms: the small loft that I was living in, which had the optical printer; and a "chemical room," like a big darkroom, where I could do all the processing. In some cases I did a whole series of variations on one roll, then hand processed it, then cut it up into its individual shots; in other cases, I'd do the cutting first and then treat the sequence in a variety of ways. In the finished film, even when a shot looks like something you've seen before, it's unique by virtue of all the individual alterations that I've made on it.

Frame enlargements from Lawrence Brose's *De Profundis* (1997). Courtesy Lawrence Brose.

When I get to the point of assembling a film, I'll hang shots on clotheslines in groups. I sit in the middle of the room where I can turn around and pick out what I need, in terms of length, color, texture, printing ratio, direction of movement, etcetera. If I can't find exactly what I want, something that works, I'll go back to the optical printer and redo shots, to get them to where I want them to be.

My background is in a very formalist, modernist tradition of experimental film. I'm interested in retaining elements of that tradition, but retaining them as a way of dealing with new material. What formal film is *about* has really changed for me. This idea of melding these different worlds—the world of very traditional experimental approaches and the world of queer theory (and other ideologies I want to explore)—is what interests me.

MacDonald: I want to come back to ideology in a moment, but I want to pursue your formal means a bit further. Because you work with the material, stage by stage, the formal process *for you* becomes part of the natural growth of the film, but people who are looking at a finished work often have no idea about the process that went into making what they're seeing, so they can't really conceptualize how the ideology is embodied in that material.

What are the processes that you use?

Brose: For the most part, they're fairly traditional extended and alternative photochemical processes. Before I began *De Profundis,* I had never processed even a still photograph, so I had to learn about processing, and then experiment and make it my own. What I've always done is learn the rules and then learn what I can do to break them. In a sense, this whole film is about breaking the rules.

MacDonald: Did your history as a piano restorer, which was work that required absolutely precise dealing with a material object, feed into this learning process?

Brose: Well, I hadn't thought of it like that. Going into piano restoration, which began with piano *tuning,* actually came out of a long period of learning meditation—this is back in the early seventies—which gave me patience and the ability to focus. Studying piano tuning is incredibly painful. You have to relearn how to hear. It takes so much time. And when you work, you're dealing with 285 strings that are interrelated, and, of course, the piano is imperfect, so you're constantly working not only to get it in tune but to set it, so that when it's played, it doesn't suddenly go back out of tune. More than anything, that work taught me to be exacting.

De Profundis is very exact—there's not a frame that's not accounted for. These are not sloppy processes. On the other hand, one of the things I detest is the charts and other instructions for using optical printers "correctly." I *don't* want to be given all of the possible "correct" options. Obviously you need to have information if you want to be able to get precisely what you want on the optical printer, but I just want to begin with the basic information. I don't want to be tied down by my training. Give me a filter range that's practical for this kind of film stock, and I'll experiment.

When I was studying piano tuning, I was also teaching blind students; and, of course, I come from my own experience of being blinded as a child and then gaining sight back only in one eye. Among other things, this means I don't have to squint when I'm looking through the camera. *[Laughter.]* My one-eyed sight limits me in one way—I live in a flat world—but it's also opened up certain opportunities. I learned from my experiences as a student and a teacher that there are two kinds of teachers: the teachers who want to make things as difficult for you as possible, to show you just how much work *they've* been through; and the other teachers, who want to demystify things. I need and want to be the second kind.

MacDonald: Where did you study film?

Brose: I studied film production at Media Study/Buffalo and at the Center for Media Study at SUNY-Buffalo from 1979 to 1983; I also studied independently with Shellie Fleming, Carl Brown, Zack Stiglicz, and Derek Jarman.

MacDonald: Talk a little more about the specific processes you use.

Brose: In the hand-processed material, I used 7378 (replaced by 3378), a high-contrast black-and-white film stock normally used for optical tracks. I used it because it gave me a lot of high-contrast material I could work with, and because it's cheap (twenty-four hundred feet for about one hundred thirty dollars). It has a low ASA, but not as low as print stock, so you can actually shoot with it. I did up to twenty-four steps in colorizing the material used in *De Profundis.* The first thing was to bleach it, which requires a lot of care. Then I used Berg color toners, which are made in Buffalo. I went to the company and asked for product support, and they gave it to me. I'm not sure they're going to give it to me again, now that they've seen the film! But for *De Profundis* I had unlimited access to their chemicals, cases of them; I used probably five or six thousand dollars' worth of chemicals.

I'd bleach a shot or a sequence, then use one color, then go back to the bleach, then to another color, and so on. I kept going back and forth between the bleach and the colors. Sometimes I worked by hand directly on the footage, but at other times, I let the image and the emulsion determine what got colorized and how. I learned to control that process very precisely. Near the end of the first part, when you hear the aphorism "I saw then at once that what is said of a man is nothing. The point is who said it," you have these high-contrast, blown-out images of the guys on the boat; their image is almost clear, but everything around the image is colorized. There the coloring refers to the aphorism: you have this empty shell of an image that is visible because of what's around it, what's "said about it."

MacDonald: This example leads right into talking about the way in which ideology is embodied by the film. Generally, the Hollywood goal is to make perfect images to reflect the perfect-looking people, in this perfect story, perfectly embodying their roles; the assumption is that identity is quite simple and singular. It strikes me that since *De Profundis* is about the *complexity* of identity—and means to function as an antidote to the Hollywood assumption—it makes perfect sense that we're seeing many layers of representation, and that we're usually deciphering an image *through* all these layers—as if identity is a mask. You don't give up identity as a concept—we see some of the same images over and over and get to know the various facets of the "personality" of the film—but we can never see any one of these facets in a simple, obvious way. Personality is seen as a complex nexus of many layers.

Brose: Wilde talks about masks in another way, of course, but I'm playing with the idea formally: the image is embedded in the process and the material; the image *is* a mask, but so is the material it's embedded in. The formal elements are constantly at work supporting the text and the ideology, but not always in obvious ways. Someone at Hamilton College last night asked, "Isn't this just too much for a viewer to see?" And my answer was, "No, it's just enough, but you need to see the film again and again." And that *is* a problem with this kind of work; we know that historically. There's rarely an opportunity for repeated viewings, even if someone were willing to go to them. *De Profundis* is usually a one-night gig.

But it was important for me to put all those elements into it, because there *are* a few people who see films multiple times, and because I think (I hope) that it all adds to that first viewing experience, even if you don't feel you're totally getting it.

MacDonald: The political content of the film is balanced by the formal beauty of your work on the filmstrip. It would be easy to see this film as just eye candy.

Brose: Oh, yeah. It's just too beautiful for its own good! Which has often been said about *me! [Laughter.]*

That's also what was said about Wilde and about the whole idea of the dandy. In this case, the film material is where the dandy resides, and yet at the same time, it's a very complex dandy. That was one of the initial issues I had to resolve early on in the process—where to locate the dandy in my film a hundred years later. Well, it became apparent that I didn't want to represent that "character" in a figurative way, yet I needed to have it present throughout the film.

MacDonald: Coming from where I come from, the length of *De Profundis* is not a problem; the film is about an hour long, and I've paid incredible amounts of money over the years to see junk films that are usually two, or two and a half, hours long. Most moviegoers accept two hours as the duration of a conventional film, regardless of the quality of the work. That *De Profundis* requires tremendous energy for its sixty-five minutes is an implicit polemic, a way of saying, "*This* is important to think about."

Also, the labor-intensive process you use to make a film is implicitly a way of paying your dues so that you can demand sixty-five minutes from the viewer. I often show students Taka Iimura's *1 to 60 Seconds* [1973], which asks that viewers spend increasing lengths of time in a darkened theater looking at nothing except numbers scratched into the celluloid that indicate how long each of the previous durations of darkness was. Students get furious, not only because of the radical confrontation of their expectations about the pace of imagery/sound in a film but because the process of *making* the film seems too easy to deserve a half hour of the viewers' time. It feels unfair to them.

You're almost puritan in the amount of work you require of yourself in order to demand the sixty-five minutes of viewing time. You "imprison" *yourself* as a laborer, and your film is "hard labor" for the viewer—a metaphor for Wilde being in prison and doing hard labor?

Brose: You don't know how many times during the making of *De Profundis* I would go to the movies and say, "God, on some level this is so easy!" (I know it *isn't* easy for commercial directors to get the shots they need or to run a huge production), and, "What I wouldn't give for a thirty-second shot!" It takes me at least a week to get thirty seconds of film I can use. The optical printer alone is so time-consuming.

So, no, in that sense I don't think sixty-five minutes is too much to ask of people; it *is* equitable. It's also true that a lot of works *don't* need much of your time as a viewer. In galleries sometimes I do find myself walking to a work and saying, "OK, I got it," and moving on quickly, even when I like the work. At other times I spend a lot of time with a piece. But film is a time-based medium, and I *do* try not to overstay my welcome—though some people might question that!

MacDonald: Last week my class and I were talking about film as a form of self-imposed imprisonment (we had looked at Buñuel's *The Exterminating Angel* [1962]), where you're in this room and you "can't" leave until the film is over. On some level your film echoes that: the middle section is the long section; it's surrounded by two sections that, together, last the same amount of time. It's structured like a building with two symmetrical wings and an entryway.

Brose: Structurally, Wilde's imprisonment—represented by the middle section—gets held together by the other two sections, which are like parentheses. I'm "imprisoning" what I see as the mistaken understanding of the "De Profundis" letter within two other dimensions of Wilde's life that I think *are* radical and exemplary: his aphorisms (his transgressive aesthetics) and his involvement in drag (queerness). The third part begins with the aphorism "A little bit of sincerity is a dangerous thing; a great deal is absolutely fatal!" which I use as Wilde critiquing Wilde (the prison letter).

MacDonald: The material reality of the two sections is very parallel—in fact there are moments where I wonder if I'm seeing exactly the same material, though it slowly grows clear that that's not the case. The soundtrack *is* fundamentally different: looped aphorisms in the first section, and, in the final section, a layering of several ongoing conversations.

Brose: There are six tracks in that final section. Ideally I would have created a kind of surround sound, where you would have all these tracks coming from different architectural points in the theater, and the viewer would be sitting in the middle of all these opposing views—but that can't happen in film, and certainly not in 16mm. I *did* try to create a different kind of sonic space, and a sense of overload that would reflect our time and that earlier one. The arguments that were going on between Wilde and Gide, and between Wilde and the Victorian society that convicted him, are still going on. But a hundred years later, we've come to a position where, partly because of what happened around Wilde, we can have voices and even the beginnings of a language with which we can begin to discuss things. Yet language fails us. Both sides of the political debate are using the same language to their own ends. I wish that the gay political agenda would have a better understanding of that and as firm a grasp of the fluidity and power of language as Wilde had—then I *would* feel represented.

The last part of the film is a different kind of experience from the first; three people are being interviewed: Agnes de Garron, Tom Chomont, and Kenny Cooper. I used them as a parallel to the "rent boys" [male prostitutes] who at Wilde's trial were brought in to help convict Wilde, even though they weren't necessarily trying to do that.

In the first part you have all of the visual imagery going by and these sound loops; and in the last part, you see *visual* loops—five sections of loops—but the soundtrack moves right along.

MacDonald: Dare I argue a Christian parallel: the first section with the aphorisms is your "gospel" according to Wilde; the second part is the imprisonment and crucifixion of Wilde for his "gospel"; and in the final section, there are apostles: men who, partly because of Wilde's leadership, have found their own voice and lead their own gay lives.

Brose: That's brilliant! One of the things I always forget to talk about in relation to Wilde is that even in prison, when he converted to Catholicism, he saw himself as crucified and as Christlike, not as a Christian repenting. It's another form of Wilde's dandyism, another performance: now he's the embodiment of Christ. This is not to say that he isn't really broken down because of the imprisonment, and because of what was going on outside: his family was taken from him, and he was bled financially to bankruptcy. He witnessed the systematic destruction of everything he had built.

But, yeah, it is a heroic story, and we're still living it and learning from it in many ways. I think the third part is about the heroism of the people who make the *other* choice—the choice *not* to repent, *not* to look at themselves as "normal" except for this "flaw"; it's about people who have found alternatives to "heterosexuality" and all the other social contracts that we can be forced into. People can say that the Fairies are just a bunch of hippies or whatever, but what I think is important is the struggle for alternatives, and the empowerment that comes from actually celebrating your difference. Their lives *are* a high point of resistance. That's something that I think is getting buried in the gay movement, and I'm afraid that some of these voices will get silenced into oblivion.

MacDonald: Your film is also a kind of compendium of the representation of gays in experimental film. For me the three early landmarks are Jean Genet's *Un Chant d'amour* [1952]; the whole saga of Kenneth Anger's films, from *Fireworks* [1947] on; and Jack Smith's *Flaming Creatures* [1963].

Brose: Jack Smith had a strong influence on this film.

MacDonald: But in a way your film includes all three—it's a prison film like Genet's; it's openly, extravagantly beautiful like Anger's films are; and it documents various forms of defiance reminiscent of Smith.

Brose: It's interesting how things influence and how they influence for different reasons. Those are three historical gay makers who were very out about their sexuality *in their work,* but not always outside the work. I remember reading an interview with Anger in *Body Politic* where he was asked, "Are you gay?" And he goes, "My god, I'm the most non-gay person I know; I'm not gay at all, I'm a manic-depressive." I do love the pageantry of Anger. But Smith comes along and gives us a different kind of pageant and of cinematic representation; and he doesn't deny himself.

What constitutes a Queer film, or a Queer object or whatever? If queerness is defiance, then I can defy even what *we're* supposed to show in film, how *gays* are "supposed to" represent themselves. The idea of an imperfect, fragmented image is as Queer as anything: it's about things being complex, unstable, indefinable.

MacDonald: You're implicitly destabilizing the nature of identity *and,* literally, destabilizing the nature of a material process that is almost always used to reconfirm the idea of a stable identity.

Brose: Right.

MacDonald: Is Agnes de Garron a Sister of Perpetual Indulgence?

Brose: Agnes was one of the founding members of the Sisters, who created this holy order, with vows and everything. One of the Sisters, Mish—short for Sister Missionary Delight—lives at Short Mountain. There are all kinds of wonderful names. In Toronto there's Sister Opiate of the Masses.

Agnes is no longer active as a Sister.

MacDonald: How did he end up in the film?

Brose: Through my friends, Keith/Kesha and Kenny Cooper; I did most of the Brooklyn shooting in their loft. They're friends with Agnes, so that was my introduction to him, and to the Faeries. They also introduced me to Mark Miller Aleksandra, another performer in the film, who is also a Queer Witch; and I met Leon Ko, the young Asian man who is the Lord Alfred Douglas figure near the end, through my John Cage portrait project, the *IMUSICIRCUS* performance in NYC (for the Guggenheim Museum). He and Alva Rogers (who was in *Daughters of the Dust,* 1992) performed Amnon Wolman's *Marilyns 93/in Cage* [1993], she as a black Marilyn Monroe and he as a Japanese S and M leather boy. Leon is a big pop star in Japan.

MacDonald: Tom Chomont's work is also about deconstructing identity. Had you known him for a while?

Brose: I've known Tom for a long time, since just after he returned from Amsterdam. His work was always amazing, and I was influenced by it, especially his hand processing.

Frame enlargements from Brose's *De Profundis* (1997). Courtesy Lawrence Brose.

What's interesting in this film, and where it's different from Tom's work, is that it isn't so much a personal film. Well, it *is* a personal film, but from a different position. I think that's why some people get a little angry with me about my use of the home movies: I have no personal investment in that material. My other works *are* very personal, but in *De Profundis* I wanted to come out and address the world.

MacDonald: You mentioned last night that you emptied the Eastman House Auditorium with this film. I know you've shown it a lot. What were the best screenings of *De Profundis?* Was the Eastman House the worst?

Brose: The Eastman House was a singular, but not entirely bad, experience. I had finished *De Profundis* just a week prior to premiering it there. So you emerge out of the madness of the darkroom with this film you've looked at only by yourself, and as the film is showing, you look around at people leaving in droves, actually fleeing the auditorium, and say, "What have I done!?" *[Laughter.]*

On some levels the Eastman House screening was a defining moment for my "presentation style." I thought, "The *only* thing we can do here is some good stand-up comedy," so after the screening, I just got up in front and said, "Well, I didn't *clear* the house, did I?" It eased the audience into having more fun in the question-answer period; those Q and As are often so grim. I had a great time with the people who were left.

The *worst* experience was at Buffalo State College, where they only had a rear-screen projection setup and tiny speakers, and couldn't really shut the lights off—horrible. And I've had everything in between. Hallwalls in Buffalo is still an incredible space for this kind of film; their new cinema is a black box, all screen at one end, and there's a decent sound system. *De Profundis* looked fantastic at Hamilton College, too; and the Millennium screening was great: we had a full house, as a result of a lot of marketing. Steven Kent, who's connected to the Mix Festival, helped market the film in New York, and we got good coverage in the gay press, the *Village Voice* and the gay sex magazines.

MacDonald: One of the most vital dimensions of avant-garde film right now seems to be Queer cinema and the gay community's support of it.

Brose: Yet, at the same time, I couldn't get *De Profundis* screened at the LA Gay and Lesbian Film Festival, at the San Francisco Gay and Lesbian Festival, in Chicago or Toronto . . . The gay and lesbian film festivals are *extremely* conservative.

MacDonald: Formally, you mean?

Brose: Formally. *De Profundis* wasn't a leather jacket love story; it didn't have a Hollywood screen kiss—so it couldn't be shown. *Stupid* movies are celebrated in the gay community—films that are just funny and easy, and affirm what people want to see as romantic images of their own lives on screen. On the whole, gay people are not any more creative or interesting, as a film audience, than most straight people—probably less.

MacDonald: Many of them do have the confidence as spectators to let their impatience be known or to leave!

Brose: Yes, *I'm* going to go have a *drink* somewhere! *[Laughter.]*

I've screened *De Profundis* at over sixty venues. I am finding that there are a lot of young, gay people interested in making more inventive films, because it fits more closely with their position in relationship to their own queerness.

The fact that you can make something in film or video without having to raise a million dollars still seems liberating. You *can* make films that are about your own labor, and you can make something important with a home-video recorder. A lot of bad stuff gets made, but I'm interested even in the failures, as people try to enunciate their positions and give some sort of voice to what they believe. It bodes well for the aliveness of the medium.

MacDonald: You're defiant as a gay filmmaker, but you're also defiant of that defiance: you're a gay *experimental* filmmaker.

Brose: Oh, absolutely.

I was outside the Millennium standing near this gay man who had the time wrong and had shown up an hour early. We got talking, and he said, "Well, you know, I've read the stuff on your film in the *Voice* and in the gay press, and I'm very intrigued. I've been very unhappy with things I've seen at the gay festivals. I think I'm just tired of narrative. It's time for me to look for other things. I can't wait to see this." So, after the screening, I see him trying to sneak out, and I grab him, and say, "So, how did you find it?" He paused and said, "Well, quite frankly, about halfway through, I found myself craving narrative." *[Laughter.]*

I said, "Well, you made it halfway through. That's a good start."

Peter Forgács

Those of us who have been involved with critical alternatives to the commercial cinema during recent decades have been forced to confront two facts. First, a century-plus of film history has accumulated an immense stockpile of critical films of all kinds, recorded on several film gauges. Second, this entire stockpile is in a process of deterioration, and there is little reason to hope that many of the most accomplished and most interesting of these films will be able to defy the ravages of decay and maintain their rightful place within film history. Partly as a result of this situation, two types of recycled cinema—that is, films made from other films—have come to seem particularly poignant. One of these is a set of films that foreground not simply the fact that film is decaying but the often sad beauty of decay itself: for example, *From the Pole to the Equator* (1987) and other films by the Italians Yervant Gianikian and Angela Ricci Lucchi; *Lyrical Nitrate* (1991) by Peter Delpeut; and *Decasia* (2002) by Bill Morrison.

In the other set of films, filmmakers have attempted to retrieve films that are particularly endangered, either because of their physical fragility or because of their compelling historical value, and to make them available to audiences in new form. Landmark instances of this approach include Alan Berliner's *A Family Album* (1987), made up of excerpts from American home movies recorded in the United State during the 1930s, 1940s, and 1950s (Alan Berliner has been interviewed for *A Critical Cinema 5*); Lynne Sachs's *Sermons and Sacred Pictures* (1989), which recycles excerpts of films made by African American Baptist preacher L. O. Taylor into an overview of his career and of the importance of filmmaking for his church and his community; and Robert A. Nakamura's *Something Strong Within* (1994), which recycles and recontextualizes home movies made by Japanese Americans imprisoned in American internment camps during World War II. The most prolific and accomplished filmmaker who uses this second approach is the Hungarian Peter Forgács. Forgács's breakthrough series of videos called *Private Hungary* and his more recent work as well, has been dedicated to the retrieval of home movies and amateur films made in Europe during the 1930s and 1940s, and to the recycling of these films into memorable excursions into places and moments generally ignored by official historians of that era.

While some of those who work with home movies and amateur films focus on the typicality of this material, the ways in which it exemplifies general historical developments or the human condition, Forgács often does considerable research into the particular films he works with so that, as he presents his version of them, he can provide us with specific information about these nonprofessional filmmakers and, often, about the family members and friends recorded in the imagery. The resulting films create a very unusual experience—somewhere between the public experience of a commercial film and the intimacy of watching home movies—during which we are able to experience, seemingly from the inside, the real lives of families not our own.

Forgács's exploration of home movies began as a way of coming to terms with his Hungarian heritage, and especially the psychic complexities of living in a rigorously totalitarian communist state, where much of what one knows and feels in private is dangerous to admit publicly. Forgács himself was for some years confined to Hungary, as a result of his active protests against Soviet domination; in time, he turned this limited mobility to his advantage in an exploration of the private lives of Hungarians.

Since the end of the cold war and the dismantling of the Iron Curtain—and Forgács's resulting personal mobility—his investigation of the lives revealed in home movies and amateur films has often extended well beyond the borders of his native land. He remains fascinated with the history of Europe leading up to and into World War II, and with the struggles of Eastern Europe with the Soviet Union in the decades following the war, as this history is revealed in the personal archives of those who took the time to document their experience.

Since so many of Forgács's videos focus on one or another dimension of war and oppression, our experience of these tapes is often gripping and sometimes emotionally harrowing. In *The Maelstrom: A Family Chronicle* (1997), for example, Forgács uses two sets of home movies: those made by Max Peereboom, the eldest son in a family of upper-middle-class Jews living in Amsterdam, and those made by Seyss-Inquart, Reich commissioner for the occupied Dutch territories after the Nazi takeover. At the conclusion of the tape, when Annie Prins, Max's high-spirited, endlessly optimistic wife, is packing for the deportation, we know that, whatever her fears and misgivings, Annie cannot know, cannot *imagine,* what lies in wait for her and her family at the conclusion of this journey—or that, soon, the imagery we are watching will be virtually all that remains of her life.

For Forgács, the people who document their experiences from the inside are the real heroes of cinema, for at least two reasons. First, the amateur filmmakers who most interest Forgács are often deeply committed to their filmmaking. In some cases, we see footage they recorded in their communities at times when all such recording was forbidden and could have led to serious consequences. In *Angelos' Film* (1999), for example, Angelos Papanastassiou made a commitment to himself to document as much of the German-Italian occupation of his native Greece as he could, knowing that were his clandestine filmmaking discovered, he and his family would surely have been arrested.

These makers are also heroes to Forgács, whether their activities were clandestine or not, even whether there was political motivation or not, because their decision to make films has resulted in our having forms of information about real lives during a particular, turbulent era, unavailable in any other form of filmmaking. The popular cinema can suggest what large numbers of people enjoyed or were moved by, when they stepped into public movie houses. The documentaries of an era can show us something about what was officially understood about the political situation of the time. And avant-garde filmmakers can suggest what some of the aesthetic trends of an era were. But home movies and other forms of amateur film are not simply a window into an earlier era; they help us understand precisely how everyday life in those places and times was both different from and similar to everyday life in our own. Of course, we recognize that in home movies, those who are filmed and those doing the filmmaking are performing their lives in accordance with the social mores of the moment, but a half century later, the very nature of these performances is revealing.

Forgács's videos often allow us insights into dimensions of everyday experience and of history that would not have been possible during the era when the films he uses were made. One particularly memorable instance has to do with the physical appearance of many of the people in the Peereboom family in *The Maelstrom,* and especially of Annie Prins. Max Peereboom's imagery of his family reveals a group of people who seem comfortable with themselves and remarkably unafraid of the camera. We see them cavorting at the beach and in other places, seemingly unconcerned with their physical appearance. Even Flora Peereboom, the mother of Max and his brothers, who is—by contemporary American standards of physical appearance promoted so vigorously by the mass media—an overweight, unattractive woman, seems quite at ease with herself and willing to be filmed in a bathing suit during horseplay with other family members. Much the same can be said of Annie Prins, who is lithe and athletic, but whose face is virtually a copy of the stereotypical Semitic face I remember seeing in anti-Semitic cartoons during my youth. In contemporary America, Annie would be considered unattractive, as "needing" a "nose job,"

Max and Annie Peereboom (*in foreground*) at their wedding in Peter Forgács's video opera *The Maelstrom: A Family Chronicle* (1997). Courtesy Peter Forgács.

but it is obvious from the home movies that she is a confident, happy person who sees herself, and is seen by her husband and the rest of her family, as very lovely. All this is put into a broader perspective when, during the second half of *The Maelstrom,* we see the Seyss-Inquart home movies. Seyss-Inquart's family is both "better-looking" than the Peereboom family and far more constrained in front of the camera. Indeed, if it were not clear they were Nazis, many viewers might consider them much more "normal" in the way they relate to each other and to being filmed.

My experience of *The Maelstrom* reveals a painful paradox: while, in the end, the Nazis were defeated (though not until they had destroyed everyone in Max and Annie's family, other than the youngest brother, Simon, who was freed from the Buchenwald concentration camp at the end of the war), their way of understanding human appearance and behavior seems—certainly in North America and apparently in increasing numbers of places—to have won. *We* see the lovely Peereboom family through a training in media imaging that seems to require nose jobs, straightened teeth, and weight reduction as requirements for being visible in public; and we can only wonder what it might be like to be as comfortable with ourselves as Annie Prins and her mother-in-law appear to be.

Forgács's videos are full of surprises, both technically and ideologically. In the "Private Hungary" series Forgács learned to work with the standard devices of nonfiction film—visual text, narration, music—but he uses each of these with unusual inventiveness. Many of his tapes have been made in collaboration with composer/musician, Tibor Szemző, whose compositions are consistently evocative and powerful. And Forgács has used a wide variety of visual text and has demonstrated an unusual sense of timing with it. Forgács sometimes calls his pieces "video operas," a term that suggests the overall musicality of his presentation of text and image, as well as the ways these tapes position the microcosmic lives of individuals within the macrocosm of societal change and cultural history.

The Danube Exodus (1998) is a particularly good example of Forgács's ability to surprise expectation. Of course, given the title, it is hardly surprising that *The Danube Exodus* tells the story of Jews escaping from Nazi-controlled Europe by means of the Danube River in 1939. But *this* exodus is only one of two stories included in the video, both of which are based on the amateur films of Captain Nándor Andrásovits, whose Danube riverboat, the *Erzsebét Királyné* (the *Queen Elizabeth*) sailed up and down the river from Bratislava to the Black Sea. This "persistent amateur filmmaker," as Forgács calls him, does record the complex goings-on onboard during what must have been an unusually tense trip down the river (the *Queen Elizabeth* was stalled for nearly a month, as Bulgarian and Romanian authorities debated whether to let the vessel and its human cargo proceed or to return the Jews to Hitler). But once the *Queen Elizabeth* does reach the Black Sea, only one story is complete, and the second begins.

"The German Exodus," as the second section of *The Danube Exodus* is titled (the first section is called "The Jewish Exodus"), occurs a year after the Jewish exodus ends, when Captain Andrásovits becomes one of a number of riverboat captains involved in the relocation of ninety-three thousand Bessarabian Germans from land on the west of the Black Sea, where nine thousand Germans had settled in 1843 with the assistance of Czar Alexander I. The Bessarabian Germans are escaping from the Russian takeover of their homeland and are transported upriver to Germany, then resettled in Poland. If at first the Bessarabians thought Germany "was Paradise itself," reality provided a painful expulsion from this Eden, first when, to their embarrassment as Christians, they were resettled in Poland on farms stolen from Polish farmers; then, when they died by the thousands during the war; and, finally, when they were forced into a second exodus, this one to western Germany, when the Soviets occupied Poland and eastern Germany at the end of the war.

While Forgács was confined to Hungary during his early years as an artist, and established his reputation by exploring the private lives of Hungarians,

his videos are thoroughly transnational in spirit. At the least, they contextual-
ize Hungarian lives within international political events; in some instances, the
crossing of national borders is a central issue. *Meanwhile, Somewhere* (1994),
made as part of The Unknown War series, produced by LA CAMERA STYLO
(Hamburg), RTBF (Charleroi), the Béla Balázs Studio (Budapest), and Hans
Bosscher (Amsterdam), is perhaps the most remarkable instance of Forgács's
transnationality. *Meanwhile, Somewhere* surveys life in a broad range of locations (the Netherlands, Belgium, France, Germany, Poland, Hungary, Austria,
Czechoslovakia, the Ukraine, Greece, Italy, and Portugal) during the years 1940
to 1943. Forgács creates a kaleidoscope of events by moving from one place to
another, from one kind of human experience to another, from one home-
movie/amateur film style to another, even from one balance of formal devices
to another—and provides viewers with an opportunity to meditate on the remarkable surrealty of what we call everyday life.

The most obvious motif in *Meanwhile, Somewhere*—many of the elements
of the film are repeated, so that we grow familiar with particular families and
particular amateur filmmakers—is a ritual punishment of a young Polish woman
and a young German man, lovers, in occupied Poland in 1941. In the nine
sequences that detail this moment of "ethnic cleansing," the man and woman
are paraded through the town, wearing signs (the young man's: "I'm the traitor
of the German people"; the young woman's: "I'm a Polish pig"); their hair is
cut off, and they are lectured to by townspeople. During these sequences Forgács
includes a formal detail that can stand as a metaphor for a crucial dimension of
his work. In the lower right-hand corner of the frame during each sequence, we
see, in a triangular insert, a tiny detail of the scene that is unfolding full-frame
before us. These details are not central to the events—at least, they are not what
the original filmmaker wanted us to notice—but Forgács' reframing of them
causes us to watch the imagery more thoroughly and helps us become aware of
the fascinating, troubling surround of these activities.

For Forgács the home movies and amateur films he has spent so many years
working with are important for the surface reality they document *and* for the
many levels of experience that are inscribed on the filmstrip, from the original
amateur filmmakers' apparent interests and assumptions, to activities of those
who surround the action that was the original filmmakers' focus, to dimensions
of this personal history that subsequent political history has awakened us to,
to the various forms of damage the filmstrip has endured. Each level of our experience of his videos can communicate interesting and important information
about the past and the present.

Forgács is a prolific videomaker. Most of his work has explored particular
collections of home movies and amateur films, but he has also made other kinds
of videos, including two that engage philosophers whose writings have been
particularly important to him: *Wittgenstein Tractatus* (1992) was inspired by

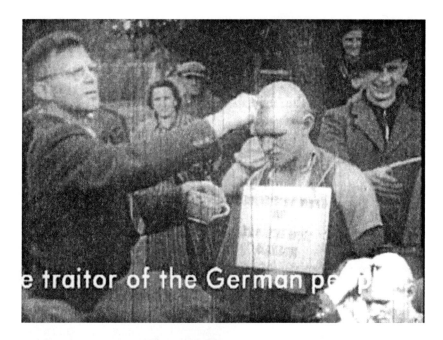

Young German man (*above*) and young Polish woman (*below*) punished for their liaison, in Forgács's *Meanwhile, Somewhere* (1994). Courtesy Peter Forgács.

Ludwig Wittgenstein's *Tractatus Logico-Philosophicus* (1922) and *Culture and Value* (1980); *A Bibó Reader* explores the life and work of Hungarian writer-statesman István Bibó.

This interview began when Forgács was a guest of the Central New York Programmers Group in October 1999 and has continued by e-mail. In our discussions I have tended to focus on tapes that are available in the United States.

MacDonald: You mentioned earlier that you were kicked out of university for political activity. Now you make an unusual kind of political film. Could you talk about your sense of political filmmaking?

Forgács: I was brought up in an intellectual family, leftist. Books were always at hand, and I loved them. I wanted to be an artist from the time I was five. The world was always very visual for me. This was the period of Leonid Ilyich Brezhnev. The Russian communist czar was not as brutal as his predecessors, but he was part of the whole frozen Communist-Nazi system.

The notion of being politically involved is very different in the States than in Eastern Europe, even today. In the sixties, during the civil rights movement and the anti–Vietnam War demonstrations, America became politically mature and recognized, for a generation at least, that civil rights movements and international politics are related. In Hungary during the sixties such movements were not fully developed, but I was taking part in left-wing cultural activities. We wanted to make a better Communism, a purer Communism. We wanted to go back to the ideals of Marx and Che Guevara and the Vietnamese peasants.

In 1972, because of this work, I was completely cut off from all Hungarian universities and institutional support. As a result, I didn't have my first one-man show in an official Hungarian institution until I was forty-five (my documentaries did begin to appear on TV when I was thirty-eight). For long years, I had no passport, so I couldn't even leave Hungary. I gave up on leftist ideals in 1973.

I never thought of myself as a resistance fighter; in Hungary it just felt like one's duty to resist Russian and Communist state control. When the Berlin Wall came down, the bubble of political activity burst for me. I don't mean I no longer cared about civil rights problems—that's the duty of all human beings—but certain kinds of resistance were no longer relevant.

My first son, Christopher, had already been born, so I had to keep myself and my family alive and had to work at various low-paying jobs. I taught for fifteen years, mostly in elementary school. I was a regular teacher for two years, but after that only worked with experimental schools. I stopped teaching finally because I realized that what I was doing in the classroom did not have an effect outside the classroom walls.

In 1978 I became a member of a minimal music group called "Group 180." I was a singer and a narrator. I also had a part-time job in a research institute.

And I was producing graphic works, illustrating and designing books, and making a lot of photographs. I lived an artist-ghetto life, which, until the mideighties, was more or less focused on a Young Artists' Club (FMK) in Budapest. Ultimately, of course, the clubs were controlled by the Communist regime, so it was an Orwellian life; but this artists' club was where I spent my time, and where I learned about minimal music, and listened to John Cage, Philip Glass, Terry Riley, and other minimalists. Conceptual art was also very hot in Hungary, and I knew about Fluxus.

Hungary is a complex society, a Western-Eastern civilization, and you could always sense—even under Soviet rule—that there was a past, a Hungarian culture, behind what you saw. I came to feel that political and economic growth and change are not the most important things, and those cultural habits and traditions and roots are more significant. Of course, this does not mean that I am a fundamentalist who wants to keep everything exactly as it is. Nevertheless, I became much more a kind of archaeologist—largely because of my inability to break free from the restrictions on my personal mobility. I could not go *elsewhere* to study culture, so I studied my own. It was a permanent *1984* in Hungary, and finding the vanishing culture of Hungary, and later of Europe, was a form of resistance. Of course, we know from Orwell that whoever controls the past, controls the present.

Somehow, my background in conceptual art and minimal music became very important, a distanced and radical motive for my studying contemporary Hungarian life. I began to collect home movies as a way of exploring the history of my culture, and after I had collected home movies for six or seven years, somebody suggested I should apply for a grant to the Film Department (it was also the film censor department) of the Ministry of Culture. The guy saw part of the home-movie collection and was amazed and interested in the things I had gathered under the name of the Private Photo and Film Archive, and I got the grant. Now the archive is a foundation.

As soon as I got the grant, I made the first *Private Hungary* pieces. This involved much research. I did interviews with the owners of the films in my archive, and with their families. It was a pleasure to do research on civilian life in Hungary during the years before and during World War II: since it was in the past, it was outside the realm of Communism.

Then I began performing with Tibor Szemző, who was the founder of Group 180.

MacDonald: Where does the name come from? Were you all "doing a one-eighty"?

Forgács: No. The name of the group was invented when they had to give their first concert. These were just young musicians coming out of the academy; they hadn't thought about names. One day, five of them were in a taxi. The piano player was a tall girl, and the others asked, "How tall are you?" She said, "180 centimeters," and the flute player, my friend, said, "I'm 180 centimeters, too."

It turned out that everybody in the taxi was 180 centimeters (well, one was 176), and that became the name of the group.

As I said, minimal music was in the air, along with Fluxus art and conceptual art. It was all the same radical change. I learned a lot at rehearsals and performances, especially about the handling of time. Tibor and I toured Europe in 1984, 1986, and 1987, doing performances. He was the composer; I was doing text, dance, and screenings. The use of music in my work is more understandable if you consider that it was performance work first.

MacDonald: The imagery was screened onstage, and you performed in front of it?

Forgács: Yes. Our performances came from Fluxus, and from psychoanalysis. They especially came from our awareness of the vanishing part of Hungarian history, from the feeling that the semantic context of Communism was not only a big lie, but was fake in every manifestation. Over the years, Tibor and I worked out, onstage, our special relationship between his music and "my" found footage; our method was an effective tool, well before I even dreamed of *The Bartos Family* [1988], the first episode of what became *Private Hungary.*

And there was also the Béla Balázs Studio, a unique organization in Eastern Europe—an *independent* film studio. "Independent" here does not mean it was not financed by the state, just that the state didn't have precensorial rights. The people who worked at the Béla Balázs Studio elected their own board; the board decided which work should be produced.

When a film was produced, the film censor did see it. There were three categories: *A, B,* and *C. A* meant a film was banned once and forever; *B* meant you could show it on a closed circuit, in cultural houses and at film clubs; and *C* meant you could go wherever you wanted and show the film.

MacDonald: But you could *make* what you wanted?

Forgács: Yes! People could make the films they wanted to make.

All the other Hungarian filmmakers in all the other studios (there were five), plus the animation studio, plus the documentary studio, had to show their proposals and scripts to those who ran the studio, and, of course, there was also a great deal of self-censorship. There was pervasive doublespeak in Hungarian film culture during that era: you might understand what I wanted to say, but you also understood that I couldn't say it directly to you because of these guys over there—but we both knew what we knew! I think it was Miklós Jancsó who originally broke through this metaphoric doublespeak.

But the Béla Balázs Studio *was* a place where independent filmmaking happened. People were making films that were unthinkable in any other Eastern European country, except for Poland—but the Polish filmmakers *left* Poland.

MacDonald: Your mentioning Fluxus opens a certain dimension of your films. Fluxus was about allowing whatever comes out to *be* the Art; it gets the artist-as-master-craftsman out of the way. Home movies do that, too.

Forgács: Exactly! What *is* a ready made? It comes from Marcel Duchamp, *The Pissoir* [*Fountain,* 1917]. And it comes from Joseph Cornell. These artists re-presented and recontextualized objects that had specific meaning within their culture, allowing us to see them in new ways. The same is true of my work with home movies. Of course, for many years, the Hungarians questioned whether my work was *art.* They thought I was just another kind of amateur home-movie-maker.

A lot of filmmakers all over the world work with home movies, and recycle other kinds of film, because they find the *surface* of culture interesting or amusing. On the other end of things is the documentary filmmaker who uses archival materials to illustrate ideas, ideology, or a particular interpretation of historic events. My approach is different from either of these.

I'm interested in going beneath the surface of the home movies and amateur films I have access to, not because I want to patronize these films or to see them merely as examples of some idea but because they reveal a level of history that is recorded in no other kind of cinema—a level of history that governments and large commercial enterprises don't see as important or valuable, but that can show us a great many things about the realities and complexities of history as it is lived by real people.

MacDonald: What originally led you to begin archiving home movies and amateur films?

Forgács: A friend of mine, Kardos Sándor, was collecting *bad* photographs; it was a kind of Fluxus collection, enormous and beautiful. He had a perceptive eye, and his collection is amazing. It had a big influence on me and on many other artists because the collection was *about* the decomposition process.

He used to say, "These are the moments when God, not man, pushed the button" of the camera. Quite inspiring. I thought I had the possibility to do something like that with film, under the cover of the cultural resurgence that was going on in Hungary; and it became a part-time job: four or six hours a week at this institution that was a safe haven for radical guys like myself, as well as for normal researchers. It didn't pay enough to live on, but it also had advantages: since there was an institution behind me now, I could advertise in the papers that I was collecting home movies and urge people to bring their home movies to me. Of course, it did not work until I started offering free video copies!

They would bring in their films, and I'd make two video copies, give them one, and keep one. I started making contracts with the people that would allow me to work with the material, and I started doing interviews with them. I went into these family histories one by one. It was in-depth, anthropological research into my own culture in my own terrain.

Another important thing was an experimental film made in 1978 by Gábor Bódy and Péter Tímár. It was titled *Private History* and was made with found footage—a very interesting and playful aesthetic film, but more about the pleasures of cinema than about the lives recorded in the found footage. Bódy was a very good filmmaker and very influential because he organized experimental filmmaking events. However, I felt more could be done with his approach.

What I saw that was still to be done had to do with the messages that come through home-movie material. What does this material reveal about the culture and the times, not just about how things *look*—but *underneath?* These films are very exciting to explore.

One other element needs to be added. Psychoanalysis is part of American culture, but it's still not part of Hungarian culture, because Communism was very thorough in killing off "decadent, bourgeois, Freudian analysis." There was a psychologist in Budapest who had been in prison because of the 1956 revolution: Ferenc Mérei. He had studied at the Sorbonne, before the war, and he taught me psychology and group therapy. I was around him for eleven years; he was my private university, the best.

To me it is a revelation to read the faces of people in home movies and the context we see them in, and to consider what this reveals about human psychology. The face is an extraordinarily sensitive surface, and these faces are not just objects like we see in Muybridge or in the Edison or Lumière films; and they are not just acting, like in Méliès films. In this case, even if it's an artificial situation, they're representing themselves. As a result, these films are full of revelatory moments about how it *was* there, about how they felt, about what they felt the need to represent. If these revelations of self are then placed in a context where you can sense the whole culture, its history and background, and how particular personalities fit into it, the results become very dynamic.

We humans are always struggling with aging and death; we are full of questions. "Granny how was it in 1929 when your father committed suicide because of the bankruptcy of his bank?" "Mama, how was it when your dad came into the U.S. and sold his cows?" "Why did you divorce?" We're always struggling with our own existential problems. We watch our children grow up, and then suddenly we see the same gestures and same "idiotic" rebellion, as *they* struggle with many of the same things.

MacDonald: A general question about your collecting and using home movies. What exactly happens to the films you find, between the time when you locate the work and when you use it in your own video? How is the material preserved?

Forgács: First, all the films are preserved by the Private Photo and Film Foundation, on Beta SP videotape. Then, most of the time, the owner gets the films back.

MacDonald: Do other moving-image artists work with this same archival material?

Forgács: Anyone can use the archive, but up until now I'm the only one who's used the material with any frequency—it's not *tasty* enough for most filmmakers. Most filmmakers have a "professional" need for crisp, clear images,

Zeppelin as premonition of German annexation of Hungary, in Forgács's *The Bartos Family* (1988). Courtesy Peter Forgács.

and since much of the archival material is scratched, and not in good shape generally, it doesn't fit to their needs.

Since 1983, I've collected 550 hours of film and transferred it onto Beta SP video.

MacDonald: How did you decide to begin *Private Hungary* with *The Bartos Family?* I assume that some of it had to do with Zoltán Bartos's inventiveness as a filmmaker and as a songwriter.

Forgács: The Zoltán Bartos film collection was a mess when his nephew, Tamás, gave it to me in 1983, following the newspaper announcement of my archives. It was a huge collection, about twenty-nine twelve- to fifteen-minute reels of film, full of interesting subjects, covering the period 1928 to 1964; and they also gave me Zoltán's songs. Not one reel of film was labeled correctly; it was like a time maze. I started with this collection because it posed the greatest challenge.

That same collection of films was known and partly used by Bódy and Tímár, the makers of *Private History* [1978]. One of Bódy's assistants at that time was my brother András, a writer and film and theater critic today, and when he saw my final *Bartos* film, he recognized the family and "confessed" to me that when he was working for Bódy, *he* was the one who messed up the labeling of the reels! We laughed about that a lot.

The widow of Ödön, the second brother, told me who was who in the imagery.

MacDonald: I'm wondering how much liberty you take with a given collection of home movies. In *The Bartos Family,* there are a number of little films within the film, many of them clearly constructed by Zoltán: *Flirt,* for example. In other instances, there are titles that I assume are yours—"Ottó" and "Zoltán"—that introduce the histories of particular Bartos family members. Did *you* create these minihistories of the family members, or did Zoltán?

Forgács: The little burlesque films in the film, like *Flirt,* were all created by Zoltán, and in those cases I kept his intertitles; all other titles and structures are mine.

MacDonald: Obviously, any given family records more or less film during different time periods, depending on what is going on in and around the family. How carefully do your films provide an analogy for the amounts of footage available? In other words, if a family has a lot of footage from 1930 to 1933 and very little from 1940 to 1943, do your videos reflect that, or do you ignore the amount of footage the makers provided you with when you construct your videos?

Forgács: I do ignore the amount of footage. The inner story line is what is most important and exciting to me. However, more film usually equals more variation. In the case of the Bartos material, Zoltán was childless, and so his subjects are widely varied. Filmmaker fathers regularly lose their interest in the world outside when their babies are born: the baby's first steps, the baby's new dress become the new and dominant subjects for the camera. This becomes boring and monotonous. So the Bartos collection was a treasure.

MacDonald: A related question: clearly, one of the themes throughout *Private Hungary* is the way in which family life is shattered by the rise of Nazism and the annexation, the Second World War, the Holocaust, and the arrival of Stalinist Russia. Often we get a more or less continuous picture of family life, which becomes increasingly disjunct as these major events engulf Hungarian society. You could visually create this idea even if you had a consistent amount of footage throughout the years, but I assume that the activity of private filmmaking does in fact reflect the traumas of the surrounding society.

Forgács: The activity and vision of private filmmaking does focus on their private lives, but, of course, indirectly it also reflects their "present historical time." I think that the relation between public and private life was radically changed *before, during,* and *after* the Second World War, and then *again* in the Communist years. And the trauma of the war experience was radically different for each class, and different for the Christian and the Jewish middle class. By 1938, the Jews were persecuted, and they were mostly destroyed by 1944. The Christians had to deal with the trauma of the lost war, of lost privilege, and then with the Soviet invasion and the trauma of dictatorship.

During those times, there was often not enough film on the market for films to be made, and also, because of the harsh Red terror in Hungary, people were not likely to film outside the family circle.

MacDonald: In *The Bartos Family,* just after we see the death of the mother, and the father crying at her grave, we meet the new wife (who we remember from earlier in the film). This sudden second marriage makes it seem as if the Bartos father had already been involved with the second wife during his first marriage. Did you mean to suggest this as a possibility, or am I letting my imagination run wild?

Forgács: That *is* my suggestion. I learned from family members that immediately after the death of the first wife of old Ármin Bartos, the second wife (Klári) divorced her own husband, Mr. Déri, the executive director under Ármin Bartos, to marry the big boss and get rich. It was so disgusting to the other family members that they were relieved when, after the war, Klári and old Bartos divorced following long years of separation.

MacDonald: Dusi and Jenő [1989] is a very strange video, in part because of the centrality of the dog in their relationship (after the first dog dies, things never seem the same), and later because of the sudden, strange arrival of the second wife, and Jenő's reading his favorite love poem at the end. This film feels almost surreal, even before the trauma of the war, the deportation of the Jews, and the devastation of Budapest. What led you to make this video the second in the series?

Forgács: If the making of *The Bartos Family* was an attempt to create "order" from what seemed a vast and confusing saga—the editing took more than three months—the footage that I used in *Dusi and Jenő* grabbed my attention the first moment I saw it; and I was able to edit this collection's clearly composed, melancholic imagery into the form you've seen, in three or four weeks. The music came later.

There was also a more personal motivation for me in this case. As you know, Budapest is a city of two parts: the Buda side, with the hills and the castle, is wealthier; the flatland Pest side is more urban, industrial, and commercial. Like Dusi and Jenő, I lived on Attila Street in Buda, about a thousand feet north of them, for twenty-eight years. I even remember the open-air restaurant that opened after the war on the place of their ruined house, and some fifteen years later, I played soccer in Tabán Park, where Dusi had walked her dog. I knew this neighborhood like the back of my hand, and from under the Buda of *my* childhood, the forgotten Atlantis, another Buda emerged through the devotion and love of Jenő's camera. Jenő must have been the opposite of Zoltán. *Dusi and Jenő* was a joy to edit.

MacDonald: Often in the *Private Hungary* videos, the immensity of social change is evoked by the *lack* of imagery. Indeed, often the larger the temporal gap, the more radical the historical-personal change. One of the implications is that major historical events—especially war, revolution, large-scale atrocities—are not exactly *personal,* at least not in the sense of "personal" suggested by home movies. It's as if they blow a hole in the personal, create wounds that must heal before an individual can rejoin domestic life.

Forgács: Thanks: very few statements so clearly communicate that aspect of my work. As in literature (see Umberto Eco), in cinematography, the *open* piece gives far more surface for the imagination than does the linear narrative. This accounts for the associative jumps in my work, the shifts from the *personal* to the *public,* back and forth, and for the frequent lack of imagery. It allows us to follow the biographical ego's, the *self's,* amnesia and its constant quest to replace the traumas with joy, with "nice things," with happiness. We become the analysts of what in effect are the amateur filmmaker's dream sketches, the listings on an intimate "CV," the trauma of memory performed. *Private Hungary* is an attempt at a new kind of film narrative, because it is always fragmented, and while the videos don't fall apart, they do include holes, vacuums, tabulae rasae, all kinds of mistakes, pauses, taboos, and black holes. These *discontinuities* offer the viewer an opportunity to reconstruct a narrative from the ruins of a filmic memory.

MacDonald: Either—Or [1989] divides into two sections: "My Friend and His Wife" and "My Daughter Baby." Was the original material divided this way?

Forgács: No. It was not divided at all. The division is my analysis of this film collection and of the game of love as revealed through the camera, especially in relation to two taboos: the first, the filmmaker's love affair—through the camera—with his friend's wife; the second, a quasi-"incestuous relationship"—again through the camera—of the father and daughter. Mr. G.'s camera expresses the father's authority over the family: it's always his choice as to what to shoot; and, of course, Baby's exhibitionism and narcissism is performed for Daddy.

The title of the piece is borrowed from Søren Kierkegaard.

MacDonald: During the second section of *Either—Or,* you use superimposed texts that function as the voice of Mr. G. Are these texts your invention? Or are they based on something in Mr. G's archive?

Forgács: The texts are completely my invention—a way to set myself *behind* Mr. G. as a narrator.

MacDonald: In the credits of this video (and others, *The Diary of Mr. N.* [1990], for example) you list János Tóth as "Expert." What was his function?

Forgács: János Tóth is a wonderful, talented director of photography and an avant-garde filmmaker. He is over seventy years old now and almost forgotten. In the sixties and seventies he photographed several successful Hungarian feature films, and he photographed Huszárik's remarkable *Elegy* [1967], a landmark of Hungarian independent cinema.

We shared a love for old cinema and home movies, and he transferred 9.5mm film onto video for me and helped me with advice from 1985 until 1991. Under better circumstances, he could have been the Hungarian Pat O'Neill: their vision is quite similar.

MacDonald: Why is "Mr. G." not identified more fully? The same question with "Mr. N." in *The Diary of Mr. N.*

Forgács: I ask the filmmakers or their families whether they agree to my using their names in my video, and in some cases their ambivalence demands quasi anonymity.

MacDonald: The family of Mr. N. is amazing. They seem to thrive despite what goes on around them. Their high energy is evident in the outdoor excursions they make and in the size of their family, which grows during the most traumatic periods in modern Hungary's history. At the end of the video, you thank Mr. N. for his "generous support of this video." How did you find this material, and assuming you had dealings with him during the making of the video, how did *he* feel about the history he had lived through?

Forgács: His name was Hideghkuty, and the most important feature in his home movies is the triptych thematic structure: family, ammunition factory, public events. This way of documentation was rare at that time. They were very kind people. Of course, as devoted Catholics, they loved a big family. We saw the *Mr. N.* film together at least three or four times. The final time, they told me, "We didn't know that our life was so interesting!"

MacDonald: At the conclusion of *The Diary of Mr. N.* we see Mr. N. and Ilona carrying apples. This seems a metaphor for the fertility of their lives together, and—since she seems very tired—a comment on the toll it's taken on her. Am I reading this the way you meant it?

Forgács: Yes, exactly.

MacDonald: Bourgeois Dictionary [1992] reminds me a bit of *Meanwhile, Somewhere*—though I don't think it's nearly as successful. Here you use several collections of home movies to move us through the major events of recent Hungarian history, using words and their meanings as a formal device to hold the diffuse history together. Of course, *Bourgeois Dictionary* does include interesting moments: the "My Sweet Parents" section, in particular; and the lovely woman we see nude in both this video and in *Meanwhile, Somewhere.*

Forgács: Bourgeois Dictionary was done after *Wittgenstein Tractatus,* and I was trying a related methodology as a way of assembling some of my favorite fragments—poems, little short stories. I agree that the result isn't as strong as *Meanwhile, Somewhere.* Sometimes I'd like to redo this or that part of a piece, or a whole piece. *Bourgeois Dictionary* is one of those.

The music is also a crucial, even dominant, dimension of *Bourgeois Dictionary.* Tibor had lost his mother earlier that year, and his passionate score fills up the empty spaces in the video. I would have preferred more silences, but I could not change Tibor's mind about the score. Music is always a major dimension of these works. Tibor and I collaborate on most every aspect of the music and on the placement of the music. It's always a negotiation between us. For *Angelos' Film,* Tibor had to recompose and rerecord the music three times before it was satisfactory to me.

MacDonald: The shot of a young girl peeing in public is a motif in your videos (and, I assume, in the home movies you have access to). But I've never seen such a shot in American home movies, at least not that I remember. So it strikes me as a particularly "European" idea. And it seems most of the time to be a little girl peeing.

Forgács: Well, first of all, *this* suggests a difference between the limits and possibilities of a written diary and a filmic one. I think Mr. G. didn't have enough self-reflection to make a written diary, but even if he'd had one, he would never *write* "my sweet daughter, Baby, pissed today at the National Gallery—oh so amusing!" But *filming* it, for Mr. G. as for other filmic fathers, is a *joke.* Of course, we know jokes may express the repressed subconscious. There is a limited time when fathers can film their human "properties": their sons and daughters. After the age of twelve, thirteen or fourteen, the children start to protest, and they disappear from the family albums or films. That's what happened here: suddenly Baby disappears from the screen; and when we see her again, she is sixteen, and climbing from one balcony to the other, a rebellious gesture.

It would require more research to find out if there is any difference between the USA and Europe in regard to this sort of imagery. But even without research, I'm quite sure it's not a question of European openness but has more to do with my luck in finding these home movies and my effort *to make them visible.*

MacDonald: Totem [1993] was a surprise for me, and seemingly a total departure for you.

Forgács: Totem is a part of one of my installation works. If you could see my other installations, this piece would not surprise you—though the content and message *is* brutal. In the installation, the film that you've seen is the stuffed pig's favorite TV program. It's my most successful installation; it's been shown in Hungary four times, and in Barcelona, Tokyo, Rome, São Paulo, New York, Graz, and in other places.

MacDonald: It's very provocative.

Forgács: It was a shock to some people, especially vegetarians; and it was also praised as a new provocation against the conventions of art. But, of course, butchering pigs is also folklore from Germany down to Serbia.

MacDonald: The inventive use of reverse is surprisingly rare in film. Walerian Borowczyk—in *Renaissance* [1963]—Jean Cocteau, and a few other filmmakers have used it successfully. Which came first, the idea of working with reverse or the idea to do *this* subject?

Forgács: Before I had made a shot, I knew this subject would work in reverse, though if you look at the film carefully—if you *can* look at it again—you'll see it's not *entirely* reverse.

MacDonald: I definitely need help with the connection between the words and the imagery. I'm not sure I understand how you mean for them to work together.

A (stuffed) hog ruminates on the slaughter of a hog, in Forgács's installation *Totem* (1993). Courtesy Peter Forgács.

Forgács: The text and all its various associations are there to drag you away from the *concrete* fact of the slaughter of the pig and onto a metaphoric level. There are many ways of reading this imagery, especially since the pig's suffering is so like a human's suffering.

MacDonald: Is there a Hungarian version of this film—or just the English version? And why the one non-English word: "Tekintély"?

Forgács: There are German, Japanese, Italian, Portuguese and Hungarian versions.

"Tekintély" means "authority." The same word appears in English once or twice in the piece. It was a mistake that I used the Hungarian in this instance, but I didn't correct it because I liked the presence of this Hungarian word as a little disturbance, as an enigma.

MacDonald: One of the things that makes your work unusual and gives your videos their energy is your implicit attitude about what culture *is.* One standard American assumption, and maybe it's broader than just American, is that when you go back to your roots, the roots get narrower and narrower and end in a single, pure ethnic heritage. For you, the energy of the history of a culture seems to be its particular *intersection* of a variety of traditions. Each particular geographic/historical place has a different set of intersections.

The Danube Exodus includes a story I didn't know. Of course, the first part of the film, about Jews escaping down the Danube, is part of a well-known history; but I didn't know that there were also, at nearly the same time and in the same place, Bessarabian Germans being displaced and going *up* the Danube, as a result of the dislocations caused by Nazi imperialism and by the war.

Forgács: In *The Danube Exodus* the Danube is a metaphor. We know the stories and myths that have grown up around the big rivers: the Mississippi, the Nile, the Ganges. A lot of avant-garde filmmakers want to play with time, or explore cinematic time and space, and frustrate the conventional viewer. But very few of them produce contemplative art. My interest, and it's maybe something typical of European cultures, or of Central European cultures, is the psychology of dreams. My work does represent particular moments, some of them new for the audience, in modern history. But in a sense, the films I make are also dream works; they're about cultural dreams and nightmares. And one can look at *The Danube Exodus* that way.

I don't use film as a pastime. I don't like pastimes. I like art and sex and raising children, and talking with other people—discourse. The ephemeral, everyday footage I'm collecting generally records idiotic pastimes, typical of middle-class life in Eastern Europe. But, on the other hand, if you think of these movies as found objects for Fluxus art, then you see that what might otherwise be *boring* can also be understood as a series of sacred moments: nonhistorical, private footage becomes historic evidence of a certain mood, of a background; a color or a gesture or a smile, or the shape of a face, reveals dimensions of a society that are never visible in public art.

My whole procedure becomes a way of my inviting you to look at what I found, to come sit beside me and think about it. Like good music, my work offers an opportunity for a contemplative experience. On the other hand, the pieces record primary facts about human history and have as many layers as dreams. You can peel them like an onion, layer by layer.

The early *Private Hungary* pieces were really experiments that I enjoyed showing to my friends. Since then, a lot of water has run down the Danube River: the river is the same, but the water is not.

MacDonald: Who saw the ship captain's film?

Forgács: He showed it to other Hungarian Danube steamer captains and also in an amateur film club in 1942. He made a little seventeen-minute version about Jewish refugees on the Danube; the outtakes were forty-seven minutes, so altogether he shot sixty minutes of the Jews on the boat.

He was interested especially in showing Orthodox Jews because in most circumstances one cannot go so near Orthodox Jews with a camera, and one Orthodox Jew would never film another Orthodox family; an unwritten law forbids it. So it was for him a kind of *anthropological* document. He's a kind of amateur anthropologist.

MacDonald: He would be condemned in American documentary discourse these days because he has not been given permission to film these people. He's there by virtue of his power over these people, and yet only *because* he exerts that power do we know them. Of course, they might not care to be known.

Forgács: That's the funny side of American life. Somebody who is a big liar can be president, and O. J. Simpson goes free, but this captain would be attacked for filming somebody without written permission.

MacDonald: You must have gotten that criticism in this country.

Forgács: Yes, sometimes I have.

There is a very important legal step that I always take: I arrange with the filmmaker or the owner of the films that all the problems relating to the people filmed in the home movies fall back on him—if there are any. But there has never been a single problem up until now, and there will be no such problems because I'm not harming people with these films.

There is a case going on now, involving a very good Polish artist, Katarzyna Kozyra, who went into a Turkish bath in Budapest, masquerading as a man, to make a video. She showed the results at the Venice Biennale, and now she will have to go to court because some people recognized themselves. But that's something else.

MacDonald: That's about money.

Forgács: No! That's about naked genitals!

Anyway, it *is* a big problem that those people in the last Balkan war who were happily cutting out the tongues and hearts of Bosnians, and cutting off the balls of the men, can still go into the cafeteria and talk about their brave acts; it's *not* a problem that a riverboat captain was shooting film on his boat. He did have a position of authority, but without his authority and his willingness to shoot film, we wouldn't have news about a certain moment in the history of ethnic cleansing. And no one would have escaped on his boat.

MacDonald: A question about your background in relation to this video. On one level, you have a Jewish heritage, but you also have a complex, non-Jewish European heritage. On some level, the two journeys in *The Danube Exodus* could be seen as an emblem of your mixed heritage.

Forgács: I *am* a Jew, by heritage, but, on the other hand, we didn't keep any kind of Jewish tradition—unfortunately. The only religion I learned was Communism, and its God at that time was Leonid Ilyich Brezhnev.

MacDonald: So on some level, Bessarabian Germans and Orthodox Jews are equally distant from you, and also equally related to you.

Forgács: There's a powerful book written by Professor Randolph Braham, a U.S. historian with a Hungarian Jewish heritage from prewar Romania, about the Hungarian Holocaust [*The Holocaust in Hungary* (New York: Columbia University Press, 1981)]. The knowledge I used in *Free Fall* [1996] developed out of this book. I was reading it and almost fainting; in fact, the video

Captain Andrásovits, the riverboat
captain and amateur filmmaker, in
Forgács's *The Danube Exodus* (1998).
Courtesy Peter Forgács.

took me years to do because his book was so painful to read. I don't want to push our interview into the Holocaust because I don't want to exploit it. But if there *is* any cultural heritage in my Jewishness, it's *Auschwitz*. I am a descendant partly of German (and partly Hungarian) Jews. This part of my family lived for hundreds and hundreds of years in Germany; they spoke German and Hungarian at home, just like those great physicists who came to your country during the Second World War and made the atomic bomb.

So, you're right, I am the river Danube; I'm the Germans *and* I'm the Jews. But I'm not the Nazi Germans and Hungarians, just like I'm not the Communist Hungarian butcher who destroys culture at any price, or the far-right Betar wing of Zionist Jews on that riverboat who were planning to kill Palestinian Arabs because the Betar ideology of settlement needed an empty land. And you're right, I'm also the German farmer who's traveling the opposite way up on the Danube, but I'm also the captain who has this distant and open-minded perception. I've internalized it all.

MacDonald: In some films you use vocal narration, as well as textual narration. Is that because the television companies that produce the videos, or show them, ask for the narration? Or are all such decisions entirely yours?

Forgács: The television people never force me to do anything. I like to use different "channels" of information—for example, to vary the vocal and textual narrations in various ways. Often, I like to repeat them like rhymes, so that they create a certain rhythm, but also to present them in conjunction with different imagery, so that the meanings of both the texts and the images continually shift and recontextualize each other.

MacDonald: There's an American film by the photographer Weegee, called *Weegee's New York* [c.1952]. Much of the film takes place on a Coney Island beach, and what comes across about that moment, at least in the film, is that the people in front of the camera seem to assume that a holiday involves a freedom from socially required appearance. Watching the film, we learn something about how earlier generations related to the camera.

Forgács: Of course, you're right, though I do think it depends on social class and on particular generations and individual choices. Your mother might not do things her mother would do.

MacDonald: Very true.

Forgács: Basically, there's a tremendous anthropological difference between the public and private behaviors of different cultures, and there are cultural barriers between generations, and between men and women. Family rituals are often different in each section of a culture. There are unanimous gestures and there are subcultural gestures. There are codes that we can read and others that we can't read. Sailors have their own codes, as do gay people. Twins have their own language. Middle-class Jews have communication codes different from middle-class Christians. The question is, who has the camera and who is recording what we're seeing? And how do the codes within which the filmmaker is working—in the case of my films, the filmmakers who recorded the home movies and the amateur films *and* the filmmaker who is re-presenting what these earlier filmmakers did—affect what we're seeing in what is recorded on the filmstrip?

The central dynamic in the films I work with is that the people making the films and the people in the films were never planning to be shown on a big public screen here in your city. They meant to have fun, to record the fun, and to see it later. Their recording is a slice out of the constant flow of time, made from a certain angle with certain material, and then it stops. These slices out of the constant, linear flow of time are full of gaps, but the filmmakers didn't care about the gaps. On the other hand, for us, the gaps, and their meanings, are part of what gets revealed by the films, once they're recycled into "my" films.

MacDonald: Since we see the films differently than their makers did, we become part of the process of constructing a story.

Forgács: Yes, but that's not only true of home-movie footage; we look at Griffith's or Dziga Vertov's work in a different way now than we did forty years ago.

MacDonald: Actually, I was thinking of Vertov last night during those moments in *The Maelstrom* where you switch from motion to still images. They remind me of similar moments in *The Man with a Movie Camera* [1929].

Forgács: Yes, but Dziga Vertov, Kuleshov, and Eisenstein were revolutionary artists committed to *destroying* the culture of czarist Russia, and I'm trying to *recover* the *citoyens* (that is, bourgeois) Hungary. Though *I* don't see myself as an agent of the bourgeoisie at all, *they* would probably see me that way.

MacDonald: I went to Riga in 1991, with the Flaherty Film Seminar. There were writers and filmmakers from the various Soviet states and various writers and filmmakers from the United States. The seminar was called "Flaherty/Vertov." What was fascinating was that the American leftists at the seminar loved Vertov but were somewhat embarrassed about Flaherty (Flaherty's romanticizing of Eskimo life and his focus on the exotic had come to seem a problem); and the representatives from the ex-Soviet states loved Flaherty and seemed to hold Vertov in contempt. Flaherty's focus on the individual was what *they* wanted.

Forgács: Yes, this example is very nice. Speaks for itself.

MacDonald: We were surprised.

Forgács: Well, before you went to Riga, you should have read Orwell. *Then* think of Dziga Vertov. If he hadn't died so early, he could have become one of the censors with the big scissors. Or, of course, he could have been executed by Stalin.

Russian Communism was a byzantine religion; it had nothing to do with Karl Marx—quite the opposite. Even if Karl Marx was quite often wrong, he *was* an enthusiastic critic of the exploitation of people. But the Soviet regime was the most exploitative form of capitalism on earth. In twenty years of building up mutant capitalism, it sacrificed millions of people. Soviet Communism was successful in industrializing, but at an incredible cost. Of course, Dziga Vertov and the avant-garde poets were not butchers, but they *were* blindly serving the devil. It might hurt some people's feelings to say it, but Vertov was Stalin's Leni Riefenstahl.

MacDonald: Stalin's, or Lenin's?

Forgács: Well, let's say Lenin, but Lenin for me is a butcher as well. I hate these little distinctions. Half a year after the revolution, Lenin executed his leftist ex-comrades because they said, "Now, what? *This* is not democracy." He just ordered them shot. Insane.

We know that the czarist regimes were awkward, underdeveloped byzantine shit. But what came afterward in Russia was just like the Cambodian Communists. What the Khmer Rouge accomplished in four years, Stalin did in twenty. What's the difference?

And I don't like the romanticizing of Bolshevik culture in the early Russian Communist films. Technically, the films are very interesting; even culturally, they're interesting. Those guys were real maestros. But I think there's also a very, very important personal responsibility not to participate in butchery, no matter what it's called. This is something Anna Akhmatova and Boris Pasternak *didn't* forget. Of course, if you're a writer, you can be quiet. You can stop serving the butchers, and no one really knows. It's harder in film.

So it may sound strange to you, but for me, Leni Riefenstahl and the Russian propaganda filmmakers are *exactly* the same.

MacDonald: I've found it particularly useful to study *Meanwhile, Somewhere* because of the way in which it surveys Europe. It provides a particularly broad sense of the terrain in which you work and helps me understand both what you're doing and what I need to understand more fully about it. How did that project develop?

Forgács: After creating the first six *Private Hungary* episodes, I became a member of INEDIT, a European association of unedited-film maniacs. This group formed as a result of an initiative by Belgian TV film director André Huet in 1990; the participants are makers, archivists, and programmers. In 1992 a number of filmmaker members of INEDIT decided to create a series of programs on dimensions of World War II that are not known, based on amateur films and home movies. We divided Europe into research zones. My fieldwork covered Eastern Europe and the Balkans. Each of us raised money for our episode. The research took more than a year.

Meanwhile, Somewhere was the third part of The Unknown War series.

MacDonald: The structure is both precise and open.

Forgács: If you look at my *Wittgenstein Tractatus,* you'll understand the background for the structure of *Meanwhile, Somewhere,* and my feeling that the traditional, educative, historically oriented, documentary approach would be useless for the patchwork of emotional comparison I was interested in. The lesson here was *not* to provide new information or to educate viewers on the viciousness of the war and the Nazis but to see the everyday banalities of life during wartime. To do this, I needed to mobilize the viewers' existing historical knowledge, but put it to a different end.

MacDonald: The punishment of the young Polish woman and the young German farmer is the central thread that holds the piece together.

Forgács: The rondo format seemed best for this material. I couldn't find a better way to show the normally invisible side of wartime than by creating a loose necklace of film poems, short stories, and moving photographs of fun and pain, of ephemeral and eternal human events and acts, taken from home movies.

MacDonald: Children are at the center of the video; during the punishment sequence, we realize how the punishment of the lovers is aimed at young people and functions as a warning for anyone who might not yet have bought into the assumption that Poles and Germans must be kept apart.

Forgács: Yes, the irrational light in the kids' eyes—the result of National Socialist teachings about the evil of sex between *Über-* and *Untermensch*—is painful.

MacDonald: The theme of social class is very strong in *Meanwhile, Somewhere.* The sequences where we see the kitchen for the Jewish workers camp at Kiszombor ends with the man shitting in the makeshift latrine; then you cut to the man, woman, and child cleaning what appears to be a shithole; *then* you cut to the Drugmans, a middle-class family.

Forgács: Actually, that isn't a shithole but a cistern full of muddy water (they pour it out to fertilize the garden). I did want viewers to associate the mud with shit. We wonder why the old woman, who must be the servant, goes down the hole; and we see how the little girl is following granny's pattern in her play, just as the little ones in the miscegenation sequence turn the punishment of the Polish girl and German boy into play.

MacDonald: One of the most interesting dimensions of *Meanwhile, Somewhere* is the critique it provides of conventional assumptions about beauty and about beauty in cinema. Throughout the video, the imagery is stunning, evocative, and moving not only because its subjects are poignant or sad or horrific but because of the way you treat the imagery. I assume you added the various tints to the material during the editing stage, as a way of emphasizing particular aspects of the imagery and as a way of helping us distinguish between different locations and peoples.

Forgács: Most of the time, the home movie tends to capture selected happy and beautiful moments of life. I consider all dimensions of a piece very carefully, including not only the particular identification of people and moments (the history of the piece) and the tinting (for providing *emotional* tone), but the use of slow motion, freeze frames, blowups; the use and design of the visual texts, and all elements and layers of the sound: voice-over, sound effects, music. Each of these is like an instrument in an orchestra.

MacDonald: There are also several full-color passages, including the gorgeous Breslau material that sings the "beauty" of National Socialism. This is the most conventionally beautiful imagery in the film (the garden most of all) and documents the ugliest political movement/system of the twentieth century. Did you mean to confront assumptions about cinematic beauty with these images?

Forgács: Yes, I did.

But let me say again, Nazism is one of the *two* ugliest systems of the last century: Stalinism was the other.

MacDonald: The overall impact of *Meanwhile, Somewhere* is to create a memorable picture, from within events, of the mix of the mundane and the horrific, the separation and connection of the many events going on across Europe during those years. The surrealism of modern life comes to the fore. At the end of *Night and Fog* [1955], Alain Resnais theorizes that the horrors of the Final Solution (at least in the form of other events like the Holocaust) are always occurring, often right next to the events of daily life—though they remain invisible to the willfully myopic. Through your process of recycling and juxtaposition, you reveal the workings of that process: we see people trying to maintain some semblance of a normal life (sometimes even a decadent life: I'm thinking of the golf) within the catastrophe of the war era.

Forgács: My first intention with this project in 1983–84 was to show my friends what I'd found in the hidden, suppressed past—the *Atlantis*—of middle Europe. My recontextualizing of home movies is not just a rereading in Derrida's sense; it's more: a moving image tells more than a text can, and in the deepest senses. There's as much cultural, personal, historic, emotional, sensual experience in the films I work with as there is in anything but the great novels of Kafka or Márquez or Bulgakov. When you fall into my work (if you're an ideal viewer!), at the same time you fall into your *own* imagination, dreams, feelings; you realize, *all this could have happened to us.* It's not an *actor* who dies; it's *him* and *her.* It's *us.*

In a dramatic narrative film, the actor never dies, only the *role.* But here it's the opposite; the real people die, but their *roles* as people doing mundane things continue in our lives.

MacDonald: One of the most dramatic moments in *The Maelstrom* is when Annie is with her stepmother during that terrifying moment when they're getting ready to be deported to Auschwitz. They don't know what we know about where they're going, of course; but it's a traumatic moment nevertheless, just because they're leaving home and don't know what comes next. And yet, Annie does not stop smiling and trying to make the best of the situation. She wants to defy being depressed—"They won't beat me down!" And of course, on another level, what she's doing plays right into the hands of the process.

the Peereboom family

spends the holidays on

the roof of their

house on Jodenbreestraat

The Peereboom family in Forgács's *The Maelstrom* (1997). Courtesy Peter Forgács.

Forgács: Yes, we know the truth, and that hurts. It's all part of the game that the Nazis created to make what they were doing seem understandable, rational. They ingeniously disguised their motives. This elaborate game was especially designed for the Dutch Jews because the Dutch Christians were protesting against the deportation of the Dutch Jews, which is clear in the film. There was even a rebellion in Rotterdam where dockworkers and students stormed the city hall and burned the lists of Jews. At one point, the Germans deported thirty thousand young Dutch Jews and among them two—related to the Peereboom family—who were in the film. Three months later the family got a letter, along with ashes, saying that their sons had had heart attacks and died in Mauthausen. Of course, this was absurd: why would young men die of heart attacks? But it was a way of not admitting what was really going on, so that others wouldn't interfere with the process. It was absolutely different with the Polish Jews; there was much less disguising of the reality.

Annie, a Dutch, middle-class Jewish woman, believes in the law. She knows that they will suffer, but why *should* she think that what we now know happened, *could* happen to her, even if she *has* heard news from Germany that terrible things are happening? The working title of *The Maelstrom* was "It Can't Happen to Us." And of course I'm exploiting the tension of the double knowledge we have as we look at these people: first, as if we were there, *and* from our position decades later. It causes tremendous tension.

You were saying this morning how shocked you and Pat were when your children were separated from you for many years. But in life we often *don't* see what's coming. When my first son was born, I never thought that his mother would have a nervous breakdown and I'd have to bring him up until he was six. I was a "revolutionary" young lad, full of optimism, and then suddenly completely tied down with a kid. We think we can secure ourselves and that nothing bad will happen. I'll drive to Ithaca today, and at the moment I'm sure there will be no car accident—but who knows? It's the same with Annie in *The Maelstrom,* packing those little things they were permitted to bring. Two socks, a mug, one pullover etcetera, and no more—but hopefully things will be okay.

Sometimes I work with much less tension because history also plays with us in a lower dynamic, one that can still surprise us out of our complacency. The painter Lichtenstein has this beautiful paradox: "When I went home, I was expecting surprise, and when there was no surprise for me, I was surprised."

In *The Maelstrom* you see Annie's hands packing the suitcase, sepia brown like in a Rembrandt engraving. Most of the film is orange-yellowish because orange is the color of the Dutch royal house: the House of Orange. Sometimes the images I work with seem like time-based paintings or engravings.

MacDonald: How did you get the Seyss-Inquart home movies? And how is it that the Peereboom home movies survived the war?

Forgács: I saw the Seyss-Inquart film (it was a confiscated war document) in the Dutch National Film Archive in 1993, when we were doing research for the Unknown War series.

As to the Peereboom home movies, they were saved by Chris, an assistant at the Boumans' shop in Vlissingen (Annie Prins was the Boumans' stepdaughter)—you can see him washing Max's car at the beginning of the video. I think Max gave that material to Chris before their deportation to Auschwitz in 1942. After the war, Simon and Chris met by accident in Amsterdam, and Simon got the films, camera, and projector back. Later, in the early fifties, Simon shot some 8mm films in the Jewish "ghost quarter" of Amsterdam.

MacDonald: If you look at old 8mm films on an 8mm projector in your living room, that's one experience; but to see the work projected large, in video, with an evocative sound track is something else. On one hand, it *is* still the original thing, but at the same time, it's more than the original because, for example, you can see the texture of the imagery in a way that they wouldn't have seen it originally. It is *now* looking at *then,* and it's *video* looking at *film,* and at times, it's still photography looking at motion photography and vice versa. The most *they* would have done is turn the projector in reverse for a joke.

Forgács: Or slow it down. Or put it away for twenty years and then show it and say, "Oh! Look at father!" Or screen it every year and create scratches—from the scratches you can tell how many times a family projected a particular film.

The scratches in the Jewish part of *The Danube Exodus* show that it was screened at least ten or fifteen times. There are no scratches on the German material. That's also part of the story of the film. In the video version you don't see the scratches all that clearly because the material went through a wet-gate system, but still the Jewish material is much scratchier than the German material.

MacDonald: At what point does Tibor Szemző become involved with the videos?

Forgács: During the early stages of editing, I listen to a lot of music in connection with the imagery—primarily the minimalist oeuvre of previous Szemző works, and Philip Glass, Steve Reich, Brian Eno. After months of editing experiments, I'm tired of the particular musical pieces I've been working with, but they become signposts for the kind of music that will work with this and that imagery. At this point, Tibor becomes a partner in the procedure—once the overall style and structure are visible. He creates a new composition for each video, working step by step, first creating musical sketches and then, working with me, finalizing the connections between image and music.

By the time Tibor joins me, I've already added in the sound effects, using a digital editing system. Of course, the final mix is supervised by a sound engineer.

MacDonald: In your videos, you create a hierarchy of filmmakers, most of whom are not even recognized as filmmakers by conventional film history but who are often heroic and sometimes cinematically accomplished in their recording of the life around them. They are your heroes.

Forgács: Yes. In *Angelos' Film,* the man behind the camera, Angelos Papanastassiou—a true twentieth-century Greek patrician, an ex-navy officer, and a successful Athens businessman—decided in the very first days of World War II to record the sufferings of his fellow Greeks and his motherland. Risking his own and his family's lives, he filmed the Nazi atrocities all through the German-Italian occupation of Greece, with a clandestine 16mm camera. Meanwhile, his daughter Loukia was born, and we follow her growth in the family. He was a courageous filmmaker, as were so many of those whose imagery I recycle: they come from various heritages and provide us with things professionals cannot.

MacDonald: One of the problems I have as an American viewer of *A Bibó Reader* [2002]—and I assume I'm not alone—is a function of my general ignorance of Hungarian history. Of course, Americans are often ignorant of their own history, and remarkably ignorant about the histories of other nations and

Simon Peereboom, who retrieved his family's home movies and made them available to Forgács, in *The Maelstrom* (1997). Courtesy Peter Forgács.

regions. But I'm often puzzled about how much of what we see in *A Bibó Reader* would be immediately recognizable to Hungarians, and how much would be generalized historical imagery for them as well as for American viewers.

Forgács: The combination of image and text offers a cultural-historical-poetical context for a Hungarian, but the text itself is probably as heavy for a Hungarian as for anyone else.

Bibó's writings were forbidden in Hungary until the mideighties. I first read him in the midseventies, during the time when I was banned from universities, and reading him was an intellectual turning point in my life. I completely dropped Marxism, which did not explain the actual, existing socialism and its exploitation, repression, and lies; and Bibó gave me a new view on the world. He was totally independent of the repressive Hungarian state party.

His ideas aren't popular even today, though he was *the* reference from 1982 until 1992. He's too heavy and too ethical for most people. The right wing and the post-Communists are equally afraid of the meaning of his writings. He is known by intellectuals but was never, and probably never will be, popularly known. However, the first public screening of *A Bibó Reader* on television had 160,000 viewers, a high number for a documentary-essay in a country with a population of only 10 million.

MacDonald: The title of the film can be read in more than one way. Most obviously, it suggests a video version of a literary anthology—like *A Faulkner Reader* or *A Kafka Reader*—but, in addition, your formal strategy in the tape demands a good bit of reading on our part: we read the titles of Bibó's major works, excerpts from the quotations the narrator reads, your indications of who this or that person is. Third, you are certainly asking us, as you do in all your videos, to "read" home-movie and amateur film imagery in ways we normally don't: that is, to read past their original functions, as a means of understanding the cultural history they embody.

Forgács: Selecting excerpts from the huge body of Bibó's works was quite difficult. I'm grateful to János Kenedi, who rediscovered Bibó for us, and introduced Bibó to me in 1973–74; he helped to create thematic "knots" of Bibó that can still create an impact today. This part of the process alone took three months.

Of course, for those who rarely or never read theoretical works, my excerpts provide a-once-in-a-lifetime encounter with Bibó; and for those of us who do read theory, the tape can function as an *appetizer,* a special nonacademic invitation and interpretation of Bibó's work.

And, yes, learning to resee the found footage through "Bibó eyeglasses" can reveal—it works this way for me—new aspects of the home movie, new aspects of my discourse on private and public history. Specifically, these ephemeral, faulty, scratchy images can't be appreciated as simple parts of a clear, single story. Do they mean anything at all? Do they help us understand what "really" happened in the past? What *is* "the past"? What *is* my memory? And what is collective memory? Or tribal memory? And do all these forms of memory correlate with one another? What is *private* and what is *public memory?* Which are the official and the nonofficial dimensions of history? All these questions are, I hope, raised by this tape, and my other tapes, and feed into an interest in doing more than just blindly accepting or avoiding the realities of our own existence.

MacDonald: Bibó seems important to you because of what seems a paradox in his thinking. He is clearly Hungarian, and he sees the history of Hungary as a particular, and important, history that, to some extent, is distinct from the histories of other European nations; but at the same time, he is entirely nonexclusive: he argues for the rights and dignity of all human beings inside and outside Hungarian society and places no value on someone's being "more Hungarian" than someone else.

Forgács: If middle Europe weren't the quagmire it is, Bibó's message could be heard more easily, but why should Bibó do better at changing his society than Socrates or Camus did in their societies? In fact, Bibó is so unique in Hungary that when I was making this film, I used to joke that he was an alien placed on Earth by a UFO.

I think he would be outraged by the new rise of Hungarian nationalism and the increasing Balkanization of the region.

MacDonald: I wonder if you know the work of Yervant Gianikian and Angela Ricci Lucchi, and if you see relationships between their work and yours.

Forgács: We are on the same ship; we sail with the same wind, and we eat the same food, chant the same prayers. Our quest is similar, and our archaeology of time is much the same.

MacDonald: When I've spoken with Gianikian and Ricci Lucchi, they've told me that when they make a film from archival material, they're usually trying to do two things: they want to be true to that material, to allow us to see what the material was saying at the time when it was made, *and* they want their use of the archival material to be a comment on current political events. Do you, also, mean for your tapes to comment on current developments? *A Bibó Reader* often seems particularly germane to the United States in the post-9/11 period.

Forgács: I like and appreciate their work, but their approach is different from mine. I can't see or feel their comments on current political events, since their work is so meditative.

I don't know how to be "true" to archival material if you touch it with an intention to do more than restore it. Of course, one tries not to create lies, but one can use a film, or the meaning of a film, for purposes very different from whatever the original purposes were (in my *Wittgenstein Tractatus,* for example, you might assume the pig you see rolling on the ground is about to be killed, but the pig is *not* killed or harmed: that imagery was from a veterinary school documentation of a case of nerve disease in a pig).

I did most of the editing for *A Bibó Reader* in the summer of 2000, so any references to recent events are accidental. It is true that there are correlations between what Bibó wrote and said and the current terrorist threats, the war hysteria, and the oversized surveillance that have come in the wake of the attack in New York.

But, on the other hand, do you realize how intolerant fundamentalist Islamic culture and religion *is?*

MacDonald: Please forgive me for asking about two other filmmakers. Do you know Alan Berliner's films? *The Family Album* [1987] seems especially related to *Private Hungary.*

Forgács: I know Alan and like his films—especially the ones on his grandfather [*Intimate Stranger,* 1991] and his father [*Nobody's Business,* 1996].

MacDonald: Some of what Bibó says reminds me of some of the films of your countryman Béla Tarr, especially *Satantango* [1994] and *The Werckmeister Harmonies* [2000]. Do you know Tarr? What do you think of his work?

Forgács: He is, along with Miklós Jancsó, the great Hungarian cinematographer-filmmaker. His way of thinking about and working with time and his uncompromising vision are very important to me.

Shirin Neshat

A native of Qazvin, Iran, Shirin Neshat finished high school and attended college in the United States, and once the Islamic revolution had transformed Iran, decided to remain in this country; she lives in New York City. In the mid-1990s, Neshat became known for a series of large photographs, *Women of Allah* (1993–97), which she designed, directed (Neshat is not a trained photographer; she hired Larry Barns, Kyong Park, and others to make her images), posed for, and decorated with poetry written in Farsi. *Women of Allah* provides a sustained rumination on the status and psyche of women in traditional Islamic cultures, using three primary elements: the black veil, modern weapons, and the written texts. The photographs are both intimate and confrontational. In each photograph Neshat appears, dressed in black, sometimes covered completely in black, facing the camera, holding a weapon. The photographs reflect both the repressed status of women in Iran and their power, as women and as Muslims; and they depict Neshat herself as a woman caught between the freedom of expression evident in the photographs and the complex demands of her Islamic heritage, where Iranian women are expected to support and sustain a revolution that frees them from Western decadence *and* represses dimensions of their individuality and creativity.

By 1998 Neshat was making films, shot in 16mm (and later in 35mm) but presented, at least at first, as gallery installations, usually organized so that the visitor to the gallery stands between the two projections, which face each other—and sometimes seem to address each other—from opposite walls. In *Turbulent* (1998), for example, a man (Shoja Azari) and a woman (Sussan Deyhim) are seen on opposite sides of the gallery space. First, the man sings a song, to the delight of an all-male audience. After his song has ended and the applause has died down, the woman performs a complex vocal piece. She has no audience and sings no lyrics, but her voice and delivery are evocative and powerful, so powerful that the man on the opposite side of the gallery seems as mesmerized by her as we are.

In the installation of *Rapture* (1999), one screen reveals a large group of men who march aggressively toward the camera, through the streets of a city in the Middle East and subsequently into and onto a fort at the edge of the ocean. On the opposite screen, a group of women, dressed in black and arranged in an arc, walk toward the camera over a rocky landscape and subsequently onto a beach, where several of the women board a small boat and set out to sea. In the final moments of *Rapture,* the men seem to signal from one side of the gallery to the women sailing into the distance—either asking the women to return or waving good-bye. In both installations Neshat focuses on the separation of the sexes in Islamic culture and on the various ways in which this traditional separation is articulated. In *Turbulent* the male singer's performance is public and verbal, whereas the woman's is wordless and solitary; in *Rapture* the men are juxtaposed with public, and particularly military, architecture, the women with the land and the sea.

In *Fervor* (2000), Neshat again uses two images, but unlike *Turbulent* and *Rapture, Fervor* is presented with the two images side by side, both as an installation and when projected (recently Neshat has been showing her double-screen installation films as theatrical works, with the two images side by side, in DVD projection). *Fervor* develops a skeletal narrative involving a man and a woman, kindred spirits apparently but separated by the restrictions of their society. At most, they glance at each other at public prayers or pass demurely by each other along country roads or on city streets. The overall design of the two juxtaposed images, combined with Neshat's use of mirror printing, creates a visually arresting maze within which the protagonists seem fated never to meet. *Fervor* is Neshat's most visually engaging and evocative film.

Soliloquy (1999) is the most overtly personal of Neshat's films. In the DVD projection we see Neshat herself in two very different cityscapes: on the left, she is dressed in black, walking in a small Middle Eastern city (it is not identified) and visiting a mosque, where she watches children play in a small pool, then seems to join some sort of ceremony with other women in black; on the right, Neshat, again dressed in black, is seen in a modern urban landscape, where she seems to have business and, in one instance, seems to come upon some sort of Christian religious service. The spectator's physical position, looking back and forth between two different worlds, echoes and embodies Neshat's psychic position, caught between her past and her present, and between her fear of losing her individuality within a traditional Islamic definition of womanhood and her feelings of separation and isolation within a modern Christian-based society.

Pulse (2001), *Possessed* (2001), and *Passage* (2001) are more convention-ally theatrical works, though they are also presented as gallery installations. In *Pulse* a single, continuous, 7½-minute tracking shot first moves forward into a darkened room (it evokes both bedroom and cell) where a woman is sitting on the floor, embracing a radio; then it tracks back out through the room. In *Possessed* a madwoman, not dressed in traditional black and with her face and hair revealed, wanders into a public square somewhere in the Middle East, then out again, leaving consternation in her wake. *Pulse* and *Possessed* suggest a dip-tych evoking dimensions of the private and public realities of women in tradi-tional Islamic cultures.

In *Passage,* a collaboration with composer Philip Glass, Neshat intercuts between a group of men solemnly carrying what looks to be the corpse of a woman, dressed in white, along an empty beach, and a circle of women, dressed in black, who are digging a hole with their hands. Nearby, a young girl makes a circle of small stones. As the men approach the circle of women, a fire behind the child (started by the child? emanating from the child?) moves in a line across the rocky landscape into the distance and in an arc behind the men and women in the foreground. Like nearly all of Neshat's films, *Passage* is a kind of cine-ritual, in this instance a ritual that seems to function as a premonition of, or at least as a kind of cine-prayer for, fundamental change in the relations of men and women. *Tooba* (2002), another double-image film, is also a ritual, shot in Mexico, in which groups of men and women, in a moun-tainous landscape, converge on a beautiful, isolated tree. Early in the film we see close-ups of a woman, apparently the spirit of the tree and of this land-scape, but by the time the groups of men and women arrive, the spirit seems to have disappeared.

Neshat's work seems to suggest, at least roughly, an ongoing transformation. *Women of Allah* reveals Neshat's anger at the traditional repression and suppres-sion of her gender and her willingness to express this anger. The two-screen installation works reveal a woman and artist torn by her diasporic identity, and between heritage and aspiration. The more recent, single-image films suggest Neshat's developing identity as a film director, certainly still empathetic with the struggles of women, but now in control of her own life and career, less torn and more ambitious.

I spoke with Neshat in New York City and subsequently by phone in Janu-ary 2003. We refined the interview by e-mail.

MacDonald: Soliloquy depicts a young woman caught between two worlds. Since you play the central character, it seems a very personal film. I know you were born in Iran and have lived in New York for some years, but I'd be grateful to know more about your history.

Neshat: I grew up in Iran in a small religious town that has now become a big city, called Qazvin. Its setting is mostly desert landscape, but it's only a few hours away from the Caspian Sea. My father was a well-known physician, a highly educated and very progressive man, with an unusual passion for agriculture and farming. I lived through his influence; he always encouraged me to be an individual, to take risks, to learn, and to see the world, as he always did. My mother was a more typical Iranian woman, with little education and committed to family and domestic life.

As a young girl, I was sent to the capital city, Tehran, to study in a Catholic boarding school, which ended up being a horrible experience.

MacDonald: What happened?

Neshat: Well, I had come from a very warm, supportive Muslim family environment, but at this Christian school, totally guarded by the Catholic nuns, I ended up feeling as if I were living in detention. I slowly became ill and developed anorexia. When I went back to my hometown after a year and a half, most people could not recognize me because I had lost so much weight.

During the late sixties and early seventies, it was felt that a Western education was a good thing. Most upper- and middle-class people; were beginning to send their sons abroad to study; but my father sent both his sons *and* daughters abroad to England and the United States. Eventually my two sisters abandoned their education, returned to Iran, and got married, whereas I ended up remaining in the U.S. and eventually developed a career. My father, of course, was very proud of me and often talked about it before he died.

MacDonald: How did you end up at Berkeley?

Neshat: When I first came to the U.S., I joined my older sisters in Los Angeles. I attended high school for one year, but when my sisters decided to move back to Iran, I found myself alone. I never liked Southern California, and during a short visit to Northern California, I fell in love with its landscape, so I moved to the Bay Area. I started by studying at Dominican College and eventually was accepted to UC-Berkeley.

I managed to stay at Berkeley long enough to earn my bachelor's degree and an M.F.A.; but the truth is I was never a good student, never a highlight. I was just getting by. In fact, I barely got accepted into the graduate school. I just wasn't ready for it, and spent two years making what I now consider mediocre art. After I graduated, I decided to abandon art altogether and didn't really get back to making art again for a good ten years—until 1990.

MacDonald: What kept you from making art?

Neshat: I felt that my ideas were confused and simply not strong enough. Also, I wasn't really inspired by the art history that I was exposed to. And when I moved from California to New York, I felt further intimidated by the contemporary art scene in New York City and found that I had neither the maturity nor the desire to pursue an art career.

I spent ten years working with an institution called the Storefront for Art and Architecture, which was founded by my ex-husband, Kyong Park. I helped him with the curatorial program but mostly as an administrator. The Storefront was a not-for-profit organization committed to presenting art and architectural programs. It was very interdisciplinary and dedicated to bringing people together from both the practical and theoretical backgrounds of architecture. I was exposed to great minds from various fields: artists, architects, philosophers, culture critics, sometimes even scientists. Working there became my true education, mostly helping me to mature and to begin to develop my own ideas and methodology. Eventually, in 1998, I left the organization.

What became the turning point of my art career was, of course, my decision to return to Iran in 1990 after eleven years (the Islamic Revolution took place in 1979); that trip and subsequent trips brought me an artistic focus: the revolution and women in relation to the revolution. Finally I had found a subject that I felt passionate about; but, more important, making art about this subject became an excuse to reconnect myself with my long-lost culture. Since then, the work has had its own natural evolution.

MacDonald: Can you talk a little about your earliest work after returning to Iran?

Neshat: My first artistic work was a body of photographs, called *Women of Allah,* focusing on the subject of the revolution and the concept of martyrdom. This series had an element of performance, as I posed for them myself. The photographs were quite minimal; a few elements were repeated over and over again, including the *female body,* a very a problematic topic in Islamic culture, as it suggests ideas of shame, sin, and sexuality; *text,* I inscribed calligraphy—poetry by Iranian women writers—directly *on* the photographs; *weapons,* obviously a symbol of violence; and, finally, the *veil,* which has been considered a symbol both of repression and of liberation—resistance against Western influence. My book *Women of Allah* [Turin: Marco Noire Editore, 1997] entirely documents this series of photographs.

MacDonald: How old were you when you left Iran?

Neshat: Seventeen. I left Iran in 1975. The revolution happened in 1979, and I didn't return until 1990, so as you can imagine, the culture had undergone a drastic transformation. I, like many Iranians who had not lived through the revolution, found this change quite shocking.

MacDonald: How did the revolution affect your family?

Neshat: Of course, everyone was affected by it, and in some ways my family was not as badly affected as others were, but the change did take a big toll on my father. He had worked very hard all his life and was just about to retire when all his benefits suddenly disappeared, so he ended up with a minimal salary. He had gained a certain social status and high respect for the relentless contributions he had made to our city through his medical and agricultural practices. Yet, during the last years of his life, he spent most of his time fighting to protect what was his. A man who thrived on world travel could no longer travel outside Iran, until just about a year before he died, when I urged the family to have a reunion in Turkey. By that time he was quite ill.

MacDonald: Were you the only member of your family who stayed in the West?

Neshat: My younger brother left right after the revolution, with many difficulties. My family helped him exit from Iran, and I managed to help him enter the United States. And now he's living in California.

MacDonald: Have you been able to stay in contact with your family, or has that been difficult?

Neshat: For a while, I was going back quite frequently, and we've met occasionally in Europe. But traveling to and from the Middle East is not as easy anymore, so mostly we try to stay in touch through telephone; we talk at least once a week.

MacDonald: You think the calls are listened to?

Neshat: I think most likely they are.

MacDonald: You were talking about your photography . . .

Neshat: Yes. At the beginning, in the nineties, when I traveled frequently to my country, I became obsessed with that experience. I found myself both fascinated and terrified by the impact of the revolution. There was so much that I didn't understand that I desperately wanted to understand. For example, I wondered how and why the revolution was formed, and what its primary ideology was. In a sense, coming to terms with this subject made me feel less distant and more a part of the community. Since then, of course, it has been an amazing process for me: every experience and question has led to many more.

Later, there were a lot of questions about the problem of translation in the "Women of Allah" photographs. My response has always been, "You have to keep in mind the context within which this work was made. I had no art career; I was not thinking about the audience, since I didn't have any; I was making this work for *myself.*"

MacDonald: I assume that if someone who knew Farsi were looking at these photographs, they could read this text and might even recognize the poetry?

Neshat: Yes, of course. Iranians not only could read and understand the meaning of the poetry but are also very familiar with the history and place of the writers in relation to Iranian society. This is something that would be impossible to translate for Westerners.

MacDonald: How did you make the transition from photography to film and video?

Neshat: I had been working with photography and the subject of the revolution since 1993, but by 1997, while I remained totally interested in the social and political realities of my country, I felt the urge to move beyond the realm

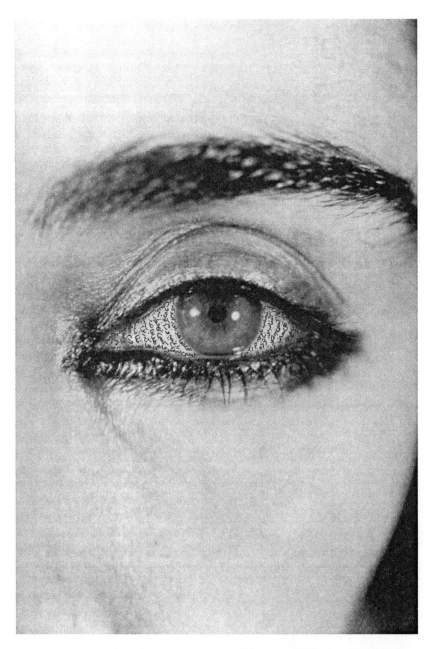

Photographs from Shirin Neshat's *Women of Allah. This page: Offered Eyes* (1993, photo taken by Plauto); *opposite page: Untitled* (1996, photograph by Kyong Park). Each photo measures approximately 40 in. × 60 in. Courtesy Barbara Gladstone Gallery.

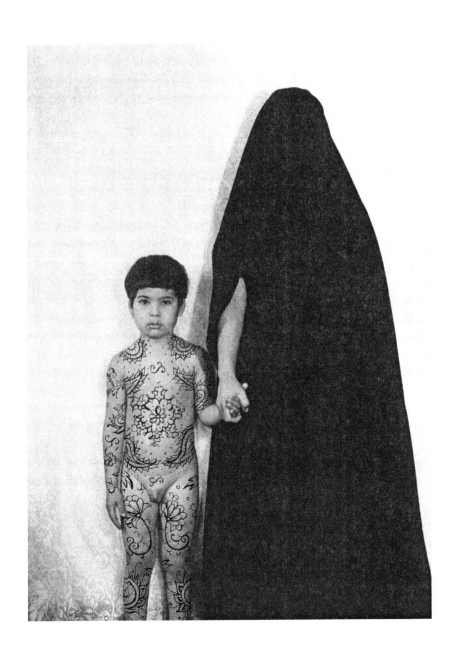

of politics and take a more philosophical approach. In thinking about refor-
mulating my concepts, I decided it was also necessary to change the medium
that I was working with. I had grown frustrated with the limitations of photography, at least in the way I was approaching it. I needed a medium that offered
me a new level of poetic lyricism that was not happening for me in photography. So I made what felt like the bold decision to shift from still photography
to the moving image. My first big attempt was a video I shot with two cam-
eramen in Istanbul.

MacDonald: Is this *Turbulent?*

Neshat: No, this was *The Shadow under the Web,* a piece with four simultaneous projections, shot in Istanbul in 1997. It was an installation that basically depicted a woman (myself), draped in black chador, running simultaneously
in four distinctly different spaces: private, public, sacred, and natural. At the
time, I was very interested in how space is defined, controlled, and divided
in Islamic cultures according to gender. For example, in traditional societies,
private spaces are considered "feminine," and public spaces are "masculine."
The Shadow under the Web, a color video that was shot in both natural landscapes and built spaces, became a big departure from my earlier black-and-
white photographs, which were very sculptural, almost monumental, and made
no use of background.

Turbulent came after *The Shadow under the Web.*

MacDonald: Even without knowing Farsi, I understand, or think I understand, *Turbulent.* It's almost a call and response, and a very generous feminist
piece: the man's singing is wonderful, and you show that he has support from
the audience, which he deserves, and then the woman responds with *her* amazing music that seems to surprise and amaze both us and him. Are these the actual
singers, lip-synching their own music?

Neshat: The female singer is Sussan Deyhim, who was lip-synching to her
own music. The male singer was Shoja Azari. Shoja had never sung; he was simply lip-synching the part. The actual singer is a very well-known Iranian
singer, Shahram Nazeri, probably the most beloved living Iranian musician who
sings classical Persian and Sufi music. He mostly sings poetry by important Iranian poets such as Hafez and Rumi. In *Turbulent* he was singing a poem by Rumi.

MacDonald: Is Sussan Deyhim singing words?

Neshat: No.

MacDonald: Often in my teaching, I use Laura Mulvey and Peter Wollen's
Riddles of the Sphinx [1977]—do you know that film?

Neshat: No.

MacDonald: It comes out of a lot of film theory and much discussion
about gender. In order to counter the usually "phallic" architecture of the film
image, Mulvey and Wollen tell the story of their protagonist exclusively with
360-degree pans, to suggest a rounded, female orientation to the world. I won-

der whether you see the auditorium space as basically phallic, and the circling around the woman as she sings as a kind of feminist response.

Neshat: That's really interesting. The main conceptual device in this film was the notion of opposites: the man, the woman; black, white; empty auditorium, full auditorium; traditional music, totally improvised music; conformity versus rebellion—and so we thought it would also be appropriate to have the camera stationary with the male singer, but circling around the female singer, particularly as she reaches the climax of her song. The fast circular camera movement around her was meant to reiterate her mental state, her "madness," her rage.

MacDonald: I like that the film doesn't end with her facing away from us, which is the position we first see her in. The man is facing us, with his straightforward look, but after we circle around her, the camera stops with her in profile. The image isn't quite the same as it was when we started.

Neshat: I wanted to reverse the situation so that at the end, she is no longer hidden. Having clearly proven herself through her unbelievable performance, she appears relieved and peaceful, whereas he comes across as shocked and at a loss.

MacDonald: Turbulent was originally meant to be seen as two images across from one another, but even though I've only seen the DVD with the two images next to each other, when the woman begins to sing, it's clearly as if the man is looking at her, so I get the sense of the original installation anyway. When you see the images side by side in any of these pieces, you can catch subtleties of parallel rhythm and graphic design that you would lose in the installation version. It's both gain and loss, either way!

Neshat: Yes. When I look at the films with the images side by side, I like how they complement each other visually; but when you have the two images projected on two opposite walls, something very interesting happens between the *viewers* and the piece. They are physically and emotionally in between the two sides, and because they cannot possibly see both images simultaneously, they must decide which side to turn to and which side to miss; and in doing so, they become the editors of the piece. *This* experience of course gets lost when the two pictures are projected side by side.

MacDonald: I found them all quite powerful the way I saw them. The only piece I've seen as an installation is *Passage,* which I saw at the Guggenheim. I like that one both ways.

Neshat: With *Passage* it made no sense, conceptually, to divide the picture into two, so everything was kept in one screen.

MacDonald: As you conceptualize a piece, how early do you bring in the collaborators?

Neshat: The process of our collaboration has been very organic in its development. It started with the making of *Turbulent* when a few of us a sort of accidentally came together. We were all Iranians living abroad, but each of us came from a different artistic field: Shoja Azari is a writer and filmmaker; Sussan Deyhim, a singer and composer; Darius Khondji, a cinematographer; Ghasem Ebrahimian, a filmmaker and a cinematographer; Shahram Karimi, a visual artist and an art director.

There was an immediate excitement in the energy of the group and how working together seemed to satisfy us both socially and artistically. I would basically generate an idea and present everyone with a storyboard. We would discuss the concept, location, and budget, and the visual form of the film. Everyone offered their criticisms of the idea. Soon a few of us would travel to find the ideal location in whichever country we decided to work in, and eventually we got busy with the production. The entire time, I remained very open to everyone's input but also felt free to reject ideas as well. Of course over time, the group came to understand my aesthetic very well, and the collaboration became more fluid.

Out of the group, Shoja Azari has been most essential in helping me through the entire process, from the conception of the idea to the postproduction work. Sussan Deyhim and I, of course, have worked together a number of times. I am very proud of our collaboration; I think my images and her music blend unusually well together.

Of course, the dynamic of this collaborative effort continues to change, as new members join and others move on. That has been the pattern. I must also mention that the other members of the group are also independently very active in their own careers, and I dedicate some of my time to helping them. Recently in Shoja Azari's film *K* (2002), I performed as an actress, helped with the production design, and was the executive producer.

MacDonald: Rapture was shot in Morocco?

Neshat: Yes.

MacDonald: Would you have shot in Iran if that had been possible? And did you choose that fort because its architecture would be well known to people in the Arab world and in Iran? Are you using the fort as a specific place or a generic place?

Neshat: It is very complicated, if not impossible, for someone like me to film in Iran, because of the controversial nature of my subjects. Also, another factor has been the ambiguity in whether I am safe in Iran or not, and I haven't wanted to take the risk. But even though I work in these other, safer countries, I pretend that I'm in Iran, and I'm very cautious about the type of architecture that I use.

In *Rapture,* I filmed in the fortress in the city of Essaouira, because this space was a relevant location for my concept. The architecture of a fortress, particularly in Islamic cultures, represents a typically male space and suggests ideas of military, war, defense—all roles associated with men. Ironically, this particular fortress was built by the Portuguese in the fifteenth century (I believe), but most Islamic cities traditionally were surrounded by walls. The city of Marrakesh is a vivid example. Another reason this fort was attractive to me is that

The men *(top)* and the women, from Neshat's *Rapture* (1999). Photographs by Larry Barnes. Courtesy Barbara Gladstone Gallery.

Orson Welles shot some scenes of his *Othello* [1951] there. Orson Welles spent a lot of time in Essaouira; he is very much loved by the local people.

In regard to the use of natural landscape, I normally choose what I consider a more generic landscape, a space that is not identified with any particular culture. For example, in *Rapture* the women were filmed in a desert that was quite plain and does not suggest a particular country.

MacDonald: Even more fully than *Turbulent, Rapture* creates a male-female point-counterpoint. When the men are chanting whatever they're chanting, the women turn their backs on them and hold up their hands as if to ward off what the men are saying; and there's that poignant ending where, and this would be particularly dramatic in a gallery space where the images would be on opposite walls, the men are waving to the women, who seem to have given up and are rowing out to sea in search of new territory. It looks like the men are waving to say, "Good-bye and good luck," *or* to say, "Please come back!"

Neshat: Exactly. I'm glad you read it like that. Making *Rapture* was a unique experience. I felt that the narrative was expressed in a kind of choreography with a special focus on form—geometric shapes. In other words, we were trying to tell the story through the physical shapes and movements of the groups of men and women in various built and natural landscapes. I particularly enjoyed the editing process and working on how the images aesthetically complemented each other. For example, at one point the men were sitting in a circle, preparing for prayer, while the women were seated in a triangular shape, praying. There were many instances where I relied on the sheer beauty and power of the image to tell my story.

Another important point about *Rapture* is that never in the entire film does the camera focus on a particular character. The narrative is always about a mass of women versus a mass of men. There is no single protagonist here. My cameraman at the time *constantly* wanted to shoot close-ups of the beautiful faces, and I kept resisting it, saying, "I'm not going to use a single shot if you do." Soon he gave up.

MacDonald: You mentioned that *Fervor* was originally designed so that the two images would be seen side-by-side. For me, as a film person, that film is particularly appealing; the way in which the two images work together is remarkable.

Neshat: Originally, my feeling was that since the subject of sexual taboo was shared by both Muslim men and women, while they were still divided, they were no longer opposites. With the superb cinematography of Ghasem Ebrahimian, I felt that both the separation and the temptation that existed between the men and women were beautifully captured.

MacDonald: How fully were the formal elements designed in advance?

Neshat: In *Fervor* the decision to put the images side by side was *not* decided at the beginning but later and only because, by accident, I saw some images next to each other in the editing room. Then I really got involved with experimenting with the mirroring effect.

MacDonald: If one reads the progression of your films, in both *Turbulent* and *Rapture,* men and women are going in different directions or are astonished at each other, but they are clearly divided into separate spaces. In *Fervor,* they're divided into separate spaces that often become one space; and then in *Passage,* it's as though the men and the women are collaborating in a ritual within the same image, to bury a certain kind of separation between them. They don't really *do* it, but they're on the verge of doing it.

Neshat: You are absolutely right. Usually the *idea* of the installation design has a direct relation to the concept. As you explained, in *Turbulent* and *Rapture* the men and women basically existed separately and were occupied differently. However, in *Fervor* and *Passage,* they came together to participate in a shared ritual, whether a public event *(Fervor)* or a funeral *(Passage).*

MacDonald: In *Fervor* the man gives the speech in front of the divided men and women. Do you have a translation of that speech?

Neshat: Yes, I do. I had a professional translation prepared and was working on subtitles, but many people, particularly English-speaking friends, recommended against it, saying, "A translation would make the film too literal; *Fervor* should be treated like an opera." So in the end I dropped the subtitles. I sometimes regret this decision, but I do try to display the translation of the speech when the film is shown as an installation.

MacDonald: Operas are now subtitled in some places.

Neshat: Yes, but I think our experience with opera is not verbal, it's visual and sonic.

MacDonald: Can you describe the speaker's oration?

Neshat: He delivers a moral speech about the subject of sin—sin that arises from desire, from the temptation for the opposite sex. He uses the story of Youssef and Zoleikha, from the Koran. As is true in the story of Adam and Eve, basically Zoleikha is blamed for seducing Youssef. The speaker is using this tale, which is illustrated by a painting in the background, as a lesson for the men and women.

This style of oratory is inspired by a very special tradition of theater in Iran, where the storyteller uses a painting as a backdrop to illustrate his story. Anyway, the speaker—it's unclear in the film whether he is a mullah, an actor, or a politician—addresses the public and warns all good Muslim men and women against adultery and urges them to repress all uncalled-for sexual tendencies. He uses the slogan "Curse upon the Satan!"

MacDonald: I have two levels of questions about *Soliloquy.* One involves the fact that you yourself play the main character, a person who seems—I don't know whether "alienated" is the right word—but at least detached from each of two places we see her in, though in somewhat different ways, *and,* on another level, who also enjoys the two places, but again in two different ways.

Public prayer meeting, in Neshat's *Fervor* (2000). Photograph by Larry Barnes. Courtesy Barbara Gladstone Gallery.

Neshat: That's a pretty good reading, actually.

MacDonald: Albany, New York, seems the place of work.

Neshat: Yes.

MacDonald: And what is the other location?

Neshat: We filmed in the eastern part of Turkey, in Mardin, a Kurdish town very close to the city of Urfa, the birthplace of Abraham, on the border of Iran and Syria, not far from Iraq. Mardin is a religious town, extremely poor and neglected, but quite beautiful. The city is made of adobe-type houses built on a small mountain in the middle of the desert. We discovered quickly that this city was quite dangerous due to the activities of both the Kurdish rebels and the Muslim fundamentalists who were apparently being trained by Iranians on the border. The Turkish government has placed a large military base there, and as you can imagine, we immediately became suspects when we arrived to make an Islamic film. We were questioned and guarded the entire time we were filming. It was the first time that I've worked with such a high level of anxiety.

MacDonald: Did you film in a single complex?

Neshat: Yes, other than one general scenic view of the city, we mostly filmed within an amazing building called "Ghasemieh," which was originally a school for the study of the Koran. However, this building, an architectural monument, has been totally neglected and abandoned; children often use it as a playground.

MacDonald: How did you decide on Albany as your other location?

Neshat: I scouted a few other American cities, such as Dallas, Texas, and a few cities in Connecticut, and ended up with Albany. My original criteria were that the city had to be typically American but not easily recognizable. I thought Albany was perfect since while it is the capital of New York State, it is not a highly visited city. For me the Rockefeller Plaza in Albany was really amazing. There were several monumental but practically abandoned buildings. I found these buildings both beautiful and oppressive at the same time, and very similar to the quality of the space in the Ghasemieh.

As you can imagine, the use of architecture became an essential aspect of *Soliloquy,* as the buildings were used to represent each culture's traditional values. It was therefore important that each culture be represented equally, in terms of beauty and grandiosity.

MacDonald: Where did you film the escalators?

Neshat: In the World Trade Center at the entrance to the PATH trains. For me the image of the long escalators, with masses of people traveling up and down, was both frightening and a reflection of the reality of modern life. We also filmed in other areas of the WTC.

MacDonald: There's a remarkable moment right at the beginning of *Soliloquy* where the trajectory of the two images seems to make a single cityscape, and then slowly the two images diverge. I'm referring to the DVD version of the piece; I've not seen the original installation, where the images would be opposite one another.

Neshat: We carefully orchestrated that opening moment. In each country, we built exactly the same-sized room and windows on top of a building. We wanted each room to face a building that would function iconically in the film. In Albany the window opened to a high-rise building, and in Mardin, the window faced a minaret. In both images the camera moved at the same speed, panning around the window to reveal the woman.

MacDonald: The black-and-white shots of the boy in the dust during the section of the film shot in Turkey are an interruption in the continuity of the film. How do those shots function for you?

Neshat: Basically, the main core of the narrative in Turkey revolves around an obscure ritual of death, a group of men and women dressed in black arriving from all sides of the building to pronounce terrible news of "death," soon to be followed with a ceremonial event which resembles something between a dance and a funeral. Here, the death was of a young boy who belonged to the female protagonist. The occasional cut to the black-and-white image of the boy was a conceptual device to reiterate this tragedy and her loss. The event was inspired by my sister, who just a year prior to the filming lost her young son. She was present with me in Turkey as we shot *Soliloquy.*

MacDonald: In the image shot in the West, when the woman goes into the modern building, she finds her way into a chapel where there are women in white. In the East she disappears and becomes invisible; *here,* she's totally visible, but alien to her situation.

Neshat: Yes, that was the intention.

MacDonald: There's also the difference that in the East the religious spaces are clearly religious spaces, but in the West, the basic space seems to be a business space, inside which there's a religious space.

Neshat: Yes. In the West I was really focusing on modernity and decided to stay away from older churches. That's why I used a very modern chapel, Saint Anna's Church in Manhattan.

MacDonald: Both *Possessed* and *Pulse* seem a little more direct than the earlier films; *Possessed* seems most like a conventional movie.

Neshat: You're right. As I said earlier, to me every one of these films has been an experiment in a direction I haven't tried before. I find it problematic to repeat the same kind of work over and over again. With *Possessed* I learned a lot. First of all, it was one of the first times that I worked with a professional actress (Shohreh Aghdashloo), so I had to spend a lot of time in character development, to create her psychosis. Also, this film has a clear linear progression, which meant that we would not be able to have as much flexibility in the editing process as we had had in the past. All of these issues became exciting and challenging for me, particularly the fact that, for a change, the cast were not treated as sculptural volumes but as real characters.

MacDonald: Possessed is very theatrical.

Neshat: Yes, absolutely. In *Possessed* the biggest aim was to explore and reveal the protagonist's state of mind—her madness, both in private and in the public domain. Her behavior continues to evolve and change from one type of emotion to another according to the space that she is inhabiting. This was a completely new experience for me.

MacDonald: Possessed reminds me a little of *Un Chant d'amour* [1952], the Jean Genet film—do you know it?

Neshat: No.

MacDonald: It's about gay men, or maybe men in general, in prison; the implication is that prison is the only place where men can express their erotic desire for each other. Imprisonment becomes, paradoxically, the one place where they are free to express a crucial dimension of themselves. *Possessed* is similar in the sense that in the society implicitly depicted in the film, madness becomes the only way in which a woman can express herself.

Neshat: That was the idea. The character here achieves her freedom through the state of madness. This of course makes direct reference to the Iranian culture, where one lives under constant social control. Therefore, the notion of individuality does pose a threat to the order of the society, since it might provoke others to demand the same thing. In this film, once the woman enters the public plaza and becomes the focus of everyone's attention, she immediately disturbs the space and divides the public into two groups: those who support her and her freedom to behave as she desires due to madness, and the others, who are insulted by her presence and furiously demand her immediate removal.

MacDonald: So we see people arguing in the square, after she leaves. Her freedom has instigated a debate.

Neshat: Exactly. She creates what we call *fetneh,* a social chaos among the people. As you said, *Possessed* is more obvious, in terms of its narrative and its message, than *Rapture* and *Passage,* which are more ambiguous and abstract. I personally prefer the latter, but I am very happy that I did the experiment that resulted in what is, so far, my most conventional film.

MacDonald: In *Pulse* I'm not sure exactly what the woman is doing. First, we see her from a distance; she's on the floor, holding something, and then as we get close to her, she seems to be holding a radio.

Neshat: Yes. We carefully organized the room so that it had the feeling of a bedroom but also resembled a prison cell. The radio becomes her access to the outside world—a tool for escape from her immediate environment. As we approach the woman, voyeuristically, we hear her voice singing along with a song on the radio. She seems to be lost in her own state of ecstasy, fantasy. The entire film was created in one uninterrupted shot from the beginning to the end, from the moment the camera entered the room with the sound of a pulse to the moment when it exits with the end of the song. There is something very erotic and sensual about this movement and her posture. There is no clear narrative, but a sort of glimpse into a private moment of this woman's life.

MacDonald: Do you think of *Possessed* and *Pulse* as a diptych: public and private?

Neshat: Well, I've never thought about them quite like that, but it is possible to draw that conclusion, especially since the two films were made at the same time with the same actress. To me the visual organization of *Pulse* is very different from the visual organization of *Possessed,* but it's true that *Pulse* does obviously reflect the *private* life, and *Possessed,* the *public* life, of the woman.

MacDonald: What led you to Mexico for *Tooba,* and what does "Tooba" mean?

Neshat: Tooba is originally a mythical character from the Koran, a woman who is also a tree, a sacred tree. After September 11, I started thinking about making a piece that focuses on the idea of a garden—a heaven. Of course, in the Islamic and Persian tradition the garden is a very important symbol in both mystical and political terms. Similar to many other cultures, in our mystical and poetic tradition, a garden is a space for spiritual transcendence, a paradise. And within our political language the garden is a place for freedom and independence. I found all those meanings very relevant at the time.

I chose Mexico when it turned out to be extremely difficult to film in Iran. I felt the urge to go to a neutral country, meaning neither Islamic nor Western. I had never visited Mexico before but was aware of the diversity in the landscape and, of course, its great culture. So I went to do location scouting in

Oaxaca, looking for that perfect tree for a garden. I found the tree—a fig tree, which *is* a sacred tree, on top of a mountain where there was no road, so we had to pave the road to get to it. We built the wall around the tree, hired local assistants, and began to cast.

MacDonald: In *Tooba,* and in *Rapture,* you worked with fairly large groups of people, who I assume were people indigenous to the places where you shot. What was the process of getting those people involved?

Neshat: Usually we hire local people as coordinators—the casting director, the project manager, a line producer. To recruit local people you need local persons who are well liked by the community and have some experience in organizing events. Then we hold an audition; people show up, and we cast. Often, it becomes very frustrating because there's a lot of competition; there are always more people than we can hire. In most cases the population is extremely poor, and of course none of them have professional acting experience, so they are interested primarily for economic reasons. I have always felt proud about this aspect of the projects, which on a modest scale are able to make an economic contribution to the local communities. In every instance, we have developed a great love for the local people and a strong bond. In the case of Morocco we have continued to collaborate with the same people on various projects.

In Mexico, we worked with native Indians, mostly older men and women. They were amazing-looking people with unusual physical strength and pride. It was a great experience working with them.

MacDonald: In *Tooba* it seems like most of the people we see coming toward the tree are men; there are a few shots where you see women, too.

Neshat: It was half and half, actually; it's just that the women couldn't keep up with the men. It was pretty strenuous running in those hills. I had every intention to have this film *not* be about gender relations.

Tooba was a film that I think many Westerners, particularly Americans, didn't quite understand.

MacDonald: How so?

Neshat: My feeling is that most Americans don't really get the poetry and symbolism of this piece. Religion and poetry don't play a big role in American culture. The language of this film is metaphoric, and one must approach it as a visual poem, not as a narrative film.

MacDonald: Of course, that's true with all the pieces.

Neshat: Yes, but there is something more tangible for the American audience in the previous pieces because of the more obvious Islamic iconography—the veil, for example. Here, I dropped all of those elements, so the piece became rather universal, while in my opinion still very Iranian.

In *our* culture, metaphoric/poetic language is the only means of expression for most of us, who are not permitted to speak freely. Poetry becomes a political statement, and the public becomes accustomed to reading in between the lines, as they say.

MacDonald: In your work, it's obvious that you understand the absurdities to which certain parties can take a spiritual idea and use it to create alienation between groups, but you haven't given up on the idea of spirit or on ritual as a spiritual process, or on art as a process of trying to heal spiritually.

Neshat: You are absolutely right.

MacDonald: In many ways, *Passage* seems related to *Rapture.*

Neshat: I think they share a similar visual and conceptual approach. For example, both narratives revolve around the relationship between crowds of people and landscapes, so both become more about choreography than anything else. Also, in both cases, visual configurations are extremely important in telling the story. For example, in *Passage,* the linear movement of the men versus the circle of women becomes very critical and rather erotic.

MacDonald: How did you happen to work with Phil Glass? And what was it like to work with him? I notice that this is the first time that your opening credit and the music credit are equal—in fact, it's Phil Glass first, *and* Shirin Neshat.

Neshat (laughter): That's just because he had also commissioned ten-minute films by three other filmmakers—Peter Greenaway [*The Man in the Bath,* 2001], Atom Egoyan [*Diaspora,* 2001], and Michal Rovner [*Notes,* 2001]—for which he could create new music and which he could accompany live with an orchestra [Glass calls the set of films *Shorts*]. The titles had to be exactly the same for each film.

I was asked by Philip Glass and his company to propose a concept for a short film, what became *Passage,* and Philip liked the proposal. I went ahead and shot the film in Morocco and started editing. I gave him a rough edit, and he started his musical composition. I remember that the first time he played his composition for me on the piano, I liked it very much. So eventually he recorded the music with a full orchestra. There were many exchanges back and forth. For example, I worked with the conductor to play down certain instruments and added the women's chant. It was a truly democratic collaboration; Philip was very supportive and sensitive to my ideas and opinions.

At the beginning I was a little worried. I thought, "He's a *man,* and he's a *Westerner.*" Of course, up to then I had worked with Sussan Deyhim, the wonderful Iranian singer and composer who often used her own voice, as well as indigenous and traditional Islamic melodies, in her compositions. Here, with Philip, I was dealing with a minimalist composer who essentially used Western sounds and instruments to create his music. But I welcomed the challenge and listened to a lot of his music before I came up with the concept.

I was concerned with another issue, which was whether Philip would deliver music which was equally as emotional as the picture. As you know, *Passage* is about a funeral, an obscure ritual of death. I have to say that by the end, I was very happy with the music. My favorite moment in *Passage* is when the camera finally goes inside the pit and reveals the women's bare hands, digging. It is a perhaps the most emotional moment of the film, and I *love* the way Philip handles the music at that point, which is very melancholic.

There was a strong and rather mixed reaction to the film when I exhibited it at Barbara Gladstone Gallery in May of 2001. There were basically two camps: there were people who *absolutely* hated it, and they said, "Oh, this is the *worst* music; you should just work with Sussan Deyhim," and there were those who said, "It's really fantastic."

MacDonald: Was *Passage* a coproduction?

Neshat: No, we produced the entire film, and Philip took care of the cost of the music. When we were done, it became *my* artwork with *his* music. He didn't want any profit from my film, and I didn't want any profit from his music, so it was a good agreement.

MacDonald: How long does it take to shoot the films? And what are the budgets like? You mentioned that you made three pieces in one trip to Morocco.

Neshat: Because of the cost involved, we try to pack it in. In *Passage* we worked with the women in the desert for three days, and the men and women on the beach for two days. So altogether five days. For *Possessed* it was about three days. *Pulse* was one night. *Soliloquy* was more complicated; we had a lot of complications in Turkey. But usually we can do our work for a film in a week—maybe less, but no more.

Turbulent cost something like twenty-thousand dollars; *Rapture* was more like a hundred thousand; *Fervor,* about the same; *Soliloquy* was expensive because we had to be in two countries—about two hundred thousand. The maximum I've ever spent is two hundred thousand; the minimum, twenty.

MacDonald: When you decided to become a filmmaker, you came to film as a gallery artist, which on a certain level is an unusual—but fortunate—way to enter the field, because—

Neshat: Do you mean "*un*fortunate"?

MacDonald: No, I mean "fortunate."

Neshat: Oh, really!

MacDonald: A number of filmmakers I've talked with in the past few years have said, "We've spent all this time and effort on these films, and the amount we get for a screening is so minuscule that it's hardly worth the effort!"

Neshat: Oh, you mean financially.

MacDonald: Yes. The gallery situation seems to be kinder financially, at least for some makers.

Neshat: Oh, yes. We can sell what we make as artworks. But you have to understand that I came to film as a visual artist, and my audience was the public who knew my photography and installation work. They understood and appreciated how my work slowly evolved from still photography to the moving image, and that although I am making films, essentially I am still working as a visual artist.

At the beginning I thought that my work wouldn't have a place in the film world, because it didn't use conventional narrative. *The Shadow under the Web,* for example, was a purely sculptural video piece. But then, of course, with *Turbulent,* the direction changed more toward cinema.

MacDonald: What was the reaction of the art world to this move toward cinema?

Neshat: At times, you do find some resistance in the art world against this blurring of boundaries. For example, *Turbulent* and *Rapture* were very well received; most critics and the public *loved* the idea of a short video installation that remained very visual but also became narrative and musical. In *Turbulent* the element of narrative was quite minimal, simply one exchange of song between the male and female singer. But soon, with *Fervor* and *Soliloquy,* the narrative became more pronounced. The more narrative the films became, the more critical the art critics became, asking whether the work is *art,* and whether it should be seen in a gallery/museum or in a movie theater.

Then came the question of taste. For a while many people were tied to the black-and-white double projections and very resistant toward my use of color or single-channel projections. And as I mentioned, some people grew very attached to Sussan Deyhim's music in my films and complained about Philip Glass's music in *Passage.* I try not to pay attention to these opinions and objections. I instinctively follow what I think is a natural progression for my ideas and experimentations. Every film for me is a new exercise and a way to expand my language as a truly multimedia artist.

MacDonald: Sharon Lockhart's career seems similar to yours.

Neshat: Yes! And in a way, Matthew Barney's, who is also working with Barbara Gladstone.

MacDonald: How did you get connected with Barbara Gladstone? And how does she work with you? It seems unusual for a gallery to be producing films.

Neshat: Barbara is a dealer who doesn't try to control an artist; she gives artists total trust and freedom.

MacDonald: Does she see a script or a storyboard?

Neshat: No. Absolutely nothing. It's extraordinary how much risk she takes. I don't think she expected herself to be a film producer; it just happened that way when her artists started to make films.

MacDonald: I understand you're working on a script. Is this a script for a narrative feature?

Neshat: Yes. I'm in the process of adapting a book, *Women without Men: A Novella* [Syracuse, N.Y.: Syracuse University Press, 1998], by a very well-known Iranian woman writer, Shahrnoush Parsipour. She is living in exile in Berkeley, California. She was imprisoned for about five years in Iran. I was lucky in finding her, and we have developed a wonderful friendship. *Women without Men* is a beautiful, surrealistic story of five different women who are all coming from oppressive backgrounds, but whose lives mysteriously converge in the countryside in Iran, in a house with a big garden. Together they try to create a paradise, their own independent society, a sort of a utopia, removed from the outside world. The only man in this community of exiles is a gardener, who is like a god figure, a wise and compassionate man who becomes a kind of guardian for these women. So obviously this is not a story about women against men. Every character in the novel is complex.

What is interesting is how eventually this community falls apart. The utopia proves impossible due to the fact that each woman contains the flaws that she is running away from in the outside world. To me this book, which is very visual, is also deeply political, philosophical, mystical, universal, and, of course, very feminist.

MacDonald: How widely has your work been seen in Iran?

Neshat: Only *Tooba* has been officially shown in Iran, recently at the Museum of Contemporary Art in Tehran. Apparently it had an enthusiastic reception. But as you can imagine, my topics are inherently problematic, so most projects are not really possible to show publicly.

MacDonald: You mentioned you are about to shoot a new short film. Where and when are you shooting?

Neshat: Yes, *The Last Word* [2003]. I'm shooting in Brooklyn, during the first week of March. For the first time I am making a film with some dialogue. It will involve two main actors and a cast of fifteen. This time, I had to write a script and develop the narrative in conventional terms.

MacDonald: Do you see this as a form of training for your feature?

Neshat: Exactly.

Ellen Spiro

By the time she made *Roam Sweet Home* (1997), the tape that marked her full maturation as a video artist, Ellen Spiro had developed a reputation as a young, gay-activist documentarian. Her first tape, *DiAna's Hair Ego* (1990), a portrait of a hair stylist and AIDS activist in rural South Carolina, was widely seen; this success was confirmed by *Greetings from Out Here* (1993), an hour-long chronicle of Spiro's travels in her native Deep South, looking for and talking with men and women who have opted against seeking the comparative anonymity and security of big-city gay communities in favor of staying at home and living openly gay lives. Spiro's early tapes reflect her unpretentious ease with her subjects, and *Greetings from Out Here,* in particular, reveals a developing sense of design reminiscent of George Kuchar's films and videos. But it was not until her second hour-long tape, this one funded by the Independent Television Service (ITVS), in Minneapolis, that Spiro's gifts found a topic that would allow her work to reach beyond the political constituency of gay activism.

Roam Sweet Home is, on one level, a continuation of the method that resulted in *Greetings from Out Here.* Again, Spiro is on the road, accompanied by her canine companion, Sam; and again, she is searching in rural America for interesting individualists. In this instance, however, Spiro's focus in the finished tape is both more diffuse and more broadly engaging. Most of *Roam Sweet Home* focuses on "Geritol gypsies," elderly wanderers of the Southwest—people at an Airstream trailer rally (actually recorded in Canada); people staying, at least temporarily, at out-of-the-way trailer parks; participants in a huge flea market in Quartzsite, Arizona—most of whom see their lives as a form of rebellion against the economic demands of more conventional society. Nearly all of those Spiro focuses on, like Spiro herself, travel with animals and seem to have developed a happy, itinerant domesticity that transforms the conventional idea of aging.

Most Americans, with the unrelenting assistance of commercial advertising, still see aging as an ongoing process of loss, as the gradual end of the good things of life. For the sweet, quirky wanderers in *Roam Sweet Home,* however, aging is a release from drudgery and restriction, an opportunity to have new experiences and to maximize the creative self. Indeed, *Roam Sweet Home* depicts their world as a cine-utopia and breathes new life into the idea of the "Old West."

Spiro sees herself as a filmmaker who works in video because its comparative inexpensiveness allows her more time for the travel and exploration necessary for her projects. But like her subjects in *Roam Sweet Home,* she has found ways of transforming what might seem a limitation into an opportunity. Spiro's dexterity with her camcorder and her evolving skill as an editor allow *Roam Sweet Home* to be one of those rare works of critical cinema that is as accessible and engaging as it is politically defiant and aesthetically accomplished.

Spiro's most recent tape, *Atomic Ed and the Black Hole* (2002), focuses on Ed Grothius, a former Los Alamos National Laboratory machinist turned atomic junk collector. "Atomic Ed" collects "nuclear waste"—nonradioactive, high-tech surplus from Los Alamos—and exhibits it in an unofficial museum of the nuclear age he calls "the Black Hole." As is true for the men and women recorded in *Roam Sweet Home,* aging for Grothius has become an opportunity for moving beyond his guilt about past failures, for overcoming limitation, and for living a more fulfilling life. For Spiro, Grothius's imagination and courage are still another example of the central quest of her work: to discover what is valuable, even productively transformative, in what conventional society and conventional media represent as beneath our notice.

I spoke with Spiro by phone in February 2002; we expanded and revised the interview on-line.

MacDonald: As a videomaker, you've always been drawn to what many might call "misfits." Does this have to do with your rebellion against your family? Or is it an extension of your family life?

Spiro: When I was young, any rebellion I ever attempted was overshadowed by that of my older brother and sister. Rebellion is the duty of preachers' kids (my father is a rabbi). By the time I became a teenager, my parents had given up on discipline; I had total freedom. Once my mother proclaimed over dinner that I had a "green thumb," to which my brother responded, "Yeah, she's really good at growing *pot!*" My mom had no idea what all those pretty green plants growing in my bedroom were. Rebellion is certainly in my blood, but I never did it just for the hell of it.

My father and my mother were also rebelling when I was young. When Dad turned forty, he bought a Harley and rode it to synagogue on Friday nights. He also acquired a pet tarantula he named Igor Arachstein, who sat on his shoulder while he watched TV. When Igor died, my dad said a prayer for him in synagogue in front of the entire congregation, never mentioning that Igor was his pet tarantula. I was holding my mouth and nose to keep from bursting out during the Yitgadel, a very solemn and serious prayer. When I was four, my mom read Betty Friedan's *The Feminine Mystique,* and—as she says—it changed her life. I think I became her living experiment in feminist practice. I was taught independence from a very young age. My mother went back to school and kept me busy for hours and hours with art supplies.

Whenever I was feeling lonely or sad, I turned to art: drawing, photography, and ad hoc construction using scavenged trash. I remember my dad taking me on motorcycle outings to search for hidden treasures in the dump, and the fright of trying to balance on the back of the Harley while holding lumber and tin for the backyard pile. I built forts where I would hide out and pretend I was a ship captain on a faraway island. My parents never said no if it involved making things.

And, thankfully, my mother forgot to teach me not to talk to strangers. Talking to strangers catalyzes all my work.

MacDonald: Were there artists in your family?

Spiro: Both my parents were raised in New Orleans in the small Jewish community there. My relatives were musicians, gamblers, shoe salesmen, and furniture makers. My paternal uncles, Ferdy and Joe Spiro, were misers who lived in a tiny, smelly hotel room together almost their entire lives. They methodically stacked their pennies into neat little towers on their dresser, beyond which were piles of cheap silverware they stole from diners. They were arrested for income tax evasion and spent several years in jail, which they loved because they got free meals and the esteemed jobs of prison librarians.

My paternal grandmother (daughter of German Jewish immigrants) was born on a farm in Brownsville, Texas, on the Texas-Mexico border. My dad tells me that she's the reason he became a rabbi—because *she* couldn't. She would stand on a milk crate and make my father sit amongst the farm animals while she preached her latest homemade sermon. If she were alive today, she might be considered a performance artist. My maternal grandfather was on a Hungarian naval ship anchored in the Gulf of Mexico, jumped ship in the middle of the night, and swam to New Orleans, with only the clothes on his back and the watch on his wrist. He was a skilled furniture builder and got a job making antique reproductions—which are now genuine antiques! My maternal great-grandfather wound up in New Orleans when his mother emigrated from Russia. She was too poor to care for him, so he wound up in a Jewish orphanage, where he learned to play the trumpet. Later he started the New Orleans Symphony, played lead trumpet in a circus band, and gave a young Al Hirt trumpet lessons. Though none of my relatives considered themselves artists, their lives were all about the creativity of survival; in some ways that's what my work is about, too.

MacDonald: Where did you get your training? What aspects of your formal or informal training have been most useful to you?

Spiro: I was exposed to photography when I was eight years old as part of a so-called talented and gifted program at my public school. We took a field trip to a darkroom, where I had a real mystical experience as I witnessed an image appearing—seemingly from nothing—onto a blank sheet of white paper sitting in a tray of liquid. By age ten I was developing film and printing pictures in my own homemade darkroom.

By the time I went to college, I knew that I should be involved in the arts, but at the University of Virginia I was lost. My dad thought I should be an architect, but my math scores were in the toilet. Fortunately, I had a photography teacher, Holly Wright—the first career artist I ever knew—who encouraged me to leave Virginia and go to Buffalo.

I dropped out of UVA during my final year and moved to Buffalo during the blizzard of 1986. Nothing ever felt more refreshing than the six feet of snow I trudged through. I was in a totally new environment with an incredible community of artists: Tony Conrad, Peter Weibel, Paul Sharits, Chris Hill, Julie Zando . . .

Imagine a tiny, run-down, *pink* storefront building in the heart of a depressed downtown Buffalo, filled with artists and filmmakers—Tony Conrad at the helm. Joints are passed, everyone is stoned, and anyone can show their latest video or film to an enthusiastic audience. Armin Heurich shows off the latest 8mm video camera and announces that it is available for *free*. Then Tony puts on one of his burnt film experiments, which we all find truly beautiful. Julie Zando shows her latest sadomasochistic lesbian psychodrama. There is some critical dialogue, lots of laughs, and the openness to consider everyone's work as interesting, somehow.

I studied with experimental filmmakers Tony Conrad and Paul Sharits in the interdisciplinary master's degree program in media studies at SUNY-Buffalo. Hollis Frampton had died, and the Vasulkas had moved to New Mexico, but their spirit and influence were very alive in Buffalo. Their names were invoked constantly, and their work was shown, studied, discussed. That experimental force still fuels many of my choices.

Chris Hill, who ran Hallwalls, and Julie Zando, who ran Squeaky Wheel Media Coalition, took me under their wings and supported my work, even some terrible crap that I'll never show to anyone—though the freedom to make terrible crap is essential to the growth of one's artistic sensibility. Learning to embrace the freedom to take ridiculous risks and embark on impossible creative adventures is the most important training I ever received—and I got it in Buffalo.

MacDonald: What came after Buffalo?

Spiro: In 1988 my political and artistic interests led me to Manhattan, where I pursued postgraduate study in the Whitney Museum Independent Study Program. I studied with Yvonne Rainer and with critics Hal Foster, Douglas Crimp, and others.

MacDonald: What was that experience like?

Spiro: I read countless critical theorists, mostly Marxists, who did *not* inspire me, probably because I couldn't understand half of what they wrote. While many students at the Whitney program got totally immersed in theory, to the point that they could sit in front of a blank canvas and think about it for a year, it had the opposite effect on me. I wanted to get out and engage in street-level reality. I'd just arrived in New York City!

Though I was born in 1964, at heart I'm a child of the sixties. I love how Marshall McLuhan talks about the present and the future and the past. I love how unrefined and spontaneous much of his writing was. McLuhan explained that people live in the rear-view mirror because it's safer; they've been there before, they feel comfort; and that anybody who looks at the present is a threat. I aspire to be one of those people who look at the present. Spontaneity is everything.

In New York City I became a founding member of DIVA-TV [Damned Interfering Video Activist Television], a collective formed to represent the AIDS crisis from the point of view of those directly affected. It was part of Act Up, which became my real postgraduate education.

MacDonald: You're part of a tradition of feminist mediamaking, but of a kind of feminism (evident early on in some of the work of Yvonne Rainer and Su Friedrich) that wants *both* to recognize political realities, even to engage them, *and* to celebrate life. And like Kathy High in her new *Animal Attraction* [2001], you repress polemic into humor, even whimsy.

Spiro: In Buffalo we often had guest artists coming through, either through Hallwalls or the University. Kathy High, Yvonne Rainer, Christine Choy, Trinh Minh-ha, and DeeDee Halleck came through town and showed their work. It was a whole new world to me; and seeing their films and videos, and meeting them in person, had a major impact. I saw that there was an amazing world of feminist filmmakers and videomakers all doing their own thing and that it was entirely accessible.

I took classes in Buffalo where I saw some incredible early feminist experimental video. Joan Jonas's *Vertical Roll* [1973] blew my mind. It was not the look or the content but the physical sensation, all that raw unapologetic anger. It was bold and uncompromising and honest. The spirit of the piece was influential: make no compromise; say what you want to say, and say it in whatever way works. I guess we are all part of some Big Movement, but I'm not good at following rules.

Sam Blumenthal, who eased Ellen Spiro's transition into New York City. Courtesy Ellen Spiro.

Kathy High was the only person I knew when I moved to Manhattan, and she immediately embraced me as a part of her community, which included a lot of feminist videomakers and filmmakers. She also got me a place to live and a job. And I barely knew her! And she hired me to work for her, as did Branda Miller and Yvonne Rainer. Not only did I become friends with these women, I became part of their creative work.

Even before I got to New York, Kathy called and asked me if I'd like to stay in a loft in Tribeca and take care of a dog, Sam, whose owner (Lyn Blumenthal) had just passed away. I said, "The dog sounds great, but what's 'a loft' and what's 'Tribeca'?" Two weeks later I'm living in a two-thousand-square-foot loft, four blocks from the World Trade Center in the not-yet-trendy Tribeca.

The dog, Sam, and I hit it off immediately. I became his foster parent, and he later accompanied me in making *Greetings from Out Here* and *Roam Sweet Home.* When people would ask me what it was like traveling alone when I was making those films, I'd look at Sam and say, "I'm not alone." Sam was no ordinary dog. In Manhattan when I'd ask, "Wanna go for a walk?" Sam would go into the kitchen, get his leash off the bottom shelf, and sit by the door, leash in mouth. When we got out on the street, Sam stopped at every intersection and waited for me. He didn't need the leash at all. He knew every fire hydrant and every pathetic little tree in Tribeca; and I quickly realized that Sam was, in fact, walking *me.* He showed me the neighborhood that had been his for ten years. Sometimes we walked half a block east to City Hall Park, sometimes three blocks west to the Hudson River, and sometimes four blocks south to the World Trade Center. We never walked north because there were fewer prime pee spots in that direction. People would recognize Sam on the street, look up at me, and wonder who the hell this person was walking Sam Blumenthal. Sam was probably a genius.

MacDonald: So how did you get started as a documentary filmmaker?

Spiro: When I moved to New York, I had no intention of making documentaries, but while documenting an AIDS quarantine controversy in South Carolina with Act Up, I met DiAna, a local African American hairdresser who'd transformed her beauty parlor into a center for AIDS and safe-sex information. Women talk about all matters personal and sexual to their hairdressers. As DiAna says in the documentary, "I'm like a priest; they confess everything to me." DiAna got involved in safe-sex education to prevent her clients, who were having unsafe sex, from dying. When I met her and saw what she was doing, I thought the whole world should know about it.

When I returned from South Carolina with footage of DiAna and her safe-sex beauty parlor, Kate Horsfield sat me down with B. Ruby Rich, then the head of the film department at the New York State Council on the Arts [NYSCA]. Ruby encouraged me to make a clip and apply to NYSCA for funding. I traded some labor for access to a three-quarter-inch editing system, made the clip and got my first grant, for fourteen thousand dollars. It seemed like a fortune, and it allowed me to master the final work on a broadcast on-line system at Downtown Community Television.

At the time, I had no clue how to make a documentary. I was very entrenched in AIDS activism and the new media coming out about it. Problem was, all the media was deadly serious, and difficult to watch. If you want to make change and reach people, you need to make media that people *want* to watch. I was moved by DiAna and her mission, *and* she made me laugh hysterically. People were scared and dying, but DiAna helped bring AIDS prevention *and* pleasure into the limelight.

I premiered *DiAna's Hair Ego,* with DiAna present, at the American Film Institute National Video Festival. From there, it went *every*where—from tiny beauty shops in Nowheresville to PBS and MoMA and the Guggenheim and around the world. DiAna herself wound up on CNN, ABC, National Public Radio, and in Washington, D.C., on a national AIDS commission.

MacDonald: If I read your work correctly, your use of video (as opposed to film) and of *medium-range* recording equipment is political, or at least media-political: you create a populist process to produce your videos.

Spiro: Well, the truth is that I don't have the patience for constant fund-raising. When I get a little grant, I stretch it as far as I can. I use grants to buy time rather than film stock. It's *time* that allows me to get what I get. I love film and video, but video is cheap, and cheap wins.

Video technology is undergoing rapid change. In my "Camcordist's Manifesto," which I wrote for the *Independent* [May 1991], I articulated my primary concerns: namely, that the notion of broadcast quality was a tool to keep people from getting their stories on television and that, really, "broadcast quality" meant anything that got broadcast. When I was advised by a supporter within PBS to lie about the acquisition format (consumer 8mm video) of *DiAna's Hair Ego,* I began to understand the political nature of "broadcast technology." Those concerns are echoed in "The Medium Is the Missed Age," also published in the *Independent* [March 2000]. I've found that the key to good video is not the lines of resolution or the number of pixels or the particular camera used, but an inventive and resourceful use of natural lighting, camera movement, and composition. A camera—video or film—is like a pencil. It can be used to create an inspired work of art, or it can be used to stab someone.

I surfed small-format video technology across fifteen years—from 8mm to Hi-8 to mini-DV and DVCAM. I find it amusing that ten-plus years after its emergence, the "indie" film world is discovering what they call "digital cinema" or "micro-cinema," and that the Sundance Film Festival waited until 2001 to have video projection. Think of all the great "films" that were never shown at Sundance simply because they were shot on video! Now, Sundance is all hyped up about video, but that boat left the dock a decade ago.

Bambi Sumpter *(left)* and DiAna DiAna, safe-sex educators in South Carolina, and the subjects of Spiro's *DiAna's Hair Ego* (1990). Courtesy Ellen Spiro.

MacDonald: Would you use more expensive technology if you could?

Spiro: Sure. I'll try anything once. I recently did a segment for HBO's *Real Sex* called "The Wrestling Party" [1999], a lesbian, nude, oil-wrestling competition in Santa Fe, New Mexico. Working with a large film crew on a relatively big budget was both liberating and frustrating. On the one hand, I felt like I had nothing to do. On the other hand, I panicked whenever the camera rolled. But it got better as we progressed, and the piece is way better than the soft porno it could have been. We ended up with a really sexy, funny little documentary that respects the subjects and does not exploit or humiliate in order to turn people on.

MacDonald: You've spent a lot of time on the road making your videos. I assume your first extended road trip was for *Greetings from Out Here.* Tell me about your life as a filmmaker-on-the-road.

Spiro: Serendipity and spontaneity are the lifeblood of my kind of filmmaking. The flip side of serendipity is misadventure, which brings its own gifts. When I realized certain situations were a little beyond my control, I would grab the camera and shoot the misadventure as it was happening.

When I was making *Greetings from Out Here,* for example, I traveled in a very cranky van that was always breaking down. In one *Greetings* scene, a mechanic explains what is wrong with my engine. He's talking about pistons moving up and down and in and out and going through the motions with his hands. I was in the backwoods of Alabama, just me and my dog, Sam, in a garage with a strange man who seemed passionate about pistons and how they go in and out and in and out. If I'd not been filming, it might have been a scary experience. But because I *was* filming, all his gestures and words ended up taking on hilarious sexual innuendo.

In making *Roam Sweet Home,* my 1967 Airstream trailer had its share of problems. The worse the problem, the crazier the adventure would become because of the parade of people that would appear to help. The section on the RV-ing women ["RV" as in recreational vehicle] in *Roam Sweet Home* is so in-depth because when I pulled into their meeting area in the middle of the Arizona desert and turned on my water, the pipes burst and flooded my trailer. Everyone came to my rescue, and we all bonded. I was suddenly one of them. They saw it as my RV-er's rite-of-passage, I guess, and were happy to participate in *Roam.*

I encountered a different kind of documentary serendipity with *Atomic Ed and the Black Hole.* That's the first piece in which I used archival footage, but I had a hell of a time getting the lab at Los Alamos to give me access to their media archive. As soon as I said I was doing something about Ed, they'd shut the door on me. I was almost ready to give up on the project when I went to my friend Jayne Loader's wedding in Dallas. Jayne was one of the directors of one of my favorite films, *The Atomic Café* [1982, co-made with Kevin Rafferty]— an inspiration for this new project. I didn't meet her husband-to-be, a Harvard physicist, until I arrived at the wedding.

After the ceremony I looked around, and I could easily tell Jayne's motley filmmaker-writer friends from Robert's tuxedo-clad physicist friends. I looked for my name tag at the tables for the motley filmmakers and didn't see it, so I glanced at another table filled with tuxedoed physicists, and there was my name tag. I sat next to a very nice man, who was telling me about his work on the big bang theory, and I asked how he liked living in Cambridge. He said that he didn't live there anymore, that he'd recently taken a position as the new deputy director of the Los Alamos National Laboratory! Then he asked me what I did, and his face turned white when I told him about my project. I told him not to worry, that I wasn't recording at the wedding. We became friends, and he gave me full access to the film archive at the lab. He single-handedly revived a project which had almost been put to rest.

My first ideas for documentaries often emerge from my desire to *go* somewhere. I cannot know what I am getting into or I'll never do it—the work is just too hard. I grew up in the South, but had to move north before I felt okay coming out of the closet. But I realized, once I was in Manhattan for a while, that I missed—in a very visceral way—the landscape, the smells, the *people* of the South. I planned *Greetings from Out Here* around my desire to hit the road and revisit the South.

I've always been drawn to tiny living spaces: forts, caves, cardboard boxes. In college I lived on a four-foot-high stairway landing, which I converted into a sort of angular cave, for two years. I never stood up. The little van I lived in during the year I made *Greetings* had everything I needed, except a shower. Everyone I met on the road wanted to see how I lived and worked in the van, and they let me use their showers. This was before digital video came on the scene, and I was using tiny Hi-8 equipment to edit. I logged all my tapes on the road, and during the logging process I'd get new ideas: certain moments would pop out and lead to new ways of connecting scenes or shooting new ones. I used the first Mac-compatible laptop, an Outbound.

Making documentaries allows me to interact with the world in a way that is more, rather than less, engaged. When I'm shooting, I'm completely immersed in what is happening in the present, working to grasp visually and aurally some gesture of those inevitably fleeting "magic" moments that might live on in a new form. It's fun, and when I'm in the middle of it, it makes me happy.

I've developed a methodology that allows meaningful stories to emerge from anyone, anywhere. The camera, if you get to know it well, becomes a kind of passport. It gives you a reason to follow your curiosity and intuition, and the power to go places you've never been. While my budgets have increased over the years, the core process has remained the same. The act of documenting other people is powerful, and one that I do not treat lightly. My small-scale crew (actually just me most of the time) results in an uninvasive process, with which I've had a lot of experience, and it allows me the time to get to know potential subjects as I would get to know a long-lost relative.

Yes, as you said at the beginning, I'm drawn to marginalized people, instinctive outsiders who are sharply critical—but in a whimsical way—of hypocritical aspects of society. I open myself to the riffs, reverberations, the trajectories of the dislocated. While few of the "stars" of my documentaries ever earned a college degree, they possess a kind of idiosyncratic intelligence which could be mistaken for mere eccentricity if not observed honestly. So, my work becomes a megaphone for seemingly ordinary people whose voices and stories might go unheard otherwise, and, rather than being a barrier, the camera becomes a bridge— an extension of myself and a vehicle to tell stories in danger of being swept under the carpet of conventional history.

MacDonald: You've certainly made clear your connection to feminist and gay communities in earlier work. But *Roam Sweet Home* and *Atomic Ed and the Black Hole* seem aimed at broader audiences. *Roam* is remarkably accessible.

Spiro: I am trying to make my work accessible—but still challenging, in a way that might change the way people think about the world. Everything I make changes *me* in some way, and that keeps me going. I use humor, eccentricity, and style to escort people through difficult subject matter. As far as I know, my audience is quite broad and diverse, because just about every American watches

TV. I would have died of boredom if I'd stayed situated in the gay and lesbian ghetto my whole life. The *world* is my ghetto.

MacDonald: It's clear that you do some creative geography in *Roam Sweet Home*. It appears to be about the Southwest, though there are images that are clearly from other locations (the sequoia tree, for example, is from California), and there's a lot of imagery that's from locales that don't declare themselves.

Spiro: The original idea, the one that ITVS and Channel Four/UK funded, was "a documentary about the permanently mobile—people, mostly older folks, living 'off the grid' and, in some cases, off the map." I started in the summer and went up to Canada to film the Airstream rally because I'd found the vintage Airstream that became my house-on-wheels and my production vehicle.

Sam was with me at that time, so a lot of the Sam footage was shot in Canada. From Canada I went through the Northwest: Idaho, Washington, Oregon. I was not as immersed in the experience of being a full-time trailer dweller at that point, so not much of that footage made it into the final piece—except for shots of Sam, who didn't become a lead character until after he died. I became so involved in mourning him (he was truly my best friend) that *Roam Sweet Home* became my tribute to him.

When I made the decision to alter my original documentary idea to include the fictional artifice of a canine narration, ITVS was not terribly happy. The quote that made it back to me from the executive director was, "Did *we* pay for the dog?" I stuck with the idea, despite what my funders thought best. I pulled through, but it was hard.

I knew that the idea of a canine narrator was a bit silly, at best; but I think *all* narrators are silly, and I wanted what Sam said to be brilliant, which is why I asked Allan Gurganus to write "Sam's voice." Allan made Sam what he was: deep, smart, insightful, poetic, funny, subversive. It was no ordinary narration. Sam was no ordinary dog.

Dogs have always been important to me. Our family dog, Eggie, was like a twin sister. I would, in fact, imagine that we *were* sisters. Having an older brother and sister who were always inflicting some form of torture upon me, I felt most secure with my connection to Eggie. Perhaps I took it too far. When I was three, I got into the habit of getting down on all fours and eating out of Eggie's bowl. My father made the mistake of telling me that if I kept eating Eggie's food, I would turn into a dog. Of course, I wanted nothing more than to *be* a dog, so I continued eating the dog food, secretly, for another year or so—which might be why I have stomach problems now! Seriously, though, dogs have taught me a lot about how to live. If you observe them, you can learn to live more freely, more fully, and more gracefully. And you can certainly learn to die in the same fashion. Sam knew all about that.

MacDonald: How long did the process of collecting the imagery for *Roam Sweet Home* take?

Ellen Spiro and Sam on the road during the shooting of *Greetings from Out Here* (1993).
Courtesy Ellen Spiro.

Spiro: I was collecting footage for over a year on the road. Some days I would
shoot nothing, other days I would shoot for hours. Sometimes it would just be
a gorgeous shot of Sam. If I got one great shot, I'd be satisfied. In Canada, when
the canola fields were blooming, vast seas of yellow flowers filled the landscape
as far as the eye could see. I shot Sam looking out, surrounded by yellow, smelling
the fields, and that became the shot where you hear my favorite words from
Sam: "I want the world for dinner." In a sense that line *was* the real meaning of
my documentary. We all know that life is short. Old people know it better
than young people do, which is why many of them have learned to live better;
but it takes a while for most people to really figure it out.

In the 1980s, when several of my twenty-something friends were dying of
AIDS, I got an up-close look at death and a deeper understanding of the
intrinsic value of life, health, and happiness. I knew I couldn't sit around waiting for life to happen. I had to eat it for dinner!

Back to your question: sometimes I would shoot things that I knew were not
relevant for the film but that intrigued me, like the site where Patty Hearst and
her Symbionese Liberation Army gang hid out in the Southern California desert.
It's not a place you can get to on paved roads; there's no signage. Some old guys
who I befriended near the Salton Sea drove me there, through bumpy miles of
salt flats and strange rock formations, in an old army jeep. The Patty Hearst

encampment is a place that, if *I* were in charge, would be a historical landmark. If nothing else, it's the location of a GAS, a great American story! When we got there, covered in salt and dust, I realized that the site would eventually get cleaned up and be no more. I shot tons of footage; if one day someone decides to make it into a historical landmark, at least there will be documentation.

I have countless little fragments of stories sitting on my shelves, tiny middles with no beginnings or ends, that never made it into anything, but might someday.

MacDonald: Roam is more fully the expression of a utopian vision of America, or really of old age, than a documentary of any particular subject.

Spiro: Thanks for getting it. I think I'm always telling multiple stories simultaneously. I provide the insider's ethnographic portrait of a marginalized subculture (aging RV-ers on the road, queer southerners, etcetera), *and* I document my personal attempt to probe the mystery, the joy, and the tragedy of existence. I'm trying to offer people a way of looking at the world that they may never have considered.

Roam Sweet Home questions a culture of materialism by looking at very happy people living on nothing. It questions the values we have in Western society, how we view work, money, family. And it looks at the inevitability of death in a context of living life to its fullest. It flips our notions of aging on their heads. By looking at the people closest to death, we actually find the people most in touch with life, living in the present and not looking backward or forward. Interspersed with these serious themes is the total hilarity and outrageousness of American "culture": the roadside signs, the giant neon cowboys, the longing for "elsewhere." One of the characters in the film, seventy-eight-year-old "Gypsy" George, says it best: "I can't say we're free spirits; we just know how the system works, and we're sidestepping the system."

There are two kinds of people who appear in my work: those who are essential to the theme (gay people, elderly people) and those who I just meet in some spontaneous encounter. The thing about traveling alone is that it gets very lonely, and all those other people out there traveling alone get lonely, too. So it's easy to find someone to talk to. When I had my little Hi-8 camera, it was only a little bit larger than my hand, and I always had it with me, always; mini-DV is the same, only better. To get the spontaneity of those moments, the camera has to be an extension of your body, and you have to be so comfortable with it that it does not draw attention to itself. For me, making video is an exchange: my subjects offer me the gift of opening up their lives, and I work to give them something back. This basic philosophy of respect, and a human-scale give-and-take, invigorates my creative work.

When I get people to sign releases, I always offer them a free video and send it to them. I've received many letters from the people in my documentaries, usually asking for more copies to give to their friends. Truth is, everyone wants to be on TV. In America that's the ultimate form of legitimation, for better or, in the case of network schlockumentaries (so-called reality TV), for worse.

After mastering the technical skills, the challenge lies in the development of one's self through the creative process. It's an approach that transforms all aspects of one's intellectual and creative life.

MacDonald: Roam Sweet Home is your *Easy Rider,* your *Natural Born Killers,* but yours is a joyous world. Did you have popular cinema, and the buddy film in particular, in mind when you were making *Roam Sweet Home?*

Spiro: Truthfully, I'm somewhat detached from popular culture, especially from television and the movies. I had Steinbeck's *Travels with Charlie* [1961] in mind when I made *Greetings from Out Here* and *Roam Sweet Home,* but not the Hollywood buddy movie. I've never been able to critically examine Hollywood, just as I've never been able to critically examine a hot fudge sundae. It tastes good while I'm eating it, but afterwards I often get a stomachache. But I did love *Thelma and Louise* [1991] and *Badlands* [1974].

MacDonald: You've been working on *Atomic Ed and the Black Hole* for a number of years. How has this new project evolved?

Spiro: All my documentaries overlap in some way or another. I was in Santa Fe shooting *Roam Sweet Home,* and I picked up one of those classified ad newspapers in a Seven-Eleven store and found an ad that read: "ATTENTION TINKERERS, INVENTORS, ARTISTS, MAD SCIENTISTS, PACKRATS! COME TO THE BLACK HOLE FOR SURPLUS FROM LOS ALAMOS NATIONAL LABORATORY." How could I resist?

I met Ed on that trip, shot some footage with him, and kept shooting every year for five years. I applied and was rejected for ITVS funding, which felt like a major setback, as I had done two successful ITVS-funded projects already *[Greetings from Out Here* and *Roam Sweet Home].* But, then, the Rockefeller Foundation and the New York State Council on the Arts surprised me with grants, and I was off and running.

In *Atomic Ed and the Black Hole* the creativity of survival is, again, the theme. How do you live with the fact that you helped build something that killed thousands of people within seconds? Atomic Ed does it by injecting humor into every part of his daily life; it's an antidote to the seriousness of the nuclear disasters he helped create and wants, more than anything, to prevent from ever happening again.

When the fire swept through Los Alamos in 2000, suddenly there was all this drama, and Atomic Ed was caught in the middle of it, literally. The Black Hole would have been destroyed if Ed and his sidekicks had not battled the fire for two straight days. Ed was arrested for refusing to evacuate the town (he was busy putting out small spot fires), and I acquired the live news coverage of his arrest. When I finished the twenty-seven-minute cut, HBO/Cinemax commissioned me to make a longer version, which I recently finished.

MacDonald: Other than grants, how have you supported yourself and your filmmaking?

Ed Grothius *(front)* and friends, focus of Spiro's *Atomic Ed and the Black Hole* (2002). Photograph by Teri Thomson Randall. Courtesy Ellen Spiro.

Spiro: With television sales, work-for-hire, digital cinematography for other people's projects, renting nine-gigabyte hard drives over the Internet (in the 1990s)—all kinds of ways. A couple of years ago, a local Austin shampoo mogul traded me a houseboat on Lake Travis in Austin in exchange for my making a video about him. I spent far too much time making *The Shampoo King* [1999], and now the houseboat motor is dead. But I enjoy wheeling and dealing, and the houseboat was fun while it lasted.

But, to get back to your point, making money and dealing with money is a creative process. I love bartering. It's fun to make money, and it's fun to spend it if you spend it gracefully. Too many artists are phobic about money and end up broke and without health insurance. I've never been able to see any glamour in poverty.

MacDonald: Have you done a lot of touring with your work? What kinds of reception have you had?

Spiro: My favorite trips have been to Deep South boonie towns, the Southwest (especially Arizona), and all my stops in Australia and New Zealand.

MacDonald: Have you ever had hostile audiences?

Spiro: I rarely get hostile audiences at in-person screenings, because those people are coming to see my work because they want to see it; but broadcasters have gotten hostile phone calls. The most came from London during the airing of *Greetings from Out Here* on Channel 4. They actually faxed the hostile comments to me! I don't know what they were thinking; it doesn't brighten your day to have someone say that you have no right to put happy gay people (is that redundant?) on television!

MacDonald: You've recently gotten tenure at the University of Texas. Can you teach *and* do the kinds of work you want to do? What's the film and video scene like in Austin?

Spiro: Teaching is great when it fuels one's work, which it does if you have time in between to make things. Teaching students to make their own docs brings another kind of pleasure—that vicarious experience of being midwife to ten or twenty short pieces during a semester. The secret to being a good teacher is allowing your students to provoke and challenge you, in the same way that your documentary subjects do. A classroom without conflict and dialogue is a place I never want to be. But I *must* have time to do my own work. Soon, I'll be teaching only one semester a year. Luckily, my dean is very supportive of my creative work. I wouldn't be there otherwise.

The film and video scene in Austin is populated by an amazing mix of wonderful weirdos all doing their own thing. Austin thinks of itself as a fringe town. Of course, as soon as a place bills itself as edgy, you know the edge is gone. But I do love Austin, despite the hype. Problem with living in any city is that nothing holds a candle to Manhattan. Manhattan is a volatile, crackling, sizzling, forever mind-blowing mix of everything that one can hope for in a city. New York does not need to inflate itself because it's *so* big there's no way for it to get any bigger. I think of New York as a third parent, really. My mom and dad sent me out into the world; I took myself to Buffalo; and Manhattan raised me from there.

MacDonald: What filmmakers and videomakers do you particularly admire? Whose work feeds yours?

Spiro: I love Alan Berliner's work, his fastidiousness and sense of rhythm. I show *Nobody's Business* [1996] every semester, and I never tire of it. That to me is a great work, something you can watch over and over and always find something new to appreciate. I love Jem Cohen's work, too. He's far less verbal than Berliner, but his images are extremely poetic, little magic fleeting glimpses of moments that nonpoets would ever notice, images that stay in your head for years. I guess all my favorite makers are poets of a sort, who are using a medium that reaches a mass audience.

And then there's George Kuchar—not a poet in the sense of the others I've mentioned, but a wild and crazy media cowboy who spits it all out and does not look back, the Jackson Pollock of video. "Meticulous" is not in Kuchar's vocabulary, but I admire his constant spewing forth of anything he feels like spewing forth. He's not bogged down. I'll never forget when he was attacked at the

Flaherty Seminar for shooting his turd going down the toilet [see Scott Mac-Donald, "Storm Chaser: An Interview with George Kuchar about the Weather Diaries," *Independent* 20, no. 6 (July 1997), for details about this event]. It was at that moment that everyone in the audience had to decide where they stood on Kuchar's work. I mentioned, before presenting *DiAna's Hair Ego* at that Flaherty, what an inspiration Kuchar had been to me, if not for the content of his work, for his use of process *as* content.

MacDonald: Do you have a sense of your next project? What would you like to do?

Spiro: Atomic Ed is going to build a museum, and I would like to make a documentary about that. Ed is trying to get Ted Turner involved, but regardless of whether Ted wants to help, I still want to make the film, *The Museum of Nuclear Waste.* And I have a *lot* of tapes, fragments of stories, on the shelves, like embryos sitting in petri dishes. I'm waiting to see which one grows into something.

You know, I almost had a nervous breakdown at the University of Virginia over what I was going to do next with my life. So I fled to Buffalo, where I figured out what I wanted to do, which is what I'd been doing since I was a child: talking to strangers, capturing the world visually, constructing things. Earlier in life, I didn't know how to make that into an adult life—I was terrified of being an adult—and then, somewhere along the way, I realized I didn't have to "grow up"!

I still have architectural cravings. I'm fascinated by alternative forms of architecture: earthships, straw bale homes, Gaudi buildings, houseboats, trailers, yurts, concrete domes, huts, submarines. If I run out of money, I'll pursue my entrepreneurial dream: a dog motel. The dogs would have an elaborate structure in which to live, and each doggie abode would be inspired by a cave—something similar to those ancient Indian caves at Bandelier National Monument in New Mexico. The dogs could stay for a day or several months or indefinitely. The longer the stay, the cheaper the rate. The motel would be great for people who travel a lot and cannot always take their dogs with them. We would cater to pit bulls, greyhounds, mutts, and other canine outcasts. The pit bulls would be sure not to let anyone in the back garden, where we would be growing massive amounts of marijuana to fund our experimental documentary projects. Just kidding!

Filmography

In the following listing, the title of each film (and video) is followed by the year in which the piece was completed; the format in which the piece was made; the length to the nearest quarter minute; and whether the piece is in black and white and/or color, silent and/or sound. Where multiple works are listed for a given year, they are arranged in alphabetical order. While I have tried to use a common format for all the filmographies, because of the disparities between the careers discussed in *A Critical Cinema 4,* some adjustments to my preferred format were requested by filmmakers or required by the nature of particular careers.

Primary rental sources are indicated in parentheses, often using the abbreviations in the following list. In some cases, a particular work is distributed by an individual or by a distributor not listed here; in these instances, the contact information is supplied with the first listing of this distributor only.

CC   Canyon Cinema, 145 Ninth Street, Suite 260, San Francisco, CA 94103; 415-626-2255; www.canyoncinema.com. Note: in my experience, Canyon Cinema is the most dependable 16mm film distributor in the United States, both in terms of its care in getting prints to exhibitors and in terms of the quality of the prints it distributes.

CFDC   Canadian Filmmakers Distribution Centre, Suite 220, 37 Hanna Ave., Toronto, Ontario, M6K 1W8 Canada; 416-588-0725; www.cfmdc.org.

EAI   Electronic Arts Intermix, 535 W. 22th Street, 5th Floor, New York, NY 10011; 212-337-0680; www.eai.org.

Facets   Facets Multimedia, 1517 W. Fullerton Ave., Chicago, IL 60614; 773-281-9075; www.facets.org.

FMC   Film-makers' Cooperative, c/o Clocktower Gallery, 108 Leonard St., New York, NY 10013; 212-267-5665; www.film-makerscoop.com.

LC   Lightcone, 12 rue des Vignoles, 75020 Paris, France; 33 (0) 1 46 59 03 12; www.lightcone.org.

LUX   LUX, 18 Shacklewell Lane, London E8 2EZ, UK; 44 (0) 20 7503 3980; www.lux.org.uk.

MoMA   Museum of Modern Art Circulating Film and Video Library, 11 W. 53rd St., New York, NY 10019; 212-708-9530.

NA   Not available, so far as I am aware.

VDB   Video Data Bank, 112 S. Michigan Ave., Chicago, IL 60603; 312-345-3550; www.vdb.org.

WMM   Women Make Movies, 462 Broadway, Suite 500WS, New York, NY 10013; 212-925-0606 ext. 320; www.wmm.com.

Chantal Akerman

I am grateful to Ivone Margulies for the Akerman filmography she included in her *Nothing Happens: Chantal Akerman's Hyperrealist Everyday* (Durham, N.C.: Duke University Press, 1996). In a number of cases I have not been able to locate distributors for Akerman's work, and a good many of her films that are available in the United States are available only as commercial videos.

Saute ma ville (Blow Up My Town). 1968. 35mm; 13 minutes; black and white; sound (commercial video).

L'Enfant aimé ou Je joue à être une femme mariée (The Beloved Child or I Play at Being a Married Woman). 1971. 16mm; 35 minutes; black and white; sound (Akerman, Chantakerman@aol.com).

La Chambre 1 (The Room 1). 1972. 16mm; 11 minutes; color; sound (Akerman).

La Chambre 2. 1972. 16mm; 7 minutes; color; silent (Akerman).

Hôtel Monterey. 1972. 16mm; 65 minutes; color; silent (LC, commercial video).

Le 15/8 (codirected with Samy Szlingerbaum). 1973. 16mm; 42 minutes; black and white; sound (Akerman).

Hanging Out Yonkers 1973. 1973. 16mm; 90 minutes; color; sound (unfinished).

Je tu il elle (I You He She). 1974. 35mm; 90 minutes; black and white; sound (commercial video, Facets).

Jeanne Dielman, 23 Quai du Commerce, 1080 Bruxelles. 1975. 35mm; 200 minutes; color; sound (New Yorker Films; 212–645–4600; www.newyorkerfilms.com).

News from Home. 1976. 16mm; 85 minutes; color; sound (Facets).

Les Rendez-vous d'Anna (Meetings with Anna). 1978. 35mm; 127 minutes; color; sound (commercial video, Facets).

Dis-moi (Tell Me). 1980. 16mm; 45 minutes; color; sound (Akerman).

Tout une nuit (All Night Long). 1982. 35mm; 89 minutes; color; sound (commercial video, Facets).

Les Années 80 (The Eighties). 1983. 35mm/video; 82 minutes; color; sound (commercial video, Facets).

L'Homme à la valise (The Man with the Suitcase). 1983. 16mm; 60 minutes; color; sound (Akerman).

Un Jour Pina m'a demandé (One Day Pina Asked Me). 1983. 16mm; 57 minutes; color; sound (Akerman).

Family Business: Chantal Akerman Speaks about Film. 1984. 16mm; 18 minutes; color; sound (Akerman).

J'ai faim, J'ai froid (I'm Hungry, I'm Cold). 1984. 16mm; 12 minutes; black and white; sound (commercial video).

Lettre de cinéaste (A Filmmaker's Letter). 1984. 16mm; 8 minutes; color; sound (Akerman).

New York, New York bis. 1984. 35mm; 8 minutes; black and white; sound (NA, lost).

Golden Eighties (aka *Window Shopping*). 1985. 35mm; 96 minutes; color; sound (commercial video, Facets).

Letters Home. 1986. Video; 100 minutes; color; sound (Akerman).

Mallet-Stevens. 1986. Video; 7 minutes; color; sound (Akerman).

Le Marteau (The Hammer). 1986. Video; 4 minutes; color; sound (Akerman).

La Paresse (Sloth). 1986. 35mm; 14 minutes; color; sound (Akerman).

Histoires d'Amérique (American Stories/*Food, Family and Philosophy*). 1988. 35mm; 92 minutes; color; sound (Akerman).

Les Trois dernières sonates de Franz Schubert (Franz Schubert's Last Three Sonatas). 1989. Video; 49 minutes; color; sound (Akerman).

Trois Strophes sur le nom de Sacher (Three Stanzas on the Name Sacher, by Henry Dutilleux). 1989. Video; 12 minutes; color; sound (Akerman).

Contre l'oubli (Lest We Forget). 1991. 35mm; 110 minutes; color; sound (Akerman).

Nuit et Jour (Night and Day). 1991. 35mm; 90 minutes; color; sound (Facets).

Le Déménagement (Moving In). 1992. 35mm; 42 minutes; black and white; sound (Akerman).

D'Est (From the East). 1993. 35mm; 107 minutes; color; sound (First Run Features, www.firstrunfeatures.com).

Portrait d'une jeune fille de la fin des années 60, à Bruxelles (Portrait of a Young Girl from the Late Sixties in Brussels). 1993. 35mm; 60 minutes; color; sound.

Chantal Akerman par Chantal Akerman (episode of *Cineastes de Notre Temps*). 1996. Video; 60 minutes; color; sound (Akerman).

Un divan à New York (A Couch in New York). 1996. 35mm; 104 minutes; color; sound (commercial video, Facets).

La Captive. 2000. 35mm; 118 minutes; color; sound (commercial video).

Sud (The South). 2000. Video; 71 minutes; color; sound (First Run Features).

De l'autre côté (From the Other Side). 2002. Video; 103 minutes; color; sound (First Run Features).

Demain en déménage. 2004. 35mm; 110 minutes; color; sound (commercial video).

Stan Brakhage

Since Brakhage's death in March 2003, a good deal of energy has been focused on assembling something like a definitive filmography of his productive career. This process is complicated not only by the fact that Brakhage was prolific—he made well over three hundred films—but by the fact that details about many of the films (completion dates and lengths, especially) have been listed differently in difference sources. Rather than compound the confusion that already exists by publishing still another tentative filmography, I am directing those interested in the shape of Brakhage's career and in the specifics of his films to Fred Camper's Web site. Camper, who has always been one of Brakhage's best and most devoted scholars, has taken upon himself the important though formidable task of providing scholars with as complete and accurate a filmography as is possible for Brakhage. This filmography will likely be under construction for some time, but Camper's Web site is and will continue to be the most definitive source for information about Brakhage's work for some time to come: http://www.fredcamper.com/Brakhage/Filmography.html.

Lawrence Brose

Light Transcends. 1981. 16mm; 3½ minutes; color; sound (Brose: www
.lawrencebrose.com).
Valley of the Obelisk. 1981. 16mm; 28 minutes; color; sound (Brose).
Winter Lady. 1981. 16mm; 12 minutes; color; silent (Brose).
Doty. 1982. 16mm; 16 minutes; color; sound (Brose).
Linda (a Portrait). 1982. 16mm; 3½ minutes; color; silent (Brose).
A Lonenight Improvisation. 1982. 16mm; 3 minutes; black and white; silent (Brose).
That's Life. 1982. 16mm; 5 minutes; black and white; sound (Brose).
By One's Own Hand. 1983. 16mm; 3½ minutes; black and white; silent (Brose).
A Peering. 1983. 16mm; 6 minutes; black and white/color; sound (Brose).
Watermark. 1983. 16mm; 6 minutes; black and white/color; silent (Brose).
Passages. 1984. 16mm; 5 minutes; black and white/color; silent (Brose).
Untitled. 1984. 16mm; 3½ minutes; black and white; silent (Brose).
No Photo Required. 1985. 16mm; 4 minutes; color; sound (Brose)
An Individual Desires Solution. 1986. Super-8mm; 13 minutes; color; sound (Brose).
Hyacinth Fire. 1989. 16mm; 40 minutes; color; sound (Brose).
Chamnan (part 1 of *Films for Music for Film*). 1990. 16mm; 13 minutes; black and
white; sound (CC, LC, LUX).
Everbest, Virgil (part 2 of *Films for Music for Film*). 1990. 16mm; 8 minutes; black
and white/color; sound (CC, LC, LUX).
Long Eyes of Earth (part 3 of *Films for Music for Film*). 1990. 16mm; 10 minutes;
black and white/color; sound (CC, LC, LUX).
Ryoanji (part 5 of *Films for Music for Film*). 1990. 16mm; 21 minutes; color; sound
(CC, LC).
Study #15 (part 6 of *Films for Music for Film*). 1990. 16mm; 1 minute; black and
white; sound (CC, LC, LUX).
War Songs (part 4 of *Films for Music for Film*). 1990. 16mm; black and white/color;
sound (CC, LC, LUX).
An Individual Desires Solution. 1991. 16mm; 16 minutes; black and white/color;
sound (CC).

CAGE: A Filmic Circus on Metaphors on Vision. 1995. Video; 50 minutes; color; sound (Brose).

De Profundis. 1997. 16mm; 65 minutes; color; sound (Brose, LC).

Abigail Child

Except the People (co-made with Jon Child). 1970. 16mm; 25 minutes; color; sound (Child, achild@mindspring.com).

Game (co-made with Jon Child). 1972. 16mm; 40 minutes; black and white; sound (Child).

Mother Story. 1973. 16mm; 5 minutes; color; sound (Child).

Savage Streets (for NBC, New York). 1973. 16mm; 28 minutes; color; sound (Child).

Working Mothers (for NBC, New York; Child believes this was the title). 1973. 16mm; 28 minutes; color; sound (NA).

Between Times (for NBC, New York). 1975. 16mm; 28 minutes; color; sound (NA).

Tar Garden. 1975. 16mm; 55 minutes; color; sound (Child).

Sisters (for NBC, New York; Child believes this was the title). 1976. 16mm; 28 minutes; color; sound (NA).

Daylight Test Section. 1977. 16mm; 4 minutes; color; silent (CC).

Peripeteia 1. 1977. 16mm; 9 minutes; color; silent (CC).

Some Exterior Presence. 1977. 16mm; 8 minutes; color; silent (CC).

Peripeteia 2. 1978. 16mm; 12 minutes; color; silent (Child).

Ornamentals. 1979. 16mm; 10 minutes; color; silent (CC, FMC).

Pacific Far East Line. 1979. 16mm; 12 minutes; color; silent (CC).

Prefaces (part 1 of *Is This What You Were Born For?*). 1981. 16mm; 10 minutes; color; sound (CC, FMC, LUX).

Mutiny (part 3 of *Is This What You Were Born For?*). 1983. 16mm; 11 minutes; color; sound (CC, FMC, LC).

Covert Action (part 4 of *Is This What You Were Born For?*). 1984. 16mm; 11 minutes; black and white; sound (CC, CFDC, FMC, LC, LUX).

Perils (part 5 of *Is This What You Were Born For?*). 1986. 16mm; 5 minutes; black and white; sound (CC, CFDC, FMC, LUX).

Mayhem (part 6 of *Is This What You Were Born For?*). 1987. 16mm; 20 minutes; black and white; sound (CC, CFDC, FMC, LUX).

Both (part 2 of *Is This What You Were Born For?*). 1988. 16mm; 3 minutes; black and white; silent (CC, FMC).

Mercy (part 7 of *Is This What You Were Born For?*). 1989. 16mm; 10 minutes; color; sound (CC, CFDC, FMC, LUX).

Swamp (with writer Sarah Schulman). 1991. Video; 33 minutes; color; sound (CC).

Swamp Songs (with composer Ikue Mori). 1991. Interactive performance video; 15 minutes; color; sound (Child).

8 Million (with composer Ikue Mori). 1992. Video; 25 minutes; color; sound (Child, LC).

Through the Looking Glass (with actress-writer Lenora Champagne). 1995. Video; 12 minutes; color; sound (Child).

B/Side. 1996. 16mm; 38 minutes; color; sound (CC, LC).

Below the New: A Russian Chronicle. 1999. Video; 25 minutes; color; sound (Child).
Surface Noise. 2000. 16mm; 18 minutes; black and white/color; sound (CC, LUX).
Dark Dark. 2001. 16mm; 16 minutes; black and white; sound (CC).
Cake and Steak. 2002. Digital video (loop); 2 minutes; color; sound (Child).
Subtalk (co-made with Benton Bainbridge and Eric Rosenzveig). 2002. Digital video; 4½ minutes; color; sound (Child).
Where the Girls Are. 2002. Digital video; 4 minutes; color; sound (Child).
Party Girls. 2003. Digital video (loop); 1½ minutes; color; sound (Child).

Peter Forgács

Forgács has made photographs, paintings, graphic pieces, performance pieces, and installations, as well as videos; the following listing includes only videos, video installations, and performances with video. For information about other media, contact Forgács: 1121 Budapest, Mese köz 10, Hungary; fax +36-1-200-76-24, forgax@axelero.hu; and Cesar Messemaker, LUMEN Film: cesarmessemaker@lumenfilm.demon.nl.

Inauguration (performed with Hámos Gusztáv and László Lugo Lugosi). 1980. Video performance at Young Artists Club.
Dixi and Pixi (performed with Dixi, Group 180, László Lugo Lugosi). 1983. Video performance at Kassak Culture Center.
Golden Age. 1985. Video; 20 minutes; color; sound (Forgács; see address above).
Iron Age. 1985. Video; 50 minutes; color; sound (Forgács).
Spinoza Ruckwerz. 1985. 35mm; 5 minutes; color; sound (Forgács).
Work Desk (performed with Tibor Szemző). 1985. Video performance.
The Portrait of Leopold Szondi. 1986. Video; 60 minutes; color; sound (Forgács).
Episodes from the Life of Professor M. F. 1987. Video; 110 minutes; color; sound (Forgács).
The Bartos Family (part 1 of *Private Hungary*). 1988. Video; 58¾ minutes; color; sound (Forgács).
Dusi and Jenő (part 2 of *Private Hungary*). 1989. Video; 45 minutes; color; sound (EAI).
Either—Or (part 3 of *Private Hungary*). 1989. Video; 43 minutes; color; sound (EAI).
The Diary of Mr. N. (part 4 of *Private Hungary*). 1990. Video; 51 minutes; color; sound (EAI).
D. Film (part 5 of *Private Hungary*). 1991. Video; 45 minutes; color; sound (Forgács).
Hungarian Video Kitchen Art. 1991. Video installation (Forgács).
Márai: Herbal. 1991. Video; 30 minutes; color; sound (Forgács).
Photographed by L. Dudás (part 6 of *Private Hungary*). 1991. Video; 45 minutes; color; sound (Forgács).
Thee A'El Greco. 1991. Video installation (Forgács).
Bourgeois Dictionary (part 7 of *Private Hungary*). 1992. Video; 49 minutes; color; sound (EAI).
The Case of My Room. 1992. Video installation (Forgács).
Two Nests and Other Things. 1992. Video installation (Forgács).

Wittgenstein Tractatus. 1992. Video; 32 minutes; color; sound (EAI).

Arizona Diary. 1993. Video; 53 minutes; color; sound (Forgács).

Culture Shavings. 1993. Video; 43 minutes; color; sound (Forgács).

Freud and Vienna (part 1 of *Conversations on Psychoanalysis*). 1993. Video; 53 minutes; color; sound (Forgács).

Hungarian Totem. 1993. Video installation (Forgács).

Psychoanalysis and Society (part 4 of *Conversations on Psychoanalysis*). 1993. Video; 55 minutes; color; sound (Forgács).

Psychoanalysis as Therapy (part 5 of *Conversations on Psychoanalysis*). 1993. Video; 58 minutes; color; sound (Forgács).

The Psychoanalytic View of Man (part 3 of *Conversations on Psychoanalysis*). 1993. Video; 55 minutes; color; sound (Forgács).

Sándor Ferenczi and the Budapest School of Psychoanalysis (part 2 of *Conversations on Psychoanalysis*). 1993. Video; 53 minutes; color; sound (Forgács).

Totem. 1993. Video; 30 minutes; color; sound (EAI).

Meanwhile, Somewhere. 1994. Video; 52 minutes; color; sound (Forgács).

The Notes of a Lady (part 8 of *Private Hungary*). 1994. Video; 48 minutes; color; sound (Forgács).

Simply Happy. 1994. Video; 46 and 72 minutes; color; sound (LUMEN Film; see address above).

Inventory. 1995. Three video installations: "Dream Inventory," "Wittgenstein Inventory," and "Totem" (Forgács).

Free Fall (part 10 of *Private Hungary*). 1996. Video; 75 minutes; color; sound (Forgács).

The Land of Nothing (part 9 of *Private Hungary*). 1996. Video; 62 minutes; color; sound (Forgács).

Class Lot (part 11 of *Private Hungary*). 1997. Video; 52 minutes; color; sound (Forgács).

The Hung Aryan. 1997. Video installation (Forgács).

Kádár's Kiss (part 12 of *Private Hungary*). 1997. Video; 52 minutes; color; sound (Forgács).

The Maelstrom: A Family Chronicle. 1997. Video; 60 minutes; color; sound (LUMEN Film).

. . . Otherwise (co-made with Zoltán Vida). 1997. Video; 2½ minutes; color; sound (Forgács).

The Danube Exodus. 1998. Video; 60 minutes; color; sound (LUMEN Film).

Angelos' Film. 1999. Video; 60 minutes; color; sound (LUMEN Film).

The Visit. 2000. Video installation (Forgács).

A Bibó Reader (part 13 of *Private Hungary*). 2001. Video; 69 minutes; color; sound (Forgács).

The Danube Exodus—the Rippling Currents of the River. 2001. DVD/video installation (Forgács).

The Bishops' Garden (part 14 of *Private Hungary*). 2002. Video; 56½ minutes; color; sound (Forgács).

Der Kaiser auf dem Spaziergang. 2003. DVD, a part of Light and Image project/ Aegina; 15½ minutes (Netherlands Filmmuseum, www.nfm.nl).

Do You Really Love Me? 2003. Video (three-screen); 33 minutes; color; sound (Forgács).

Mutual Analysis. 2003. Video; 12 minutes; color; sound (Forgács).

Jill Godmilow

Tales (co-made with Cassandra Gerstein). 1969. 16mm; 70 minutes; color; sound (NA).

Antonia: A Portrait of the Woman (co-made with Judy Collins). 1974. 16mm; 58 minutes; color; sound (Direct Cinema; 310-636-8200; directcinema.com; Facets; Pioneer Entertainment [DVD]).

Nevelson in Process (co-made with Susan Fanshel). 1976. 16mm; 30 minutes; color; Sound (Home Vision Entertainment, Media for the Arts).

The Popovich Brothers of South Chicago. 1977. 16mm; 60 minutes; color; sound (Facets).

The Odyssey Tapes (co-made with Susan Fanshel). 1978. Video; 30 minutes; color; sound (MoMA).

The Vigil. 1979. Video; 40 minutes; color; sound (NA).

With Grotowski, at Nienadowka. 1979. Video; 60 minutes; color; sound (NA).

Far from Poland. 1984. 16mm; 110 minutes; color; sound (WMM, Facets).

Waiting for the Moon. 1987. 35mm; 88 minutes; color; sound (Facets).

Roy Cohn/Jack Smith. 1995. 16mm; 88 minutes; color; sound (Facets, Godmilow: Jill.Godmilow.l@nd.edu).

What's Underground about Marshmallows: Ron Vawter Performs Jack Smith. 1996. 16mm; 60 minutes; color; sound (Facets).

What Farocki Taught. 1998. 16mm; 30 minutes; color; sound (MoMA, VDB).

Lear '97 Archive (Condensed). 2002. A 3-disk DVD; 180 minutes; color; sound (Facets, Godmilow)

Peter Kubelka

Mosaik im Vertrauen. 1955. 16mm; 16½ minutes; black and white/color; silent (CC, CD [Cinedoc/Paris Films Coop; www.cinedoc.org], FMC, LC, LUX, Sixpack [Neubaugasse 45/13, P.O. Box 197, A-1071 Vienna, Austria; 43-1-526-09-90-0; www.sixpackfilm.com; in USA: Ralph McKay, amovie@earthlink.net]).

Adebar. 1957. 35mm/16mm; 1½ minutes; black and white; sound (CC, CD, FMC, LC, LUX, Sixpack).

Schwechater. 1958. 35mm/16mm; 1 minute; color; sound (CC, CD, FMC, LC, LUX, Sixpack).

Arnulf Rainer. 1960. 6½ minutes; black and white; sound (CC, CD, FMC, LC, LUX, Sixpack).

Unsere Afrikareise (Our Trip to Africa). 1966. 16mm; 2½ minutes; color; sound (CC, CD, FMC, LC, LUX, Sixpack).

Pause! 1977. 16mm; 11¾ minutes; color; sound (CC, CD, FMC, Sixpack).

Jim McBride

David Holzman's Diary. 1967. 16mm; 74 minutes; black and white; sound (Facets, Direct Cinema; 310-636-8200; directcinema.com).

My Girlfriend's Wedding. 1969. 16mm; c. 60 minutes; color; sound (NA).

Glen and Randa (director/co-screenplay). 1971. 16mm; 94 minutes; color; sound (Facets).

Pictures from Life's Other Side. 1972. 16mm; c. 60 minutes; black and white; sound (NA).

Hot Times (McBride's title: *A Hard Day for Archie;* director/screenplay). 1974. 35mm; 80 minutes; color; sound.

Breathless (director/co-screenplay). 1983. 35mm; 105 minutes; color; sound (commercial video).

"The Once and Future King" (episode of *The Twilight Zone*). 1986. 35mm; c. 30 minutes; color; sound.

The Big Easy. 1987. 35mm; 101 minutes; color; sound (commercial video: Vidmark/Trimark).

Great Balls of Fire! (director/co-screenplay). 1989. 35mm; 108 minutes; color; sound (commercial video: Orion Home Video).

"Daddy's Little Girl" (episode of *The Wonder Years*). 1990. 35mm; c. 30 minutes; color; sound.

"The Glee Club" (episode of *The Wonder Years*). 1990. 35mm; c. 30 minutes; color; sound.

Blood Ties (pilot for Fox TV). 1991. 35mm; 84 minutes; color; sound (commercial video: New Horizons Home Video).

"Christmas Party" (episode of *The Wonder Years*). c. 1991. 35mm; c. 30 minutes; color; sound.

The Wrong Man. 1993. 35mm; 104 minutes; color; sound (commercial video: Paramount).

Uncovered (The Flemish Board) (director/co-screenplay). 1994. 35mm; 107 minutes; color; sound (commercial video).

"Fearless" (episode of *The Fallen Angels,* Showtime). 1995. 35mm; c. 30 minutes; color; sound.

The Informant (aka *Field of Blood,* Showtime). 1996. 35mm; 105 minutes; color; sound (commercial video: Paramount).

Pronto (Showtime). 1996. 35mm; 100 minutes; color; sound (Paramount).

Dead by Midnight (ABC). 1997. 35mm; c. 90 minutes; color; sound.

The Informant (Showtime). 1997. 35mm; 106 minutes; color; sound (Paramount).

Meat Loaf: To Hell and Back (VH-1). 2000. 35mm; 90 minutes; color; sound (Paramount).

"Brotherhood" (episode of *Six Feet Under*) 2001. 35mm; 60 minutes; color; sound (commercial video: HBO Home Video).

Shirin Neshat

The Shadow under the Web. 1997. Four-screen video installation; color; sound (Barbara Gladstone Gallery, 515 West 24th St., New York, NY 10011; 212-206-9300).

Turbulent. 1998. 16mm/2-screen installation; 10 minutes; black and white; sound (Barbara Gladstone).

Rapture. 1999. 16mm/2-screen installation; 13 minutes; black and white; sound (Barbara Gladstone).

Soliloquy. 1999. 16mm/2-screen installation; 17 minutes; color; sound (Barbara Gladstone).

Fervor. 2000. 16mm/2-screen installation; 10 minutes; black and white; sound (Barbara Gladstone).

Passage. 2001. 35mm/installation; 11½ minutes; color; sound (Barbara Gladstone).

Possessed. 2001. 35mm/installation; 12 minutes; black and white; sound (Barbara Gladstone).

Pulse. 2001. 16mm/installation; 7½ minutes; black and white; sound (Barbara Gladstone).

Tooba. 2002. 35mm/2-screen installation; 12¾ minutes; color; sound (Barbara Gladstone).

The Last Word. 2003. 35mm; 20 minutes; color; sound (Barbara Gladstone).

Mahdokht. 2004. 35mm/3-screen installation; 11 minutes; color; sound (Barbara Gladstone).

Ellen Spiro

DiAna's Hair Ego. 1990. Video; 28 minutes; color; sound (VDB, WMM).

(In)Visible Women (co-made with Marina Alvarez). 1991. Video; 28 minutes; color; sound (VDB, WMM).

Greetings from Out Here. 1993. Video; 56 minutes; color; sound (VDB).

Roam Sweet Home. 1997. Video; 56 minutes; color; sound (VDB).

The Shampoo King. 1998. Video; 15 minutes; color; sound (Spiro, spirovich@yahoo.com).

Speak Out. 1998. Video; 30 minutes; color; sound (Spiro).

Texas Splash Bash. 1999. Video; 15 minutes; color; sound (Spiro).

"The Wrestling Party" (episode of *Real Sex*). 1999. Video; 15 minutes; color; sound (HBO).

Atomic Ed and the Black Hole. 2002. Video; 39 minutes; color; sound (HBO, VDB).

Chuck Workman

Workman has worked in a variety of ways. For years, he produced and directed advertisements; and he made trailers for such feature films as *Close Encounters of the Third Kind; 1941; Paris, Texas; Salvador; Star Wars;* and *The Wiz.* I am including as complete a listing of his work in various capacities as I can assemble—but much of his early and more recent commercial work is left out of this listing.

As editor:

Monday's Child (directed by Leopoldo Torre-Nilsson). 1967.

The Traitors of San Angel (directed by Leopoldo Torre-Nilsson). 1967.

The Designers (documentary on the making of *Goodbye, Mr. Chips* [1969]). 1969. 35mm; 30 minutes; color; sound (MGM).

With Respect to Mr. Lester (promotional documentary on Richard Lester). 1970. 35mm; 20 minutes; color; sound (United Artists).

As director of special sequences and/or montages:

Cuba Crossing (also known as *Kill Castro, The Mercenaries, Sweet Dirty Tony, Key West Crossing* [directed by Christopher Cain; Workman also directed additional sequences and reedited the film]). 1980. 35mm; 90 minutes; color; sound (Facets).

Protocol (directed by Herbert Ross). 1984. 35mm; 100 minutes; color; sound (Warner Brothers).

Stalin (directed by Ivan Passer). 1992. 35mm; 173 minutes; color; sound (HBO).

And the Band Played On (directed by Roger Spottiswoode). 1993. 35mm; 140 minutes; color; sound (HBO).

As director/filmmaker:

The Money. 1975. 35mm; 90 minutes; color; sound (Independent International; released in DVD in 2003 as *The Atlantic City Jackpot* [Wellspring, www .wellspring.com]).

The Making of The Deep. 1977. 16mm; 50 minutes; color; sound (Columbia).

The Director and the Actor (produced for Eastman Kodak and the Directors Guild of America). 1984. 16mm. 22 minutes; color; sound (MoMA)

The Director and the Image (produced for Eastman Kodak and the Directors Guild of America). 1984. 16mm. 22 minutes; color; sound (MoMA).

The Game (documentary short, broadcast on the Discovery Channel). 1984. 16mm; 17 minutes; color; sound (Calliope Films, Calliopefilmsofc@aol.com).

Stoogemania. 1984. 35mm. 88 minutes; color; sound (Atlantic Releasing, Paramount Video).

Precious Images (produced for Directors Guild of America). 1986. 35mm; 7 minutes; color; sound (MoMA).

1988–2003: Montage tributes to Robert Wise, Woody Allen, Stanley Kubrick, Walter Matthau, Claire Trevor, and George Sidney.

The Best Show in Town (history of Paramount Pictures, made for its 75th anniversary). 1988. 35mm; 20 minutes; color; sound (Paramount).

Words (produced for the Writers Guild of America). 1988. 35mm; 13 minutes; color; sound (MoMA).

And the Winner Is (history of Academy of Motion Picture Arts and Sciences made for its 50th anniversary). 1989. 35mm; 20 minutes; color; sound (Academy of Motion Picture Arts and Sciences [AMPAS], www.ampas.org).

Pieces of Silver (produced for Eastman Kodak). 1989. 35mm; 7 minutes; color; sound (MoMA).

The Great Movie Ride (finale film, Disney World Studio Tour). 1990. 70mm; 5 minutes; color; sound.

Superstar: The Life and Times of Andy Warhol. 1990. 35mm; 87 minutes; color; sound (Wellspring).

Alfred Hitchcock Exhibit (Universal Studios Tour). 1991. 35mm; 6 minutes; color; sound.

The First Time (montage for 63rd Academy Awards show). 1991. Video; 6 minutes; color; sound (AMPAS).

Opening comedy segment for 64th Academy Awards show. 1992. Video; 5¼ minutes; color; sound (AMPAS).

Michael Jackson—History. 1993. Video; 4 minutes; color; sound (Calliope Films).

Not Us. 1993. 16mm; 10 minutes; color; sound (Calliope Films).

Emmy Awards opening sequence. 1994. Video; 5 minutes; color; sound (Calliope Films).

Emmy Awards opening sequence. 1995. Video; 5 minutes; color; sound (Calliope Films).

The First Hundred Years. 1996. 35mm/video; 88 minutes; color; sound (HBO).

Michael Jackson tour intermission film. 1996. Video; 7 minutes; color; sound.

One Hundred Years at the Movies. 1996. Video; 10 minutes; color; sound (Turner Classic Movies)

That Good Night. 1996. 35mm; 11 minutes; color; sound (Calliope Films).

"Mad about You" (retrospective piece for television show *Mad about You*). 1997. Video; 23 minutes; color; sound (Columbia Television).

The Story of X. 1998. Video; 82 minutes; color; sound (Playboy Channel).

Bugs Bunny's Retrospective. 1999. 35mm; 3¾ minutes; color; sound (Warner Bros.).

Nickelodeon Television anniversary montage. 1999. Video; 6 minutes; color; sound (Nickelodeon).

Putting It Together (opening montage and song by Bernadette Peters for 66th Academy Awards show). 1999. 35mm/video; 5 minutes; color; sound (AMPAS).

The Source. 1999. 35mm; 89 minutes; color; sound (Wellspring).

You Must Remember This (compilation history of Warner Brothers). 1999. Video; 10 minutes; color; sound (Warner Home Video).

History of the World (for 72nd Academy Awards show). 2000. Video; 5 minutes; color; sound (AMPAS).

A House on a Hill. 2001. 35mm; 89 minutes; color; sound (Abramorama).

Charlie Chaplin Tribute. 2002. Video; 9 minutes; color; sound (Warner Home Video).

None but Honest and Wise Men. 2002. Video; 50 minutes; color; sound (White House Historical Association).

The Spirit of America. 2002. 35mm; 3 minutes; color; sound (Calliope Films).

The Actor's Life. 2003. Video; 78 minutes; color; sound (Calliope Films).

Presidents Day: A Day for Us All (for U.S. Department of Education). 2003. Video; 30 minutes; color; sound.

Bob Hope Tribute (for 76th Academy Awards show). 2004. Video; 2 minutes; color; sound (AMPAS).

Martin Luther King, Jr.: The Making of a Dream (for U.S. Department of Education). 2004. Video; 30 minutes; color; sound.

Bibliography

While the preceding filmographies are as complete and up-to-date as I am able to make them, this bibliography means only to provide an entry into the discourse on critical cinema in general and on those filmmakers interviewed for *A Critical Cinema 4*. *A Critical Cinema, A Critical Cinema 2,* and *A Critical Cinema 3* also include listings of general references; the following is an addendum to them. If a publication included in an earlier bibliography is referenced in the text of *A Critical Cinema 4,* bibliographical information is repeated with the reference. If a reference is cited in full in the General References section, it is given in shortened form in the individual filmmaker bibliographies.

General References

Dixon, Wheeler Winston. *The Exploding Eye: A Re-visionary History of 1960s American Experimental Cinema.* Albany: State University of New York Press, 1997.

Elder, R. Bruce. *A Body of Vision: Representations of the Body in Recent Film and Poetry.* Waterloo, Ontario: Wilfrid Laurier University Press, 1997.

Fischer, Lucy. *Cinematernity: Film, Motherhood, Genre.* Princeton, N.J.: Princeton University Press, 1996.

Grant, Barry Keith, and Jeannette Sloniowski, eds. *Documenting the Documentary: Close Readings of Documentary Film and Video.* Detroit, Mich.: Wayne State University Press, 1998.

High, Kathy, and Liss Platt. *Landscape(s). FELIX* 2, no. 1 (1995).

High, Kathy, and Maria Venuto. *Voyeurism (fin de siecle). FELIX* 2, no. 2 (1999).

Hoberman, J., and Edward Leffingwell, eds. *Wait for Me at the Bottom of the Pool: The Writings of Jack Smith.* New York: High Risk, 1997.

Hoolboom, Mike. *Inside the Pleasure Dome: Fringe Film in Canada.* 2nd ed. Toronto: Coach House Books, 2001.

Kilchesty, Albert, ed. *Big As Life: An American History of 8mm Films.* New York: Museum of Modern Art; San Francisco: San Francisco Cinematheque, 1998. Catalogue for a traveling show of 8mm films, February 1998 to December 1999.

MacDonald, Scott. *Cinema 16: Documents toward a History of the Film Society.* Philadelphia: Temple University Press, 2003.

———. "Experimental Cinema in the 1980s." In *A New Pot of Gold: Hollywood under the Electronic Rainbow, 1980–1989,* ed. Stephen Prince, 390–444. Vol. 10 of *History of the American Cinema.* New York: Scribner's, 2000.

———. *The Garden in the Machine: A Field Guide to Independent Films about Place.* Berkeley and Los Angeles: University of California Press, 2001.

Marks, Laura U. *The Skin of the Film: Intercultural Cinema, Embodiment, and the Senses.* Durham, N.C.: Duke University Press, 2000.

———. *Touch: Sensuous Theory and Multisensory Media.* Minneapolis: University of Minnesota Press, 2002.

Rees, A. L. *A History of Experimental Film and Video: From the Canonical Avant-Garde to Contemporary British Practice.* London: British Film Institute, 1999.

Reinke, Steve, and Tom Taylor, eds.. *Lux: A Decade of Artists' Film and Video.* Toronto: Pleasure Dome/YYZ Books, 2000.

Rich, Ruby. *Chick Flicks: Theories and Memories of the Feminist Film Movement.* Durham, N.C.: Duke University Press, 1998.

Russell, Catherine. *Experimental Ethnography: The Work of Film in the Age of Video.* Durham, N.C.: Duke University Press, 1999.

Sitney, P. Adams. *Visionary Film: The American Avant-Garde, 1943–2000.* 3rd ed. New York: Oxford University Press, 2002.

Zimmermann, Patricia R. *States of Emergency: Documentaries, Wars, Democracies.* Minneapolis: University of Minnesota Press, 2000.

Chantal Akerman

Camera Obscura. "Chantal Akerman on Jeanne Dielman: Excerpts from an Interview with *Camera Obscura,* November 1976." *Camera Obscura,* no. 2 (fall 1977): 118–21.

Jenkins, Janet, ed. *Bordering on Fiction: Chantal Akerman's D'Est.* Catalogue for a traveling exhibition of Akerman's *D'Est,* published by the Walker Art Center in Minneapolis in 1995. Includes essays by Akerman, Catherine David, Kathy Halbreich and Bruce Jenkins, and Michael Tarantino.

Margulies, Ivone. *Nothing Happens: Chantal Akerman's Hyperrealist Everyday.* Durham, N.C.: Duke University Press, 1996. Includes an extensive bibliography of writing by and about Akerman.

Stan Brakhage

Brabner, Wendy. *Stan Brakhage: A Guide to References and Resources.* Boston: G. K. Hall, 1983.

Brakhage, Stan. *The Brakhage Lectures: George Méliès, David Wark Griffith, Carl Theodore Dreyer, Sergei Eisenstein.* Chicago: Good Lion, 1972.

_____. *Brakhage Scrapbook: Collected Writings, 1964–1980.* Edited by Robert A. Haller. New Paltz, N.Y.: Documentext, 1982.

_____. *Essential Brakhage: Selected Writings on Filmmaking by Stan Brakhage.* Edited by Bruce R. McPherson. Kingston, N.Y.: Documentext, 2001.

_____. *Film at Wit's End: Eight Avant-Garde Filmmakers.* Kingston, N.Y.: McPherson/Documentext, 1989.

_____. *Film Biographies.* Berkeley: Turtle Island, 1977.

_____. *I. . . . Sleeping.* Edited by Robert A. Haller. Staten Island, N.Y.: Island Cinema Resources; Rochester, N.Y.: Visual Studies Workshop, 1988.

_____. "Letter to Yves Kovacs (On Surrealism)" and "Letter to Ronna Page (On Music)." In *The Avant-Garde Film: A Reader of Theory and Criticism,* ed. P. Adams Sitney, 129–38. New York: New York University Press, 1978.

_____. *Metaphors on Vision.* Special issue of *Film Culture,* no. 30 (fall 1963), ed. P. Adams Sitney.

_____. *A Moving Picture Giving and Taking Book.* West Newbury, Mass.: Frontier Press, 1971.

_____. *Telling Time.* Edited by Bruce McPherson. Kingston, N.Y.: Documentext, 2003.

Camper, Fred. Camper is one of the leading writers on Brakhage, though his writing is generally made available on-line. See Camper's Web site for a bibliography of his writing on Brakhage, along with a range of other Brakhage resources: http://www.fredcamper.com/Film/BrakhageL.html.

Elder, R. Bruce. "The Body As Universe in Stan Brakhage's Early Films," and "The Cognitive Body—The Films of Amy Greenfield and Another View of the Films of Stan Brakhage." In *A Body of Vision: Representations of the Body in Recent Film and Poetry.* Waterloo, Ontario: Wilfred Laurier, 1997.

_____. *The Films of Stan Brakhage in the American Tradition of Ezra Pound, Gertrude Stein, and Charles Olson.* Waterloo, Ontario: Wilfred Laurier, 1998.

James, David. "The Filmmaker as Poet." Chapter 2 of *Allegories of Cinema: American Film in the Sixties.* Princeton, N.J.: Princeton University Press, 1989.

Keller, Marjorie. *The Untutored Eye: Childhood in the Films of Cocteau, Cornell, and Brakhage.* Rutherford, N.J.: Associated University Presses, 1986.

MacDonald, Scott. "Avant-Gardens" and "Benedictions/New Frontiers." Chapters 3 and 11 of *The Garden in the Machine.*

Michelson, Annette, ed. "Eisenstein/Brakhage." Special issue, *Artforum* 11, no. 5 (January 1973). Includes essays by Michelson, Paul Arthur, Phoebe Cohen, and Fred Camper and an interview with Stan and Jane Brakhage by Hollis Frampton.

Nesthus, Marie. "A Crucible of Document: The Sequence Films of Stan Brakhage, 1968–1984." Ph.D. diss., New York University, 1999.

Sitney, P. Adams. "The Lyrical Film," "Major Mythopoeia," and "The Seventies." Chapters 6, 7, and 13 of *Visionary Film*.
_____. "Whoever Sees God Dies: Cinematic Epiphanies." Chapter 9 of *Modernist Montage: The Obscurity of Vision in Cinema and Literature*. New York: Columbia University Press, 1990.
Steinhoff, Eirik, ed. "Stan Brakhage: Correspondences." Special issue, *Chicago Review* 47, no. 4 (winter 2001); 48, no. 1 (spring 2002). Includes letters and other writings by Brakhage; articles by Fred Camper, Jean Cocteau, Guy Davenport, Nathaniel Dorsky, Robert Kelly, Marie Nesthus, Kristin Prevallet, John Pruitt, Jennifer Reeves, and P. Adams Sitney; and a conversation between Steve Anker and Michael McClure.
Wees, William C. " 'Giving Sight to the Medium': Stan Brakhage." Chapter 4 of *Light Moving in Time: Studies in the Visual Aesthetics of Avant-Garde Film*. Berkeley and Los Angeles: University of California Press, 1992.

Lawrence Brose

Brennan, Donald, and Zack Stiglicz. "The Visionary Art of Filmmaker Lawrence Brose" (an interview). *Lightstruck* 7, no. 4 (summer 1991): 23–38.
Ferber, Lawrence. "Lawrence Brose/*De Profundis*." *Independent* 21, no. 6 (July 1998): 7–8.
Licata, Elizabeth. "Scoring Film." *Afterimage* 25, no. 7 (July/August 1998): 15.
Tejada, Roberto. "*De Produndis*/Lawrence Brose." Catalogue essay for a show of Brose's film stills, at Big Orbit Gallery, Buffalo, New York, from September 22 to October 27, 2001.

Abigail Child

Child, Abigail. "Being a Witness: A Poetic Meditation on *B/Side*." In Reinke and Taylor, *Lux: A Decade of Artists' Film and Video*, 165–84. Toronto: YYZ Books and Pleasure Dome, 2000.
_____, ed. *Canyon Cinemanews* 15, no. 7 (1977). Also one of several editors for issue 1978, no. 6; 1979, no. 1; 1979, nos. 2–3, nos. 5–6.
_____. *Mob* (collected poetry). Oakland: O Press, 1994.
_____. *A Motive for Mayhem* (collected poetry). Hartford, Conn.: Potes and Poets Press, 1989.
_____. *Scatter Matrix* (collected poetry). New York: Roof Books, 1996.
_____. "Sound Talk." *Cinematograph*, no. 5 (1993): 25–28.
_____. "Truth Serum." *Cinematograph*, no. 4 (1991): 43–52.
Keller, Marjorie. "Is This What You Were Born For?" *Xdream* 1, no. 1 (autumn 1986): 1–5.
Kotz, Lisa. "An Unrequited Desire for the Sublime: Looking at Lesbian Representation across the Works of Abigail Child, Cecilia Dougherty, and Su Friedrich." In

Queer Looks: Perspectives on Lesbian and Gay Film and Video, ed. Martha Gever, John Greyson, and Pratibha Parmar, 86–102. New York: Routledge, 1993.

MacDonald, Scott. "Experimental Cinema in the 1980s." In Prince, *A New Pot of Gold,* 430–31.

Raymond, Monica. "The Pastoral in Abigail Child's *Covert Action* and *Mayhem.*" *Cinematograph* 3 (1988): 61–64.

Sitney, P. Adams. *Visionary Film,* 421–24.

Tamblyn, Christine. "No More Nice Girls: Recent Transgressive Feminist Art." *Art Journal* 5, no. 2 (summer 1991): 53–57.

Peter Forgács

Wees, William C. "Old Images, New Meanings: Recontextualizing Archival Footage of Nazism and the Holocaust." *Spectator* 4, no. 1 (fall 1999/winter 2000): 70–76.

Jill Godmilow

Miller, Lynn C. "[Un]documenting History: An Interview with Jill Godmilow." *Text Performance Quarterly* 7 (July 1997): 273–87.

Patterson, Wendy. "Far from Documentary: An Interview with Jill Godmilow." *Afterimage* 13, no. 7 (February 1986): 4–7.

Rabinowitz, Paula. "National Bodies: Gender, Sexuality, and Terror in Feminist Counter-documentaries." Chapter 8 of *They Must Be Represented: The Politics of Documentary.* New York: Verso, 1994.

Rosenthal, Alan. *The Documentary Conscience: A Casebook in Film Making* (Chapter 22: "Antonia" [an interview with Godmilow]). Berkeley and Los Angeles: University of California Press, 1980.

Shapiro, Ann-Louise. "Jill Godmilow, in Conversation with Ann-Louise Shapiro." *History and Theory* 36, no. 4 (1997): 80–101.

Peter Kubelka

Arnold, Martin, and Peter Tscherkassky. "Peter Kubelka." In *Austrian Avant-Garde Cinema, 1955–1993.* Catalogue for a traveling exhibition of films curated by Steve Anker, 50–55. Vienna: Sixpack Film, 1994.

Kubelka, Peter. "The Theory of Metrical Film." In *The Avant-Garde Film: A Reader of Theory and Criticism,* ed. P. Adams Sitney, 139–59. New York: Anthology Film Archives/New York University Press, 1978.

Mekas, Jonas. "Interview with Peter Kubelka." *Film Culture,* no. 44 (1967): 42–47. Reprinted in *Film Culture Reader,* ed. P. Adams Sitney, 285–99. New York: Praeger, 1970.

____. "Interview with Peter Kubelka." In *Structural Film Anthology,* ed. Peter Gidal, 98–108. London: British Film Institute, 1978.

____. *Movie Journal: The Rise of a New American Cinema, 1959–1971,* 114, 145, 198, 258–60, 262, 298, 347, 374, 376. New York: Macmillan, 1972.

Russell, Catherine. *Experimental Ethnography: The Work of Film in the Age of Video,* 125–35. Durham, N.C.: Duke University Press, 1999.

Sitney, P. Adams. *Visionary Film,* 283–92.

Jim McBride

Bershen, Wanda. *"David Holzman's Diary/Portrait of Jason."* In *The American New Wave, 1958–1967,* ed. Bruce Jenkins and Melinda Ward, 63–69. Catalogue for a touring show organized by Media Study/Buffalo and the Walker Art Center in 1982.

Carson, L. M. Kit. *David Holzman's Diary: A Screenplay by L. M. Kit Carson from a Film by Jim McBride.* New York: Farrar, Straus and Giroux, 1970.

Gelmis, Joseph. *The Film Director As Superstar* (interview with McBride). Garden City, N.Y.: Doubleday, 1970.

Motion Picture. "On Independent Film Distribution" (conversation with Ricky Leacock, Jonas Mekas, and Jim McBride—plus a letter from McBride). *Motion Picture,* no. 1 (spring/summer 1986): 16–17.

Shirin Neshat

Azari, Shoja. "An Inside Look at Shirin Neshat's Art." In *Shirin Neshat,* catalogue for an exhibition of photographs and films, May 28 to July 31, 2002, at the Centre for Contemporary Art Ujazdowski Castle, Warsaw.

Camper, Fred. "Closed to Interpretation." *Chicago Reader,* February 26, 1999.

____. "Houses Divided." *Chicago Reader,* July 9, 1999.

Women of Allah. Catalogue for a retrospective of Neshat's photography. Turin: Marco Noire Editore, 1997.

Zaya, Octavio. "Q & A Shirin Neshat." *Creative Camera,* no. 342 (October/November 1996): 18.

P. Adams Sitney

Sitney has been a remarkably productive editor and scholar for more than forty years. He founded and edited *Filmwise* and subsequently edited and regularly contributed to *Film Culture* during the years when it was the most crucial publication in the field of alternative cinema. His contributions to journals and catalogues are too numerous to include here, but I have listed his books and chapters of books.

Jenkins, Bruce. "A Case against 'Structural Film.'" *Journal of the University Film Association* 33, no. 2 (spring 1981): 9–14.

Mellencamp, Patricia. *Indiscretions: Avant-Garde Film, Video, & Feminism,* 17–33. Bloomington: Indiana University Press, 1990.

Sitney, P. Adams. "Autobiography in Avant-Garde Film." *Millennium* 1, no. 1 (winter 1977–78): 60–105.

——, ed. *The Avant-Garde Film: A Reader of Theory and Criticism.* New York: New York University Press, 1978.

——, ed. *The Essential Cinema: Essays on the Films in the Collection of Anthology Film Archives.* New York: Anthology Film Archives/New York University Press, 1975.

——, ed. *Film Culture Reader.* New York: Praeger, 1970.

——. "Landscape in the Cinema: The Rhythms of the World and the Camera." In *Landscape, Natural Beauty, and the Arts,* ed. Ivan Gaskell and Salim Kemal, 103–26. New York: Cambridge University Press, 1993.

——. *Modernist Montage: The Obscurity of Vision in Cinema and Literature.* New York: Columbia University Press, 1990.

——. *Visionary Film: The American Avant-Garde, 1943–2000.* 3rd ed. New York: Oxford University Press, 2002.

Ellen Spiro

Cagle, Chris. "Imaging the Queer South: Southern Lesbian and Gay Documentary." In *Between the Sheets, in the Streets: Queer, Lesbian, Gay Documentary,* ed. Cynthia Fuchs and Chris Holmlund, 30–45. Minneapolis: University of Minnesota Press, 1997.

MacDonald, Scott. "Re-envisioning the American West." *American Studies* 39 (spring 1998): 115–46. Reprinted as chapter 4 of *The Garden in the Machine.*

Spiro, Ellen. "The Medium Is the Missed Age." *Independent* 23, no. 2 (March 2000): 11.

——. "Outlaws through the Lens of Corporate America." *Cinematograph,* no. 4 (1991): 180–83.

——. "What to Wear on Your Video Activist Outing: A Camcordist's Manifesto." *Independent* 14, no. 3 (May 1991): 10.

Chuck Workman

MacDonald, Scott. "I *Love* the Audience: An Interview with Chuck Workman." *Film Quarterly* 57 (fall 2003): 2–12.

Acknowledgments of Permissions

I am grateful to the following journals for permission to include (usually revised, expanded versions of) essays and interviews:

Film Quarterly, for "The Filmmaker as Visionary: Excerpts from an Interview with Stan Brakhage," vol. 56, no. 3 (spring 2003): 2–11; "I *Love* the Audience: An Interview with Chuck Workman," vol. 57, no. 1 (fall 2003): 2–12; "His African Journey: An Interview with Peter Kubelka," vol. 57, no. 3 (spring 2004): 2–12.

Public Culture, for "Pioneering Spirit: An Interview with Ellen Spiro," vol. 14, no. 3 (fall 2002): 468–75.

Feminist Studies, for "Interview with Shirin Neshat," 30, no. 4 (winter 2004–5).

Index

Page numbers in *italics* indicate figures.

Text: 10/12 Times New Roman
Display: Helvetica
Compositor: IBT Global
Printer and binder: IBT Global